Appalachian Ohio and
the Civil War, 1862–1863

Appalachian Ohio and the Civil War, 1862–1863

by

SUSAN G. HALL

McFarland & Company, Inc., Publishers
Jefferson, North Carolina, and London

Library of Congress Cataloguing-in-Publication Data

Hall, Susan G., 1941–
Appalachian Ohio and the Civil War, 1862–1863 / by Susan G. Hall.
p.   cm.
ISBN 0-7864-0866-9 (illustrated case : 50# alkaline paper) ∞
Includes bibliographical references (p.   ) and index.
1. Harrison County (Ohio) — History — 19th century.   2. Appalachian Region —
History — 19th century.   3. Ohio — History — Civil War, 1861–1865 — Social
aspects.   4. United States — History — Civil War, 1861–1865 — Social aspects.
5. Harrison County (Ohio) — Social conditions — 19th century.   6. Appalachian
Region — Social conditions — 19th century.   I. Title.
F497.H5H18 2000   977.1'608 — dc21   00-56061

British Library cataloguing data are available

On the front cover: Background map reproduced from the Ohio
Historical Society. Foreground image ©2000 Index Stock.
On the back cover: A typical 1862 town home in Cadiz, Ohio.
(Harper and Brothers, 1890)

Manufactured in the United States of America

McFarland & Company, Inc., Publishers
Box 611, Jefferson, North Carolina 28640
www.mcfarlandpub.com

Contents

Preface

From summer to summer, 1862–63 brought the crucial battles and political events which shaped the Civil War and the nation subsequently, and altered societies in many ways, not only in the South. This narrative history of a community in Appalachian east Ohio delineates a people's experience of the war at home and in the armies fighting in Kentucky, Tennessee, Mississippi, and Virginia, in a year that fomented a powerful peace movement in Ohio, and meanwhile changed its farmboys, carpenters, scholars, and ministers into hardened soldiers laying destruction around them.

Harrison County and its county seat of Cadiz sat in the center of its political and military districts, which extended west from the state border on the upper Ohio River, so its history records activities, active people, and soldiers of this area — Jefferson, Belmont, Carroll, Tuscarawas, and Guernsey counties.

With a focus on a small society, we can see the interlinkage of personal life, culture, economy, politics, and military attitudes which gave it character and operated in a year of momentous events.

Aspects of all these, for instance, generated the sudden emotional fervor of 1862 recruiting. They were all at work in the bitter division of the community that soon followed, between the war-supporters and the anti-war "copperheads." They were meshed also in the perspectives which soldiers conveyed home in their letters, their views of the armies and of the places and people of the South they encountered. They together propelled the first cavalry company from this, George Armstrong Custer's native county, in 1863 to ride off for the Western Territories, and inspired a young local editor's puff of these "brave and jolly" fellows: "if they ever come in contact with the 'big injuns' they will quickly learn them the art of 'skedaddling.'"[1]

A well-informed people, with daily national news from their rail and telegraph lines, these Ohioans were yet in ways quite provincial. Most lived on farms, many in ancestral log houses, and kept old customs. None were sequestered from home-grown manners and fashions. Of social strata elsewhere in the

1

country they were little aware, even though Virginia plantations began only thirty miles away. Educated but provincial soldiers became avid reporters on the South they discovered.

To compare their viewpoints with more objective records of the varied societies they visited, this account draws information from the 1860 census and local histories. Behind the differences among the Ohio community and most of the others, ranging from the Shenandoah Valley to the Kentucky bluegrass to the Cumberland basin in Tennessee, lay a historic common origin; they had been established around the turn of the century in the waves of western movement which carried recent Scots-Irish immigrants, with Germans and English behind them, beyond the mountains to open lands. From a shared ancestral culture, these settlements had evolved in divergent paths, all differently enlightened and benighted, each to its own character, and course in the war.

Among some soldiers' discoveries was their first astonished vision of young women in white dresses. Neither the "Victorian" modes of the East nor the aristocratic styles of the South elevated, and enclosed, women in the Ohio neighborhoods, within which they had diverse work, opportunities, and associations. The expansion of the war increased the private and public responsibilities they undertook. This history includes their participations.

A grass-roots study has relevances to general history of the war. It tracks the varied and shifting motivations of individual soldiers over time, giving a different perspective on their ideals and politics from that of James M. McPher-

son's analysis in *For Cause & Comrades: Why Men Fought in the Civil War* (1997); and it far extends the range of mutual influence between home and army. Second, it specifies the rise of war opposition in the Copperhead movement which had its center in Ohio and its champion in Ohio's Clement L. Vallandigham, and which seemed to promise Confederate success in early 1863. The active Copperheads of this county were, contrary to usual generalizations about backward Ohio "butternuts," men of wealth and influence.

Moreover, Vallandigham's opponent in the House of Representatives and on the national stump was Rep. John A. Bingham, whose home was Cadiz. Bingham is a shadowy figure in histories that center on Lincoln, although as a leading member of the House Judiciary Committee in 1861 and 1862 he forged key Republican war measures, and he knew Lincoln personally — to what extent can merely be guessed from the spare facts that Lincoln interviewed him for his views on Edwin Stanton, a Cadiz attorney early in his career, as prospective Secretary of War,[2] and that Lincoln in August 1863 consulted Bingham to find a "little short act" of Congress which Stanton needed to locate.[3] According to Bingham himself, after he met Lincoln in 1861, he freely, often visited him, and influenced him in decisions including the issuing of the Emancipation Proclamation.[4] In the annals of east Ohio, Bingham has an imposing presence as everyone's hero or demonic villain.

Bingham's — and Vallandigham's — main role was that of orator: the significance of oratory can be illuminated within a view of the society and culture of the audience; within a narrative, its effects can be traced. Bingham's orations at home and in Congress were plentiful and powerful in 1862–63, and the scope of this history shows their connections.

Third, both James M. McPherson, in *Abraham Lincoln and the Second American Revolution* (1990), and Garry Wills, in *Lincoln at Gettysburg: The Words That Remade America* (1992), contend that Lincoln singlehandedly changed the concept of Constitutional Union to one of a people as nation; and Wills argues that Lincoln "altered the document" of the Constitution "from within" in the Gettysburg Address, implicitly asserting the Declaration of Independence and its premise of equality as the founding document, in "one of the most daring acts of open-air sleight of hand ever witnessed by the unsuspecting."[5] Months before Lincoln eloquently formulated this shift, however, the questions and changes behind it were pronounced in the debates that raged through local Ohio politics, and in letters soldiers wrote.

Political changes occurred to people of Harrison County not as one speech, but many, and through neighborhood scenes: of farmers riding in armed bands to meetings, wives of soldiers pleading for support for their children, an editor holed up with his side-armed friends awaiting a mob, men racing to defend their town from Morgan's Confederate cavalry, and local African-American men learning to drill on the town street in preparation for joining the Fifty-fifth Massachusetts Regiment.

In ways, this community's experience was representative of the North's; otherwise, it resembled that of the divided core of the country, in Appalachia.

This agricultural county, with just over 19,000 in total population in 1860, had sent off almost 6 percent of its population to the Union army by September 1862. Since all were white males as were voters, a comparison with 1860 election figures is relevant. An "estimated 90 percent of Ohio's voters turned out" for this election[6]; and the number who did not vote can discount the difference between voters and the volunteers of under voting age. The county had 3,622 voters in 1860, so the 1,100 volunteers exceed one-fourth of the mature males. They were more than one-third of the 3,287 men aged 18 to 45 counted in the 1862 military assessment. On the other hand, these men had wide political differences before the rebellion began. A majority of 60 percent voted for Lincoln, the same percentage as in the country's far north, above the 41st parallel — in Ohio, the Western Reserve, settled by New Englanders.[7] Only 21 percent voted with the far-majority of Democrats of the North who favored Douglas; only 1 percent with Bell's Union party that won Virginia, Kentucky, and Tennessee; but 18 percent with the Democrats of the Deep South — giving Breckinridge in this county the same portion of votes he received in the nation as a whole.[8]

The late county historian John S. Campbell often wondered why so many volunteered, and why especially so many went from the neighborhood near Cadiz known as Irish Ridge. In 1862, Nancy D. Mitchell, my great-grandmother, was a twenty-year-old "girl" of Irish Ridge who saved letters from the soldier "boys" who wrote her. From these, genealogical information, letters and accounts in the two newspapers of Cadiz, and military reports, an unusual background and chronicle emerge. Who these people were, who fought so vigorously over and in the war, shaped their participation. Their culture, society, and economy provided the interests which provoked their bitter divisions and supplied their overall unity. Their long-established family relationships framed their views and prospects. The important ties of soldiers to their homes, however, were seriously threatened and sometimes broken. The customary courtships needed to settle sons and daughters, and supply gossip, were disrupted. Because of these separations, letters replaced conversations; and Nancy's correspondences with her brother, friends, and potential suitors reveal the role of ordinary young women in making and keeping the ties that bound the family and society.

The war significantly altered this society. It broadly instructed, and undercut, a provincial people. Many soldiers did not return, many who did return were disabled or addicted to drink, many others soon moved westward in Ohio, and to Iowa, Missouri, and Kansas; and well-off farmers expanded their lands, wool profits, and wealth. Moreover, during the war, soldiers brought plague illnesses home to their families and neighborhoods; and after it, young women remaining in them found no husbands; some families literally "died out." The Irish Ridge would never again be the vibrant, full, and varied neighborhood of Nancy's youth.

Sources

To give a representative picture of the Ohio people in this history, I have drawn upon their own words and contemporary records; these are not always consistent or accurate. Census rolls and regimental rosters, for instance, frequently disagree in names and ages they list. Census figures have discrepancies in different published accounts and tallies. Military reports vary. I have chosen to use the account, among such variations, closest to home: census figures from the local newspapers, for example, rather than those compiled and published in Washington.

Where my descriptions from such sources pertain to individuals, they cannot be completely reliable, as a definitive genealogy or biography would require. Neither would I claim that the accounts of people written by those who knew them are entirely creditable — especially not the malicious tales. Longstanding personal acquaintance, however, played a considerable part in shaping the allegiances and animosities in this society, affecting everything from individual morality to political action to military conduct. Some gossip and rumor are necessary to represent the personal drama men and women perceived as their experience; that is their purpose here, not the defamation of any individual.

Similarly, this work quotes insults published in the local newspapers, including offensive racial epithets and derogations. Ugly racist language was not commonly, thoughtlessly used as an unchallenged convention in this area; rather, it was employed deliberately by some, for purposes this history investigates. To suppress such language here would conceal and distort the political and social reality: especially, the rancor of the politics, and the blatant prejudice of numerous whites which African-American residents endured, and which in 1863 they countered, with military steps.

The published sources are quoted with literary accuracy. The private letters are quoted with some modifications to render them readable; punctuation in some of them was omitted or has faded, and other mechanics were obscure in unpracticed handwriting. The widely varying literacy of these writers will readily appear despite my minor changes — also, the grammar and pronunciation of the vernacular of the area, from which its orators and educated writers drew colorful language.

In the following chapters, sources will be cited within the text in Modern Language Association style, with author or brief title and page number in parentheses. The full information on each source appears in the Works Cited list. Abbreviated titles will appear for local newspapers and such standard works as the *Official Records* (*OR*) and *Dictionary of American Biography* (*DAB*). Where descriptions of individuals are based on census rolls, citation of the many page numbers would swamp the text; the names and census pages can be located in alphabetical indexes of the localities: the reader will find these listed together in the Works Cited under U. S. Census, by the state indexed. Statistics on the counties surveyed here, drawn from three compilations of the 1860 census, are alphabetically arranged by state and county in three volumes listed under U. S. Census in the Works: *Population*, *Manufactures*, and *Agriculture*, the last of which includes separate sections list-

ing agricultural production, acres and value of farm lands, slaveholders and slaves, and numbers of farms of various acreages. For Harrison County residents, in addition, descriptions are drawn from burial, marriage, and genealogical records which are alphabetically arranged and indexed in Hanna's *Historical Collection*; from the 1862 map and business directory of the county by Jacob Jarvis and those of 1875 by J. A. Caldwell; from regimental rosters; and from advertisements of the time in the local newspapers.

The local weekly newspapers consisted of four dense pages, following the same general pattern of national and state news (and most soldiers' letters) on the first two, editorials and local news on the third, continuations and advertising on the fourth; page numbers are omitted here, but the day and month of the issue cited for each article, with these abbreviations for months: Ja, F, Mr, Ap, My, Je, Jl, Ag, S, O, N, D. With parenthetical references to dated sources, a running chronology keeps the reader's place in time.

The research for this work has had the help of many libraries and their librarians. It began about thirty years ago, in the Cadiz Public Library, now the Puskarich, whose historical collection I have continued to consult. The Ohio State Historical Society furnished the microfilm of the Cadiz newspapers, and permission to quote from them. Its collection includes the John A. Bingham papers. Its librarians have generously assisted me on several visits in locating materials from the state archives. Louisville, Kentucky, has provided me resources and expert guidance in a superb array of complementary libraries: The Filson Club Historical Society, Louisville Free Public Library, Louisville Presbyterian Theological Seminary, Sons of the American Revolution Genealogical Library, Southern Baptist Theological Seminary, and the University of Louisville Libraries. The Cincinnati Historical Society Library and Public Library of Cincinnati and Hamilton County furnished access to Ohio regimental rosters and area history.

Numerous other libraries, historical societies, visitors' centers, and national parks have aided me, as I have followed the soldiers of east Ohio to their camps and battlefields. In particular, tours and reenactments at the Perryville

Battlefield, a Kentucky park, shaped my understanding. The Belle Boyd Museum and Berkeley County Historical Society of Martinsburg, West Virginia, offered many relevant materials; I especially thank its director, Don C. Wood, for generously sharing his expertise during my visit. West Virginians Charles Head of Mt. Storm and C. Laurin Swisher of New Creek gave me invaluable historic details of their areas when I, a total stranger, knocked on their doors at the suggestions of their post offices.

Most of all, I owe inexpressible gratitude — and apologies — to my family, who for many years have spent "vacations" with me in graveyards and on battlefields.

Notes

1. Frank Hatton, *Cadiz Republican* 24 June 1863.
2. Benjamin P. Thomas and Harold M. Hyman, *Stanton: The Life and Times of Lincoln's Secretary of War* (New York: Knopf, 1962), 136.
3. "Indorsement on Note of Secretary Stanton," Aug. 25, 1863, *Abraham Lincoln: Complete Works*, Ed. John G. Nicolay and John Hay (New York: Century, 1894), 2: 395–96.
4. Erving E. Beauregard, *Bingham of the Hills: Politician and Diplomat Extraordinary*, American University Studies Ser. 9: History; vol. 68 (New York: Peter Lang, 1989) 58–59, 73–74.
5. Garry Wills, *Lincoln at Gettysburg: The Words That Remade America* (New York: Touchstone-Simon & Schuster, 1992), 38.
6. Nat Brandt, *The Town That Started the Civil War* (New York: Laurel-Dell, 1991), 239.
7. James M. McPherson, *Battle Cry of Freedom: The Civil War Era* (New York: Oxford UP, 1988) 232.
8. The figures come from the *Cadiz Democratic Sentinel* 14 Nov. 1860; and David Wallechinsky and Irving Wallace, *The People's Almanac* (Garden City, NY: Doubleday, 1975) 287. This local newspaper will subsequently be referred to as the *Sentinel*, or abbreviated *CDS*. The other newspaper will be abbreviated similarly.

Chapter 1

The Land and Its People

West of the Ohio River where it could often be forded near Wheeling and Steubenville, a long, high ridge runs among the steep hills, early a pathway of buffalo, Indians, soldiers, and settlers through the forest of oak, walnut, and sugar maple. The ridge divides the headwaters for Short Creek to rush the twenty-four miles east to the Ohio, from those of the Stillwater creeks that flow through the gentler slopes to the west, and north to Lake Erie. In 1862 the virgin forest stood in groves, fringes, and hollow woods, and the ridge overlooked its surrounding country of curvaceous hills, all rippled and cleft by myriad springs, and dropping with their streams into winding hollows and valleys.

This cool and rainy precipitous land of shallow, clayey soil did not appeal to the early developers of Ohio land, who sought farmlands on the broad valleys and plains to the west. But groups of families were waiting nearby across the river in Pennsylvania and Virginia for the territory and the land office in Steubenville to open. Around 1800 they streamed up the trails to join the few squatters in the forest and the deer, bears, and wolves. Here they found land they could own and could clear into a higher version of the ancestral hilly homelands from which their forbearers had been driven by persecution and high rents, in the Western Lowlands of Scotland and subsequently the English-owned plantation farms in Northern Ireland. The spring-fed slopes would make superb sheep pasture. And for fires, instead of chopping peat from bogs, they could pick coal from outcroppings in the vales.

In 1862 the hills were spread in rich pasture grass crisscrossed by hedgerows and lanes, and tufted with large flocks of sheep; well over 100,000 sheep resided in the county. The slopes in summer were a patchwork in shifting hues of green, gold, blue, and brown, in fields of hay, oats, wheat, flax, and corn. Along the lanes sat the log houses most families still lived in, frame houses of the same side-chimney design, with lean-to kitchen rooms added to the rear, and tenant cabins. Close behind farmhouses rose large barns, and the clusters of sheep-folds, smoke houses, pig pens,

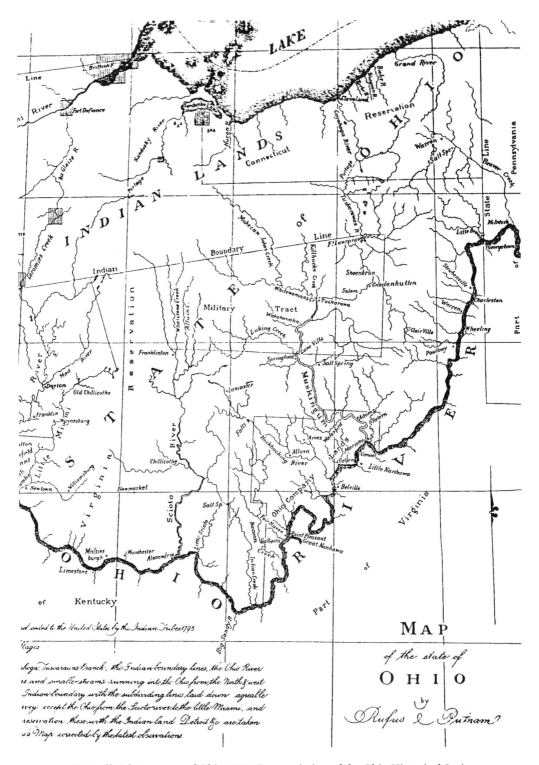

First official state map of Ohio, 1804. By permission of the Ohio Historical Society.

and spring houses, flanked by orchards, berry patches, and gardens. Into the center of this thriving, a branch railroad climbed through a northern valley; from the height of the dividing ridge, its train of cars appeared "a little toy affair, a child's plaything, playing Bo-Peep as it dodged in and about the hillocks" (Howe 174).

The first settlers were part of the vast migrations of Scots-Irish called "swarmings," by which much of the Shenandoah Valley, Kentucky, the Carolinas, and Ohio were populated. Yet they seem to have been a particular part, in a pattern somewhat different from those who settled east of the Allegheny and Appalachian Mountains, who are described in James G. Leyburn's *The Scotch-Irish: A Social History* (1962). Surely they had the same history in the Lowlands of violent upheaval between 1662 and 1679, when King Charles II revoked the Solemn League and Covenant of 1643 and imposed episcopal government on the Church of Scotland. The Presbyterians known as Covenanters revolted in guerrilla tactics and battle with the army, before their defeat and dispersal; during and after this chaos, area Scots and surviving Covenanters moved in thousands to the Ulster counties. There they endured, under minor discrimination, until in 1703 the Test Act debarred Presbyterians from ministry and office-holding, and then the English landlords began doubling and tripling the farm rents; massive emigrations to the American Colonies proceeded throughout the century (Leyburn 105–7, 162–5).

In America they found themselves often unwelcome in settlements, and generally pressed into the frontier, where they met Indian attacks. According to Leyburn, they were in Pennsylvania an "impetuous" people who provoked the Indians, seized upon lands without permission or payment, and took "tempestuous" interest in local politics; and a restless people who moved frequently, seemingly compulsively, leaving good farmlands to the better farmers, the Germans, who followed them (190–1, 199–200). As the pioneers of Harrison County came from the south-western border of Pennsylvania, in Washington and Fayette counties, such a description implies they were "backsettlers" like those Crèvecoeur describes in his 1782 *Letters from An American Farmer*: men degenerated to "ferocious, gloomy, and unsociable" hunters, often idle and inebriated, more savage than Indians, with slothful wives and children, in families cut off from manners and religion (565–6).

The principal first families who settled in Harrison County, however, brought with them a rigidly organized Scottish religion, and some Pennsylvania neighbors who were fervent Methodists. Too, they were rapidly joined by people of a kindred Presbyterian sect from various Pennsylvania areas, and by people coming as directly as they could from both Ireland and Scotland themselves. The portion of the ridge where Nancy D. Mitchell lived was known as Irish Ridge because so many of its settlers came in person from the "old sod." Considering the state of communications and transportation into wilderness Ohio in 1800, and the rigors of farming in the virgin timber, this migration differs from the usual Scots-Irish history in America.

Typical 1862 country home. Source: J.A. Caldwell, *Caldwell's Atlas of Harrison Co., Ohio.* Condit, Ohio: n.p., 1875.

The large families who took lands on and by the ridge in the center of the county were Associate Reformed Presbyterians (ARP). On a large eastern projection of the ridge arose the village Cadiz, laid out in 1804, to which the first missionary preachers of this church came, where lots for a log meeting house were purchased in 1812, and the congregation with its elders and pastor was established in 1813. Its churchyard was the town's burial ground. For six years after the county was organized in 1813, the courts met in the ARP church (Hanna 139–41, 109).

Meanwhile, a more rustic set of Presbyterian dissenters had arrived. They were Associate Presbyterians (AP), known as the "Seceders." A section of this body had earlier merged with the Reformed to constitute the Associate Reformed. Crèvecoeur termed Seceders "the most enthusiastic of all sectaries," fierce zealots, who when together, not divided among and pacified by German and Dutch settlers, would "cabal and mingle religious pride with worldly obstinacy" (564). On a hillside north of the village the Seceders built a "tent," a high platform about six-feet square, sided waist high like a pulpit, with a roof to shelter the preacher from rains, while the congregants sat on logs under the trees in long services. They formally organized in 1813, but met at their tent, or, in winter, in houses or the courthouse, until 1830 (Hanna 145)—

seemingly unable to agree on building a church.

The mainline Presbyterian denomination had a minister and two congregations in the far east of the county from 1804, but only organized a congregation in Cadiz in 1816 and received a minister in 1822 (Hanna 157–8). They subsequently became "Old School Presbyterians" (OSP) after a national schism in 1837 divided these defenders of the "old Calvinism" from the modifying New England theology — and abolitionism — of the church in the East and in Ohio's Western Reserve area. This split "coincided in the main with the racial demarcation between the Scotch and Scotch-Irish," the latter dominating the Upper Ohio Valley and the Old School Presbyterians (McKinney 250–1).

The extent to which the region was unusually dominated by the dissenting Scots-Irish character is reflected in the rationale of the first attorney to settle in Cadiz. Walter B. Beebe wrote to his parents in Connecticut in 1813 that after a 500-mile tour of Ohio he had chosen this "old settlement" to set up his law practice among "Virginians, Pennsylvanians, Germans, Scotch, and Irish, who are more litigious and quarrelsome than the Yankees are, and pay their money more freely" to sue each other (Hanna 108). The ARP and AP had a strong presence in the area, although in the nation they were minuscule. The Presbyterians had 513 ministers in the Colonies in 1776 (Leyburn 283). In 1802 the ARP had only 34 ministers in the country, only 100 congregations with 5,250 communicant members. The AP in 1801 had merely 14 ministers, in 21 congregations with 2,400 members (Glasgow 23). The mainline

Presbyterian Church of Cadiz enrolled most of the Yankee and other professionals who followed Beebe to Cadiz as the county's population swelled to 20,916 by 1830, many other newcomers from Pennsylvania, Virginia, and Maryland, and numerous former ARPs and APs; in 1851 it was supposed the largest Presbyterian congregation in Ohio (Hanna 100). Yet the largest congregation in town in 1861, according to the *Cadiz Republican* editor, a Methodist, was that of the merged ARPs and APs, who in 1858 became the United Presbyterians.

At the time of this merger, the ARP and AP listed ten different congregations within the county (Glasgow 370), and they — especially the AP — had earlier lost ministers and congregations in local schisms. In 1860 there were eight Old School Presbyterian churches, and one "Free Presbyterian" church, which had separated from the OSP to militate against slavery.

In local Civil War history, the differences of these churches, alike descended from the Church of Scotland, were pronounced as their members most vocally debated and caviled. The particular religion of the AP charted John A. Bingham's political course into and through the war, Erving E. Beauregard has shown ("Chief" 409; *Bingham* 3–4, 16).

This early county society and its influence persisted among many other settlers. The large families of Dickersons, Dunlaps, and Crumleys who brought Methodism to the center and south of the area had come through Virginia and Maryland to Fayette County, Pennsylvania, in association with the Scots-Irish Oglevees, whose marriages varied between

AP and Methodist. On Irish Ridge they met the Holmes family, who were among the more than 5,000 descendants in America by 1790 of the Rev. Obadiah Holmes, an English immigrant whom the Puritans whipped out of Salem, Massachusetts, in 1651 for his Baptist opinions; this family had moved through Rhode Island, New Jersey, and Virginia, and up Short Creek to the ridge, and joined Dickerson's Methodists (Hanna 519).

The early Quaker establishment of Mount Pleasant, above Short Creek just east of the county, brought anti-slavery Virginians into the area and also African Americans. In 1813, the boy William Cooper Howells, who would become the father of writer William Dean Howells, crossed the mountains with his parents on a Quaker wagon train, which an African-American family joined in Pennsylvania for the journey to Jefferson County, Ohio. In the 1820s with Quaker sponsorship, five families, including Christians, Binfords, and Williams, freed from slavery, came from Virginia to become farmers on eighty acres in Stock township of Harrison County (Reed, Greer 3–4). This migration from the east and settlement continued. In 1860, a family who prospered on a farm worth $5,200 in Short Creek township, listed as black on the census, had come from Virginia through Pennsylvania: James Jackson, 63, his wife Anne, 58, Samuel, 25, and Sarah, 20, were Virginia-born; Joseph, 18, was born in Pennsylvania; Lydia and David, 16, were born in Ohio. A longer journey was that of James Manly, born in North Carolina in 1826, whose daughter Jane E. was born in Maryland in 1852; in 1860 he owned a Cadiz township farm worth $1,000; with his Ohio-born wife Anne, 39, he had two sons, James, 3, and Joseph H., 2; and he housed a farm laborer, Nathan Carter, 21.

There is evidence, discussed in Chapter 25, that the principal Virginia origin of eastern Ohio African Americans was Loudon County, an area of large plantations of aristocratic families, and also small farms of Quakers, bordering the Potomac River and near the National Road through Maryland to the west. In frontier Ohio they, like the Howells from Wales, found a very different society. In 1825, when William was eighteen and the eldest of seven children, the Howells moved to a 160-acre farm in southwestern Harrison County, in the Stillwater creek area between Freeport and Moorfield, purchased with the father's $600 inheritance. It had good soil, Howells recalled, but not one acre that was level. The families of the region lived alike in log cabins or houses; the cabin into which the Howells moved was eighteen by twenty feet, with a loft above for sleeping on the floor. Neighbors commonly helped in raising buildings, and the Howells soon had a somewhat larger log house and a log barn of two pens twenty-four feet square joined by beams and a roof, in the double-crib design on all the farms. Work in the steep fields — which the Howells departed after a few seasons — took all hands; women especially harvested and prepared the flax, and if a family had older daughters but not sons, the girls planted, hoed, raked hay, and did all other farm labor but the heaviest tasks alongside their fathers. People joined together in corn-husking and

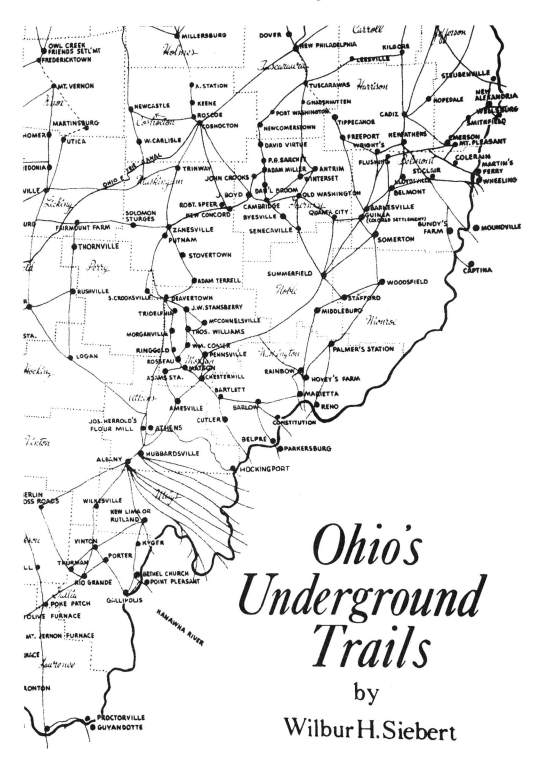

Underground railroad of Southeastern Ohio. By permission of Long's Book Company.

threshing parties, at which both women and men drank the whiskey from their stills, passed in jugs. Social discussion had its dominant subject in religion, with members of the three Presbyterian sects arguing predestination or free will with each other and with the Quakers and Methodists. The principal fault of this democratic society, Howells remembered, was the slander which their very free talking emitted (Howells 110–25, 152–8).

An "underground railroad" for escaping slaves came to pass up Short Creek and through Cadiz, north to Salem, on to Canada. Black families settled in the county where they were welcomed, mostly in Quaker localities or those of AP and ARP ministers or elders, such as the village founded in 1817 by the AP Rev. John Walker for Franklin College — New Athens — and near Charles Warfel's mill on the creek below Irish Ridge. In Cadiz they formed an African Methodist church in 1852. A few years later, the AP minister Jonathan McCready started a Sabbath School for religious instruction of their children (Hanna 150). In 1860 the town, according to the census, had 106 residents of African-American descent along with its 1060 whites (*CDS* 14 N 1861).

To the north and west of the county came many German families, having passed through Maryland; among these were the Custers who in 1839 produced George Armstrong Custer. Custer taught school on Irish Ridge in 1856–57, drove boisterous sleigh rides with Joe Dickerson, and joined in the evening debates of the "Wide Awake Exhibitional Society" in nearby Science Hill schoolhouse, before receiving the appointment to attend West Point. According to Charles B. Wallace, Bingham only recommended the young Democrat at the behest of the father of Mary Holland, with whom Custer had earlier fallen in love and dallied in the "trundle-bed," the fireside bed, of her home, where he was boarding (39, 35).

Among all these settlers during the years passed many Methodist revivals which swept people of varied ancestries into their chapels. In Cadiz, these began in meetings from 1806 usually at the home of Brother James Simpson; his son later preached his first sermons in the small frame church, and as Bishop Matthew Simpson he was a nationally eminent preacher, a friend of President Lincoln, and the speaker of his burial oration (Hanna 163).

In 1860, the county had twenty-six Methodist churches, two African Methodist, three Friends, four Disciples, four Lutheran, and five United Brethren churches (*CDS* 14 N 1861).

Religion particularly figured in ante-bellum politics of the area because the dissenting Presbyterians acted as a "church militant" in opposing slavery. The AP, from its first county ministry in 1815 under Rev. John Walker, had ardent abolitionist leadership. The ARP took up the issue of slavery as a Synod body in 1826, and their Synod of the West in 1830 urged members to free any slaves they held as soon as these people could maintain themselves in freedom. The ARP had followed Scots-Irish geographic migration patterns, pushing to the frontier fringe in the Carolinas, but without being able to settle in Virginia, so that in 1822 their southern members were too distant to attend general meetings and therefore withdrew; this small denomination exists through the South, except Virginia, today. Prior to the ARP move to eastern Ohio, ARP had established themselves numerously in Kentucky, and the Kentucky ARPs migrated into western Ohio and founded their Synod of the West, centered at Xenia (Harper 77). In Kentucky the ARP churches disappeared by 1858, probably a result of the antislavery stand.

The form of action on abolition the Cadiz AP church took around 1840 and the merged UP body declared in 1858 stemmed from the Scottish legacy. It began locally with an 1839 motion presented to the elders by Thomas Lee: "Resolved. That all members of the Secession Church who approve a resolution passed at a political meeting, held on Cadiz on the 15th day of May, A.D. 1839, approving of the course pursued by the State and National Administration on the subject of abolition, are guilty of a breach of the moral law, and the principles of the Secession Church." Opposition to the national policy in 1839 would require men to join the Liberty Party then being formed — whose platform was abolition — and depart from the Whigs or Democrats, who were abetting southerners by barring with a "gag rule" any discussion of slavery from the House. The elders' voting first produced a tie; a month later, a negative; a month afterward, a positive vote. Subsequently, the congregation, at least those who remained in it, pledged a "Solemn Covenant" on abolition, a long vow made "before God, angels, and men," with their "hands lifted up to the Most High God" (Hanna 149).

"Covenant" is of course a ubiquitous term among all Biblical believers. But it had special implications for the APs and ARPs when they codified their combined church in 1858. Among the Articles of the UP Church and the five principles they proclaimed separated them from other Presbyterians were condemnation of slaveholding and a requirement of "covenanting": "public and explicit covenanting with God is a moral duty under the gospel dispensation" (Harper 405, 79). As UPs they regarded themselves as "bound by the engagements of our reforming ancestors, in the National Covenant, and Solemn League and Covenant." They added a defensive hedge between them and the covenanting ancestors: in pledging "public and social covenanting," "we are not to be understood as expressing our approval of every thing connected with these transactions, as entered into by them" (Harper 128). The church *Manual* traces the history of the Reformed Church to a "community" that existed well before the ARP and AP were organized in 1743 and 1733 in Scotland: "It adhered tenaciously to the covenanted attainments achieved during the reformation period of 1638–1649, and became a distinct religious community after the Revolution Settlement of 1688. Many of her members suffered persecution and martyrdom at the hands of a tyrannical government as a reward for fidelity to covenant engagements. The embers of true devotion to Scriptural principles were sacredly kept alive by coventicles, society meetings and correspondence, without ministerial oversight or ecclesiastical jurisdiction, until 1743" (Glasgow 9).

The idea and image of covenanting in the minds of most literate mid-

THE SIMPSON HOME IN CADIZ, OHIO.

Typical 1862 town home. Source: George R. Crooks, *The Life of Bishop Matthew Simpson*. New York: Harper and Brothers, 1890.

nineteenth-century Americans were hardly favorable notions. The extremely popular historical novels of Sir Walter Scott, to which are often attributed Southern romantic fashions of chivalry and dueling, included one novel vividly depicting the Covenanters — as not glamorous but horrendous figures. *Old Mortality* (1816) is a colorful adventure and romance of titled gentry constructed on a detailed panorama of Scottish society and history, which is buttressed by Scott's verifying introduction, to show the fate of fanatic, ruthless peasants who, in Scott's words, saw "massacre as God's justice." His Covenanters are wild, raving canters in hillside preachings of their divine election to

defy authority; ignorant bigots who cannot communicate in civil discourse or make the least adjustment to a civil society; and terroristic rebels bent on anarchy. Their mobs, in Scott's novel, have few survivors: only "Old Mortality" who wanders the countryside for thirty years with his chisel, keeping the gravestones of slaughtered Covenanters inscribed, and the "Cameronians" he sometimes visits. By "Cameronians" Scott referred to the "sect of Reformed Presbyterians," labeling them as an extremist party of rebellion (Calder 525 n, 5).

Scott's pictures — of disruptive fanatics who would try to overthrow government rather than accept compromise — were no doubt in the heads of some progressive Harrison Countians when the "Covenanters" rose up among them, especially Presbyterians whose Scottish ancestors had endured civil war.

Personal quarrels, too, had arisen early among the struggling, interdependent Scots-Irish settlers, and persisted in their politics. John Ritchey, for instance, who owned two large farms on Irish Ridge in 1860, sketched his long feud with his McFadden neighbors, Irish natives of Coote Hill, County Cavan, when Ritchey in 1891 yet stood like "some stal- wart elm or oak" "in the green and fer- tile field" and the other pioneers had been chopped down. Ritchey's parents had been persuaded by a neighbor in Ire- land to come to Harrison County and live on his land. The family arrived in 1805, built a log cabin and a saw mill, and produced lumber for new settlers. They, like McFaddens, belonged to the ARP church. The parents died when John was sixteen, leaving ten children. He went to live and work on the neigh- boring farm of George McFadden; in six

A Harrison County farm, in 1875. Source: *Caldwell's Atlas.*

A Harrison County farm, in 1875. Source: *Caldwell's Atlas.*

years of labor he assumed he was earning his parents' land. McFadden was also bringing up a young niece, and "a mutual attachment soon sprung up." In 1834 Ann was only seventeen, under age to marry in Ohio, but she and John eloped to Pennsylvania and married there. On their return, McFadden would not grant John his land, and "would not suffer them to depart," so John worked for McFadden until his death brought the inheritance. John and Ann became Presbyterians; John, a staunch Jacksonian Democrat (Beers 49–50). The feud went to court in the 1850s after one of John Ritchey's barns burned, and he charged a McFadden with setting it afire. In a move that must have enraged Ritchey,

McFadden engaged Congressman Bingham to defend him; the testimony Bingham took from neighbors to exonerate McFadden records his rare practice of ordinary law in a nearly illegible scrawl among his papers.

Into the 1860s, characteristics of the Calvinistic Scots-Irish society prevailed. Gravestones were plain slate tablets, most inscribed with the years, months, and days of the deceased's life, to carry out the injunction of Psalms 90:12, "So teach *us* to number our days, that we may apply our *hearts* unto wisdom." Visual display, such as architecture, reflected the limitations of a practical frontier people "unmindful of man-made beauty or of any need for it" (Leyburn 151). In Cadiz, frame and brick structures lined up end to end, fronting directly on the walkway of the street. The most elaborate public building was the courthouse built around 1819, the scene of the rallies of "thousands" in 1863. It was brick, forty-five-feet square, with a closed entry porch just large enough for passageway, three steps above ground. Its embellishments were capped, arched windows and an octagonal belfry on its four-sided roof, topped by a high octagonal spire that looked like a dunce cap. The most elegant church, the Presbyterian, was brick with plain rectangular windows lined up on its two stories, the front and

THE OLD COURT-HOUSE AT CADIZ.

Courthouse of Harrison County. Source: *The Life of Bishop Matthew Simpson.*

Franklin College. Source: *Caldwell's Atlas.*

rear walls rising to conceal the roof be-hind stairstep battlements. A few brick houses were ornamented with rudimenta-ry touches of Federal architecture around windows and doors. By contrast, the town of New Lisbon, built up at the same time only forty miles north — the boyhood home of Clement L. Vallandigham — had many embellished old brick houses set in lawns, and a graceful English-country-style Episcopalian church. In the Harrison countryside, the Dickerson Chapel on Irish Ridge, built 1854, was considered a model, and remains one, of rustic carpen-try; the narrow, shuttered windows on its rectangular sides have triangular tops, and the entry belfry abutting one corner is square, with a four-gabled roof.

Not a "graven image" was to be seen, as is evident in the earliest letter Nancy

D. Mitchell preserved, from Samuel Thompson Gray. He was a nephew of the Samuel Cochran family on Irish Ridge, and had probably been her schoolmas-ter. In October 1861, twenty-three years old, he took charge of a school in Dela-ware County, north of Columbus, where his aunt lived, earning money for his ed-ucation at Franklin College. In Delaware he had seen the Roman Catholic cathe-dral, a "beautiful building" which was "however spoiled by a great Roman Cross that modern relic of ignorance su-perstition and a species of Idolatry"; and cemetery with monuments "all in the shape of a Cross and mostly colored Black a grand emblem of … supersti-tious Faith."

His letter also compared the two rural areas in that he considered the

Eastern Cadiz Township in 1862. Source: Jacob Jarvis, *Harrison County, Ohio Land Ownership Map*. Compiled by Mary Hovorka Beebe. Ashland, Ohio: Mary Beebe, 1985.

Delaware County Fair "a complete fiz-
zle," and found parties similar except
that Delaware boys were backward and
never danced. He requested a long letter
with news of the fair and the ridge.

A prevalent taste and talent for debate and lengthy argument can also be
traced to the Calvinistic sects, whose
ministers delivered several long exege-
ses of scripture from both Testaments
every Sabbath, and examined members
on the sermons and catechism, and the
social experience of contending with
these people. Matters that elsewhere
were privileged and private became
public, and public entertainment. In
one instance, the Universalists, a
church of New England's individualis-
tic intellectuals, gained adherents in
Cadiz, and to advance this reasonable
religion they brought in their skilled
proponent, who challenged the AP
minister Jonathan McCready to answer
him. This 1857 debate went on from a
Tuesday morning into Friday evening,
by which time the Universalists were
"repelled, routed, and overcome"
(Hanna 150) probably by exhaustion
and futility in this forum.

Another instance of public engagement came at a trial in which Edwin
Stanton made his greatest impression on
Cadiz, where he first practiced law. He
represented a young woman in a civil
suit for damages "for seduction under
promise of marriage." She had borne a
daughter by the son of a neighbor farmer,
and fellow church member. A large
crowd gathered for the trial, and Stanton
courted publicity; he walked with his
client from the hotel, carrying her child
into the courtroom. He made a forceful
argument to the jury and won their ver-

dict. One source of the sympathy for this
young woman was a traditional allow-
ance for sexual intimacy between engaged couples, who in the AP church
had been required to post banns of marriage, a betrothal contract. She expected
to marry the father, and brought charges
only on the day he planned to marry another. She was more vindicated than disgraced by the trial, as she later married
another man (Shotwell 75–7).

Another trial reflects some racial attitudes, and the fertile ground for dispute among a people used to arguments
over terms and definitions. In 1861 a
ridge farmer took his and his brother-
in-law's sheep west to a farm he rented
in Muskingum County, an area largely
settled by ARP and AP families from
Harrison (Porter vii). All spring, he wrote
back, he had been too "throng" by work
to write or settle his debts in Cadiz; but
all that week he had spent attending the
trial of a man they knew, "Colored man
for marrying White woman." The man
on the 1860 census was a single farm
laborer, listed as mulatto. But the trial
brought forth "a big time," and the "Court
cleared him" because they "could not
prove any African blood in him." Nancy
D. Mitchell's family's only notable contribution to local history was the long
service of her uncle Daniel Mitchell as an
elder in the AP and then UP church. The
family followed an evident custom of
naming children for uncles, aunts, and
parents which makes Mitchell and other
names in records indistinguishable; and
solely the unusual name of Nancy's father, Rudolf, leads to the genealogy contributed by her probable uncle Robert,
who neglected to mention the names of
his eight brothers and three sisters who

had died. This Robert lived in 1891 on the ridge northwest of Cadiz in Archer township, in a "commodious brick residence" beside the small log cabin built by his father John; it was this log cabin Nancy visited in Archer in the 1860s, nearby her Hines cousins, because Robert's mother was Mary Hines, daughter of the German-born Rudolf Hines, a Revolutionary War veteran. John and Mary Mitchell, Robert recorded, were AP members (Beers 221). One of his sisters was Elizabeth, who married James Megaw. Nancy's uncles Thomas and Andrew were other Mitchell brothers, living in 1862; David, Hugh, James, and John H. were surely the others, because they were buried in the Ridge graveyard west of Cadiz, where their parents lie, in 1847, victims of that year's "Seceder Fever," an epidemic of violent fever that raged principally in this congregation, and severely tested its providential doctrines, which forbade funeral eulogy or benediction over the grave (Hanna 146).

The relatives of Nancy D.'s mother on Irish Ridge were numerous families who particularized their last names by spelling them every different way they could, as Ferral, Ferrel, Farral. Nancy Farel Mitchell was five years older than Rudolf, born in Ohio in 1812, a daughter or granddaughter of Nancy and Peter Farel from Ireland. Peter in 1850 lived with Nancy and Rudolf and their children, a schoolteacher of 104 years.

Others on Irish Ridge coped with the perplexities and legal difficulties of their identical names by titling themselves by nativity, as "John McFadden (Irish)," or parentage, as "Samuel Dickerson of Asa."

In the county in 1860, the central and eastern townships of Scots-Irish settlement had the sharpest political division. The Democrats in them voted for Breckinridge and his platform to extend slaveholding, while the more German areas north and west favored Douglas, although despising, Charles Allen claimed, "his doctrines and heresies." The election of Lincoln endangered the nation, Allen concluded, but Providence had denied him a Congress that would pass any of his measures (*CDS* 14 N 1860).

Differences were set aside, however, on Valentine's Day of 1861, "considerable of a day in these parts! A live President or a President elect had never passed through this county before." "Early on that morning, everybody in this section was on tip-toe for the Junction. Six cars, as full as they could hold, went down from Cadiz, besides large numbers had gathered in from all parts of the surrounding country" (*CDS* 20 F 1861). They were "all wondering what Old Abe would look like, whether he looked, spoke, acted and ate like other people. On the road people were coming in from every hilltop and every valley, with the same anxiety depicted in their countenances and the same curiosity beaming from every feature ... until the scream of the old iron horse broke upon the ears of the impatient crowd, and announced the approach of the object of the commotion, when a rush was made for the platform of the Parks House, the hillside above and the track behind the cars. The door of the rear car was opened by Judge Jewett, who stepped upon the platform, followed by an individual looking like anything else than the original of so many pictures scattered over the country, yet instinctively all knew it was Old Abe himself, when a shout went up from the throats of near two thousand people that made the welkin ring. Old men took off their hats and shouted lustily — young men yelled and shouted as Young America can only do. The ladies waved their handkerchiefs and smiled audibly; never before did such a tumultuous shout reverberate from peak to peak of those old hills and roll in such thundering echoes down the fertile valley.

"What did Old Abe look like? He is a tall, rather spare man, with fair skin, dark hair and whiskers, broad high forehead, with sparkling eyes and tolerably capacious mouth. All who saw him was pleased with him, and he looks to possess courage, firmness and decision of character to suit the times, while his genial, smiling countenance lit up with enthusiasm indicates an abundant flow of good humor and old fashioned kindness.... After the tumult had subsided he spoke a few words to the people, thanking them for their kind reception, and stated that there were a great many stopping places between his home and Washington, and if he stopped to make a speech at every one he would not get to Washington until after the Inauguration, and that would not suit him. He had but time to thank them most heartily for this kind and cordial greeting and bid them farewell, when he was ushered into the dining room of the Parks House and partook of a most magnificent and sumptuous repast, such as we read about being served up in the banqueting halls of the gouty monarch of 'the olden time,' prepared by Mr. Cady and his excellent lady, than whom none know better how to tempt the appetite of the lovers of good living.

"Dinner over the President and suit repaired to the cars again, and Old Abe said he should return thanks to Harrison County for a most excellent dinner, when the train moved off, the President elect smiling and bowing to the crowd, who sent up cheer after cheer, and many a heart-felt aspiration went up to heaven for the safety and well-being of honest Old Abe and the Union — that the dark storm cloud which lowers in the Southern horizon may be rolled back, and the sun of liberty leap out from the midst of the tempest and shed its genial rays once more upon a united, happy, contented, and fraternal people" (*CR* 20 F 1861).

Chapter 2

Fourth of July 1862: "The War Is Almost Over Now"

An unfortunate visitor met the gamut of attitudes and manners on the streets of Cadiz in 1862. Editor Allen entitled his account "Pseudo Philanthropy": "Last week a large, stout buck African came to Cadiz from Columbus, with unexceptional testimonials from prominent Republicans in that place, on a begging tour for money to buy his children, who are now in slavery. Here was an excellent opportunity to carry into practical operation some of the superabundant philanthropy of the nigger lovers of this section. As he told a plausible story, he gathered quite a number of quarters and half dollars about town. But everybody referred him to an eminent Divine of one of our churches, who they said, had devoted all his life to uttering antislavery tirades.... Go to him, by all means he will give you a big lift, and let you collect money after service on Sunday. With high expectation our colored friend sought the parson, and laid the case before him. It was answered that he did not believe in *buying* the slaves free, and that no collection should be taken up in *his* church, and that he would not give him any aid whatever, no sir, not a red. In order to bring this conduct out in a strong light, we have only to say that the darkey applied to another divine in town, who never made a political sermon in his life, and he not only gave him pecuniary aid, but helped him in his ministerial capacity at church." (*CDS* 2 Ap 1862).

The next week, the UP minister replied, "I am not in the habit of paying any attention to such attacks.... The coarseness of the writer sufficiently betrayeth itself, as well as his recklessness of statement. The writer and those who will believe his statements, ... Such will like this, both in style and spirit. The very first line contains their shibboleth ... They see the proportions of their beloved slavery waning rapidly, and cannot be comforted and are mad.... O! how it *galls* them to see their quondam associates driven to the wall by our brave Yankee boys. They are groaning inwardly, but now, thank God, things are not as they were. Loyalty is popular now, and they must, with the best face they can wear, drift with the mighty current. The halcyon days for them are gone, and they are mad, so look out, ye abolitionists! You are the cause of all this....

"Now in all this pile of hyperbole there is one grain of truth not very creditable to that writer — viz: that everybody *sent* the colored man to me and other antislavery men, as they have always done, (giving nothing themselves) so that if we give nothing they can cry 'hypocrites' and if we give they can call us 'nigger lovers,' &c. Now I envy not that man his wretched heart who can take enjoyment from inquiring into what others do that he may have the satisfaction of proclaiming it upon the house tops. — The colored man said he was questioned closely immediately after he was in town, no doubt by the writer. How natural the description of David, 'They hide, they lurk, they mark my steps, waiting my soul to kill.'...

"The story of the colored man, for aught I know, is true. It was to the effect that having been a slave himself he bought his freedom for a large sum, and came to Columbus, Ohio, to raise money by work and begging to buy his family, consisting of a wife and five children, held by a widow lady in Staunton, Western Va., by the name of Mrs. Crawford. Represents Mrs. C. as a Unionist and a member of the Presbyterian church. He succeeded in raising money to buy his wife and babe at $650 and a little boy at $1109, and now has $1000 more, and is trying to raise the balance to buy the re-maining three who are between the ages of 15 and 18 or 19. Mrs. Crawford being loyal and *pious*, and being compelled, of course, by the circumstances surrounding her to be a slaveholder much against her will — ... this pious Sarah, in view of our war times, is willing to be relieved of this burden and relieved her grip of these three human souls for the paltry sum of $3200.... I told the colored man that it was an outrageous price.... I told him I had for some time been rejoicing in the belief that slavery was doomed, — was of the opinion that before a year rolled round he could get his children for little or nothing....

"One thing more I said — for I will yet be more vile in the eyes of proslaveryism. I told him I would give him five dollars if he would go and steal them. Horribile dictu! Dishevel your hair and rend your garments, ye proslavery Scribes and Pharisees, hypocrites! Ye have heard the blasphemy, what need ye any further witness? If it were blasphemy against God you could stand, but it is against diabolism....

"The writer of that, too, has his church [Allen was a Presbyterian] and persists in making invidious comparisons. And were it not for his persistent devotion to it, one might almost doubt whether he is an insidious enemy or an indiscreet friend. Now is it not decidedly cool for him to boast of their contributing and twit us for not contributing to rescue three souls from the avaricious grasp of one of their own members. Shame! ... J. S. McCready" (*CR* 9 Ap 1862).

Local society expected vituperation in politics, especially from Allen, a prominent figure with, a Mitchell letter noted, the greatest belly ever seen.

Support for the war was not at issue; to Ohioans the war seemed nearly over, as a long article Allen reprinted from the *Ohio Cultivator* in June proclaimed; and the time seemed at hand to pursue the moral and political course that would bring about justice after the imminent victories of the Union armies closing on Richmond and Corinth, Mississippi.

Party differences concerning this justice did not interfere with mutual celebrations of the Fourth of July. A letter to the *Sentinel* vowed: "Let us celebrate it with guns, martial music, bonfires and every thing.... Let gun powder be used freely.... Let us eat every thing we should eat; drink every thing we should drink" (25 Je). In a more temperate mode, the Cadiz Presbyterian and UP Sunday Schools gathered a large crowd in the nearby oak grove to hear Mayor John S. Pearce, a handsome young attorney, Democrat, and proud new father, read the Declaration of Independence; and to hear speeches by the Rev. J. S. McCready, the Rev. David Craig, and the banker R. M. Lyons, superintendent of the Presbyterian Sunday School. They listened, by Allen's account, to the suitable addresses and ignored any that contained abolitionism. Then from the tables they filled themselves with the "good things of life" and visited, while "the children were in the best of humor" (CR, CDS 9 Jl). The sun was shining after a cold, rainy spring that had lasted into June; farmers were beginning to cut the green hay that had flourished; and wool sales were brisk — the fine wools were bought, and Walter Beebe had sold 12,000 pounds of medium wool at 45¢ each, 12¢ more than last year, as these sales commenced.

On this day, the Mitchells' neighbor Abram Holmes, Jr., was in Columbus at the Democratic State Convention organized by Clement Vallandigham, to promote a quick end to war through election of Democrats in the fall. The premise of the county Democrats, as attorney Josiah Estep had proposed it in their meeting a week before, was to sustain the government in putting down rebellion. But a bold young speaker then arose to decry the recent Congressional act abolishing slavery in Washington, D.C., to blame prior Republican opposition to territorial extensions of slavery for causing the war, to claim the salvation of the country depended on continuing slavery, and to declare the South was fighting for its rights, and could not be subdued. This supporter of Vallandigham's principles, attorney Philip Donahue, became one of the four Convention delegates (CR 2 Jl).

On the Fourth of July, the citizens generally were proud of their county's contribution to the armies which seemed close to victory; but they had surrendered few men to death, or even much danger; and they had faint acquaintance with the realities of the war. They had early mustered men enthusiastically in response to Bingham's 13 April 1861 message: "Fort Sumpter has been battered down by the traitor hoards of the South. It is the first battle upon this continent and of this century waged in defense of chattel slavery.... I repeat now what I said in my place as your Representative last January, — the question of to-day is not whether the constitution of our country shall be amended, but whether the constitution shall be maintained. Upon the solution of this question depends the fate of the Republic. President Lincoln ... will, I trust, soon summon the loyal citizens ... to the rescue of a violated constitution; let them come as the winds come, when the forests are rending; let them come as the waves come, when the navies are stranding." A week later Bingham addressed a crowd overfilling the courthouse seats and stirred them to roaring. They hauled the rusty cannon up out of storage and thundered charges across the hills. Two days later, a volunteer company was on the street with "General" Warfel, the mill owner, former State Senator, and an officer in the militia of olden days, introducing drill. On 27 April, a hundred men left for camp, after a prayer meeting in the courthouse and presentation of a New Testament, pin cushion, and needle-case (McGavran 30-33).

These men were three-month volunteers in the 13th Regiment O.V.I. (Ohio Volunteer Infantry) Many, like William Pittenger, came home at the end of that time in camp. Others reenlisted in two companies of the 13th, or in a company raised in the county for the 30th. Company H of the 13th, under Capt. R. R. Henderson, titled themselves the "Cadiz Guards." Capt. Castill of the original company led another. This regiment by January 1862 was only half-filled, advertising for 500 needed recruits. In the 30th a company under Capt. David Cunningham called themselves the "Harrison Guards." Among them were Hiram Dickerson, Jr., and Joseph Dickerson, Jr., of Irish Ridge. In December 1861, Company C of the 43rd left under Capt. Moses J. Urquhart. During 1861 the county had sent just over "half her proportion as required by

the State," a deficit subjecting citizens to the "taunts and jeers" from the counties surrounding (*CR* 8 Ja 1862).

In the winter, however, two more companies were raised, one for the 74th by Albion Bostwick, son-in-law of editor Richard Hatton and a Mexican War veteran; another for the 69th. Several boys ran away from home in January to join Bostwick, including Hatton's son Frank and seventeen-year-old J. W. Gallaher, who enjoyed four months in camp before his father took him out of service and back to the farm (Beers 222).

Training in drill took months for these men who, at home, had never marched. After training, they were mostly assigned where reliable guards were needed, among people who needed to be convinced Union soldiers were peacekeepers, not fearsome warriors. In July 1861 the 13th joined the Army of Occupation of Western Virginia, guarding the railroad near Grafton against bridge burning. The 30th went to Sutton, Western Virginia, in September, with only 444 men enrolled, to guard the depot and the trains between Grafton and Charleston. On 21 September Col. W. S. Smith led the 13th on a charge during the small battle at Carnifax Ferry on the Gauley River; their march through a ravine of rocks and dense laurel turned the line to the shape of a *U*, and when an enemy or accidental gunshot sounded, the 13th blindly, in panic opened fire on each other, killing 2, wounding 30. In their next action on 16 November, they pursued the Confederate forces of Gen. Floyd "scouting most cautiously" (*OR* 1.2.225, 586; 1.5.140, 278).

In December the 13th were sent to Kentucky to join Buell's army and move south. On 6 April 1862 they camped above Pittsburg Landing, Tennessee, and marched to the front of the battle of Shiloh to join Gen. Nelson's line on the left. This murderous running battle showed many Union cowards, but reports home of regiments that ran did not include the 13th. The Cadiz Guards had 3 killed and 7 wounded, including Capt. Henderson; but news of the loss came with the consolation of apparent great victory, because the Confederate army retreated south. By July, the 13th were in Huntsville, Alabama, among the Union forces trapping and besieging Bragg's Confederate army (*OR* 1.10.365–6; 1.16.593).

The 30th remained in the Western Virginia mountains, guarding ferries in the New River gorge, occasionally chasing rebel bands, and moving south in the effort to construct telegraph lines through the wilderness; in July, they were guarding communications around Flat Top Mountain, near present-day Beckley (*OR* 1.12.127). The 43rd, after a winter in camp, enjoyed a steamship ride down the "Grand Ohio" to Cairo, before an excited trek through the woods to near New Madrid, Missouri, 13 March, where rebel gunboats lobbed shells at them for two days, but missed them. The enemy vacated the town in the night; and the 43rd participated in a significant conquest with the major complaint, according a letter from Arch J. Sampson, of having had to lie on their muskets all night in the rain. They had passed by a few "large slave plantations," of which he observed only that the soil was rich, deep, but probably unhealthful (*CR* 26 Mr). Thereafter, they marched south amid the army, and camped in front of Corinth, Mississippi, by 13 May.

The 69th and 74th moved from training camp only late in April to Nashville, Tennessee, and its vicinity, where they guarded bridges and took the police duties of provost guards. Capt. Bostwick reported home that they had marched 200 miles in the area, chasing rebels, taking down disunion flags, and having speeches. They also provided a "good example" against fears of "Hessians, Yankee Invaders, and Lincolnites" with their Sabbath services, in which they formed themselves as a hollow square and invited visitors inside (*CR* 2 Jl, 11 Je).

At home, people still thought of battles in distant, naïve curiosity, which the *Cadiz Republican* addressed with an article on 2 July, "What Is A Battle, You Ask?" It began, "You have often wondered whether the men wore their overcoats, knapsacks, haversacks, and carry their blankets, when going into battle. That depends upon circumstances.... You also wonder whether the regiments fire regularly in volleys or whether each man fires as fast as he can." Usually, it answered, the regiment fires only upon their officers' specific commands. The distance between this writer and any battle created his impression of its sounds: "You hear a drop, drop, drop as a few of the skirmishers fire, followed by a rattle and roll which sounds like the falling of a building, just as some of you have heard a brick wall tumble at a great fire." The untypical battle he described seems to derive from either the tactics recommended for front-line skirmishers who have had to run from a cavalry attack and have to reassemble (Heitman 137), or a recent fight at Front Royal, Virginia, in which Confederate infantry reportedly charged in a hollow square formation, single file front and rear, double files on the sides, with fixed bayonets; and the fleeing Union soldiers were attacked on three sides by Stonewall Jackson's cavalry (*CR* 4 Je, 18 Je).

Moreover, only in the past few weeks had the county begun to learn, with shock, the peril of disease in the army. Francis M. McConnell died in Nashville 22 June of typhoid fever. His obituary, written by a friend, paid respect to "the alacrity with which he responded to his country's call to his duty — disregarding the social tie that bound him to home…" (*CR* 9 Jl). Will Reid, also of the 69th, eighteen-year-old son of a New Athens minister, too died of typhoid. His fellow members of the Philo Society at Franklin College, including A. A. McConnell and John Finley Oglevee, draped their hall in black and resolved to wear badges of mourning for thirty days. His father submitted to the *Cadiz Republican* a letter Will had written during his fever, in which Will wandered seeking liver pills and medical care for almost two weeks before receiving any — too late, his father bitterly complained (25 Je).

In summer 1862 people were also largely ignorant of the conditions and motives in society of the South. The apparent approach of Union victory raised fears that escaping or liberated slaves would soon cross the Ohio in overwhelming numbers. In the past month the Ohio legislature had considered a law proposed to ban black immigrants from entering the state. The "Union" majority, of Republicans and Democrats joined in a war-time Union party, refused, in Allen's words, "to pass a law to prevent the State of Ohio from being overrun with the lazy, worthless runaway negroes of the South"; while Bingham, in House debate, said he welcomed the "'great numbers of the unfortunate race who were fleeing to Ohio, and he hoped the great exodus would continue!'" Allen added, "Send him round! Let the finger of scorn be pointed at him! Let every white laboring man in the State avoid him as they would a viper!" (*CDS* 25 Je). Hatton noted a shifting sentiment: men in the county who previously "rode into office by professing extreme antislavery sentiments" had come to "speak as sneeringly of Abolitionists as the meanest locofoco rebel sympathizer" (*CR* 25 Je).

Chapter 3

"'Lay on McDuff' &c"

In the Fields, Streets, Saloons

After the Fourth of July, startling reports came up the Cadiz Branch and telegraph wires, and out the lanes, to the families pressed in the heaviest work of harvesting, as the hay all had to be cut rapidly "when in the milk," raked up, covered from dews, spread out and turned over several days to cure it, then hauled to the barns (*CR* 11 Je).

Word of reversals for the army advancing on Richmond seeped out from a succession of contradictory accounts from the Virginia peninsula, which the Cadiz papers of 9 July traced. Having to set type by hand all week for their issues, the editors set reports as they received them. Thus people first heard of the Battle Before Richmond as on the *Cadiz Republican's* page one: "Splendid Victory — Stonewall Jackson's Army Defeated … Retrograde Movement Continued by Order of Gen. McClellan." Page three brought the Baltimore reporter's wires that the army had been fighting for four days and had retreated seventeen miles; later, that in six days it had lost 12,000

soldiers; later, 20,000; finally, that on 4 July Gen. McClellan addressed his troops in Washington announcing a victory with no loss.

Amid the news of McClellan's rout from the peninsula appeared notices of the approaching income taxes to pay for the war; of the President's call for 300,000 volunteers; and of Gov. Tod's call for 25,000 men to fill existing regiments and 40,000 for Ohio's proportion of the 300,000.

The same week, another shock hit Irish Ridge. From Flat Top Mountain in Western Virginia, where the air could be presumed wholesome, came a dispatch that Hiram Dickerson, Jr., had died of disease. Further grievous, his body could not be brought home to the churchyard on his family farm. He was buried on the remote mountain.

In Cadiz war news filtered through the bustle of business and pleasures. Wool sales continued brisk, bringing up to 50¢ a pound. A new attraction was the soda fountain Sam Ferguson had installed in his confectionery, "just what's been needed in this place for a long time," where gentlemen were encouraged to take their wives and sweethearts: "Now's the time for ice cream, soda water, oranges, lemons, etc." (*CR* 11 Je).

At the "Ice Cream Saloon," young men and women could debate the knotty problems posed in the *Sentinel's* regular "Scientific" columns. In these, local schoolteachers with pen names such as "Secant," "Cotangent," "&," and "tab." challenged current textbook principles, and submitted original questions and theories they considered more significant than the authorities'. Under discussion this month were two long treatises by "tab." on "Grammatical Blunders," in which he sought to re-establish nouns upon his new lengthy postulates of definition, which included "archetypes." In addition, the problem presented by "&" had remained unsolved: "If the earth is 7912 miles in diameter, how high above its surface must the eye be placed, in order to see all of it?" Differing intricate geometrical diagrams for the eye-in-space were offered by Tangent and by Inquirer. Inquirer then added this perplexing issue: "Considering the etymology of *deleble* [*sic*] and *indelible*, as also that of *parsnip* and *turnip*, why the difference in orthography?" (*CDS* 16 Jl).

Meanwhile, from the law office above George & Bro. Grocery, a new public diversion emerged. Attorney Stewart-Beebe Shotwell, at forty-three, had been a leader in the old Whig Party, then the Republican, then the war-time Union party which had absorbed most local Democrats. Now, with reorganizations pending to steer renewed recruiting and nominations for the fall elections, he sensed his powerbase was

crumbling. Some county Republicans, particularly Richard Hatton, had not given up their name or separate meetings, as he had expected, but worked in tandem with his Union party and kept on championing Republican leaders, like John A. Bingham, and their efforts to liberate slaves and even put them into military service. These aims offended many of his Union Democrats, and in recent weeks Charles Allen had sponsored a revival of Democrats (*CR* 28 My) which could lure them from Shotwell's camp entirely.

In mid-July the county Military Committee formed with Estep, Pearce, Lyons, Hatton, and Allen, without Shotwell; and Hatton in his paper supported the Union party in the state, but advocated a Republican ticket for the county, rejecting a "mongrel" party that would cater to "Locos" and not re-elect Bingham (*CR* 16 Jl). Thereupon Shotwell embarked on a campaign against Hatton. He took a ledger to the auditor's office, searched, and copied the accounts over eleven years of Hatton's pay for printing county work. Then he appeared "daily, at the corners of the streets, in the stores, and at other public places making an exhibit of the same to passers-by." "Our old friend," Hatton lamented, "has become our bitterest personal enemy." Shotwell charged that Hatton had made a "fortune" off the county. In two columns, Hatton defensively detailed his business, claiming he had never made, in totality, a profit over $200 a year. "He's trying to crush us out or compel us to cease our opposition to his Union party — himself and one locofoco." Shotwell was "incensed," Hatton wrote, because Republicans denied his and

Jamison's demand that their Union committee alone campaign. Shotwell "has set himself up as Dictator" for the county and "woe be to the Republican who stands in opposition to that indomitable, self-willed individual. Already the edict has gone forth that we are to be crushed out.... We have no tears, however.... 'Lay on McDuff' &c." (30 Jl).

["And damn'd be him that first cries "Hold, enough!"" (*Macbeth* V.viii.33-34)] Here Hatton infelicitously cast himself as Macbeth in his losing fight, and misspelled the valorous hero as a Scots-Irish cousin. The "Bloodhound," as he came to call Shotwell, did not relent.

Recruiting

Having such entertainments, Cadiz gave little attention to recruiting this month. Allen predicted that recruiting would proceed only after Congress showed people that the war had the sole purpose of restoring "the Union as it was and the Constitution as it is." The first officer commissioned to recruit for a new 98th regiment hardly stirred enthusiasm. He was Wm. P. Saunders, a fifty-five-year-old member of a storekeeping family in Hopedale, who had been a recruiter for various regiments, a service for which men were sometimes paid by captains raising companies. His notice announced "Richmond Must Be Taken" and warned that "if we do not volunteer, we will be drafted" (*CDS, CR* 16 Jl).

By this time, "shocking scenes" were reported from the recent battlefield, of our mutilated soldiers left in the woods and swamps; and dis-

patches came that Morgan's 2,800 guerilla cavalry were in the Kentucky Bluegrass, stealing horses, destroying property, and occupying towns, while an attack on our force at Murfreesboro, Tennessee, had led to its surrender.

During the next week, with military rallies scheduled to begin 24 July, with Shotwell, Estep, and others vying to address them, and Bingham coming home to speak, Allen overcame his reluctance about recruiting. A committee for the five-county district met at Steubenville, with Mayor John S. Pearce its secretary. There Estep successfully proposed that each county supply men to the new 98th in proportion to its population, thus: Carroll 125, Harrison 150, Jefferson 200, Tuscarawas 255, and Belmont 270. The man transferring to lead the 98th was a long-time Democrat friend of Allen, at thirty-seven, a prominent Steubenville attorney, a Mason, a "perfect gentleman," a devoted husband and father of two little boys. He had served one year in the Mexican War and the past one as major, then lieutenant colonel of the 25th Ohio. In its service in Western Virginia, he had led 700 men to Huntersville, fought off 600 cavalry, and driven two infantry companies from the town. In this, he made a January march of 102 miles in six days, to thirty miles deeper into enemy-held territory than had before been attempted. In April he had led eight companies of various infantry regiments and a cavalry company to meet over 1,000 attacking rebels and cavalry at Monterey; after a brief skirmish, the rebels retreated (*OR* 1.5.497-8; 1.12.1. 422-3). George Webster would become colonel of the 98th.

Interestingly, Webster had previously set some of Cadiz to marching. He had come to give a speech for Douglas in the 1860 campaign, to a gathering mostly of Breckinridge Democrats and Republicans in front of the courthouse. The Republican club of "Wide Awakes" (who it seems had previously engaged the courthouse for their meeting) assembled, "beat their drums," and paraded discourteously through Webster's audience (who may have selected the occasion to disrupt the Wide Awakes) (*CDS* 10 O 1860).

The 98th's second regimental leader had been a captain in the 43rd Ohio and had been rumored to be so disgusted with service he wanted to resign; but Allen had reason to encourage his leadership in the army. At home in St. Clairsville, Christian Poorman, 36, had been the abolitionist editor of the influential Belmont County *Chronicle*. Allen publicly commended his energy and "temperate habits."

The man who suddenly ascended to the position of major was John S. Pearce, 30. "Major Pearce we all know to be a social, jovial, clever fellow." Allen became confident the county could raise 150 men in two companies in the next twenty days (23 Jl). Allen also became, upon the Democrat Pearce's resignation, the mayor of Cadiz (*CR* 30 Jl). Then he left on a vacation, probably in the quiet village of Freeport where his aged father lived, and put his foreman W. H. Arnold in charge of the *Sentinel* (*CDS* 6 Ag).

Despite the offer of a $100 bounty, one-fourth to be paid when the regiment filled, and one month's pay of $13 in advance, and the threat that drafted men would earn only $11, moreover have no

voice in the election of their officers (*CR* 23 Jl), Wm. Saunders had enrolled only one man, Martin Overholt, when the rallies began. At the first, Thursday evening in the courthouse, Christian Poorman spoke, but none enrolled. The next evening John A. Bingham addressed a courthouse meeting, with like result. On Saturday, however, one man of Cadiz, John C. Norris, 25, signed up.

He was evidently a patriotic, popular, and enterprising man, of remarkably good looks, Nancy observed in a later letter as she contrasted them with his habits (perhaps drinking and irreligion). During the war he courted, and married, Jeanette, the daughter of the very wealthy farmer Walter Beebe, despite her family's great opposition. Soon after enlisting, John C. Norris joined Saunders as a recruiting officer; and it seems that he set about persuading convivial town companions to enroll.

On 29 July, a volunteer came forward from a different quarter: James W. Dickerson, 21, a younger brother of Joe, and cousin of the dead Hiram, Jr.

Meetings began around the townships on 30 July, twenty-two of them, nightly except Sundays, from New Athens, Laceyville, Deersville, New Market (Scio), Smyrna, to Love's School House in Archer on 8 August, with a grand rally to finish on Saturday morning in Cadiz. Bingham, Lewis Lewton (Bingham's law partner), Estep, Shotwell, Pearce, and Lyons rode around the county making speeches, urging men to do their duty in defense of the country, or the Constitution. Propitious for the various-minded speakers were three new acts of President Lincoln. He had replaced McClellan with Halleck as

General-in-Chief. He had signed the Confiscation Bill freeing slaves of people in rebellion who came within Union lines, and allowing the President to employ them, a measure Bingham had introduced, along with an emancipation bill that lost (*CR* 4 Je). At this time, on the other hand, relatively few slaves of active rebels lodged within Union occupation; and the taking of Richmond, which appeared the necessary, sufficient military stroke to end rebellion, would not affect much territory nor many slaves. Moreover, Lincoln had newly appealed to the slave-holding Border States, revoking a general's proclamation of emancipation in his vicinity, supporting federal reimbursement for gradual emancipation, and proposing an emigration of blacks to South America (*CR* 30 Jl).

New Athens, with its Franklin College, was an abolition and Bingham stronghold; it had already sent numbers to the war, and after Bingham spoke there, so many students left to enlist that the college nearly emptied of all but its few young women. It remained a mere skeletal school until the end of the war. Nancy's neighbor on the next farm, John Finley Oglevee, 22, who was in his last term and an advanced mathematician; Samuel Thompson Gray, 24; Abram Holmes, and others left its halls.

Bingham's oratorical effects in the 1862 recruiting through the area were described by the editor of the Noble County *Republican*, after their military committee invited him to speak at their meetings: "Prior to the holding of meetings, volunteering was a low ebb, and indeed, the most sanguine among us were in a state almost of despondency.

No sooner had Mr. Bingham come among us than a marked change took place. Under the earnest, powerful, convincing pleadings of Mr. B. in behalf of our bleeding country, the scales fell from the eyes of many who have opposed the war from conscientious motives." The "great statesman" expounded the "real issue at stake," the country. Upon "learning" this the old and young men "gathered round this Champion of Freedom and the Right" to contribute money or life "for the preservation of the Union, the Constitution and the enforcement of the Laws" (*CR* 20 Ag). These last phrases had political reference as they quoted the 1860 slogan of the Constitutional Union party, in its support for the Tennessee slaveholder Bell against Lincoln (McPherson, *Battle Cry* 219-20).

People journeyed to hear Bingham's speeches, which were long, unwritten, seemingly spontaneous orations. On 30 July Thomas, eighteen-year-old son of the Kyles on Short Creek, enlisted, with his father's consent.

Several of his neighbors soon joined, Tom Stringer, Robert Booth, and Robert Hagan. Around Charlestown, at Warfel's mill, two Finney sons, George Adams, and others enlisted. From Irish Ridge Bill McBride followed Jim Dickerson, then John Pennock and his younger brother Richard, George and Asa Glaisner, and Bill Moffitt, a married laborer of 27 who had three children. Another laboring ridge father, John Penn, 43, signed on to be the company wagoner.

By 6 August, forty to fifty were promised to the 98th. Anderson P. Lacey and George A. Voorhees joined the recruiting officers, and enrolled men in the west and north of the county as the meetings and speeches progressed — pairs of McKirahans, McMaths, and Quigleys.

The last township meeting of the series on 8 August in Archer drew more sons from Irish Ridge. Robert Mitchell evidently wanted to join, but his family thought him too young at eighteen, and vulnerable. He was known to his cousins as "little Robert," probably to distinguish him from his Robert uncle and cousins, and because he was immature in general. They were suspicious of the company he might keep with Norris' friends. His parents no doubt came to consent to his going because they trusted Jim Dickerson, Finley Oglevee, and Thompson Gray to look after Robert, expected a long, disciplined training under Cols. Webster and Poorman in "the beautiful and healthy camp at Mingo, near Steubenville" (CR 6 Ag), and took a further, compelling encouragement: on this evening Ira Dickerson, Hiram Jr.'s younger brother, joined the company.

The next morning, Saturday, on "a glorious day in Cadiz," a crowd of "two to three thousand" men assembled. John C. Norris soon had names to fill the company, including those of William A. Pittenger, 20 — the seventh volunteer to leave Hatton's office (CR 6 Ag) — James M. Crawford, 19, who worked at the Sentinel, and John D. Norris, 29. "About one o'clock the Cadiz Brass Band took position on the capacious stand erected on the Public Square, and the meeting was organized by calling Josiah M. Estep to the chair. After music by the band, Mr. Estep announced the purpose of the meeting and introduced Rev. Butts, a new recruit." Butts said he "did not intend making a speech — the time for speaking had passed &c. He made, however, a patriotic appeal to the men of Harrison, in behalf of our bleeding country, and called upon them to go with him to its rescue. After he drew tears from many eyes 'unused to the melting mood,' he took from his pocket a Roll, and invited those willing to enter the service with him to come forward and sign." Fifteen to twenty promptly signed. Lt. Col. Poorman then spoke, although hoarse from two weeks of "incessant speaking," and Major Pearce gave a brief address (CR 13 Ag).

Anthony Butts, 30, was a Methodist preacher on the Deersville Ridge circuit west of Cadiz, and he brought in young men by twos, threes, and fours from its families — Hines, Poulsons, Birneys, McKinnies, Pattersons, Barretts, McCombs, and more. He would make a "fighting captain," Hatton recommended, on the basis of his speech. He soon had about 115 young men wanting to serve with him, and so, his own company.

At the same time, Col. Dan McCook, of the "Fighting McCooks" of Carrolton, whose older brother Maj. Gen. Robert, while riding in an ambulance, had recently been murdered by guerrillas near Selma, Alabama, was recruiting in the area. James T. Holmes of the Science Hill family had become, after graduation from Franklin College, President of Richmond College in Jefferson County; he led out twenty-eight of his students there into McCook's 52nd Ohio (Stewart 199), and also his brother Abram.

Another recruiting drama transpired in the UP church. Nancy's congregation sat under the arched ceiling, which they had painted blue like the heavenly vault, below the high, staircased pulpit where their black-cloaked minister gave a "patriotic" sermon; and then before them Mr. McCready disrobed, revealing himself clothed in an army uniform. He had a commission to raise a company. The boys and men who soon joined it came largely from his congregation. One of the first was Nancy's cousin John L., elder Daniel's son, at 24 a schoolteacher like his sisters Nancy K. and Martha, the most promising young man of the family. Two brothers of Finley Oglevee quickly joined it: Hugh, 23, and James W., 20. Elisha Hargrave of Nancy's neighborhood, and two each of the Haverfields, Loves, and Herveys entered. From the farm above hers, Frank P. Grove enrolled, listing an age inferior to his thirty-four years, at which he was a year older than McCready — and then his nephew, Frank McNary, 18. A younger brother of McCready came from Pennsylvania to his company.

By 20 August the county had added between 400 to 500 men to the 619 volunteers it had already sent, and recruiting was still going on, with extended meetings. Two full companies had gone to camp with Norris and Butts. Voorhees had a full company, Richard M. Lyons had seventy to eighty men enrolled, and McCready was calling through his congregation and around the countryside. Over 1,100 men of the fewer than 20,000 men, women, and children in the labor-pressed agricultural county had become volunteers in the army (*CR* 20 Ag).

Alongside this effort, citizens were asked to pledge money to pay soldiers' bounties and support their families. A long list of subscribers appeared in the *CR*, followed by names of four men who had been solicited but refused to contribute — at the top was Walter Beebe (20 Ag).

At the same time, the county assessors enrolled all men aged 18 to 45 in case a draft became necessary, or the state militia should be re-assembled. The latter possibility had seemed, to some leading Democrats, a great threat this summer. Allen had printed numerous warnings. They followed from the 4 July speech of Vallandigham, carried in the *Sentinel* 6 August, which reported a plan to call up the militia and denounced it as a scheme to suppress Democratic meetings and newspapers, to kidnap and arrest editors. As Democrats rallied to military meetings and regiments, however, such fears subsided. Mayor Allen returned to his paper to load it with articles about the "Warfare on the President," articles which supported Lincoln against the abolitionist Republicans pressing him to declare emancipation, and which clearly supposed Lincoln did not favor emancipation except with emigration to foreign colonies, and would take no such action if the war ended soon (13 Ag, 20 Ag, 27 Ag). This "Warfare on the President" provided another motive for anti-abolitionists to join and cheer Father Abraham's 300,000.

The Union party cause advanced. Besides his military speaking engagements, Stewart-Beebe Shotwell found time for more "street harangues." Specifically, he charged that Hatton had triply overcharged the county. Hatton denied it, with details of his costs for paper and labor. Shotwell now meant to "starve us out," he squealed, but counterattacked that Shotwell had "accumulated a *fortune* by *skinning* his clients, and *oppressing* the unfortunate" (6 Ag). This was vitriol; but Shotwell did weekly advertise that he gave "especial and prompt attention to Collecting, business of Executors, … Titles to Real Estates, … and loaning and investment of money." His name often appeared as the attorney handling foreclosures and auctions of property. The county Republicans met on 18 August in one convention with Shotwell's Union party. There together they resolved their approval of the course of Rep. Bingham, saying "Well done, good and faithful servant," and pledged to nominate him for re-election (*CR* 20 Ag).

This unanimity probably touched on the bottom line, or shoal that pressed so many men this month toward the military rapids: local men of any political standing wanted to avoid a draft, for which they would be blamed. They were grateful to Bingham for his having orated men into serving the call of the President, from divergent and, in some regards, momentarily propulsive reasons to support Lincoln. Volunteers of differing ages and backgrounds had of course varying motives in this quick enrollment, from impulses to join brothers and friends in adventure, to the "deep conviction of duty, after mature and prayerful reflection" — as McCready's decision was described by Rev. Wm. Wishart — of being called "in the providence of God" to demonstrate "the sincerity of his faith and profession" by sharing with young men the work and dangers in the "strife between liberty and slavery." Yet the force which swept so many together was the power of oratory, as attributed to Bingham and, on occasion, Butts.

Oratory was the high art of this culture. Oratory marks a culture still oral in orientation, not refined to reliance on printed text, not separated from communal sense and action by the critical, individualizing perspective raised on print. These citizens of 1862 were not, in other words, the individualist Americans Ralph Waldo Emerson defined or, perhaps, created with his pithy essays on self-reliance. When Lincoln in the Gettysburg Address, as Garry Wills demonstrates, radically altered public address, he changed its model from long oration to Emersonian text, and in effect its audience from the crowd to the reflective individual.

Politically, the impetus of oration seems quite significant, especially in view of the dramatic changes in men's responses to Bingham. For all its apparent social power over people in its hearing, however deeply it moves them at the time, an oration's vocal impression must fade in memory, and its elaborated connections of reason and sentiment fray. The mutability of response probably arose less from insincerity than from the shifting wind of time in which oratory raises its tornado in the forest, to extend McGavran's metaphor describing Bingham's 1861 rallying speech: it would deafen those within its power to the usual surrounds of their fears and interests; stir them to the roots of their beliefs; and then depart, replaced by other weather, with no lasting effects on the trees — unless they were felled.

Into the "Gorgeous Procession"

Early on the Monday morning of the Union party convention, Robert

Mitchell's family joined the crowd of well over 1,000 at the depot (*CR* 20 Ag) to see his company off to camp. It was not a rending occasion for them, since they could ride the cars to the camp to visit, and plan to do so for months; some families, like Nancy's, accompanied their boys, to inspect the place before they left them there. Other recruits were far from chaperoned; on the train Nancy noticed the boisterous drunkenness of several who had evidently caroused all night.

They rode through the ravines and tunnels, through the steaming brick city of Steubenville with its wool and felting mills, and south along the river to the camp. It sat on the Mingo Flats, a broad bank near an island where the Mingo Indians had crossed and camped.

The early business was electing officers. Men commissioned to recruit who entered service customarily were granted the top positions, and John C. Norris became Captain, Wm. Saunders, 1st Lt. Other officers chosen represent early recruits from various county neighborhoods or friends of Norris. John W. Carson became 2nd Lt.; John H. Reaves, 1st Sergeant; Martin Overholt, William McBride, William A. Pittenger, and James M. Crawford among the corporals. John Finley Oglevee and Thompson Gray were privates just like young Robert Mitchell and Thomas Kyle. Jim Dickerson, however, was made the Color Sergeant, to carry the flag for Webster's entire regiment.

This company, with some reason, felt it represented Webster's favorite best men. As Co. C, it would stand in line-of-battle formation in the center of the regiment. During a drill it claimed notice by the Steubenville *Herald* as "phys-

ically well-developed and remarkably uniform in size — not tall but compact … educated young men, every fifth man competent to represent a district or teach an academy" (*CDS* 27 Ag). This uniformity in height implies that friends and neighbors who had arrived together in groups would stay in the same proximities, as the company was early lined up by height to form ranks and squads; this basic military assignment did not much revise prior associations, and Bill McBride stood near Robert as his corporal.

Rev. Anthony Butts, among his many "professors of religion" (*CR* 20 Ag), became Captain of Co. F when they arrived on Tuesday; Anderson Lacey, 1st Lt.; and Fletcher McCullough, 2nd Lt.

Norris, Butts, and their officers hardly had time to learn, much less teach, the basics of drill in camp; within hours of their arrival they were ordered to "the front" in Kentucky, and left the following Saturday.

Not only were rebel forces in the central Bluegrass, they had taken East Tennessee and neared Cumberland Gap; all of Kentucky seemed in danger (*CR* 20 Ag). The alarms of John H. Morgan's recent exploits had brought local readers a curious description of "the Guerrilla": his force "embraces men from Texas, Miss., Georgia, and Kentucky, of desperate character, but obedient to his will, as is the lion to his master. A few of them are gentlemen, but the majority would as soon cut a man's throat as to take a chew of tobacco." He himself was said to be courteous, never angered; dark-complexioned with a mustache and chin whiskers, wearing a low-crowned black felt hat with its wide crown raised on one side by a silver crescent; before the war, his business was that of a Cincinnati faro bank — he "was engaged in picking up 'seeds,' as verdant people who accompanied him to the gambling houses were familiarly called" (*CR* 13 Ag).

Toward such unaccountable warriors the verdant soldiers rushed in confidence. As they lined up at the train, young ladies brought them a silk flag. Miss Annie Bennett addressed them: "Volunteers from Harrison County — the young ladies of the Cadiz Schools — the place where many of you have long resided — have appointed me, in their behalf, to tender you this beautiful flag — the banner of our Country. They feel assured that in your hands it will never be dishonored. You are performing a noble duty, and they offer it as a token of their regard. Take it — keep it — never let it trail in the dust before your enemies, but let its beautiful folds float o'er the battlefield in victory. May it be an incentive to deeds of prowess for the re-establishment of our government over every foot of its former dominion. We shall watch you and rejoice in your successes — God bless you — and protect you."

Captain Norris responded: "Young ladies of Cadiz — In behalf and as representative of one hundred brave men, I accept the beautiful flag.... God bless you! And here in your presence and before high heaven, I pledge you ... that this flag shall never be dishonored in their hands — that it will be returned unsullied, unstained — and that all that brave hearts and strong hands can do, will be done.... But this is no time for words.... We are ordered to the field. A part of our regiment is already on the cars.... Ladies, God bless you!" After three great cheers for the ladies, and three returned by the Cadizians, they boarded and "hurried off by the 'iron horse' to new scenes" (*CR* 27 Ag).

Moses Urquhart went with this regiment as captain of Co. D, most from Belmont County. Company G, under Captain Hugh Ferguson, had mostly Harrison men according to a note John S. Campbell left on the roster in the Cadiz library. The remaining companies from Harrison entered the 126th, as Co. A under George W. Voorhees; C under Richard M. Lyons, which included Nancy's cousin Samuel Hines, 19; and H under Jonathan S. McCready.

While Confederate armies attacked Kentucky, they also upsurged in the East, in the Shenandoah Valley and near Washington. The 30th, including Joe Dickerson, left Flat Top Mountain for Washington. The Dickersons never were able to bring Hiram Jr.'s body home, but after the war he was reburied in Arlington National Cemetery.

McCready's company, the last to go, was to leave Thursday morning 28 August, and to avoid any repetition of the indecorous departure by some of Norris' men, he summoned his to the courthouse the evening before (*CR* 27 Ag), to sleep on hard benches and process soberly to the depot. There they and the families gathered for a solemn leave-taking, but beside the tracks in Dewey's field a novel festivity roared.

Van Amburgh's Mammoth Menagerie came in an "immense procession nearly a mile long" up the street to advertise the two shows that day in a six-center-pole tent. At the head of the "Gorgeous Procession" a steam calliope tootled. Behind it a cornet band played. Then appeared four elephants, with acrobats; ponies that would dance; horses in "new silver mounted harness" pulling "gorgeously painted cages," with lions, tigers, a panther, leopards, California grizzly bears that would dance, an "African bison," antelope, wart hog, ocelot, zebra, llama, birds including a condor and a parrot, monkeys, and more (*CDS* 20 Ag). With lion tamers dressed as Roman gladiators, it promised an excitement to divert Cadiz from thoughts of departed soldiers: recently in Monongahala, Pennsylvania, its huge tiger had escaped and driven the shrieking audience to and fro in the tent, and when Van Amburgh chased the tiger back into the cage, it floored him, and presided with its paw upon him for some time (*CDS* 3 S).

Chapter 4

Kentucky: The School for the Soldier

The dry weather that had speeded the hay and grain harvesting ended with refreshing showers for the hills, but the rest of the region stayed in a long drought, shriveling the rivers fordable in many places, and inviting rebel raiders and armies north, to alarm even Indiana. On 23 August the 98th expected to ride to the camp near Columbus and receive their bounty pay, but instead they steamed across the hills and plains of Ohio to Cincinnati, where they debarked with many "anxious inquiries," such as "where are there any barracks in Cincinnati?" to which the only answers were "to rank right face, march." That night they crossed the river on a ferry to Covington, where fear of attack by Morgan's Cavalry had impelled citizens to mount defenses and stand guard on the Kentucky heights. The 98th officers "started around the city to hunt up quarters," as James M. Crawford reported: "Our company, along with three or four others, was taken to the Court House, where we were allowed to spread our

blankets and unstring our knapsacks, having carried the last-named article for about three hours; and we being tired out, having been confined in the cars all day, and it being about 11 o'clock, were glad enough when the order was given to break ranks."

What appeared to them at daylight was foreign to their eyes. The city had been built by Marylanders and Bavarian Germans. The courthouse was an elegant white Greek Revival temple with a graduated clock tower above it, topped with a story-tall statue of George Washington. Mansions of old families had columned porticos and the inset porches of Italianate loggias. The bulk of the city of 16,550, however, gave it the appearance of a city on the Rhine, with the graceful high spires of many churches, and neatly crafted brick homes set in walled or fenced gardens. Here were numerous breweries, sausage houses, and German bakeries (Federal Writers'). The Ohioans found a palatable acquaintance.

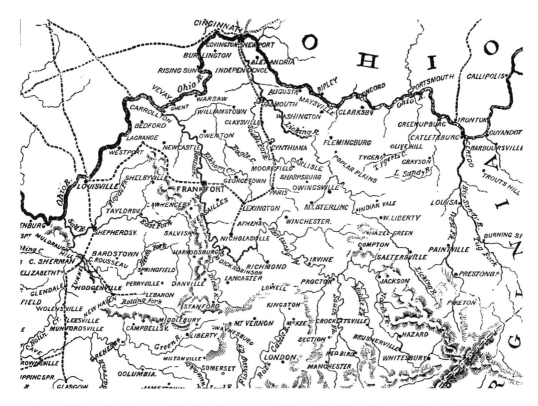

Central Kentucky. Source: Alfred H. Guernsey and Henry M. Alden, *Harper's Pictorial History of the Civil War.* New York: Harper and Brothers, 1866. Reprint Fairfax Press-Barre, n.d.

"On Sunday morning, the citizens of Covington prepared us a reception meal, which was something we had not looked for, but, as unexpected as it was, we were all prepared for it and I can assure you that we did it ample justice, for it was somewhat *better* than army rations. When through eating, each company gave three cheers for the citizens of Covington.

"At noon the citizens came round to the different quarters of the companies and invited the boys to come and get their meals with them. Myself and two or three others were invited to a private house on Garrard street to dinner, and I can say that we could not have had more hospitality shown to us at home, where we were known, than was shown to us here. I think, to take the citizens of Kentucky generally, they are more social and show more hospitality to strangers than the citizens of our own State — Ohio. The volunteers of the 98th will never forget the kindness and tender care shown them by the citizens of Covington; especially the ladies, for wherever we went for a meal we had the most urgent solicitations to return again. The reporter of the Cincinnati *Times* tried to make out that it was an imposition on the people of the city but they deny it…" (*CDS* 10 S).

The newspaper criticism brought a reply from Col. George Webster, to the *Cincinnati Commercial* 27 August; it describes the family situation of his recruits, and illustrates his concern for them which made him a revered leader: "Permit me to correct a statement in this evening's *Times*, relative to billeting troops upon the citizens of Covington.

"The 98th reached here on Sunday morning, and were furnished by the patriotic citizens with an excellent breakfast in a public hall. Companies have since been garrisoned in different parts of town, and the Quartermaster being provided with a full supply of Commissary stores, has furnished everything required of them since.

"The good citizens, however, have been most profuse in privately supplying a considerable portion of the men with the best the market affords. I am aware that this is a serious tax, but do not know how to prevent it.— The serious charge that the Quartermaster pockets the value of rations not consumed is a mistake....

"Every Ohio reg. (except 98th & 105th) has been paid by the bounty when mustered in, as promised by the Government.— The 98th was mustered in the 23rd inst. but no funds were furnished to pay the bounty. It was hurried to Lexington under promise that an officer would follow with funds. One half the men have families, whom they were not permitted to provide for, or even see, after going to camp. They relied upon this bounty ($27) for support, and *now need it*. If the regiment leaves without it, and the muster rolls go to Washington, or Columbus, it will not be paid until November, if then....

"I have sent two messengers and numerous dispatches to Columbus.... Gov. Tod has done all for me in his power, under the am't of business pressing....

"The regiment has no tents, and therefore is quartered in public halls, etc. We are exceedingly anxious to get into the field, and relieve the hospitable citizens of Covington to tax themselves on our account. Geo. Webster, Col. 98th Reg.O.V.I." (*CDS* 3 S).

While Webster held his new regiment here, one from Indiana rushed onward; they received their pay in Kentucky, but no food for almost a week, except what they could steal. Another fresh Ohio unit, the 95th, had a "gloryhound" colonel who pressured authorities to advance it, so that, undrilled, it soon stood, and fell, in the front of battle (Lambert 22, 86).

On 28 August Webster's men were paid and ordered to pack their knapsacks. Crawford detailed the novelty of handling army gear: "I hunted my 'traps,' packed my 'bureau,' and then started around with some others to call on our acquaintances to thank them for their kindness, and bid them adieu. We left Covington with the good will of the citizens and their wishes for our success and safe return. At 6 o'clock P.M. we were formed into line, knapsacks slung, arms in our hands, and all of our 'harness' on, which altogether is not a small load for a mule, leaving a human being out of the question, and marched to the depot, where we received ten rounds of cartridges apiece. We were then put on board a train of freight cars, something like a drove of cattle, except that we had seats to set on.— There were about fifty of us in each car. At about 10 o'clock P.M., we bade farewell to the city amid the cheers of the citizens, the boys all regretting to leave such a fine city, such a sociable people, and, among the smaller things, such good fare for army rations.

As we were marching through the streets I thought I heard quite a compliment to the ladies of Cadiz: such remarks as, 'What a beautiful banner!' 'Take care of that splendid and glorious banner!' We had it flying at the head of our column, and carried by our 1st Corporal Robert Booth, a splendid specimen of the 'Buckeye Boys.' We all answered that we would do our best to return it unsullied and unstained.

"We slept but little last night, for the boys were in too close quarters to sleep with much comfort, being packed in so closely that we could not lay down, and having had ammunition dealt out to us, some were on the lookout for something to do, for we did not know but what some of Morgan's horse would be burning bridges or bushwhacking on our route. We arrived at Paris, Ky., just at daylight, the train sitting on a trussel bridge nearly a quarter mile long, so the boys could not leave the cars, but had a good view of the city. We stopped again at a small station 9 miles north of Lexington, where we had our first taste of hard crackers, which were a little softer than a limestone, requiring good teeth, a good jaw, and plenty of water to wash them down without sticking in or cutting our throats. We arrived here at about 10 o'clock this morning, 12 hours being the time it took us to make the 100 miles, the distance between Covington and Lexington. We are encamped about half a mile north of the city, in a large and beautiful grove, with nothing to complain of but scarcity of water. We passed through some of the most beautiful farms that I ever saw, between Paris and Lexington; the soil in its composition is limestone. There are very few sick in the 98th, but two or three in our company — one, Mr. Battin, is in the hospital, but I think will soon be able to join us. We are expecting to leave soon. James M. Crawford" (*CDS* 10 S).

From the fabled Bluegrass farms had come the first thoroughbred cattle in Harrison County. Robert R. Cochran proudly described, in a short 1875 family history, his 1858 purchase from "Jeremiah Duncan, of Paris, Bourbon County, Kentucky, the cow Arabella, and a thorough-bred champion bull" from Woodford County. Robert included names of their descendants also — rather than his own (Caldwell 7).

The former *Republican* foreman, William A. Pittenger, recounted for it the 98th's journey, with the details that the company of "Webster Guards" also lodged in the Market House, had their "beautiful repast" in the Armory, and in fact "lived in luxury" in Covington. He placed the camp in Lexington near the city cemetery, "where is the Clay monument, whose columns tower higher than the quiet, honorable resting place of the great statesman, Henry Clay" (*CR* 10 S).

This monument gave an imposing, and ironical, introduction to the funerary art that was unknown at home. The Great Compromiser had labored to prevent the rift which brought these soldiers, who had studied his speeches in school, to his city. His tomb on the knoll was a massive pyramid, the base for a high stone pillar rising to a capital of spearpoints, flowers, and winged wheels; the cupola of a magnolia cone; and the likeness of Clay addressing an audience on high.

There were five new regiments at Camp Clay, including the 52nd Ohio with Abram Holmes and his brother.

The next day, Saturday, its flag flew at the headquarters, with their bold title of "McCook's Avengers," honoring their colonel's late brother. Col. Dan McCook was in charge this 30 August, because the commander of the army in Kentucky had dashed off in the night on report of an enemy force approaching his two new brigades at Richmond, southeast of Lexington twenty-six miles. He sent an order for them to retreat to Lancaster, and left orders for the regiments except McCook's to follow him there; but Mc-Cook had subsequent orders from headquarters in Cincinnati to send all his men to Richmond. There was no telegraph to Richmond, and neither could McCook contact his general, as he with an aide spurred to Lancaster, and turned east to the sound of artillery fire (*OR* 1.16.2.460; 1.16.1.908). McCook sent regiments down the Richmond road this afternoon and evening as reinforcements, with the 98th regiment the last to go.

Maj. Gen. William "Bull" Nelson had arrived only 24 August to take charge, after the Confederate army escaped from Buell's Union forces by railroad and headed north. He was assembling his new regiments for training at various strategic towns. Reports came of enemy moving in the rugged mountains southeast; but the Union force at Cumberland Gap had not been attacked, and no other route seemed accessible to an army of any size (Lambert 40).

His 6,500 men at Richmond had not learned the basic motions of handling their muskets, nor the movements to form a line of battle out of the columns of the march, nor the procedures of moving and shooting within a company (Lambert 24-25); they had not

begun the lessons that were simplified into a new primer in question-and-answer form, *The School For The Soldier* (Van Ness). The infantry under Kirby Smith which attacked them had only 350 more men, but they were veterans so tough and resolute that they had pulled their artillery over heights their mules could not manage, so skilled in movement and firing that they seemed to represent 20,000 (Lambert 236, 8). By the time Gen. Nelson rode to his troops in the afternoon, they were fleeing in a mob. He managed to threaten some two thousand into lines; and they "stood about three rounds when, struck by a panic, they fled" (*OR* 1.16.1.909). He himself was shot but managed to escape, while Smith's cavalry took 3,500 prisoners (Lambert 156).

At midnight the 98th started toward Richmond to "reinforce Gen. Nelson," Wesley Poulson of Butts's company recounted. "On the way we met all the baggage wagons of Nelson's brigade coming towards Lexington, for the purpose of making themselves clear should Nelson be defeated the next day. Many inquiries were made of the wagoners by soldiers of our brigade, but scarcely any two agreed as to the result. They were very much excited and some said to us we had better march the other way which proved to be true. We met a great many soldiers who had been in the battle; some were wounded and others had run from the field. The most of them seemed very much disheartened. Some that were the last to leave the battle field said that Nelson had surrendered, and that there were 20,000 rebels coming to meet us with about 5,000 undrilled men. We traveled 13 miles...."

Here they reached the high palisades on the Kentucky River above Clay's Ferry and, halfway to Richmond, stopped to rest. With morning's light they looked across this gorge and "could see the enemy's picketts on the opposite hill, watching our movements," Pittenger wrote. "As there were only three Regiments in our force, we were compelled to retreat, and after one hour started bound for Lexington" (*CR* 17 S). By 7:30 A.M. Smith's whole Confederate army, cavalry, infantry, and artillery, could be seen from the palisades "streaming north unopposed toward Clay's Ferry" (Lambert 159). "We could see," Poulson continued, "the rebels plain enough marching toward us. The brigade was then turned into an orchard to rest a little, and in a few minutes we could plainly see the rebels trying to surround us. The men were told to eat something and prepare to march. The men were very tired being unused to marching, yet they must go on or be taken prisoner, and neither one was very pleasant. To make it more disagreeable, it rained on us for several miles of the way back. The roads were very slippery and the men (many having no oil cloth blankets) were wet as they could be.

"Some gave out and had to stop by the way, however all got back to Camp during the night and next day. None were taken prisoner.

"When we came in Lexington the people were astonished to see us back, having been told by the stragglers we had met in the morning that we were all cut to pieces and taken prisoner" (*CR* 17 S).

Citizens were in a frenzy, getting their money out of the bank, packing up, and heading for the safer countryside, as the city was ordered evacuated. The army garrison was loading its supplies onto railroad cars and a wagon train for Louisville, and piling what it could not carry away for bonfires. Gen. Nelson passed through on his way to Cincinnati to recuperate, and Gen. Wright supervised the exodus into the next day, leaving at 5:00 P.M. for Louisville (Lambert 179).

The last units to depart were the novice soldiers of the 98th and 52nd Ohio. They did not leave Lexington until nightfall. The 52nd stood in line outside the city watching Kirby Smith's army advance on it. As they crossed the city to get away, Morgan's cavalry rode into the streets of Lexington (Stewart 15). Neither regiment had wagons. The 52nd "pressed into service" some carriages remaining in town to haul knapsacks, but the 98th had to leave their tents, blankets, and all supplies behind. Their two sutlers, from St. Clairsville, had to desert all the new goods they had purchased for their store.

Morgan's riders followed them in close pursuit. Nevertheless, when they were several miles from Lexington, the 98th's Co. B, from Belmont County, realized they had left their flag in camp, and their Captain Joseph Mitchell led ten of his men back within the enemy campfires to retrieve it. By sunrise the regiments had paced the sixteen miles east to Versailles, and they did not halt but trudged on to Frankfort (*CR* 17 S).

They had some difficulty finding their way on this journey through the Bluegrass lanes. Major John Pearce yet lacked a horse, and had to borrow Adjutant Ellis Kennon's to ascertain directions ahead; and when Kennon "took it affoot" he became lost from the regiment, yet he found his way to Frankfort hours before they got there (*CR* 17 S). They walked at least the 78 miles Poulson counted, up to the 123 Stewart recalled. What they could learn from the residents was distinctly unhelpful, especially as they had to search for water in the hot, droughted countryside. On one veranda a "matronly woman" sat, promising that a "bubbling spring" rose a few hundred yards from her across a ravine and cornfield; when an officer and three comrades took a cautious entry into the corn, they discovered a squad of rebel cavalry were there, making prisoners of the regiments' boys as fast as the woman sent them over. At a roadside well, they found the chain and bucket had been removed, and the thirsty crowd desperately ventured into the well. Tommy White of Ferguson's Co. G, 98th, slipped and fell to the bottom — fortunately feet-first, and into water only a foot and a half deep. He got down on his knees and "like Gideon's three hundred soldiers of Bible story, lapped the water with his tongue, and climbing the rugged wall, went on his way rejoicing" (Stewart 17-18).

Men fell by the wayside in the duress, as they plodded eighteen hours of each twenty-four under dread of Morgan and threats from Gen. Nelson's staff, their escorts. The hapless sutlers left them at Frankfort to go home, and took to Covington a sickened boy of Butts's, Robert Peck, 19, who died there on 5 September. They expected attack whenever they stopped. McCook had "two brass field pieces" his men set up each day by the road as they paused, unaware the caisson was empty of ammunition. The farms alongside were occupied by Morgan's riders, who continued to collect fellows who wandered in search of water; the 52nd had twenty-six men taken prisoner along the way, among them, Sergeant Abram Holmes. The many who fell behind or staggered aside from the forced march in exhaustion were treated to the discipline of Nelson's army regulars — "tied to the battery wagons or beaten by the sword" (Stewart 17-18).

Meanwhile, the Harrison County soldiers of the 30th had encountered their first real battlefield. On Friday morning they, with Gen. Pope's huge army, had crossed Bull Run to the site of the war's first contest, and marched forward into the cannonfire from Stonewall Jackson's force. Victory seemed near, and they moved through the woods to get aside the enemy and cut off its possible retreat through an unfinished railway cut. There, however, they found the enemy in place, and its attack drove them back. The next day they stood under artillery fire to reinforce the right, until their army's left caved in, and its withdrawal turned into the full retreat of Pope's army from Second Bull Run (*OR* 1.12.2.421-3).

The other retreaters limped toward Louisville hardly the glorious band they had expected to be. To any citizens who peered out at them, they must have resembled a prison gang more than guardian soldiers. Without provisions, in a hostile land, harried by the enemy's horsemen and oncoming army, the scholars of Franklin College might ruefully have recalled their introduction to military leadership in their first-year reading in Greek of the *Anabasis*

(Beauregard, *Old Franklin* 67), wherein Xenophon recounts the comparable situation of the Greek army fleeing from Babylon after defeat, which he transformed with one speech to the model of the marching, and foraging, democracy.

These Ohioans did not stray to the barns they passed, but they outpaced Xenophon's twenty miles a day. They were hard-pressed even as they neared Louisville, when they lined up on the road at 3 A.M. on Friday, in expectation of an attack. A few of them that morning conceived a new stratagem, but it did not affect military discipline. Two of Jefferson County's Co. G, 52nd, went off to a farmhouse with the hope they could hire a team and driver for their trip. They found three of Norris' 98th men ahead of them with the same notion, and the farmer ready with his team and wagon. The five of them paid and rode past their miserable comrades for four miles, at which point they reached officers of the 98th who ordered their three to dismount. The other two rolled on for another mile, where they found Nelson's officers, who repositioned them in the harsh discipline of the rear guard regulars all the nine miles onward (Stewart 18).

"The men seem very stupid today," Wesley Poulson wrote from a camp near Louisville the next day, 6 September, where they were getting new knapsacks and supplies. "The nights are cool here and days very hot. I think it is healthy here if there were not so many together. No word from home since we left Steubenville, except one letter … and I am pretty sure if any of the rest had received one we would have heard them rejoicing…" (*CR* 17 S).

Wm. Pittenger reported on 8 September: "We have been hurried over the ground rather fast the last 4 to 5 days…. I can say without hesitancy that Co. C has decidedly the best Captain in the 98th and admitted by others. In Capt. Norris we have utmost confidence, that he'll stand by us and with us, and not a man in the Co. but who will stand by him and obey him with a willing heart. Long live the Captain of the 'Webster Guards.' …We are in a dense woods between two hills, and it seems as if we are shut out from all creation, where we can neither hear nor see what's going on in the world. The boys are all wishing for Cadiz papers in order to learn the news. They hope to hear of some people at home being 'pressed' into service ere long.

"The Captain has today gone to the city and we expect some news when he returns" (*CR* 17 S).

They were in the heights east of the city, probably in the fairgrounds, part of 17,000 new infantry arriving to defend it as Kirby Smith's army occupied the center of the state, and Bragg's larger force entered its south, headed toward Louisville (Hafendorfer 41).

By 12 September the 98th had moved to a camp on the flats south of the city, near a farm below the Germantown streets named "Sneed's Hens" (*Views of Louisville* 127), and Robert Mitchell wrote home. By this time he did not know where he was, and headed his note "Camp buall near Lexington." It may have been the first letter he had ever written, and it lacked any form of address or punctuation. "I am well at preasant. we goet plenty to eate at preasant. this is a nice place to be. we have our tents up we will stay here a while. i expect there is abot 60 thousand troops here know. tom kyle went to get somthing to eat and he got three turkeys and hid them and went back to get some peaches to eate and the man seen him and drwed his pistol on him. Kyle run then for life for fear he would be shot and came back and told what he had done and him 5 or 6 more went back and run him [the farmer] in the hous and loct himselfe up.

"i like this place first strate. we drill 6 hors a day. there is not a hil to besene here. the timber is very poor here. I wont right nomore til you rgh me a lter. i have hade none yet. Robert Mict. I want you to send me some postage stamps. Well I Will right some more. i was out side of the Guard and got a drink of cider. we cannot get unles we hav a bucket or hour canteen. there is a goonay [simpleton] goes out that and stayes allday. right soon. Robert Mitch it is know dinner time."

Discipline among the new troops here was not up to Nelson's standards. The multitudinous saloons were ordered to close; but, according to the *Louisville Daily Journal*, many kept their back doors open; notices that appeared in the paper for officers and soldiers to report to camp imply that many found resorts elsewhere. In camps, the training drills must have concentrated on military appearance in parade, because the commander, Gen. Cruft, who had been in charge of a brigade at Richmond, planned to present the troops to the city in a Grand Inspection on Monday, 15 Sept.

A day before it, on 14 Sept., Bragg's army, marching far ahead of the Union army under Buell which was pursuing it, surprised the forts at Munfordville only seventy-five miles south, that guarded the rail bridge on the Green River and the pike to Louisville, and began to surround them.

That same day, the Harrison men of the 30th marched up the winding road on South Mountain, Maryland, to its steep heights, where hidden cannon blasted them with shrapnel. They charged up open fields to the stone walls concealing the enemy, and fought their way to the gap, where near sundown their leader, General Jesse Reno, was shot dead. The next morning the enemy had gone; the way was clear into the broad valley of Antietam Creek (*OR* 1.19.1.469).

The new soldiers in Louisville marched down Broadway on its southern border for military review, then paraded through the downtown and Main Street, past the stores and warehouses of goods at this principal port of steamboat trade, and ferry junction with Indiana. The parade was blasted by heat, and became a spectacle of fallen soldiers. According to Pittenger, they "marched about twelve miles in all. The day was extremely hot, and many a brave soldier boy seen laying by the wayside, utterly worn out.... Louisville is rather a pleasant city, and the citizens, as a majority, are very patriotic and generous. During our march through the city, large crowds gathered upon the streets to see us, and many a good old 'flag of the free' was cast to the breeze before us. Many little children" waved small flags and cried "Hurrah for the Union." Yet "I have no doubt there are many Secesh in the city who looked upon us with utter contempt…. I hope they are few, as … who would treat the troops who have come to their deliverance thus would be fool or knave." From Co. C four went to the hospital — "R. J. Shaw, Mr. Clark (called Doc Clark), John Pennock, Thomas Sloan."

The *Daily Journal* the next day observed that at least five fell with obvious "symptoms of sun stroke" and no attention by their own surgeons before they were carried to the military hospital. Its editor, George D. Prentice, did not respond to the occasion as its military organizers had intended, and he took alarm at both the citizens and their defenders: "The people of Louisville do not seem to have a just appreciation of their present position. They are inexcusably supine at a time when rebel cannon are thundering almost on the very confines of our county…." Placing an army of 30,000 with Bragg at Glasgow, thirty miles closer than Buell's at Bowling Green, and 20,000 "armed and desperate men" occupying the Bluegrass, he found the city had no preparations for defense except that "masses of brave but undisciplined Indianaians are thrown upon her suburbs, men who are fresh from the harvest-fields," and "untaught soldiers of Illinois."

Louisville was not "supine" because it had many secessionist sympathizers to welcome the Confederate army. It supported the Union, on which its trade depended; its Louisville Legion had already given distinguished service to Sherman's army. But even in this emergency, the civic mind turned on the theme that perennially dominated its self-reflection, and fixed its eyes on the rival it watched with a kind of jealous obsession, alter-

nately a competitive emulation and a disdain — Cincinnati, the upstart city that had bustled ahead to seize the title and position of Queen City of the West. Under the present threat of attack, Cincinnati had rushed into every measure of martial law, and sent its men with spades and old squirrel-hunting guns across a pontoon bridge to the heights above Covington. Louisvillians, according to Prentice, were regarding the Cincinnatians' excited exertions with amusement and mockery, when they should be following their example: "If we do not prepare ourselves — if Louisville is not fortified, it will be taken and given up to Confederate pillage and magnanimity…. Let the work commence immediately. Let every able-bodied man go at it. Stop all business; close all hotels and send officers and soldiers to their camps…. We rode on Saturday around the new camp ground of Gen. James S. Jackson's Division, a superb location, its right flank on the Bardstown road and its left on the Shelby[ville] pike, upon either of which the whole force can be readily swung, but it needs fortifications…."

The next day, 17 Sept., Gen. Nelson returned to Louisville to take charge of the defense of Louisville, and began the work Prentice had urged.

On this day in Maryland, the 30th forded Antietam Creek upstream from the stone bridge "under a shower of grape" from enemy batteries, and began charging through a cornfield and plowed field toward the hillcrest above Sharpsburg. The immense battle drove the Confederates to the brink of a retreat, until reinforcements arrived for them, but not for Burnside's troops, who were forced back across the fields until the dense smoke became night (*OR* 1.19.1.463).

The next morning the 98th came to the campground of Gen. James Jackson (previously a Kentucky cavalry commander) that Prentice had surveyed. Whereas his troops had faced east at that time, Nelson "swung" them to anticipate attack from Bragg's army and the city itself. Louisville suddenly aroused, with these cannon pointed on their heads. Here, however, a new battery such as the 19th Indiana could hardly conduct its needed artillery practice; just below the hill other troops were building entrenchments, and a half-mile farther, the city streets began. The 98th pitched their "tents in the very suburbs, and in full view of the city," Pittenger wrote on this day. "Our present position is a fine one, being posted to support the 19th Indiana Battery, which is being planted on the hill immediately above us, and commanding this city. You would naturally suppose from this that we are expecting an engagement here…. The news received here this morning reports that Rebels have captured Mumfordsville, about 75 miles from here, and have opened the way for an advance upon Louisville. It is learned, also, they are moving in this direction, and it may be that they will attempt to make a dash upon us, capture the city, and drive us from our position. But I think such a movement would but result in the utter capture, rout or annihilation of their army . Yet, if they have decided to come, there is but one response from the boys of the 98th: 'Come on, ye ruthless invaders of Kentucky soil, and the best we have will be given unto you…. Look where you may from where we are now

situated, there can be seen the tents of the soldiers of the Union" (*CR* 1 O).

Maj. Gen. Nelson was not so optimistic as Corp. Bill Pittenger. With Bragg's army only hours away on 22 Sept., Nelson ordered all women and children to leave the city; he summoned all men to military service, and prepared to arrest the noncompliant. He vowed to fight to the end, then set fire to the city, retire to the Indiana shore with his cannon, turn them on Louisville and "reduce it to rubble" (McDonough 191). The city became a "blaze of excitement." Stores closed and citizens expected attack within forty-eight hours (*CR* 24 S). They loaded carriages and handcarts, or bundled their goods to carry, and crowded to the wharves seeking ferries and flatboats to Indiana, in a melee of escape (*Views of Louisville* 120-1).

The edge of the Louisville Highlands where the 98th dug rifle pits afforded a great vantage point for artillery should the city be invaded, but its elevated ground had been cultivated since 1848 for the far-different prospect of the beautiful rural cemetery, a place for uplifting contemplation of harmonized nature and art in, as Louisville titled Cave Hill, the "City of the Dead." With the picturesque design of English garden landscape, its lanes wound through an arboretum. One of the finest instances in the country of the Grecian- and Transcendentalist-inspired rural cemeteries (see Garry Wills 63-75), Cave Hill also rose with tombstones in all shapes of funerary imagery, sculpted with admirable art — graven angels, lambs, flowers, urns, feathered doves, babies in seashells.

"I visited a few days ago the City

Cemetery," Pittenger wrote on 29 Sept., "near our camping ground. Up to within a few weeks past it presented a beautiful and grand appearance scarcely imaginable, but the rude hand of desolation has been laid upon it, and now its beauty is destroyed, many of its costly tombstones leveled to the earth, its rare shrubbery torn in pieces and scattered around.... A rifle pit has been dug through the entire length of the Cemetery. I noticed a plain but beautiful grave, which desolation's hand had not reached. 'Twas the long, quiet home of a youthful defender of his country's cause. His name was beautifully inscribed upon the marble front, and will live as long as his country shall live, ... Thomas Martin, and was wounded at Shiloh, and died of his wounds. He was only 19 years old."

That the Webster Guards had become gravediggers Pittenger did not report home, but they were digging up corpses and standing guard at night in trenches through the graveyard, according to a letter from Robert Mitchell; and the men were increasingly sick.

Bragg's army had lost its opportunity for swift conquest, however. Buell's, as James Crawford wrote on 28 Sept., "was too fast for him, having arrived here the same day Bragg reached Bardstown [25 Sept.], about 20 miles from this place." Among Buell's troops were the 13th Ohio and its Co. H. "One was John Bayless of Cadiz, rest from different parts of Harrison County. They looked well except for clothes, not having had a change of clothing since they left Battle Creek, 36 days before they reached here, having marched 361 miles in that time. Lieut. T. L. Carnahan has charge of the Co., Capt. Henderson having been pro-

moted to Major of the 121st" (*CDS* 8 O). Pittenger detailed the visit: "Your correspondent in company with James M. Crawford started for their camp, which is about three miles from here. The day was rainy and disagreeable but we were eager and undaunted. Although 'twas happiness to see the members of this company who have survived the war thus far and have passed through the fiery ordeal of battle, ... Yet a feeling of sorrow and of pain was caused to fill our breasts at the remembrance of some of our young friends, their 'comrades in arms,' who have passed from earth away.... The Co. now musters about 50 or 60 fit for duty."

They met "'Jack' Barnes, who is still on hands like a thousands of brick ... full of life and merriment," Johnny Clifford and Frank Mealy, "as great old chaps" as they were in Cadiz, "our old friend and fellow typo, Samuel Moffitt," chief bugler of the regiment (son of the Methodist minister on Irish Ridge), the two Hatton boys, John and Harris (sons of William Hatton), "those three bright Cadiz larks, John Bayless, John Randals and Milton Bryan," "merry boys of the old gay circle," James Crumley and Edward Young, who could eat the rations of five men, and the other "Cadiz Guards."

Of the "Webster Guards," ten were in the hospital, several more in poor health. "An accident, the first in the Company, occurred last night. By the accidental discharge of his gun, Corp. Ennis received a shot through his right hand. It will most likely render him unfit for duty for some time at least, and perhaps for all time." With so little training, John Ennis may have shot himself by accident; or, having already visited the hospital, he may have felt so sick of the army after this month that he chose to exit. He stayed in Louisville until discharged for disability in January.

Pittenger continued: "Considerable excitement was manifested in camp yesterday on account of the death of Maj. Gen. Nelson ... at the hands of Brig. Gen. Jeff. C. Davis of [Indiana]. The difficulty was in regard to the manner in which General Nelson used a portion of the [Indiana] troops at the battle of Richmond, Ky. Nelson struck Davis several times in the face, after which his antagonist immediately borrowed a pistol and shot him, killing him almost instantly.... The people generally justify Davis in the act, as far as I can learn." Davis, with political friends, was never tried; and the loss to Buell's army of Nelson would soon become evident in the Battle of Perryville.

"In regard to whereabouts of Bragg, not certain. Cavalry says they are not nearer than 18-20 miles. Our men captured 11 prisoners last night and brought them to camp. A hard looking set of creatures. Only one has a regular suit of military clothes.

"We rec'd *Republican* last Saturday. Sorry to hear of the death of Duffield and wounding of Fogle" at Antietam (*CR* 15 O).

On Wednesday, 1 Oct., they left Louisville to find and fight Bragg's and Kirby Smith's armies. By this time, many of the regiment were too sick from their recent ordeals to march, and stayed behind in Louisville hospitals: Lt. Col. Poorman placed their number at about 100 (*CR* 10 D), but Adjutant Kennon thought it was over 300 (*Belmont Chronicle* 13 N).

Chapter 5

"Most Respected Friend Nancy"

Nancy D. Mitchell's first army correspondent was fourteen years older than she, a carpenter, fellow member of the UP church, from a former ARP family on an adjacent farm. Francis Pringle Grove did not live there, however, but with a sister and her husband David Braden in Charlestown, near Warfel's mill. His two brothers, Thomas and Will, farmed the 108 acres of their widowed mother. His friendship with Nancy was a recent development, perhaps even connected to his preparations for leaving with their minister's company. A year before, one of his older brothers-in-law had been urging him to press his courtship and marry another woman; and Thompson Gray, in his letter to Nancy, asked how she liked dancing with Kyle.

At Camp Steubenville, Frank began a diary, recording the company's election of McCready as captain; his first guard duty, which brought him a headache so that he got a replacement; the usual two sermons on Sabbath, at ten and three o'-clock, the first by Capt. McCready on "Escodis" 20:8, the commandment to keep the Sabbath holy, the second on Matthew 6:20; and on Monday, the election of other officers. They chose Thomas H. Smith 1st Lieutenant on the first ballot. Candidates and votes for 2nd Lt. were John Mitchell with 3, J. Bricker 2, Thomas McKinney 19, Moses Conaway 18, and F. P. Grove 8. The second ballot between the two leaders gave McKinney the office. Then rain dampened the politicking, and they decided the Captain should appoint the other officers. In the days following, Frank noted visitors everyday, his mother, brothers, the Bradens and niece Maggie Braden, his other sisters' families of Mc-Narys and Hawthorns, his nephew Francis G. Patton, and the ladies and girls from Piney Fork and Shortcreek who "set a splendid dinner" and "set us a grand dinner."

Nevertheless, Frank complained to Nancy of his fare. The spelling in his letters echoes the region's accent and its background: close and high vowels, so that *there* sounded as *thare*, *get* as *git*; elaborations, often nasal, of vowel sounds into diphthongs and even triphthongs; lengthened and stressed consonants, especially *r*s, retreated from the Scottish burr.

Camp Steubenville, 6 September 1862: "Most respected friend Nancy, It is with pleasure that I address you this morning. Perhaps you have been looking for a letter from me before this time and it may be that I ought to have written sooner, but I thought as thare was some of the folkes down from your neighborhood all most every day you would be likely to hear from me often — Well Nancy I am enjoying my usual health and am enjoying myself as well as I expected. I nead not tell you any thing about our way of liveing for you have seen how we live here — We had neither knives forks nor plates till yesterday we drawed some & hired two Darkies for to cook and it appears more like liveing now we git plenty to eat if only it was cooked right. We drawed our equipage yesterday. we have Austrian rifles. And if you had been here yesterday eavening to see the Regiment out on dress parade with our bayonets glittering in the sun you would have thought we looked like fighting. we have drawed part of our clothing but not all. We do not know how long we will stay here but my opinion is that we will stay here several days for the Phasician was round yesterday and ordered our quarters all to be cleaned out every day and kept in good order. The Regiment is not full yet. it is said thare is between seven & eight hundred here. Our Company took in a squad of men from Tuscarawways County which raised our number to about 84 men — We had our officers elected but when we took in this squad we had to give up our second lieutenant and take thair man for second lieutenant so that Thomas McKinney is second sargant now instead. I have got the humble office of 5th Corporal. the greatest advantage in this is I will not have to stand guard & I will get 2.00 per month more than a Private. John Mitchell is 5th Sargant. I nead not tell you who all the officers are for thair names will be in the papers and you can see them thare. When have you heard from Robert. When you write to me tell me whare he is & how he is gitting along, if he is still in Cincinnati. I think we will git to see him afterwhile. The Ladies of Stubanville belonging to the Soldiers Aid society visited the camp yesterday and presented the soldiers with pin cushions & needle cases. Thare is Ladies in camp every day that I am acquainted with so that we won't git lonesome here but after we git away whare they are all strangers we will think more about home. I will have to stop writing for it is allmost time to go on drill. If I saw you I would have a great deal more to say than I have to write. Please write soon and give me all the news. If we stay here long I would be glad to see you down here for I have not much hopes of gitting home on a furlow. Nothing more at present. but remain your Friend. F. P. Grove"

The next day, the new chaplain, J. K. Andrews, a Steubenville UP minister, preached from Romans; the afternoon sermon expounded Psalms 20:4-5 ("in the name of our God we will set up our banners"). Monday, "Mrs. Mitchell & Nancy D. Mitchell came on the train. we had a pleasant time." Tuesday, Lizzy Kyle and her father visited.

On 22 September, Frank began another letter: "Camp Parkersburg Verginia, Most Respected Friend, I have seated myself on the bank of the little Kanawha river to address you this morning. though we are seperated by hills and vallies yet by the blessing of the pen we can communicate our thoughts to each other. Well Nancy I suppose you wonder whare I am by this time. I will give you a little history of our Journey here. We left Camp Stubanville on last Thursday the 18th about 9 Oclock in the morning and went from thare to Bellair. we had to wride in open cars and it was a dreadful dusty dirty wride. we crossed the river at Bellair and got on the Baltimore & Ohio railroad. here they put us in old freight cars. we then started for Grafton about 12 Oclock that night a distance of 100 miles. We then took the road to Parkersburgh a distance of 104 miles and arrived here about 12 the next day, Friday. part of the road we traveled after night but what I saw of it was the roughest road I ever saw. It was what I would call the underground railroad for we passed through 23 tunnels going from Grafton to Parkersburgh. I stood the trip first rate altho we had pretty hard fare. we had nothing to eat but some dry crackers. I am enjoying my usual health but I dont like this plaice as well as Camp Stubanville. thare is no Ladies visits us here I see no familliar faices except those of our own Regiment. the Camp is on the suburbs of the town on the bank of the Little Kanawha River. thare is part of two Verginia Regiments here besides us. thare is lots of secesh round here. thare is squads of Soldiers camped all al-

long the Railroad to keep them from tairing up the track. And we keep a picket Guard about 3 miles out from Camp. Sept. 24th. Well Nancy, I suppose you will think I have been a long time writeing this letter. but I will explain the reason. Yesterday I was put on the Picket Guard so I had to stop writeing. The way the Guards are placed thare are a certain number of Guards detailed each day, in the morning they are drawn up in line and one corporal and three privates sent to each poast. they are sent out different roads for two or three miles and stationed at such places as crossroads or forks of road. we have to take one days rations along and stay for 24 hours. we are not allowed to let any one pass us without a writen pass from headquarters. at night two sleeps while two watches so we take it by turns. We had a good station yesterday it was about 2 miles from Camp down the river at the forks of a road thare was 6 or 8 houses close round us. lots of Women thare but verry few men. they said the men is away in the union army. they ware verry kind to us. they gave us pies and milk and cooked chickens for us. so we fared first rate only we had to ly under a walnut-tree all night. [The green-coated nuts, larger and heavier than golf balls, would be falling on them all night.] And if the enemy come — Jump up fire on them and run to the bushes. nothing more on that subject — Well Nancy how are you enjoying yourself have you been at any singings lately. I hope you will enjoy yourself. well has your dhalias come out in bloom yet if so are they nice ones. Oh Nancy how I would like to call in some eavening and spend a few hours with you. When I am on Picket Guart at night away in some lonly plaice how my thoughts run back to home and loved ones thare, but I trust I will not be forgotten by those I left behind. I suppose the Fare will come off in a few days. I would like to be thare but what's the use of talking I can't go. Thare has a large amount of Artillary & artillary men come in today. we are looking for a fight here some of these days. [The day they arrived, a large force with the Confederate Gen. Floyd was reported nearby, Frank noted, and "forty rounds of Cartridges ishued this eavening a fight expected."] Please answer this soon and give me all the news. tell me when you heard from Robert whare he is and how he is gitting along. One of our Boys got in a bad scrape. James Stewart that lived at McAdamses was found sleeping on Guard last night. he was Courtmarshaled and put on duty for 20 days picking stones & bones off the Camp ground with a guard oaver him all the time and has his victuiles carried to him & has to sleep in the guard house at night. but I dont want it made known who wrote home about him. Please write soon. Direct your letter.... Yours truely Your sincere friend F. P. Grove"

Chapter 6

"Here I Am Bound to Blaze"

In the Light of Nature

At first, Cadiz took a diversion from war talk in ridiculous jokes that occupied the wits of the unrecruited: "We will take the fire out of you. How do you live?" "I ain't particular, as the oyster said when they asked him whether he'd be fried or roasted." — "What do you follow? "Anything that comes in my way, as the locomotive said when he run over a man." — "What's your business?" "That's various, as the cat said when she stole the chicken." — "That's nearer the line, I suppose." "Altogether in my line, as the rope said when choking the pirate." — and on and on.

"If I hear any more absurd comparisons," Allen complained, "I will give you twelve months. I'm done, as the beefstake said to the cook" (*CDS* 10 S).

While Jonathan McCready pondered the manual's intricate instructions for heels, insteps, toes, knees, hips, and fingernails that should create a marching man, his congregation decided to support his military mission by keeping him their minister, pledging "as evi-dence that we fully acquiesce in the course he has pursued" to continue collecting his salary for him (*CDS* 10 S). On the political front, the District Union Convention in Cambridge on 28 August nominated John A. Bingham for reelection, who accepted with the promise to uphold the President's use of force against secession, including Congress's recent "sweeping confiscation and emancipation" measures to make armed rebels contribute to the expenses of ending their rebellion (*CR* 10 S). Thereafter, the county's united advocacy that had just rallied 500 sons and fathers into the army rapidly broke, as the congressional election turned into a referendum on the war, while its escalating violence and consequences whiplashed opinions.

The district Democrats met at Antrim, Guernsey County, 3 September. The delegate there from Greene Township was Nancy's uncle Thomas Mitchell. Both the Greene men and Editor Allen expected nomination of a "Union Democrat," opposed to secession and also to the abolition tactics of the present Congress, seeing in both obstacles to "peaceful adjustment" of the country's dispute (*CDS* 3 S). The county's delegates, however, voted for Philip Donahue, who had urged sympathy for the South and its rightful separation in preference to subjection. The convention became, according to Allen, who was its secretary, "a spontaneous uprising of more than *one thousand* people, collected without any drumming of any kind," and its first ballot chose Joseph W. White, who made a "statesman-like speech" (*CDS* 10 S). White was, by Hatton's account, a second-rate Cambridge attorney, Donahue's intellectual inferior, and "one of the most rabid, bitter, pro-slavery Democrats in the District" (*CR* 10 S).

Allen crammed his papers this month with articles in tiny type condemning the record of the "fanatic Abolition Congress" and Bingham, and proclaiming that Lincoln rejected their emancipation projects. His cultural offerings subtly challenged the ethical grounds of abolitionism. "Limited Vision," from the *Congregationalist*, warned, "Who, investigating the smallest subject, has not soon come to those inevitable borders—'thus far shalt thou go, and no further'—which hedge about the mysteries of life and nature?" Not only are heaven's suns and stars incomprehensible in their "dust of worlds," but also a fly or flower is beyond our understanding. Look at a cat, and reflect on the gulf between its mind and ours; so, "How do we know what an angel may see in a tree?" (*CDS* 3 S). One should not, by implication, presume to judge or change the inequalities of slavery. The "Scientific" columns attacked people's "Grammatical Blunders" in auxiliary verbs, espe-

cially their confusion of time, possibility, purpose, and duty exemplified in uses of "shall" and "should" that misconstrued a future wish as a present duty. Grammarians had "entirely overlooked" futurity, tab. maintained (*CDS* 10 S). The language itself seemingly needed his fundamental overhaul before it should move the independent thinkers he addressed to any further consideration. Later, tab. produced an "Orthographical Problem" pretending to extract "every elementary sound" in the language within only sixteen letters, the garble being an abolitionist pronouncement of "rebholeushion" (*CDS* 1 O).

Meanwhile, "with the suddenness of a thunderclap," came alarming reports of the immense rebel force only thirty miles from Washington, three days of slaughterous battle, and retreat of Pope's army from Bull Run; of the "Terrible Battle" near Richmond, Ky., the surrender of Lexington, and the movement of Bragg's army to Bowling Green which indicated it could strike the Ohio River Valley (*CDS* 3 S). In the next week, the rebels took Frederick and Hagerstown, Md., invaded Pennsylvania near Hanover, attacked the Federal rail garrisons at Harpers Ferry and Martinsburg, Va., and threatened Ohio. "OHIO INVADED BY REBELS," Allen headlined. Near Ravenswood, Western Virginia, downriver from Parkersburg, Jenkins and his "Bushwhackers" had crossed at Bluffington Island, ridden to the village of Racine, and shot three citizens. Gallipolis expected attack (*CDS* 10 S).

The county military committee issued orders in a flurry, trying at once to organize militia companies, recruit more volunteers, and avoid drafting men.

They directed all men between eighteen and forty-five not exempt from duty to meet in their polling places on Friday, and enroll their township quotas. After tabulations of the assessors' militia rolls and recruitments, it appeared that 211 to 213 men were lacking to make up the governor's requirement of army service by 40 percent of the militia number. Only Cadiz and North townships had exceeded this quota, and the others were deficient. The county had sent, in total, 1,101 men into service out of its 3,287 militia enrollment, 33.5 percent in these figures, which have discrepancies in Allen's totalings, and another ambiguity in that they may, or may not, include men recently exempted from service.

The nearing emergencies of war seem to have countered the prior recruiting enthusiasm. Many men discovered they were congenitally indisposed to military activity: "Judging from the number who have applied to Surgeon McBean for exemption on account of disability," Allen surmised, "we think Harrison county will soon be able to muster a brigade of Invalids. There are more sick men than we have ever seen before in this section.—Their sighs and groans are truly pitiful. Men who never thought of getting sick before, are now almost on the verge of the grave. 'Tis heart-rending! Humanity can hardly bear up under it! Some are troubled with almost every disease ever mentioned on a 'quack' doctor's list of diseases. Deaf, dumb, blind, halt, lame, spavined, ringboned, rheumatic, and deformed." He recommended that "some blatant, fierce Abolition-war man, who was among the first to apply, be appointed to the command." By 6 Sept., 195 were exempt with a surgeon's certificate: 36 in Short Creek alone, 13 percent of its eligible men; 22 in German, 10 percent; 20 in Stock, 16 percent (*CDS* 10 S).

Mobilization in the townships began with gatherings that were, in Harrison character, political meetings. James C. Love called the militia of Archer to order and first appointed a committee including Samuel Holland to draft resolutions. The militia resolved that in the present crisis Archer would do her duty and defend the state borders; that they supported the President; that they protested "editors acting as dictating generals"; and, finally, that they would elect officers and meet every Saturday afternoon for drill. The leaders, prominently Democrats, directed their letter to the *Sentinel* (24 S).

Dissension flared among Republicans. "A Conservative Republican" addressed others "who have never bowed the knee to the Baal of Abolitionism. Can they vote for John A. Bingham for Congress, and ever again pretend to be a lover of the country? If they do, they will have to stifle every feeling of honor and love for the Constitution and laws which they have hitherto professed." Since the war began, "his voice has been heard in the councils for the Nation, and it has always been to distract and divide." With "great swelling words" imitative of the traitorous secessionists, he "has been crying for general emancipation." This Conservative believed Lincoln adhered to the principles protecting slavery proposed by the 1860 Crittenden Compromise, which the Union State Convention had adopted, and Bingham pronounced a "DAMNABLE HERESY!" He vowed to vote for White (*CDS* 10 S).

In the next week's news, the upper Ohio Valley came in range of invasion from a force of 5,000 to 10,000 in Western Virginia. The Federals on the Gauley River had retreated east, evacuated Charleston, which was, in this frightening account, shelled until only two houses remained, and withdrawn down the Kanawha. Local militia were rushing to Gallipolis. A battle proceeded at Hagerstown, Md.; and from Harper's Ferry, only cannonfire was heard. In Pittenger's and Poulson's letters, readers confronted the near-capture and rout of their own soldiers. They winced at the "Horrible Blunder — Battle Scenes" from Maryland where over a hundred men of the 3rd Michigan were shot in the backs by an Indiana regiment overlapping them from the rear. And reports of the dire aftermath of the Bull Run battle told of Union soldiers left in the woods and bushes for eight days dying of thirst, hunger, and putrefaction of wounds (*CR* 17 S).

In Cadiz, men prepared to meet the foe with accustomed ceremony. Several hundred from the townships assembled Saturday with "*Maj.s* Allen and Magee," to hear Estep's call and march with the drum and fife to the fairgrounds, where they had "some" drill, three speeches, a dinner set by the ladies, and a parade back with banners flying.

The Major with the great paunch no doubt made a conspicuous figure on the march, and had political reason to do so. By now one of the parties' arguments concerned which one had supported the war effort. Hatton charged that many Democrats had not contributed money because they favored the rebelling South and Vallandigham's state platform (*CR*

17 S). Allen countered with a long rebuke of Hatton, Bingham, and abolitionists' participation, in which he claimed that Estep's speeches had raised the volunteers, not Bingham's abolition harangues (24 S).

This was tangential to the basic controversy, which spread in bitterness. Hatton summarized it and in one remark pointed out a seal of silence which had kept the county together in effort, and now opened to its disarray. Before his criticism of non-supportive Democrats, Hatton devoted long praise to J. M. Estep, and observed that Estep had never discussed the causes of the present war (17 S). It might seem incredible that a political leader could lengthily urge others to fight against the rebellion without ever interpreting what had brought it about; but prior and subsequent events imply many shared this rather ahistorical and limited view — which had sufficed in a war presumed to be restricted in length and scope. And it closely parallels, of course, the immediacy in the common Confederate motivation of home-defense, among people who had little knowledge of or participation in the leading politics of wealthy planters.

Only now, amid escalating loss and danger from the war, the cause of it became generally a crucial issue. Many Democrats were charging, falsely, Hatton said, that it was an "Abolition war, brought about by the Republican party." Around the district their editors loaded their presses with Bingham's record, especially one quotation. They took this choice piece from the Tuscarawas *Advocate*. Bingham, in the House, had delivered a rhetorical flourish which, as they quoted it, sounded disunionist: "Who, in the name of Heaven, wants the cotton States in the Union, or in any other place than the state of perdition, if slavery is to continue." Bingham's full finish was this: "if they are to be in the Union *on the condition* that, from day to day, from generation to generation, and from age to age, this new civilizer of the children of Dahomey, shall continue, and be upheld by the Whole Power of the Government." Hatton reported that the Tuscarawas editor Patrick later granted he had mistaken Bingham's meaning, and printed a correction; but other papers continued to reprint the first attack (17 S, 1 O). Allen did so, and also decried Hatton's account of Patrick (24 S). The *Advocate*, by the way, had reprinted a Bingham speech for confiscation in June, commended his "bold" course, and labeled any not in sympathy with him as traitorous (*CR* 18 Je). This incident indicates, most of all, the heated swirl of the charges on Bingham and his supporters. Allen termed him a "traitorous disunionist," an ultra-abolitionist in favor of Negroes liberated, coming to Ohio, voting, and holding office. Bingham allegedly had recently boasted to his friends in Cadiz that he and his friends had inaugurated the war, and vowed it would never end until slavery and the "Slave Aristocracy" were obliterated (24 S).

One Bingham fan responded with a comical reply to the "Conservative Republican." Its satiric barbs mimicked the arguments of a long quarrel, but in particular the letter burlesqued the ejaculatory style of Allen. "A Consarned Damphool" asked, "Can you vote for John A. Bingham…and expect afterwards to be saved?" Bingham has abili-

ty, and "such a qualification has always been considered as *unconstitutional* with *us*, and if now adopted as a principle would lead to the utter extermination of OUR race, and consequently to *abolition*— which we consider as far *worse*, for we would better be *exterminated* than *abolished*. (We are also opposed to *eradication*.) We must adhere to *our* ancient prerogatives, if *we die* by it, which would be far better than other alternatives, both for *us* and for the *country*. *To die* for one's country is SWEET, but to be eternally abolished is *abominable* to think of." Bingham has experience which "might be of advantage to the country at this time; but what is that to *us*?—Better the country and everybody else should go to the *Devil* than that *we*, who have always maintained a high character for 'PERSISTency,'" should act contrary to our "*Constitutional construction*." Bingham "is himself an abolitionist…. He is in favor of depriving the 'angels' who are in rebellion of their property; and especially of their slaves…. This would be a double sort of abolitionism; it would free 'niggers' and destroy the rebellion. *We* could never stand it — yes, it might prove a sort of triple abolitionism. It would kill *our horse*; we'd have nothing to ride. Ye Gods! Brethren think of this…. The fall, if we get thrown, might so shock us as to bring us to the rational state…. *I* see it. What! have a country and a Union without Slavery! The Union may be a very good thing, but what would it be worth without any *horse* in it for us to ride? … We would rebel against *Davis* if he should interfere with it." Lastly, Bingham opposes compromise with rebels-in-arms, and so offends Donahue,

Phillips, and "*our* Constitution" (*CR* 24 S). Matthew Phillips was a substantial farmer to whom Hatton would allude as "the Squire of Athens."

Philip Donahue wrote up the speech he had given county Democrats at their recent convention, to correct Hatton's report of it. The Republicans had influenced people's minds over years so as to make Union impossible, he charged. They incited the Northern "section," a Vallandigham term, to "seize upon the government, through the ballot box, and conduct it, independent of the wishes of the South." Thus they took in a majority of the North, "by which means a Northern Confederacy was formed, which naturally resulted in the formation of a Southern Confederacy...." They built up "a national feeling peculiar to the North alone, which naturally resulted in a national feeling peculiar to the South." War can never redirect these "national feelings." New "doctrines and measures" must allow reorganization — no "revolutionary" doctrines or changes in "institutions that are well established and fixed," unless they are so gradual as to be "insensible." A view of the actions of this Congress "in the light of nature (which is the miniature through which everything should be examined)" showed it "had designs against the nation" (*CDS* 24 S).

Thus Donahue revised the concept of the Union government to a "Northern Confederacy," implied patriotic fervor stemmed from a sectional presumption, and deprecated the war "in the light of nature."

The cost of driving the Confederates from the fields of Maryland on 17 September came home slowly, beginning

with the arrival on the 22nd of Charles P. Dewey and the body of Adjutant Charles L. Duffield, from Capt. David Cunningham's company of the 30th. Duffield had been shot twice, in the thigh and through the stomach, and died the next day. Dewey counted three dead, including Lt. Furbay from Georgetown, four wounded in the company (*CR* 24 S). The total Union losses were estimated at 1,200 killed, not over 6,000 wounded; 3,000 rebels left dead on the field had been buried. But soldiers had fallen in stacks and piles on this bloodiest day in the war, to be found and counted gradually, up to the casualties of about 13,000 Federal and 10,000 Confederate soldiers. Cunningham would report that six more than Dewey thought had wounds (8 O). Almost a week after the battle, Samuel and Margaret George of Cadiz learned their youngest son had been killed — wounded in the thigh, then shot through the breast while being carried off the field — "murdered by rebel assassins" — his body not found for two days — and after all this time, his brother Thomas had to go and search for his remains (*CR* 1 O).

Twenty-one-year-old Albert had left home a year before, against his parents' wishes; the day after Capt. Cunningham swore him into the 30th, he wrote them that he felt a duty to his country, and asked their forgiveness; this letter became his obituary (*CDS* 15 O). He came home in a coffin two weeks after the battle, in the evening, and a large crowd then followed him to the new cemetery outside town "in the solemn hours of the night, with the pale moon looking sadly down, and the solemn tolling of the funeral bell speaking to them in mournful accents, that mortality was being lost" (*CDS* 8 O).

"We are drifting into savage and retaliatory warfare," warned an article from the *Christian Examiner* Hatton printed on his front page. The policy of the "defensive war" to reoccupy U.S. arsenals and forts has failed, intensified the rebellion, and put immense armies long in the field — "dangerous magazines in a republic," producers of moral degradation, so that we "shall have ere long, a saturnalia of vice and crimes" (1 O). Casting Democratic ballots would do more to save yourselves and your country, a *Crisis* article in the *Sentinel* urged, than "can be done for these sublime objects on the gory fields of battle, with mourning and wretchedness as counterparts.... If you are charged with want of spirit and courage, send the slanderer to the field where leaden bullets will test the courage of the most bloody minded.... If you are charged with want of love of country, ask if he who loves best his wife and children is the one who strikes with the arrows of death!" (24 S). In Washington township, which had just sent 41 men into service (22 percent of its eligible men), the military committee now reported contributors to the soldiers' bounties and families' support: twenty-eight of those asked had refused to give anything, almost 18 percent of the total solicited (*CR* 1 O).

"A Great Fair Promised"

On 22 Sept. President Lincoln issued the Emancipation Proclamation, declaring freedom the next January for all slaves in rebelling states, and proposing congressional action to compensate the other slave-holding states if they abolished slavery. He referenced his Proclamation to the Confiscation and D.C. Emancipation acts, for which Bingham had prominently argued. The *Republican* announced the country's rejoicing in the "dawn of a new era" (1 O). The "conservatives," however, were stunned, then outraged.

The heated politics attended, yet could not dominate, the gathering of thousands at the County Fair, held the first three days of October at Cadiz, advertised as the showcase of "the greatest wool-growing county in the United States," its stock, produce, and crafts (*CR* 24 S). To the fairgrounds men, women, and children brought their works for judging by leading citizens, vying for premiums that totaled $2,000, the numerous awards set in rank of community value.

Here they raced their horses for the fair's richest purses — $25 for the fastest trotter, $10 to Thomas S. Mitchell in third place. Contests for Fast Racking or Pacing, Fast Walking horses, and Fancy Matched Pairs won $10 and $5 firsts. The Horse Department awarded $18 to Updegraff and Delaney for the Sweepstakes Stallion, $10 to John Cunningham's second place. Competitions for saddle and draft horses of all descriptions rewarded horsemen; J. T. Updegraff with ten premiums, Craig Hamilton two for his draft horses, T. H. Dickerson one for his two-year-old mare, Jacob Poulson one for his Spring Colt.

The sheep farmers showed bucks and pens of five ewes of all age categories among three breeds. For Saxony sheep, John McFadden (Irish) took many of the $5 to $2 premiums, John Singer passing him for the best pen of year-old ewes and ewe lambs, John N. Haverfield besting him for the best buck lamb, Applegate McFadden, Wm. Eagleson, and T. J. Meholm taking prizes for old bucks. The Spanish (Merino) sheep of Robt. Perrine, Asa Dickerson, and Eagleson dominated their division. The Silesians of John C. Jamison, John Singer, and Rezin Holmes starred in theirs. The most interesting exhibition sheep were surely the fat muttons, not only for their size, but also for the requirement that the owners post accounts of their method of feeding.

The cattle premiums were much swept by Wm. Hedges and Isaac Thomas, but Martin S. Jamison won $5 for a three-year-old bull, Thomas Mc-Fadden $2 for an ox, Thompson Mc-Fadden $2 for a younger ox, and Samuel McFadden (Irish) $1 for a pair of working steers.

Joseph Clendening had both premium Jacks; Thompson McFadden had two of the winning mules. There was even less competition in the hog department — a contest for boars, in which Isaac Thomas took $5, S. B. Lukins $3, and one for breeding sows and litter that brought John McFadden (Irish) $5, John Quigley $3.

Poultry won only 50¢. James Keesey's pea fowls, ducks, and geese took honors. Susan Case brought the winning pair of Bramah Pootra, Julia Wier the native chickens. Other breeds shown were Ahanghai, Java Bantram, and Cochin China.

The Mechanic Arts displayed the equipment crafted in the county: two-horse carriages, for the best of which John McFadden (Irish) won $8, George Wright $5; two-horse wagons, S. Kenedy $5, John Clifford $3; sewing machines,

R. G. Martin $3, R. C. Ladd $2; corn shellers; wheat drills; general ploughs; corn ploughs, E. Laizure $2; horse rakes; reapers, E. Laizure $5; mowers, C. Aultman & Co. $5; reaper and mowers combined, C. Aultman $5; harrows; cider mill and presses. J. M. Robinson made the best cooking stove for wood, parlor stove, and coal grate cast front, each $2; J. M. Paul surpassed him for the coal cook stove. Robinson's door hinges won 50¢; E. Laizure's horse shoes and David Peterman's horse shoe nails earned the same. Thomas Phillips, Jr., took first premiums of $3 and $2 for Gents' Fine and Coarse Boots and Ladies Summer Walking Shoes; John Rea won two seconds, and Henry Hagadorn another. Hagadorn earned $2 for leather with his two calfskins. W. N. Carson bested the cooper ware of pork barrels, flour barrels, and churns, $1 each. Carpenters contended in panel doors, for which O. Slemmons gained $2; armed rocking chairs and sets of parlor chairs, earning L. F. Grider $3 each; and sets of split-bottom chairs, bringing Jacob Cassell only $1. Here John Rea the shoemaker showed his painting of Specimen Graining that merited $3.

The best loaves of bread earned $3 for C. Wagoner, $2 and $1 for Martha Rea; fresh butter $2 for Ruth Cope, $1.50 for Susan Case; 10 lb. cheese $1.50 for John Simpson, 75¢ for Nancy Ross; light cakes $1 for C. Wagoner, 50¢ for Mattie Carnahan; sponge cakes $1 for Ellen Jamison; and Rusk Pastry premiums of $1 to 50¢ for Isabella Clark and Susan Case; bacon $1 and 50¢ for Wm. Boggs; gallons of soft soap, 3 lb. of hard soap, and gingerbread, prizes for Isabella Gordon.

In the Floral and Vegetable Halls they arrayed their harvest wealth. Fruit in 40, 20, and 10 varieties, $2 and $1 premiums, won in all by Isaac Thomas, plus those for apples, along with J. B. Jamison and Elizabeth Carrick. Peaches, pears, quinces, plums in five varieties, grapes in eight, prizes in the last taken by E. Laizure and Joseph Sharon. Pecks of dried peaches and apples from the growers. Crops in half-bushels: red wheat, for $1; white wheat; buckwheat, won by John N. Haverfield; oats; seed corn. Pecks of timothy seed, won by James N. Haverfield, and clover seed. The best half-bushel of sweet potatoes took $1.50, of potatoes $1. William S. Grove got $2 for his potatoes in three varieties, William Lukins $1. Mrs. Mary Warfel earned the 50¢ first for her sample tomatoes. Mary E. Hilligas' rhubarb took first place. Others arrayed their beets, cabbages, pumpkins, carrots, parsnips, millet, braided corn ears, and broom corn.

In the numerous contests of preserves, Ellen Jamison won $1 for her peach, Martha Rea 50¢. Sarah Cochran took 50¢ for her peach jelly and $1 for her raspberry. Malinda Warfel got a 50¢ second for her spiced apples, and Jane Cochran the same for spiced plums.

In the panoply of needlework and bedclothes, Elizabeth Robb gained $2 for a quilt, Elizabeth Bond $1; Fannie Lisle $1 for a counterpane, Jennie Lisle 50¢; Mary E. Hilligas $1 for a shirt. Among the double-woven coverlets Mary Dickerson's took $1, Adam Dunlap's 50¢; of homemade linen tablecloths, W. B. Beebe's entry $1, Agnes Mealy 50¢; in pairs of linen sheets, C. Ehrhart $1, Ellen Jamison 50¢. Ellen's pair of pillow slips

earned a second and 25¢. Of the five-yard lengths of homemade linen O. Ehrhart's merited $1, Adam Porter's 50¢; of the ten-yards homemade woolen flannel, Jane Dickerson (of Asa) bested others for $2. Nancy Hammond's rag carpet won $1.50, Julia Smiley's 75¢. Knitted woolen stockings, socks, mitts, and gloves also competed.

The regular categories of arts exhibited were few: photographs, for which Linnie Shank took $1, W. B. Beebe 50¢; Ambrotype, H. Davis 50¢; oil painting, Anna Cooper $1; watercolor painting, W. H. Culbertson $1; pen drawings and pencil drawings, each J. P. Johnson $1.

Women and some men entered other creations in the Unenumerated Articles for Females, for which about 200 premiums were awarded. Only four in the Floral Hall went to flowers—the scarlet verbena, rose geranium, and Isabella Gordon's fuchsia and tea rose. Along with dried fruits, marmalades, cherry catsup, watermelon molasses, rice molasses, cherry wine, dewberry butter, picnic cakes, tomato jam, tomato honey, tomato figs, the Union jelly of Sarah Cochran, the Moravian cake and watermelon wine of Mary E. Hilligas, the dried currants of Thomas Hilligas, the Queen cake of Isabella Gordon, the hockled flax of Susan Clark, they displayed items that show they valued their handicraft more than "Victorian" modesty. Mary E. Hilligas brought her Bosomed Chemise to win 50¢; Bell Cady her tatting night dress for 75¢; Ada Cady her ruffled drawers for 25¢. Also to be seen and compared were the tatting drawers, tatting chemise, shellwork cotton stockings, and linen stockings. Anna

Cooper showed off her photograph album to win 75¢; Nettie Beebe, 50¢. Other prized possessions appeared. Mrs. Charles Allen exhibited her canary bird, which triumphed over H. Dallas'.

The Unenumerated Articles for Males, about 100 premiums, included basket willow, barometers, thermometers, designs for a farm house, James Keesey's Hillside Plough, John Rea's axe handle and boy's sled, Joseph Sharon's hayladders, Martha Chaney's straw hat, Master Harry Barrett's Hobby Horse, Tommy Hilligas' powder horn, wooden chair, and moss house, Samuel Warfel's folding rocking chair, Willie George's model log cabin, William Cady's plum seed chain, Anna Cooper's writing desk, H. Dallas' "California Tomato," cocoa nut-dipper, and cat, E. Laizure's sugar cane mill and "Tire Upsetter."

Among the curiosities brought forth were an engraved shell, a variety of shells, "Congress Gaiters," a Military Sash, Zoave Cap, case of amputating instruments, and white squirrel.

Allen reported that "*the* attraction" was the Floral Hall which thousands visited. The most exciting incident was a trotting match between two fast horses. The large crowd "preserved the best order, and, considering the excitement of the times, there were very few fights. We overheard one excited individual call another a secessionist, and ... we beheld him stretching his full length on the green sward, his fall accelerated by a well directed blow between the eyes" (*CDS* 8 O).

Monstrous Depths

As the county flocked to town they found posted at the courthouse a dire

new display — the list of the 206 men drafted. Among them were the county's State Representative, John Latham; fifteen from Archer, including Thomas M. Mitchell and John Hines; twenty-six from Short Creek, including Isaac and Lewis Furbay of the late Lieutenant's family, Jesse and John Singer, James L. Hawthorn, and Rezin Holmes; thirteen in Athens, with Samuel M. Dickerson, Samuel Dunlap, and Joshua B. Phillips, most likely the son of the "Squire" Matthew Phillips. They had to report 7 Oct. for transportation to Camp Zanesville (*CR* 8 O).

For evening entertainment at the courthouse, fairgoers had a Democratic meeting on Thursday, with speakers congressional candidate Joseph W. White and A. W. Patrick of Tuscarawas — the editor who had first castigated Bingham's "cotton states" line — and on Friday a scheduled address by Bingham.

The secretary of the state Union Party had already repudiated Bingham for abolitionism and endorsed White, in a letter Allen placed at the head of his paper for two weeks, so his many new subscribers could read it (24 S, 1 O). Lincoln's Proclamation provoked a furor to direct at Bingham. It struck at the Constitution and felled the nation to the pit-bottom of its existence, in the *Crisis* interpretation: "Sad is our fate and monstrous the depths." A rebuke to the "Consarned Damphool" claimed that conservative Republicans did not "love the negro race above their country" and would not "sacrifice" it to benefit negroes. Bingham, this writer charged, spoke on one subject only, "the everlasting negro." "When all patriots prayed for Compromise," he and his class sneered at them for "weak knees," "determined to stand by their ultra opinions though the land should be drenched in blood, and ruin would be the fate of the nation." "John A. Bingham *don't want the Union restored to day*. He said so on the 12th of March 1862, in his place in Congress...." Conservative Republicans wanted the Union restored, he wrote, and slavery treated like "other institutions in rebellious states," not preferred, not disturbed. He vowed he could not vote for Bingham: "The blood of his countrymen stains his hands, and he stands responsible for all the influence he has and is exerting to prolong and embitter this strife" (*CDS* 1 O).

Bingham was a hypocrite, Allen charged, who at home knew no man but his ultra-fanatic friends while he won nomination, then went about the district speaking abolition or conservatism depending on the community's inclination. He complained of being called an abolitionist in spite of his advocacies of the liberation of four million slaves, among which he had promised "these children of oppression will make such an exodus from the house of their bondage as the world had not seen since the exodus of God's people, which the dark-eyed daughters of Israel celebrated in that sublime song: 'The Lord hath triumphed gloriously; the horse and his rider hath He thrown into the sea.'" This exodus loomed, to some in the promised land of the sheep-herders, as a certain dreadful influx. The *New Philadelphia Democrat* predicted the "practical effect" of "Bingham's Emancipation Schemes." First, the army would "set to freeing niggers instead of fighting for the Union." Past his-

tory proved every slave freed came north, and Ohio's portion would be one-fifth — 800,000. Tuscarawas' share would be 8,000 black immigrants. Furthermore, in another entire column, this editor calculated the tax each township would pay to purchase the freedom of the border-state slaves who would come. Allen in reprinting these claimed Harrison could expect a comparable influx and tax (1 O).

In such terms could Bingham expect to be pilloried at the Democratic meeting, a pillory chopped out of his own podium. He cast about, it seems, to contend; but had history, on which he had always based his moral-political arguments, ever been revised so radically so fast?

Usually Bingham when at home prepared for speaking in private meditation. He sequestered himself, according to Walter Gaston Shotwell, from his cousin-wife Amanda and their six young children, under a windowed ventilation dome on his rooftop, on the high edge of the town hill. There he could survey the sheep-flocked hills and primeval forest groves which inspired his descriptions — in conjunction with the poetry of the Bible and the English Romantics he and Amanda had long read (230).

On this occasion, Bingham prepared a defensive stratagem so ineffectual that W. G. Shotwell's characterization of him as artless and undesigning seems acute. He drew up a list of questions for Joseph White, as though White should deign to answer or even acknowledge them, as though White might face challenge in the House or some tribunal of justice. While White was a guest in Allen's house before the meeting, so Allen complained, Bingham showed himself no gentleman by sending these questions to White through a "lackey."

At the crowded courthouse the speakers calumniated Bingham full tilt. One of Bingham's "tools," the "notorious disunion Abolitionist" John Haverfield, and then others, protested by interrupting White and Patrick, until "Mr. Estep had to get up and give Bingham's dirty dogs" a severe rebuke. "Mr. White and Mr. Patrick showed up Bingham's record in such a light Thursday night and laid his wounds so bare" that he and his "lackeys" present "were fearful that mortification would take place in less than twenty-four hours if salve was not immediately applied." Despite their meeting scheduled for the next night, their "only remedy was for Bingham to get up at the close" and "beg for the privilege of saying something in reply. The 'statesman' spoke about two hours....He twisted and turned and frothed, went forward and backwards, and done every thing but reply to arguments" of White and Patrick. "Poor Bingham, we pitied him. His case was so hopeless that he looked perfectly distressed." His days in Congress would be finished at the end of the term in March, Allen predicted. The next night, the Republicans had no speech, and drew so few they "did not even light up the house" (*CDS* 8 O).

Unfortunately, the *Republican* for this week, with any opposing account, has disappeared. That the meeting provoked extreme reactions can be seen, however, in a warning Allen issued: "There has been instances, within a few days, in this community, of persons attempting to do mob violence. They should abstain ... even if Lewton, Bingham's law partner, should offer half-grown boys 25 cents apiece to commit mob violence, or the officers of the law ... should say that they 'would not be on hands'.... If violence is committed on one, it will not end there, but become universal" (8 O). Hatton subsequently warned men carrying loaded guns in the town streets that they could accidentally fire (15 O).

When the irate drafted men came to Cadiz, some people in the area predicted they would attack Bingham's home. Allen denied this threat, reported in Steubenville. The drafted went to camp along with J. M. Estep and other commissioners, and prospective substitutes. For the latter, the market "was brisk for a few days." "They commanded prices ranging from $200 to $400." In the region, only Jefferson and Guernsey counties had met their quotas through volunteers. In Belmont 101 were drafted, Coshocton 198, Muskingum 317, Noble 376, and Tuscarawas 431 (*CDS* 15 O).

Allen's paper greeted the drafted with "The Great Issue" proclaimed in its basest new terms: are the people of the district "willing to be taxed to buy the slaves of the South?" Joseph White stood opposed, and Bingham "anxious that the wooly-headed contrabands" should be freed at the expense of white men. "Every vote cast for Bingham is an invitation to every splay-footed, bandy-shanked, hump-backed ... contraband of the South to come north to be a terror and pest..." (8 O).

The leading article of this issue was a notable two-column "Army Correspondence" written from Headquarters near

Sharpsburg 25 Sept. from "C." It began, "*Friend Sentinel*: — The strict censorship of the press which has lately been adopted by the government has rendered it difficult, if not dangerous, for me to keep you posted with reference to the movements of this army. Matters of general interest and importance, after becoming facts of history, should not be withheld from the public." It ended, "The proclamation of the President in reference to emancipation was received in camp last night, and so far as my observation extends, it produces *universal dissatisfaction*." Allen identified the writer on page three: "Every person should read Capt. [George Armstrong] Custer's letter....It is the best description of the great battle in Maryland that we have read." The twenty-two-year-old Custer had become an aide to Gen. McClellan following his solo reconnaissance fording of the Chicahominy River in May, had accompanied

Brig. Gen. Alfred Pleasanton, with cavalry and artillery, to near Sharpsburg on 15 Sept. (*OR* 1.19.1.210), and so observed the entire action from the first "grand sight" of the rebel lines through the "fourteen-hours of continuous hard fighting" on an unprecedented open field. He pictured for the reader the sweep of battle, and drew the successive actions into a narrative that subtly effected his underlying purpose — justification of McClellan when he did not reinforce his attacking troops or pursue battle with the enemy. In sending to Harrison County, no longer his home, this vindication of the Democrat McClellan, framed with criticism of Lincoln's administration, Custer joined the campaign against Bingham, his former sponsor. My full argument of this motive, and a transcript of Custer's letter, has been published in the *Ohioana Quarterly*.

Chapter 7

Nancy's News

In autumn the men on the farms harvested their barley and corn, women picked and preserved the apples and vegetables, and children returned to the schoolhouses, along with older youths who had not yet completed the common school curriculum. Nancy Mitchell at twenty still went to school when she could; as the oldest of six children, often needed at home, she was far behind her cousin of the same age Martha (Mat), who had been teaching for at least two years. On evenings the main social events of the countryside began, occasions that fostered courting in a free and casual manner; these were "singings" held at the schoolhouses, open to all. Young women went to these without escorts, and in the course of the evening some found men to accompany them home and visit with them privately — unless other youths in the household harassed them.

The "singing" itself had a rustic exuberance, far different from playing and singing songs with a parlor piano. The "singing" was not meant to please listeners, but to rouse the gathered in a more athletic or spiritual than aesthetic musical contest. Traveling singing masters taught people to vocalize in the interval pitches named fa-sol-la-me, represented by separate shape notes in this music. Nancy named a local teacher, in a letter, "Crabbed Old Sammy." This kind of music and instruction dated to the 1720s in America, but had been replaced in the East, and come to flourish in the rural West and South by the time *The Southern Harmony* was compiled, by William Walker, in 1835. It preserved the Renaissance psalmody and polyphony from the Genevan Psalter (Wilcox iv) of 1551, and added American folk and gospel hymns. It prevailed where music did not rely on, and was not keyed to the regulated pitches and harmonies of pianos. As Nancy's church yet sang only psalms, with men as leaders and no instrument, the modes of shape-note singing probably represented their familiar music; here the war wrought a considerable change, as men returned having learned standard melodies, and while they were absent, women had needed to form the choir; the women

72

who undertook this were likely piano-trained, and a few years afterward, the church installed an organ.

In the singings, the tenor part carried the main tune. Women with voices in the lower range joined men in this part, and others could sing the lead an octave higher. Men with low voices sang the bass line; women sang the treble part, in which they could be joined on a lower octave by men; and some tunes had a fourth part, which too could be sung on alternate octaves. Thus the three or four lines sounded in as many as seven differently pitched parts. The bass, treble, and fourth lines each sang a melodic counterpart to the main tune which aimed more at its own interest than at a harmonic accompaniment subservient to the central tune. They also frequently moved with disparate rhythms between the notes ending each text line. On these long notes the parts joined in a chord, frequently blaring a discord, and between these end-notes discords flared, especially in the differing syncopations.

The singers synchronized their parts not by accord to a dominating melody, but by following the leader as he literally beat time. On some object before him he would strike his finger, then the heel of his hand, before raising his fist, then casting out his open hand at shoulder height, to dramatize the meter that should regulate the group. This failing, the dissonances would of course defy any resolution, and result in more cacophony than any "hootings of the midnight bird," to which Walker compared the loud singing uncultivated singers favored (ix, xxix).

These voices contending throughout the whole range of pitches sounded like a great band of bagpipes. With such martial breadth, driving beat, and bass bellows, the chorus in a major key proclaimed the "Jubilee" ("O tell me no more of this world's vain store! The time for such trifles with me is now o'er"). In minor keys the chorus blasted discords on all mortal hopes and sounded the alarm: "When Gabriel's awful trump shall sound, ... Comets blaze, Sinners raise, Dread amaze, Horrors seize The guilty sons of Adam's race..." ("Mississippi").

As a prelude to romancing, the singing rang out either a dire caution, or the emboldenment of desperation. Afterward, in autumn, courting couples on their moonlit ways to the fireside had another aural accompaniment, from the surrounding pastures and pens. The thousands of ewes on the hills were coming into heat. A farmer with hundreds who would have to assist them in birthing in the spring, and foster their lambs — for both require extensive help at the time — had to time breeding carefully so that he and his family and farmhands, if he had any, could attend to all the forthcoming lambs. Therefore, he selectively kept the rams at bay, in wait of mating at a time convenient for the farmer. The insistent calls of the balked rams and the plaintive cries of the ewes blared a counterpart "singing."

From Nancy D. Mitchell to Frank P. Grove, 4 Oct.: "Very kind Friend, Yours of the 22nd and 24th of last month came duly to hand and its contents perused with Eager interest and pleasure as all your productions are and it is with much pleasure that I sit down to answer the Epistle of so kind a friend. You will no doubt wonder why I did not answer it sooner, But I will tell you the reason. I was going to write to you when I heard John had come home and intended going back on Monday. [Capt. Mc-Cready had given John Mitchell, Thomas McKinney, and the other officers a week-end furlough.] So I came to the conclusion I would not write untill after the Fair and let you know how I got along there and send it with him and you will likely get it as soon as if I had written sooner and sent it by mail. But I must tell you about the Fair. Well, Frank I thought it was the poorest one I was ever at. Whether every person thought so I don't know. But a good many thought so I am sure. O it was so dusty it almost choked me. And O if that was all I would not have cared. I did not enjoy myself atall, But I did not expect to before I went. Still I was fool enough to go. The Floral hall was about as nice as usual. I did not go to see the stock nor I did not go to see them running ther horses. All the pleasure I had was meeting some familiar faces whom I had not seen for a long time. But when I think of those faces that I would like to have greeted there were not and whose loving footsteps may ne'er enter the threshhold of 'Sweet home' it makes my heart ache. But although the zenith of our nations Sky looks dark I trust it is but the prelude of a brighter one and I hope the day is not far distant when you and my dear brother will be returned home in safety. Well I will tell you about the draft. It came off the 1st of Oct. They drafted about 200 in this County. Most of them married men. Ths Mitchell is one that is drafted. I feel sorry for him he hates it so bad but I am in hopes he will be rejected. Samuel Dickerson (that is Joe's

son) is another. They take it so hard and no wonder because all his sons are gone now and he was all the help he had. [Samuel, eighteen, was the youngest brother of Joe and James W.]

"There are a few secesh drafted, that's good don't you say so? I heard that some of them said they would 'wade in blood' before they would go. But the Governor says any man can be exempt by paying two hundred dollars. This may not be true. If it is I think it is a mean act of the Gov because those that are rich can stay at home and the poor will have to go and fight for their property.

"I feel so disappointed that they did'ent draft in Cadiz. But they say there will be another draft before long and I hope some of the young men of Cadiz township will be pressed into the Service. Such as are 'rebel sympathisers' you know some of them? There was none drafted in Charlestown. (is not this the poorest writing you ever saw but my eyes are ful of dirt I cannot see) You wanted to know how I am enjoying myself, not very well, I have not been at any singings since you went away. There was one at Irish Ridge and two at Science Hill. One was there last night. [Afterwards, Mc-Cready's sergeants] Albrt Harrison and John went to Holmes and your brother went to my Uncles. [John Mitchell accompanied Sally Holmes home, and William Grove went home with Mat.] I believe that is all I heard about it. Thats not very much is it? John waited on his Sally the time of the Fair. I think he was there on Thursday night. Frank my Dahlias are all dead. They did not bloom worth a hoote. There might have been some nice ones on them but the frost came so soon it killed them. Oh Frank how I would like to see you but who knows how long the time may be ere we shall meet again. But I trust God will protect you from the missiles of death and bring you home again. I had a letter from Rob last Thursday. He was at Louisville then but they had orders to prepare five or six days rations. Some thought they are going to take Lexington but he said he did'ent want to march back there again. he said there were about 130 thousand troops. The 13th Ohio Regt is there, he said he saw T L Carnahan. B F Morris is there also he belongs to the same brigade that the 98th does. He said that he, [Finley] Oglevee and [Corp. William] Clyde were put on double duty for missing Roll Call 'but we did'ent care' he said. They have to get up at 3 o'clock every morning and stand in the Rifle pits till daylight. They cut clear through a cemetery. They would lift the dead and dig a little hole and put them in. [Nancy's next report might seem to represent soldiers' exaggerations. The 98th had encountered Kentucky soldiers much taller than they, such as Generals Nelson, Jackson, and Terrill. But the account of the giant is accurate. He was the legendary Jim Porter, a tavern keeper; Cave Hill has a hillside tomb for him today, below the ridge of the rifle pit.] They dug up a man that was 7 feet 8 inches long. (Oh they cannot let the dead rest. I am afraid you will never read this letter it is such poor writing.

"Well Frank I must tell you how the girls in Charlestown are getting along. You have heard before this that Harriet and Malinda Warfel are teaching school at Red Hill [on the Wheeling road above Charlestown]. Maggie Braden told me that Malinda had a beau home with her from the Fair on Thursday night. She didn't know who he was. Oh I must not forget to tell you Mary Jane had one wait on her at the Fair. His name was Alex Barriklow. They both kept pretty quiet you had better think. Ellen Mitchell and Tom Shirey have some good times I guess. She appears to enjoy herself. O Mat says Gabriel has sounded his trumpet again good for him. [Gabriel Holland has been calling on Mat's sister Ellen.]

"I have had all the work to do for three weeks, Mother not being well but she is beginning to help me some now. its too bad what do you say about it. Well you will think this is the poorest letter you ever read and you wont be mistaken I got my eyes so full of dust yesterday that I can hardly see.

"Well Frank I got my likeness taken for you but it is such a poor one that I wont send it. one of the eyes looks a great deal paler than the other. I did not notice it till I came home. Davis had the toothach and he was so cross that he did not care what he done. But I'll get a photagraph the next time and I shall send it in the next letter I write to you. [In a studio such as Davis', mirrors magnified light from a skylight to glare on the subject, who had to stare into the camera during the slow exposure. Eyes frequently moved or blinked — but usually both together.]

"Oh when did you hear from Mary Cope? [John evidently told Nancy of this letter to Frank.] I hope you will not believe what she told you about me for it is a falsehood whoever the author of it is or may be. I blame Mary for not telling

you last winter before she left but perhaps she knows her own business best.
They say Rob Christy is going to be married before three weeks to M G Love.
May happiness be ever theirs. Well it is
getting late and I must bring this poor
letter to a close hoping you will excuse
me for not writing sooner and be assured
I will not be so long again. Please remember me soon by another letter and
excuse careless bad writing. For the present Farewell, Your true Friend, N D
Mitchell. I was so disappointed when
John came home that you were not
along"

On this Saturday night, the young
people went to another singing; and subsequent rumors suggest that one of Mc-
Cready's officers had a farewell visit with
Mat Mitchell which resulted in reports
they were engaged to be married.

Chapter 8

Perryville: "Nobody Sees a Battle"

Col. George Webster's 98th Ohio came to stand in the center of the Battle of Perryville, a ferocious fight which in diverse ways turned the course of Kentucky and the Civil War. Their battleground has only recently been added to that in the Perryville Battlefield State Park, not yet intently investigated for its landmarks. The military history of this battle continues to be studied. It has been described by Kenneth Hafendorfer in successive editions of his *Perryville: Battle for Kentucky*.

The middle action, however, has been represented from incomplete and conflicting reports in the *Official Records*. In referring to these, I will cite them by writer and page in *OR* I.16.1. Several letters from the 98th, quoted in this chapter, add closer descriptions. Unlike *OR* reports, these letters were not scribed with an eye toward military approval or advancement.

Buell's reorganized army took up a pursuit of Bragg's army over four different routes from Louisville. The

Third Corps marched south-east directly toward Bardstown and Bragg's main force. The Second Corps moved south before turning east. The First, under Maj. Gen. Alexander McCook, sent one division east through Shelbyville toward Frankfort and Kirby Smith's army, where the new Confederate government of Kentucky prepared to inaugurate its governor. A division under Brig. Gen. Lovell Rousseau and another under Brig. Gen. James S. Jackson took a route between the Frankfort and Bardstown pikes, through Taylorsville. Jackson's troops were all new recruits, in a brigade under Brig. Gen. Wm. R. Terrill and another commanded by the 98th's Col. George Webster.

Buell, to speed his army's pursuit, ordered the soldiers to carry all their equipment, including knapsacks, cookware, and oilcloths, resulting in the tremendous loads they soon strewed along the road, as Wesley Poulson, 98th, reported on 3 Oct. from a ridge near Taylorsville: "Wednesday Oct. 1st we left

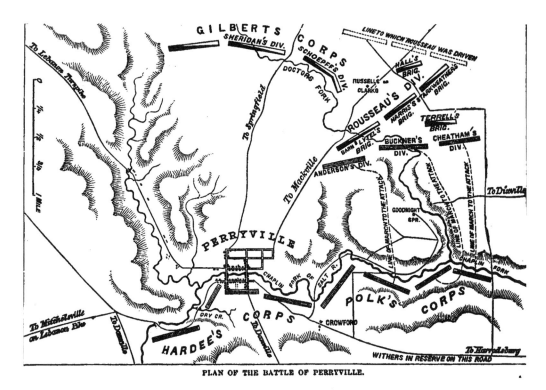

An official map of the Battle of Perryville. Source: *Harper's Pictorial History.*

Louisville about 10 o'clock, having been out on picket the night before, and being tired and sleepy in the morning you will not wonder when I say we were tired and sleepy at sundown after marching about 13 miles carrying about sixty pounds as near as I could guess when we started but before we stopped a little spell it felt like it was at least 20 lbs. heavier.

"We encamped for the night, and at 3 o'clock in the morning we had to get up and stand with our arms until day, when we were allowed to make fire and cook breakfast.

"At ten minutes before eight we were again marching. Some did not carry so much this time, having dispensed with a part, needless to say how. We marched till about 3 o'clock in the evening when it commenced raining. We were halted a spell, and then marched on, it raining on us till after four. As water was scarce we could get none to camp near till we had traveled about 18 miles, which kept us till after night a spell. A little before night it began to rain, and rained on us till we were in camp. It stopped raining a little before we went to bed. I was awakened about 3 o'clock in the morning by a little rain which fell in my face, and shortly after it rained very hard, making us very wet and uncomfortable. In the morning we marched without getting time to dry our clothes, which made our loads much heavier. I tell you there were a few blankets left on that field, and not a very few either! My load was fifteen pounds heavier by the water that was in it, I know, and had we marched all day, some of it would have been left by the way, but we only marched one and a half miles when we encamped, and will stay till tomorrow, I think, and perhaps longer. Where we are going we know not. — Some think to fight, some think we are going to Cumberland Gap &c. Reports are here that there is skirmishing between our men and some of Bragg's forces. I do not think it is true. I have seen no rebels in arms yet, and doubt whether they are so plenty in Kentucky as reported.

"...Captain [Butts] rode part of the way, not being able to march so far after being sick. — The boys are all doing well that came with us. They are getting a good rest now, if we have to march, which I think is likely, for we are drawing five days rations. Some of the boys were left behind at Louisville, and will no doubt be well cared for. I have not room to give all the names, and will just say that they are well off to what we are, as far as care is concerned.

"We have had but one death in our company yet....We are about 30 miles southeast of Louisville, and 20 miles from the place where the rebels are said to be. We got some letters from home to day, which revived the boys considerably. I got three, and felt rich, but did not get all that are on the way, for I got one little one from father, and he said he had written a big one for me, a few days before, which I have not yet received.

"The regiment is going up Salt River. I can see Salt River now, just by raising my eyes. It is very low at present. I have not time to write more now, but may, at a future time, if spared. Yours, &c., W. S. P." (*CR* 15 O)

Soon McCook and his 12,500 men were close behind Bragg's southeastern

retreat, hearing fire from his rear-guard cavalry. The new soldiers expected their first battle fast on the heels of every report — until wearied by false alarms and the lengthening harsh march.

After crossing the Salt River, they climbed into the increasingly rocky hills south, beyond the gulch of the Chaplin River, a rough, scarcely habitated country of few wagon roads through the dry woods and ravines, where "the men were compelled to drink foul pool water, and could get very little of that," Lt. Col. Poorman wrote the *Belmont Chronicle* (23 O). They were preceded to this stagnant water by the hogs of the area and the horses and mules of cavalry and artillery ahead of them. They wound through these poor, droughted steeps to Willisburg, thence to Mackville, a narrow crossroads where the creek was dry. By this night, 7 Oct., the rations were depleted. Many of McCook's men had only hard corn picked from the few parched fields on the way. Their journey the next morning has been known as the "Dry Canteen March."

Col. Webster, however, somehow provided his men with fresh beef, and advice to collect water, which his attentive soldiers took. Robert Mitchell and friends probably did not heed this, as he later wrote Nancy that he thought the threats of imminent fighting had been only more attempts to "fool" them. Wesley Poulson, among Butts's dutiful soldiers, did prepare, as he recounted: "at about daybreak we were aroused from slumbers by the beat of the drum and ordered to be ready for marching in forty minutes, which is rather a short time to prepare and eat breakfast, but as I have often heard it said 'A short horse is eas-

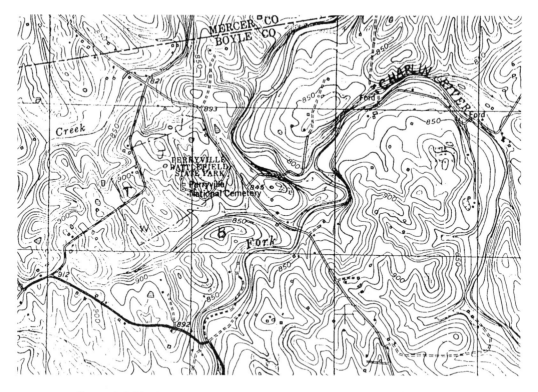

Perryville Battlefield, showing the positions of Gen. Jackson (J), Gen Terrill (T), Col. Webster (W), and a rebel battery (B). Source: U.S. Geological Survey.

ily carried,' so it was with our breakfast that morning, which consisted of crackers, fresh beef, and coffee which was made by taking some water from a goose pond near, (which was the only water we could get there) putting it over the fire till it commenced to boil, then putting in some coffee to give it a different flavor from that of the water.

"The evening before the Lieut. Col. told us to have our canteens filled with water ready to march early in the morning, for we would have to fight for it before we get any more. I with four other boys from our company took several canteens and went back as near as I can guess a mile and three quarters to a spring which I had seen as I came that way in the evening. This was between

the hours of ten and twelve.— We each filled his six canteens and then started for camp, where with tired limbs we at last arrived, having as our pay three pints of spring water for the trouble of walking three and a half miles.

"Breakfast over and we prepared for the march to Perryville, which we commenced about sunrise or shortly after, having as we were told ten miles to march.

"We had not gone far when the roaring of cannon was heard distinctly, and we knew that something shortly was to be done either in the way of fighting or running. A few of the boys began to get sick when we heard the sound of the cannon but most of them seemed to walk with more ease, as if there were springs in their legs. Every mile we advanced the more distinct became the sound, and the more frequent also. As we neared the field we met many citizens, male and female, old and young, leaving the neighborhood for fear they would get hurt. Most of them seemed much excited, some shouting for joy at seeing our division, and others crying at the thought perhaps of their homes being taken as the battle ground, their houses destroyed, their stock killed, &c."

In this march, Poorman reported, "The 98th was designated as the advance regiment; but, as Jackson's division was composed almost exclusively of new troops, Gen. McCook desired him to give the advance to Gen. Rousseau, with his old veterans, which was done; and in this order we arrived, after a very hard, dry, dusty march, about noon in front of the town, after having driven the enemies pickets and advance posts several miles before us" (*BC* 23 O).

It was an excruciating trip for the "Webster Guards." Robert wrote Nancy on 31 Oct.: "we had not gon far before we hurd the roaring of the canon it was about 9 miles to the bale field we had not gon more than 2 miles til order came to put out hour skirmerish and Co was sent out the rough country i never seen before there was lots of them give out i was never near give out in my life before." Norris' company, that is, had to spread out in a line perpendicular to the regiment on the road, and advance cross-country alongside, to guard its left flank, as fast as heavily burdened men with loaded muskets could be driven up and down the steep hills, bluffs, rock- and bramble-filled ravines. Parched from the outset, in a hot morning sun, they were

liable to literally blood-boiling heat stroke. Ira Dickerson probably fell insensible from this scrambling skirmish line, so he was missing and not located or identified for days afterward.

And, as they neared the blasting cannon, some other few evidently felt their bravado "give out," and turned as a squad to venture in the opposite direction.

The Mackville road to Perryville snaked up a steep woods to a high ridge overlooking the valley of the winding Chaplin River and the hollows of its branch creeks. Gilbert's corps of the army was already in place on these Chaplin Heights, from about 500 yards to the right of the road (*OR* McCook 1039). "Between twelve and one o'clock," Poulson estimated, "we came in sight of our battery which was at that time engaged. I looked in the direction they were firing, but could see no rebels. I could see the smoke of their battery rising above the trees, but the leaves were so thick we could not see a man.

"Their battery was nearly a mile from ours at that time.

"The ridge upon which our line was being formed extended nearly north and south. The rebels were east of us on another ridge. When we got to the top of the ridge we were ordered to file right and we went southward along the ridge some two or three hundred yards then we filed left into a piece of woodland. There we received orders to pile our knapsacks and set a guard over them. We were then taken back nearly to the road we had come up and there filed left into a cornfield. The corn was in shock. After loading our pieces we were ordered to rest. While we were in this cornfield the firing became more rapid.—Several other batteries were opened on each side and it seemed that the rebels were trying to get up farther north so as to turn our left flank."

The cannon in front of the 98th as they waited belonged to two brigades of Rousseau's division. Rousseau's third brigade and two batteries arrived about three-quarters of a mile north and slightly west on the ridge heights, behind a crook in the lane across them known as the Benton Road. McCook was placing Jackson's division on high places between Rousseau's batteries. He sent the six-cannon 19th Indiana Battery under Capt. Samuel Harris, and Webster's command, out an eastward projection of the heights. In front of Harris' battery, skirmishers of Rousseau's 33rd Ohio went down the valley toward Doctors Creek in search of water, and encountered enemy cavalry. These batteries north of the waiting 98th fired on the cavalry until they disappeared.

Meanwhile, McCook led Gen. Jackson to a high knob farther north of Harris' battery and Webster's position, across a wooded outcrop and hollow from it, in front of Rousseau's division under Starkweather; McCook directed Gen. Terrill's battery and brigade to this knob, which to the north overlooked a bend of the Chaplin River where McCook planned to secure water.

McCook had seen enemy infantry only in the morning, and then skirmishing with Gilbert's corps in the valley on his right, and driven off before he rode over two miles to report to Gen. Buell, who was recuperating from a fall; neither expected a battle that day. Mc-

Cook assigned Webster's new troops to the position of reserves, according to him, "to the left of Russell's house," his headquarters on the Mackville-Perryville road near the Benton lane, "and in the rear of the center of Rousseau's line, on the right" (OR 1040).

Rousseau however had only one regiment, the 33rd Ohio, in front of Webster when Bragg's whole army, having moved invisibly in the valley, began its attack aimed at Harris' battery, which appeared to form the flank of the Union army. Moreover, the new soldiers of the 98th were not even in position before the massed infantry attack forced the 33rd back, to about a half-mile in front of Harris' battery. The Tennessee and Mississippi veterans had climbed the steep bluff of the Chaplin River, and they rose suddenly in front of McCook's center, above the hollows and fields between them and his lines, only 90 to 100 yards away (OR Oldershaw 1060). As they charged toward Harris' battery, though, they came under fire from both his cannon and those of Parsons, in Terrill's brigade, on the northward knob; this latter battery and the new troops being rushed to defend it became their foremost target.

These recruits and most of their officers had scant experience even in camp drill. Moving them across unknown, uneven ground among crowd and commotion presented a challenge, and trying to insert them as a line of battle while under attack invited disaster. To move to the left and forward while maintaining basic formation, troops must march by right-facing and then wheeling into their line; if they proceed by a left-face march and then have to turn to the right, they find their officers between them and the enemy, as happened when two of Gen. Terrill's new regiments first raced to Parsons' battery and faced the enemy "rear rank in front, which produced much confusion" (*OR* Anderson 1062-63). Here as Gen. Jackson worked to direct his cannon and musketry on the charging rebels, two bullets pierced his right breast, killing him.

The barrages of this attack came to the ears of the 98th in the cornfield. They were not eager for the "glory" of battle, not prepared by training or education to be warriors. A fair sample of their progressive schooling, alongside girls, may well be McGuffey's Fifth Reader of 1853, which represents modern warfare vividly in the anonymous verse "The Warrior's Wreath" (of human gore) and prose "Evils of War," which states, "Nobody sees a battle" for it is a "job" which men do "without daring to look upon"— a "continuous reciprocal murder," mutilation, and torture in which men are maddened to rabid brutes by their feverish thirst: a symptom these former schoolboys and teachers now felt.

Wesley Poulson reflected, "This was rather a serious position to occupy, for we were looking to see a messenger with an order for our regiment to fall in line of battle. At about half past two as near as I can guess we saw Col. Webster's aid [Lt. John T. Collins of Co. E 98th] coming in rather an exciting manner. He had lost his hat by some means, and his hair was flying as he came running up to Lieut. Col. Poorman. We readily guessed his errand, and were soon marching toward the scene of carnage.

"I can not say how the rest of the boys felt about that time, but I know my heart was beating more rapidly than common, and I *think theirs were too.*

"We soon found that we were intended to support Capt. Harris' battery.— Five of the companies of our reg't were put to the right and five to the left of this battery, which consisted of four [actually six] rifled twelve pounders. We were then ordered to lie close to the ground till we got further orders. We had seen no rebels yet. We knew they were near though, for the shells were bursting around, and solid shot were making the soil fly, near us."

Evidently the enemy attacks on Terrill's brigade and battery to the left, and on Rousseau's to the right, had progressed by the time the 98th came to Webster's position on the high ridge, since the rebels had been able to plant a battery close before them. It fired from a knob which rose above the hollow woods that fell from the ridge into the valley, and it was "posted on a hill half a mile distant to the right of Harris' battery, occupying a position nearly enfilading the Ninety-eighth Ohio and Eightieth Indiana Regiments," as Lt. Ellis E. Kennon of the 98th reported (*OR* 1067).

In addition to the tumult of positioning new troops on the field under cannonfire, two other factors promoted the confusion implied by discrepancies in reports. In regard to Terrill's and Webster's brigades, "It must be remembered that the position of the two batteries forming our right and left was taken without regard to the line of infantry battle. Yet our entire force, with the exception of two regiments, was formed between the two, and from the contracted space and from the fact that all men and most of the officers ... were without experience in such matters, they many times went up in line of battle four, five, and six deep, and delivered their fire" (*OR* Oldershaw 1061). According to Kennon, the 98th was ordered to form right of the battery, but could not all get into two-rank line of battle there, seemingly because the ground fell rapidly into the wooded ravine on the right, so the left wing had to line up in the rear of the right wing. Both Robert's Co. C and Poulson's Co. F were in the right wing, thus little aware of the left's movements. Another impact of emergency came as the rebel attack killed Gen. Jackson and Col. Webster received orders to "take command of his entire brigade," while the battery where Jackson fell was overrun by the enemy (*OR* Oldershaw 1060).

Of Webster's brigade, the 80th Indiana were placed left of Harris' six cannons on the ridge crest, the 50th and 121st Ohio "in the ravine to the left and rear" of the battery by 2:30 P.M. (*OR* Strickland 1068-9). In minutes, Webster sent the 121st over the wooded rise to his left to support Parson's battery there. En route, they had "some considerable delay" from poor guidance; they were not formed in line before that battery was captured and the enemy massed before them; they "abandoned their position in bad order" and retreated "some distance to the rear" before they lined up again and began to fire (*OR* Kennon 1067). Thus they must have joined in with Rousseau's troops under Starkweather, behind the Benton lane; and Webster had lost one-fourth of his brigade from the position he was assigned to defend.

At 3 P.M. Webster sent all but two companies of the 50th Ohio left around the 80th Indiana and forward through the woods to charge the advancing enemy. Thereupon the 50th's colonel himself fled to the rear and crouched behind a stump (*OR* Oldershaw 1062), leaving his Lt. Col. Strickland to command his regiment over a fence into a cornfield ravine, driving rebels back at this point. Since the 50th was from this time nearly surrounded by enemy, it is possible they were hidden from them by corn or ravine.

At the same time, Webster sent the left wing of the 98th to aid Terrill's men, over the hill to their left (*OR* Kennon 1067). Lt. Col. Poorman led these five companies to the left, at 3:30 by his account; as they arrived where directed, they were ordered back (*BC* 23 O).

Gen. Terrill had attempted to reform the new troops who had left the fallen Jackson and Parsons' battery, first 60 to 100 yards behind it and a broken fence, then behind Rousseau's battery under Bush, trying to make a stand until McCook could get Gen. Gilbert to send reinforcements from his corps. Meanwhile, he was under attack from both his front and his left flank. Quickly Terrill was struck; a piece of shell carved out part of his lung and put him near death. His brigade had fought less than an hour and was shattered (*OR* Anderson 1063; Hall 1065). Terrill's mortal wounding left Col. George Webster ranking commander of the far-flung division, the last of its three leaders, who, when together the night previous, had philosophized that their new soldiers would find no reason to take fright in battle, because among Buell's vast army, death for any one of them was extremely improbable (Hafendorfer 123).

To the 98th this battle on their left had been audible but invisible. They could see the 33rd and 2nd Ohio of Rousseau's division below them on the rippling rises fending off successive rebel charges, and his troops on the hill to their right firing at enemy approaches through the cornfield there. As Poorman wrote the next day, "no sooner was one [enemy] regiment or brigade driven back than its place was supplied by a fresh one; and from the time of our arrival in front of them until nightfall, their regiments, fresh from their reserve, could be seen filing over the hilltops in our front, and moving forward, carrying their black flag, and waving it defiantly in front of our exhausted, worn-out, but brave and undaunted columns" (*BC* 23 O).

His first battle came to Robert as a sickening shock: "they ordred us to halt I felt bad and then we was ordered to lay down and then I saw the rebles a coming out of the woods rite across a big hollow and then the rebals commsed fire on us and then the bulets commsed whis around us the firs man i saw shot a canon ball take his arm of and next i saw one of hour Co shot through the head and fell dead and then we had to give back in to the woods and then we was all scatered every whare hour Cap gave orders to raley on the flag and then came the hard fighting…" (31 O).

Wesley Poulson first observed the spectacle of battle with the distance of curiosity, in detail he remembered analytically: "We saw before we had been lying long in that position a swarm of rebels come out of the woods about half

a mile in front of us. When they got into open land and lines dressed they started on double-quick shouting and hollowing like wild men, thinking I suppose to scare us and make us run, but it had the opposite effect and only made us grasp our rifles more firmly. About this time the musketry was brought into action on by [*sic*] both sides by regiments that were coming in contact. Our battery kept them back from us for a considerable while, and during this time the shell, solid shot and rifle balls were flying over us. Some high up in the air and some so low as to occasionally make us strike the ground with our noses. One shell burst in the air I suppose some thirty feet above us and a piece of it or some of its contents went into the ground about 15 inches from my head. A cannon ball passed over my back which I am quite sure would have struck me had I been standing up. I thought when I heard it coming that it would strike my head. I shut my eyes expecting to feel it, but had the pleasure of hearing it whistle over me, and afterwards saw the dust fly to the rear of our company some distance.

"Some of the boys were sleeping notwithstanding all the noise that was being made. For my part I could not sleep. There was too much to be *seen* and a prospect of to [*sic*] much to be *done* for sleep to bother me.

"To our right was a regiment which was engaged, and I could see their men fall some to rise no more, and others to be carried away by their comrades. I could plainly see the blood on some of them as they were carried back to the Surgeon. I could see the rebel's flag on the next hill [to the right] and occasionally the heads of the rebels, when they would rise to shoot at the reg't mentioned. They however took good care to hide their bodies, and their heads are so *little* that they are rather difficult to hit."

As the enemy charged McCook's troops on both his flanks and now started moving a massive drive at his center, where Poulson lay, they raised a remarkable stampede from the ravines and woods before him: "I saw horses without riders, running for life. I saw hogs, pigs and rabbits, all running toward our line, scared to insensibility almost, by the advancing rebels."

These animals probably veered from the battery and regiment's lines into the woods below and behind them. The hogs would return to reclaim their fields, and feed on the bodies left there.

The next scene Poulson recounted is remarkable but problematic. The barn he described has been placed, by Hafendorfer's maps, across and below the rightward hill, where Poulson would not have been able to see it from Harris' battery ridge. Poulson's account could stem from recollections he heard from other soldiers, especially of the 3rd or 10th Ohio. This barn, on the other hand, could have been on a height of the hill he did observe; Col. John Beatty of the 3rd located his "line of battle extending along the crest of the hill and passing near to and somewhat beyond a large barn filled with hay" (*OR* 1058), and his report of the fire there assigns it a place in the battle just in accord with the sequence of Poulson's narrative: "To our right a few hundred yards was a barn that had been fired by a shell from the rebels after they had made several attempts to fire it with a torch and the

torch bearer shot before he got near it, one of whom when mortally wounded threw the torch toward the barn, but had not power to send it far enough to execute his wish. Their object was to throw our men into confusion, for the barn was just in our line and could not be burned without troubling our men considerably. The 10th Ohio regiment was partly on each side of the barn and the brave boys maintained their position till their faces were scorched by the heat of the ascending flames. They were forced to fall back some distance" (*CR* 18 Mr 1863).

By the time of this retreat, Rousseau's 33rd and 2nd Ohio had withdrawn from the slopes in front of Harris' battery and the 98th, out of ammunition; Rousseau's batteries to the right had drawn back on the ridge, to the woods near the Mackville and Benton roads; there stood the ammunition wagons where Rousseau's men gathered to resupply themselves. Rousseau's troops were retreating to this wooded area behind the cornfield (*OR* Harris 1050).

Poulson's account of the charge before him reflects his innocence of fundamental battle tactics, as he interpreted the convention of the skirmish line to be a nefarious scheme of sharpshooters, in part because of his complete dependence as a novice soldier upon following orders: "During this time the 98th was lying on the ground watching the movements of the rebels in front of us. They finally concluded to make a charge on our battery. Their sharpshooters were deployed and in advance of their columns some forty or fifty yards, for the purpose, I suppose, of 'picking off' our commanding officers, so we could not have the benefit of their commands in the conflict which they expected would follow.

"To make the capture of our battery doubly sure they sent a regiment to flank ours on the right. The flanking regiment kept behind a hill from us and we were entirely unconscious of this movement until they were opposite the right wing of our regiment. During this time we were watching the line in front of us. It was a grand sight to see. The line was composed of some of Bragg's best disciplined troops — The men kept in excellent order, and when our battery would belch forth solid shot or shell at them, the line would fall as if all the men were linked together. As soon as the shot or shell struck they would rise at a word from their commander, and march forward till they again would see the smoke and again prostrate themselves to the earth. They seemed not to notice the men killed and wounded, but boldly marched on leaving them behind, and keeping their ranks well closed. They were marching down a declivity and we could plainly see the killed and wounded left behind. One shell burst in their line that killed and wounded at least twelve men. This shell was fired just after they arose and I suppose they did not like to lie down and get up more than once in the same place. The line moved on and there on the hillside was the little lot of rebels some still in death and others rolling in agony caused by their wounds. Rebels as they were and deserving death as they did, the sight truly made me feel sorry for them, and had I not known their object in coming toward us, I should really have pitied them. This all took place in less time than it has taken me to write about it."

Gen. McCook rode from his left-flank lines behind the Benton lane, where Starkweather's brigade and the retreated troops of Terrill were holding off the enemy, to the right, seemingly between 3:30 and 4:00, "only in time to see it turned by a large force of the enemy." He "then ordered Colonel Webster, of the Ninety-eighth Ohio, to move his troops to the right and repel this attack, if possible." McCook's report gave scant mention of Webster's command after this, probably because McCook was occupied in the defense of the crossroad area where his ammunition was, where Rousseau's batteries and regiments contended with enemy attacks. McCook, that is, was subsequently far to the right and rear of Webster and out of touch with him. Nevertheless, McCook's report praised the 98th along with the 94th Ohio solely among the new regiments, for "deeds of heroism" (*OR* 1040, 1042).

How far did the right wing of the 98th move to the right to meet the rebel charge? Hafendorfer charts this move as simply a swing to the right to face the hollow woods below, so its line remained on the slope of Harris' battery. An 1877 map, however, drawn under orders of Maj. Gen. George H. Thomas, who was second in command of Buell's army at Perryville, shows Webster engaged over the crest of the hill to the right of his battery, even beyond the Mackville Road — in clear sight of the burning barn wherever it stood in this area (Ruger map). Some estimate of the distance and direction the 98th moved may be made from Poulson's narrative. In it, also, we find the reason Poulson was one of the few who indeed could look upon this central action of the battle.

As the rebel flank attack approached, Webster had only the right wing of the 98th on the right of his battery. He, not Lt. Col. Poorman as Poulson thought, ordered these men to their feet, since when Poorman and the left wing returned, the right was already "beginning to fall back under the murdurous fire of the enemy, who had completely flanked us," Poorman wrote (*BC* 23 O). These rebels were "right of the Nineteenth Battery in a corn field" (*OR* Kennon 1067) which stretched over the hill beyond the hollow woods. McCook and Webster saw "the steady approach though the corn of a flag with a black ball in the center of a white ground" to the edge of the corn, where the enemy opened fire, as the 98th ran through the woods to line up (*OR* Oldershaw 1060-61).

The attack on Webster's right coincided with a massive charge up the hill against his front. The 80th Indiana left of the battery were firing on these Confederates when the 2nd Ohio, depleted of men and ammunition, fell back and "marched over" the 80th. Webster's men were probably so densely packed that the 2nd could not get around them. Subsequently, Webster ordered the 80th Indiana, while under fire, to turn its line so as to face the flank attack, so that its left end stood against the battery; this regiment suffered 157 casualties in the battle. Meanwhile, Webster ordered his battery to retreat (*OR* Kennon 1067). But only two cannon were hauled off before the drivers and cannoneers deserted (Poorman *BC* 23 O).

Poulson recounted, "When Lieut. Col. Poorman [*sic*] first saw the regiment which was flanking us he called for attention and we instantly sprang to our feet. We were now facing eastward toward the advancing line of rebels. We were ordered to 'right face, forward march' and then to 'file right.' This placed us with our left flank toward the advancing line (which was now ascending the hill on which our battery was placed) and our face toward the regiment that was flanking us. Firing now commenced on both sides. One of company F was struck the first fire. The ball striking him in the face just below the left eye. Seeing his face so covered with blood and hearing the mournful noise he made seemed to strengthen my nerves till I felt revengeful.

"We were within about 80 or 90 yards I think, of them. I shot three times from this place and then moved to where the company had gone, which was some 60 yards. They received orders for this move which was made on 'double quick.' I thought they were running from the rebels, and would not go till I saw the Captain [Butts] make a motion with his hand for me and three or four others to come on. On the way to them I halted long enough to take aim and shoot once and then reload my rifle, and when I got to them I shot the 5th and last time. I think I was not more than 50 or 60 yards from the one I shot at last. He fell, but whether I or some one else hit him no one could tell.

"We were here formed into line having been thrown somewhat into confusion by the excitement of the movement."

This "double-quick" motion seems to be the one recalled in Robert's sequence of the events when he described first falling back into the woods, being scattered, and rallying on the flag with Captain Norris, before the "hard fighting." If so, it accords with Poorman's description of bringing the left wing up as the right wing was recoiling from the flank attack. Another correlation appears in a letter to the *Tuscarawas Advocate* from John P. Brisben, Orderly Sergeant of Co. K, 98th, written three days after the battle. He was among the left wing and "placed on the left of the" 80th Indiana as the "enemy came up near the battery in three columns, when the left wing was ordered back to the battery. When the two wings were coming together, the 80th Indiana fell back and ran through our regiment, throwing it into confusion, and before the regiment was brought under command rebels were pouring their bullets into us like hail. We fronted toward them and held our position until dusk" (*TA* 24 O).

Kennon reported that the 80th Indiana, after shifting to face the flank attack, was "ordered" to move 200 yards to the rear, and its Lt. Col. then took command also of the 2nd Ohio, which accompanied it. Later, during the 98th's defense of the battery, Kennon, the brigade adjutant, was ordered to take the 80th into line on a hill 400 yards to the rear, which duty occupied him as the battle ended (*OR* 1067-68).

Kennon was not with the 80th Indiana early in this attack; he was among Co. B of the 98th, on its far left wing, as he spoke with "Poor little George Thompson" of St. Clairsville about the "very hot time" coming very soon; and minutes later Kennon stopped and looked upon George's pale face upturned, "poor little slim arms" lying still by his side, and his blood "slowly trick-

ling from the fatal wound" in the top of his head (*BC* 13 N). If the 80th Indiana "ran" back, we have an explanation for Col. Leonard Harris' account of Webster in this stage of the battle. Harris, 2nd Ohio, in command of Rousseau's brigade that included the 2nd, 33rd, and 94th Ohio plus 38th Indiana, was "in the woods at the rear of the cornfield" when he met the retreated 2nd and encountered Webster "rallying a regiment of his brigade which was in confusion," assisted him, and "requested him to form in the rear" of the 33rd and 10th Ohio, so his other troops could resupply their ammunition. Webster did this with the "portion" of his brigade which appeared here, probably the 80th Indiana; after Harris' brigade's next retreat, the 50th Ohio joined them (*OR* Harris 1050-51).

Webster must have galloped after the 80th Indiana and gotten them to stall in a swarm on the wooded height where Rousseau's regiments were retreating, where he and Col. Harris directed them to form lines again. Meanwhile, only the 98th and two companies of the 50th Ohio remained to fight in front and on the right of the four cannon which the battery drivers and cannoneers had deserted. Webster then must have dashed off from the 80th Indiana and back to his regiment near the cannon, because someone commanded them into a desperate defense at this point. The novice soldiers of the 98th began to fire the cannon on the attacking rebels; and they were detailed to load and fire them in a selection of men that Poorman's and Brisben's accounts disagree upon — so implying it was not Lt. Col. Poorman who ordered men to work the cannon, but Webster. Poorman cited Capt. Norris, of Robert's Co. C, with some of his men, and Lt. Woodmansee and eight to ten privates of Co. B as the new gunners. Brisben numbered six from each B, C, G, and four from his K.

Wesley Poulson did not make it back to the ridge where the cannon stood. He described what happened during the flank attack, after the confused "double-quick" movement of falling back into the hollow woods to the right of the battery: "Orders were given to march forward and after marching as near as I can guess some thirty yards, just as I was making a step with my right leg it was struck about three inches below the knee joint with a large rifle ball instantly shivering both bones. I set my rifle down *very quick* to keep me from falling and with it hopped out of the way so as to let the rest of the regiment pass. I then lay down, and it so happened that near where I was stood a stump.—I lay down by this with my head toward it so as to bring it between me and the line of advancing rebels who were now firing rapidly at us. There was fortunately for me a rail pile between me and the regiment that had flanked ours. I heard several balls strike the stump and heard the splinters knocked from the rails but received no further injury myself.

"I made no noise when shot, of which I am conscious, and got out of the ranks....

"In less than five minutes after I was wounded the rebels were all round me shooting at the Union men. One shot several times off the stump by which I lay. His gun rested on the stump with the barrel extended over me, having bayonet fixed and gleaming, and had I made signs of life he perhaps would have used his bayonet on me. When he had fired a few times, our men (a regiment from Illinois, I think) made them run and then came down as far as where I lay. I told the boys to *'give them fits.'* They replied they would and then wanted to carry me off, but I refused to let them, saying to them *use your guns* and let me alone.

"As soon as the rebels [of the flank attack] ran, I cut the string off my canteen and tied it around my leg so as to stop the blood from flowing so freely, and I have no doubt but some other boys might have saved their lives by the same means. I believe in half an hour longer had I [not] done this I would have lost so much blood, that death would have followed shortly."

Then the enemy concentrated its attack on the 98th. Poulson observed the close fighting which ensued: "In a few moments our line was driven back and the *dirty, greasy* rebels were around me. This time the most of them passed me and went up nearer our men, and it seemed to me as if the firing was all at the same place, the lines were so near each other.

"Some of the rebels were afraid to go near and were hid behind trees bushes and whatever was near. The rebel color bearer came up opposite to where I lay and within almost twenty feet of me. He there placed the staff on the ground and remained, I suppose, some twenty minutes in that position. He was a portly looking man and better clad than most of the rebels were. Many of them were bare-footed, hatless and without a coat, and their shirts and pants seemed considerably the worse of wear and tear. The most of them, however, were well supplied that night by robbing the dead 'yankees' as they call them.

"The dead and wounded that I could see were considerable mixed, and to about this proportion: one Union man to three rebels. The rebels were on this ground near me longer and lost more men there. One large fat rebel fell near me that had a furrow made along the top of his head from front to back by a rifle ball, and the jar he received when he fell caused the brain to protrude, the entire length of the furrow. I never saw him stir after he fell. His head was within a yard of my feet."

In Poorman's account, after the left wing joined the recoiling right, "We succeeded in rallying the men and reforming them as they fell back to the ridge in the rear...." This was probably the ridge where the cannon stood, which the 98th fired, since McCook reported these four cannon were lost to the enemy only at 6:00 (*OR* 1041). Near this point, most likely, after leading his men all afternoon "wherever the fight waged the hottest," at "about 5 o'clock in the evening," Col. George Webster "was shot through the small of the back, the ball passing above and through the right hip bone and through his bowels, lodging in front in his left side. He fell from his horse and was carried from the field, his wound examined by the Surgeon, and he carried to the rear and well cared for; but there was no hope in his case, and he died [the next] morning at about 5 o'clock" (*BC* 23 O). Poorman alone gave a description of his wound and care. He later wrote that Webster was struck near day's end while encouraging his brigade (*BC* 30 O).

Webster was likely riding in front of and facing his regiment, urging them

to stand against the oncoming rebels. One can infer that he himself was engaged in the fighting, and had his revolver in his hand when he fell, so that it flew away from him and into enemy hands, because his revolver was only recovered months later, on another battleground, after a defeat of rebel troops in Tennessee (*CDS* 29 Ap 1863). Too, Webster's mount was lost; he was riding Kennon's horse, which had already been "shot in the breast" before Kennon got off it (*BC* 13 N).

Moreover, from this point on, the action of the 98th can be understood from the fact that they were bereft of higher command, cut off from their division and Rousseau's, and really forgotten by the generals in charge. Col. Harris, as he reported, thought Webster had removed to Harris' lines far in the rear, which continued to retreat. Thus was the 98th left in the fore of McCook's corps, just as Poorman wrote, "where they nobly stood up for an hour and a half under the fire of several regiments of the enemy, after every other [Union] regiment had fallen back on the right and left of it, and until their ammunition was completely exhausted, when they were relieved by night and an Indiana regiment of Thomas' [*sic*] division, that had cooly formed in our rear — refusing our appeal for assistance because *their* General had not ordered them to advance, whilst our ranks were being fearfully thinned" (*BC* 23 O). Poorman was so unconversant with the higher command of Buell's army that he did not know it was Gen. Gilbert who headed the nearby corps sending reinforcements to McCook's. It seems that the 98th persisted much as they had in marching on toward Richmond, in despite of common sense and, here, a tragic, wasteful loss of life, because they and their officers awaited orders to retreat, while others, seeing themselves overwhelmed and nearly surrounded, promptly removed to the rear. Their stand, however, balked the Confederate charge while McCook's battered troops withdrew and concentrated, and reinforcements from Gilbert came to fight.

These men and boys were so untrained that, as Poulson shows, they had difficulty giving and receiving orders, and mistook any backward movement as "running." It is amazing that in the confusion and under cannon and veterans' musket fire, they formed up and made a stand, loaded and shot rapidly enough to hold off the much-practiced enemy. Poorman gave some instances of their "hard fighting": "Jerry Stinard, of Co. B, got a good position, kneeled down on his knee, and fired his 40 rounds of ammunition without getting up. John Kilgore, of Co. G, was wounded five times, in the face and body four times. He continued to load and fire with the greatest coolness after he had been hit four times, and shot away all his ammunition.— Lieut. Fribly, of Co. K, took a musket of a killed man and went into the ranks, was badly wounded in the shoulder, but loaded and fired five times after he was wounded and until he was so reduced by loss of blood as to be unable longer to stand. Captain Parrish of the same Company—which suffered more in killed than any company in the regiment—after one of his Lieutenants was killed and the other wounded, continued to encourage his men and urge them to stand to the work" (BC 30 O). Kennon,

writing to his wife, estimated that 5,000 of the enemy, in succession, charged the 98th at the battery, and described the ground there as "literally covered with their dead" (St. Clairsville Gazette 16 O).

As Hafendorfer charts the battle from Confederate reports, the forces of Cleburne made the flank attack on the 98th, and divisions under Wood, Donelson, and Stewart swept up the valley and onto the ridges where the 98th fought. Subsequently, Confederate reinforcements for Cheatham's division, which earlier had captured Parsons' battery, advanced. They were Liddell's brigade, accompanied by Maj. Gen. Leonidas Polk. They started forward in twilight, and proceeded across the front of McCook's retreating corps; when they stopped at night they had captured McCook's papers, baggage, and Russell house headquarters near the Mackville-Benton crossroads (OR Hardee 1121). Somewhere in this final charge over the darkening smoky hollows and rises, Liddell's brigade came upon the 98th. It may have transpired near the crossroads, with the 98th drawn back into line there in front of Illinois and Indiana regiments who had come as reinforcements from Gilbert's corps—if Poorman and Major John S. Pearce accurately identified the troops nearby.

At dusk, as Major Pearce told the story in Cadiz, "One of the rebel regiments had advanced up a ravine unperceived and commenced firing upon the 98th. Maj. Pearce supposing it to be an Illinois Regiment, which was in close proximity, rode up and begged them for God's sake to cease firing on their friends. An officer rode up to him and inquired who he was. He replied that he was Major of the 98th Ohio. Then, said the officer, you are my prisoner.—The officer to whom Maj. Pearce surrendered proved to be Gen. Polk" (*CR* 29 O). "You are killing your friends!" sounded in the confusion as Liddell's Arkansas troops accidentally mingled near the crossroads with the 22nd Indiana and 59th Illinois of Gooding's brigade, Gilbert's corps, both sides fearing they were firing upon their comrades. Gen. Polk rode to stop this shooting, discovered that he had met the Indiana colonel, brazenly ordered him to cease firing, and returned to his own side, where he orchestrated a "slaughter" of the Indiana regiment (Hafendorfer 368-69). The 98th probably received the same treatment from their "friends." But Maj. Pearce found a gentlemanly reception; he was taken fifteen miles to Harrodsburg and only there "relieved of his horse, sword, pistols, &c." and paroled, so he could proceed home to await exchange, seeming "well pleased with the service" (*CR* 29 O).

If this coincidence places the 98th at the battle's end near Gooding's brigade and the Russell house, it shows they were driven back and far to their right by the final Confederate charges of Wood's and Liddell's forces. McCook's other troops had retreated behind the Benton-Mackville crossroads long before this, and at 6:30 P.M. were through with fighting (Hafendorfer 352-353).

On the ridge of the Chaplin Heights, "Night closed over the scene while the battle still raged," the correspondent of the *New York Herald* wrote at midnight, using a stump for his desk, beginning his battle sketch "with the din of battle yet ringing in my ears, and the low grating sound of the spade on all sides, where wearied braves are toiling by the bright moonlight in burying their fallen companions." He reported that "in leading his brigade up to the fight Col. Webster was seriously wounded" and that "desperate fighting" occurred when "*Four to one the enemy pressed this little column; but they could not force them back.*" The field for a half-mile was "covered all over with the slain, and the suffering wounded were trodden beneath the feet of the contending forces" (*CDS* 22 O).

Meanwhile, Wesley Poulson met the opponents of his life, limb, and Wesleyan virtue: "Night came and the storm ceased. I could still hear noise enough made by the wounded of both sides.

"Shortly after sunset some of the rebels were running round to gather up guns, revolvers, watches, bowie knives, &c. They came to where I lay and asked me where I was from, to which regiment I belonged, how long the regiment had been in service, and a great many other questions. They took my gun, carried it about ten yards and set it against the fence with many others, intending to haul them away....

"One rebel Lieutenant asked me if I had a revolver. I told him yes. He then asked where it was. I told him that I had given it to our wagoner the day before to haul till I called for it again, and he replied, 'I wish to God you had it with you, I would soon have one.' I am very glad I have *not* got it said I.

"One asked me when I had had any water to drink. Not since noon, said I. He said he would give me his canteen, which was full of water, for mine without a drop in it. I told him I was willing and we exchanged. It was now dark. They said they would be back in a short time with a wagon to take me to a hospital. I told them just to leave me there and not bother about moving me. To this they would not assent, saying that there would be more fighting the next day, and I would get hurt" (*CR* 18 Mr 1863).

"At the time promised the rebels came with a wagon and either four small horses or four mules....They asked me how I was wounded, and where; if I thought it would have to come off, if I thought it would get well so that I could go into service again, if I would like to be in another battle, if I had enough of fighting, and many such questions as these. All of which I answered readily. I told them if I ever got fit for duty again I wanted to have another chance at the rebels. To this, one replied very crusty like, 'we're not rebels, we're confederates you *damn Yankee*.' I'm no Yankee, but a *Union man*, said I.

"They concluded to take me prisoner....

"Two men lifted me up so that two who were in the wagon could reach me and take me in. One of the latter sat down and told me to lean against his breast, which I did; he then held me there as warmly and tenderly as my own brother could have done. He told one of the Union boys, (there were four besides myself in the wagon) to hold my foot and keep my leg stretched so as to keep the pieces of bone from cutting the flesh so as not to give me pain. He seemed very sorry that so many poor fellows were killed and wounded. He sympathized with me and even shed tears, some of which fell on me. He said he was a con-

script and was forced into the army."

They passed full hospitals for five and a half miles — every house and yard full of wounded rebels.

"I was taken to the porch and laid on it. The rebels formed a circle around me and quizzed me for two hours I think.

"The Surgeon tried to make me drink a half pint of whiskey, but could not succeed. I was too anxious to see and *know* what was going on, for to get drunk, as they wished me. I told them I was a temperance man and intended to be one till I died, be that time long or short. Most of the rebels got very drunk, and such a wicked set of men I never was with before and do not desire to be again.

"As far as acts were concerned they used me well, and in speaking they used very rough language, but it appeared to be natural for them to use that kind. I attribute it mostly to their ignorance....

"I did not sleep very much that night. I was suffering wonderfully all night. My leg was *very painful indeed*. They furnished me plenty of water and I kept it wet and cool as possible, for I knew the cooler I could keep it the better it would be for me. In the morning my leg was swollen badly and the rebel Surgeon said it would have to be taken off. He was preparing to amputate it after breakfast, but when about ready to begin the operation there was an order came for them to be ready to march in a few minutes....

"When all had been quiet a short time, the owner of the house (who had been forced to leave it) came, and he staid there to wait on us. He brought us food the best he could, supplied us with water, talked friendly to us and did all in his power to make us comfortable. He said he was a Union man and I believe he was. He said he owned no slaves and was opposed to the institution of Slavery.

"I expected to lie there on that porch till mortification would take place in my leg and kill me...

"Sometime before noon three Surgeons came, and I being on the porch was noticed first. They soon decided that my leg must be taken off or I must die soon. They gave me Chloriform, amputated my leg about an inch and a half above the knee joint. I was then taken in an ambulance back to Perryville. I was then taken to the Methodist church, which became hospital No. 5, where I remained..." (*CR* 15 Ap 1863).

On this rainy morning the remnant of the 98th stood in line again, "ready for a renewal of the fight," with Buell and his other two corps this time "on hand; but the day passed slowly away without any engagement, and at night we learn the enemy have fallen back, and we are in possession of the town" (*BC* 23 O). The fact that Poorman learned of the rebel retreat only at night suggests he was yet at distance from whatever command Webster's scattered brigade had received, and any official intelligence; also, that these soldiers spent a miserable day expecting to fight and witnessing the scene Robert recalled as he ended his account to Nancy of the battle: "the sores is someing if yo could see the wounded craling of [crawling off] the bale field." He closed, "Write soon Write soon Write every day yo can."

On the fields of bale below, the dead and maimed waited among the slaughtered horses while flocks of buzzards gathered to pick, and herds of swine to gnaw and guzzle flesh indiscriminately. On this night of 9 Oct. Poorman wrote that Major Pearce and about fifty others of the regiment were missing. He named only thirty-five, and they included some, like John D. Norris, 29, of Capt. Norris' company, who would be found dead, but did not name Ira Dickerson and others who had fallen on the way or otherwise disappeared. The two known dead in this company were likely those Robert had at first seen having an arm swept off by a cannon shot and struck in the head — John B. Ramsey, 21, of Hopedale and Benjamin M. King, 22, of Moorefield. Capt. John Norris himself had been shot in the leg; William Heberling in the thigh; Robert Hagan, leg; Thomas J. Stringer, knee; Oliver Randles, "jaw bone"; George A. Adams and Thomas Glandon, "slightly"; and Thomas P. Kyle, Robert's neighbor who had purloined the farmer's turkey and peaches, in the arm.

The roster of Capt. Norris' company was not kept accurately, so it would be impossible to tell how many actually had injuries or deserted.

In Capt. Butts' company, Corp. Enoch Conaway, 18, Robert A. Clark, 26, and William J. Cummings, 20, were known dead. Sergeants Allen McCormick and John L. Erwin were wounded; Levi Hollingsworth, John T. McCombs, and David Palmer were "slightly" wounded; Corp. Theodore McKinney, Nelson L. Birney, Hugh A. Birney, James B. Holloway, George McIlroy, Wesley "Miner" Rogers, William Todd, John W. Cummings, and John W. Walker were wounded "severely"; and three, including Wesley Poulson, were missing.

Capt. Parrish's K of Tuscarawas had six killed, sixteen wounded, and seven missing.

On 9 Oct., Poorman knew of 27 dead, 155 wounded, and 35 missing. Kennon's official report of 18 Oct. numbered 35 killed, 162 wounded, and 35 yet missing in the 98th. These 229 casualties represent by official records almost 28 percent of the 98th's men, near to if not the highest casualty ratio among regiments in the battle. However, a number of the 98th did not enter the battle, having been left behind sick: Kennon calculated that one-third of those who fought were casualties (*BC* 13 N). In Webster's brigade the 80th Indiana had 25 killed, 116 wounded, 16 missing for 21 percent of its men; the 50th Ohio, 22, 32, and 79 for 20 percent; the 121st Ohio, 3, 23, and 16 at 5 percent.

McCook's men stayed on the field while Buell's other two corps moved through Perryville after the retreating rebels. Only the second day after the battle could the 98th search the mangled, bloated, blackened bodies in the fields and woods for their comrades. This day Ellis Kennon wrote his "Very Dear Wife" that through "the providence of God" he escaped unharmed from a battle "terrible beyond the power of description"— "my first experience, and I pray God it may be my last." Some 14,000 of our army gave no assistance, which was "Infamous, while our poor boys were falling one after another until the very ground was redened with their life's blood." He with many others would mourn their brave General Webster, who had treated him with great kindness.

Lt. Louis Woodmansee of Co. B wrote to his wife that he was unscratched

although "one bullet passed through his hat, and several through his clothes." He and fifty others of the 98th had buried twenty-one of the regiment, in a row. They marked the graves of George Thompson and others they knew, so their bodies could be "readily obtained"— if families could journey to unearth and carry them home.

From Capt. Cordner's Co. E came an estimate of 2 killed, 22 wounded, and 2 missing — one "supposed to be killed," the other "probably killed" (*SCG* 16 O).

They spent these days and nights in cold rain without tents, and many uninjured soon fell ill. The wounded of both armies, meanwhile, filled houses and churches for miles around. In the Perryville Methodist Church, Poulson wrote, "there were, for the first week, about 90 wounded men, and few only, who read this, have any correct idea of a house filled with such sufferers. There were almost every discription of wounds to be found there, men struck in so many different places, from the top of the head to the end of the toes...."

"We lay the first night on the floor.—Next day we were provided with some straw and in a few days we had bed ticks and bunks....Our fare was at first very coarse and rather scarce also...."

"The ladies of Perryville visited us daily and not unfrequently brought us something nice to eat, and papers, books and magazines to read.

"At first three Surgeons were kept in hospital no. 5 and had plenty to do." The one who remained earned Poulson's "*heartfelt gratitude.*" J. L. Stockdale of Kentucky had led a Union home guard of seventy men who, when Bragg's army occupied their area, hid in the woods and "bushwhacked the rebels" until the battle. Then he emerged to be a "kind, attentive," and respected surgeon. "Notwithstanding all that could be done, I saw twenty two carried out of that house lifeless" from wounds or wounds plus disease (*CR* 15 Ap 1863).

Poulson saw his regiment for the last time as it passed through Perryville. By 13 Oct. the 98th had marched the fifteen miles northeast to Harrodsburg, where Poorman again wrote the *Chronicle*, with more complaints against his army. Christian Poorman, the former abolitionist editor, did not spare his military superiors any criticism, as Kennon would do in his official report. He castigated with more bitterness the failure of Gilbert's corps to join the battle, and added that "we are being moved too slow to overtake or even keep up with" the rebels. The officers and men felt "something radically wrong in the management" of their army, deplorable and disheartening to them. They had orders to march this morning at 7:00 after the enemy, reported 38 miles ahead (*BC* 30 O).

Thereafter they marched southeast to Danville, taking a triangular route twice the distance of a direct one from Perryville, as Poorman complained, thence to Stanford and on 16 Oct. to just past Crab Orchard, where the Wilderness Road became a rocky trail up the mountains. Here Poorman boiled. Needed surgeons, ambulances, and medical supplies had been sent from Ohio with Secretary Kennon to care for its soldiers wounded at Perryville, and in Louisville "they were very cooly informed by the Post wiseacres"—"leeches"—"that there had been no battle fought, but there had been a *slight skir-*

mish" between pickets, "and that there were already on the ground two doctors for every wounded man, and they refused to permit the surgeons who had volunteered their aid to pass through the lines, except as *servants of officers*....I learn that the very successful Gen. Don Carlos Buell also calls the fight a 'Reconnoisance'" in which he had no opportunity to fight. Bitterly, Poorman totalled the cost of this "skirmish," at one-eighth of those engaged, one-third of some regiments, 7,000 men of both sides. As for surplus surgeons, the three of the 98th "had 164 wounded men" to care for, while surgeons of other regiments had as many also.

Poorman earlier had predicted that with the loss of Jackson and Webster, the 98th would not receive the credit it deserved for its fighting. Now, on 19 Oct., he railed at the emerging accounts, which have come to dominate *Official Records* reports from McCook's corps. He attributed them to "penny-a-liners in Gen. Rousseau's Division who are evidently encouraged, if not employed, to puff and blow that brave but vain General into notoriety," to "injure the reputation of others" to "increase the reputation of their beau ideal." They attributed all effective fighting to Rousseau's Division, whereas Webster's men fought "nearly an hour after Rousseau fell back three hundred yards from their line, and permitted them to occupy a position on the right" front, which was the last attacked.

The 98th had waited since this morning to move into a fight in front of them, but later seen rebel prisoners marched past them from one at the Wildcat Mountain twenty miles southeast. Poorman accurately predicted that Buell's army could not continue a large scale pursuit, because it could not get supplies or transport them over the worn-out road to Cumberland Gap, especially as the rebels ahead were burning its bridges and felling the forest across it (*BC* 30 O).

Thus ended Bragg's Kentucky campaign, in which the retreat was probably his and Kirby Smith's greatest accomplishment. He had taken advantage of the deep gorge of the Dick's (or Dix) River, crossing it early, defending its few possible fords, keeping his artillery on its higher eastern bluffs to fend off Buell's advance. Meanwhile, Smith's men drove the wealth of the Bluegrass they had for a month assembled, and the Federal foodstuffs, munitions, and supplies from Camp Dick Robinson, in a wagon train twenty miles long, including 4,000 new Federal wagons captured at Richmond, over the rugged hills and mountains to Tennessee. Great herds of Kentucky livestock of all kinds accompanied them (Hafendorfer 428). Bragg later claimed that his campaign supplied his army and the central Confederacy for the year to come.

During these days John Hunt Morgan and his cavalry rode over the Bluegrass again, behind Buell, threatening Buell's wagon trains of rations, the rail lines, and the Federal storehouses at Lebanon. The 98th were soon tramping again across the Kentucky hills to guard this beleaguered town, arriving on 24 Oct.

Poorman was promoted to Colonel of the 98th, and made commandant of the garrison at Lebanon — work enough for three men, Kennon wrote. For his brave leadership at Perryville (where he had been somewhat hurt falling from his horse, shot dead beneath him), he "would never get the credit" he deserved, except in his men's loyalty (*BC* 13 N). His reward, and his men's, was a post that was doomed to be the pit of Kentucky's war misery. Perhaps the army esteemed it a safe haven and worthy occupation for Poorman's pen and moral outrage.

Chapter 9

Correspondences

Just as Christian Poorman, in the army, kept on editorializing, Jonathan S. McCready attempted to follow his calling as a minister, while learning and teaching to his men the craft of marching and killing. They also were unlikely soldiers, many old by army standards, and numerously poor tenant farmers. In a sermon pertinent to their situation, and the widespread defeats of their army, McCready preached at Camp Parkersburg on 5 Oct., according to Frank Grove's diary, on "Whare *is* the Lord God of Elijah." This was the question of the old ploughman Elisha, who had never been his own master and was jeered by children for his bald head, when stranded on the far bank of the River Jordan after Elijah's departure, and in need of miracles to become Israel's prophet during civil war (2 Kings 2:14). McCready himself had been able to leave the plough only through an accident which he believed "sent of God, to change the course of my life." The oldest of the six children of Hugh and Nancy McCready of near New Galilee, Pennsylvania, he was destined by his father to work on the family farm, and could not leave to go to school, until when he was nineteen his shoulder dislocated, and his father allowed him to go away: "Here I would set up my pillar and write upon it — Ebenezer"— the stone memorializing God's help in victory in 1 Samuel 7:12. In preaching, McCready spoke plainly, in a "logical and energetic" style, with "a familiar, conversational manner, but sometimes warming into deep or intense feeling" (Wishart 223-25).

The piety of McCready and his followers did not transpose easily to life in even a small army camp, where the 126th gradually assembled with the 6th and 11th Virginia regiments and a battery, to guard the railroad from Jenkins' Confederates. James W. Oglevee wrote on 17 Oct.: "Well friend Nancy, I am about writing you, as I promised. What to say first I hardly know, for so many things occurs to my mind at the same time, that it throws me in a state of confusion. I have witnessed many things since I left my quiet home which causes painful reflection.

"Profanity is one of the leading passions of the souldier.

"Although our company is almost yet not entirely guiltless of that crime. How sad it seemes that so many of our noble youths must thus be lost & ruined for want of one firm resolve. True the temptations of camp are many, yet they all can be overcome. The Sabath in many respects is spent as well for all & much better for some as when at home, but in other respects I am sorry to say that the Holy Day of rest is not observed as it should be.

"We have bible class every Sabath which is attended with a goodly number which causes it to be very interesting. The explinations as given by the Captain are most satisfactory.

"…I have been out on picket duty three times. The first time I was out I was stationed south of town in rather a poor part of the country. I had a conversation with a secesh ladie. She expressed greate confidence in the Southern Confedercy; thought the time was not far distant when President Davis could rule his government in peace.

"The other times I was at the same post about 1 mile from camp. There I met friends to the Union & to the Union Souldier. I formed acquaintence with four ladies while there. Two by the names of Jones & two by the name of Williams. They are Dixie gals. Befour I was aware they hat almost won my affections by their kindness. I was compelled to respect them for a friend in a friendless land cannot be too highly esteemed.

"The men in this part are universaly McClellan lovers. They think there is no other man like him. When the news reached here that he (McClellan) was re-moved I was at Mr. Williams as he read the dispatch he almost bit himself. Well Nancy I would like to see you and have a social chat but that cannot be so now.

"…I received word from home yesterday & was quite glad to hear that Mother is better. I supose you are as uneasy about the 98 Regt as I am as we have each a brother in it. I saw a list of the wounded in a Cincinnati paper today but neather Roberts or Finleys name war there recorded. But I must close. Pleas write soon as a letter is the only thing that brakes the spell of monotony to which a soldiers life is subjected. So good by — Pleas excuse all errors, for they are many.

"Give my love to all enquiring friends especially to your Mother. J. W. Oglevee"

The same day, Frank Grove addressed Nancy: "Respected Friend,…Oh how glad I was to receive it a letter from the hand of one I esteem above all others. You may think that I am flattering you. (But honor to whom honor is due. I must say it is the best letter I have received since I left home and I am shure it is the longest one. I did not miss a word in it for I read it oaver & oaver both with feelings of Joy and sorrow. No doubt you have been looking for an answer before this….I am kept busy all most all the time it is nothing but drill drill allmost all the time. We don't much more than git in some times and git our guns laid away till we are called out again. This is the way Soldiers are hurried a long till the first thing they know they are hurried clear out of the world. I was out on Picket guard last night and do not feel verry well today. So I went to the Captain and got excused from drill this afternoon partly on account of not being well and partly for the purpose of writing this letter.— I was sorry to hear of your Mother being sick and you haveing all the work to do. You must not work too hard and git sick too. I imagine I see you flying round thare. Have you heard from Robert since the battle. I have been watching the papers verry close to see if thare was any of my acquaintance killed or wounded but I have not seen any account of any yet except Captain Noras. I hope the rest are all safe. Oh Nancy this thing of war is a horrible thing. And just to think how some rush in to Battle unprepared for eternity with oathes & curses upon thair lips. Nancy you have but a feint Idea of the wickedness and profanity of the Soldiers. I have been often kept from falling asleep Just by oathes and curses of the worst caracter and perhaps it would be the first thing that would greet my ears when I awoke. Oh Nancy I am sorry that likeness was spoiled for I would like so well to see it but I hope you will send me one yet. You can send me a photograph in a letter and I would Just as leave have it.— I intended to git some photographs taken to send home to my friends but have not got it done yet. I have not written to Mary Cope yet perhaps I will some time when I have nothing else to do— Elisha Hargrave has got a couple of letters from hur since we came there. You need not be uneasy about what she told me about you for it had no effect on me. I will believe you before Mrs. McAdams or her either. John Mitchell and the rest of the boys of your acquintance are all well. But I must stop writeing for I think it will keep you busy to read some of this. The next time I will try and write you a

longer letter. I will be pleased to hear from you as soon as convenient. Excuse bad writing and especially that big blot I made. Your Friend for ever, F. P Grove"

Clearly, absence made Frank's heart grow fonder of Nancy, especially as a writer of letters full of news of home, and a vigorous young woman he could picture on the farm "flying round thare" doing all her and her mother's work.

As a correspondent, Nancy had a mentor in her cousin Nancy K., Daniel Mitchell's eldest daughter, who at twenty-six was teaching school nineteen miles west in Londonderry, where several uncles' families lived. Only one of Nancy K.'s letters survives, but in it a voluble woman sketched the range of her life, from concern with public affairs to boisterous courting activities: "Oct. Monday the 20th 1862, My good cousin Nannie, … Oh Nan I was *so* glad to hear from you. it does me so much good to get a letter from home or from my good friends…. I received a letter from Mattie Saturday and a *good long* one it was that is the kind of letters I like don't you! Oh I was so glad to hear that Thomas was rejected [in the draft]. I was afraid that they would take him but I *just wish* they had kept Dick Philips and all such rebels as he. Oh Nan but I am sorry that Bingham is defeated. I almost cryed when I heard it. Oh what will become of our land if we have such bad men in power. I fear there are evil days in store for us yet. but *one* good thing Valandigham did not get elected. Uncle Russ says he could almost give Bingham up for the sake of keeping Valandigham from getting elected.

"Well Nan it is noon and James Karr [Kerr] is here and he has been trying to whip me so I put him out of the door and told him to go so he has left for Freeport. I am getting along as usual in school — very well as far as I know. I have 21 scholars enrolled. I have some of the kindest little girls that ever I saw. They bring me apples and peaches nearly every day. I have just three weeks to teach. Then I will make tracks for home. Well Nan I have not heard from Robert yet. I have been looking for a letter for some time but have been disappointed so far. Oh but I would like to hear from him. Uncle Andys have not heard from Thomas since the battle. We heard that the 97th regt which he is in was all cut to pieces but I do not know whether it is so or not. [The 97th was in Crittenden's corps, not in action at Perryville.] They are very uneasy about him. Uncle Tidricks have not heard from their boys either since the battle. Aunt is very near crazy about them she has been sick for a week. I was sorry to hear of the 98th regt being in the battle. Oh Nan was you not uneasy about Rob. It appears to me he never seemed to me as when I heard of the battle. I was very uneasy about them all until I heard about them. poor Col Webster fell in the battle poor fellow. Oh wont they miss him especially Norrises Co. have you got a letter from Rob since the battle there has no letter come here since the battle but one that man wrote that he hoped God would preserve him from ever seeing another such a battle. I heard Saturday that McCreadys Co was in a battle & that there was 26 of his men killed but I do not believe it at all. I had a letter from D. C. Tidrick & Frank Grove last week & they were all safe then. Well Nan school is out and I seat myself in the parlor to finish my letter. Nan I

would like to see you it seems a long time since I left home. I do not enjoy myself as well here as I did last winter yet I feel almost at home here too; but I have a dread of something on my mind all the time which makes me feel melancholy very often. I have not visited very much yet....There is to be a contest in Derry at the close of school....I expect to tend it and hear that *Man* of mine speak. Nan I wish you were here to go. Oh Nan that Mr. Frame is gone to war. I saw him at church at Derry last Sabbath week and he came up and shook hands and talked a long time. I bid him good bye in the evening I thought he was going to kiss me before the preacher and all but he did not. he told me to give his compliments to you....Nan I think you should write to him Nan I tell you I never saw him look as well as he did with his uniform on and I thought him sharper than ever he was before. I very near fell in love with him being he was going to war. I believe that makes me like evry one of the boys better that go to war than those that do not go.... Wm. Lawrence was here the night of the fair ... but I was at uncle Lawrence and missed all the fun of plaguing them [cousin Jennie and Lawrence] and had no beaux either. that is so Nan. Nan you wanted to know how Joe and I get along. Well some times he walks befor me and sometimes behind me. but I do not have any correspondence at all. I have not spoke to him only to say how you do for three weeks....I was sorry to hear of Mrs. Oglevee's illness poor woman she has a long time of suffering indeed. Jennie sends her compliments to you. Well Nan I am making poor writing here and crooked at that. I was sitting up last night with a sick woman and I did not sleep one wink all night so I feel very sleepy to day. the woman has the consumption she is very low her name is McClune but you do not know her. Jennie is just starting to sit up with her to night. they live on uncles place. well it is getting very near dark and I must write some to Ellen to. well I will sent them both together with James to Cadiz in the morning....write and tell me all the news. I remain Your affectionate cousin, Nannie K. Mitchell"

The charitable custom of sitting up with neighbors and tenants who were lengthily ill with active tuberculosis supplies one reason this bacterial infection was latently widespread in the area. Mrs. Oglevee's long sickness was also consumption. Any prolonged exposure to the airborne TB organisms could introduce them to healthy lungs; but most people developed no evident illness. Their immune systems defended them, or they endured an infection which, in nine of ten cases, the body sealed off in the scar tissue of a tubercle, where it remained dormant. In children, the infection often lodged in a growing bone, or in lymph nodes of the neck which would, after a winter of malnourishment, swell and even burst in the chronic disease called "scrofula." Usually, only the stress of hardship or another illness unleashed the latent TB into active attack. The disease was recognized in 1862 only in its advanced damage to the lungs, a stage in which TB was 50 percent fatal (Merck 131-32).

On 21 Oct., the 126th regiment moved by railroad to Cumberland, Maryland. Nancy D. addressed a letter there on 28 Oct.: "My dear friend Frank,...In your letter you said you had been on picket guard & was not very well & Mat Mitchell received a letter from John since stating you were not any better. I was indeed sorry to hear such bad news. But I sincerely hope you have recovered ere this. Its bad enough to be sick when at home but how much worse to be sick away from home in a friendless land.

"I have a very sore throat today which makes me feel rather dull so if this letter is not interesting (which I know it will not be) you will have to excuse me. My mind is so confused I hardly know what to write.

"The weather here for the last two or three days has been quite stormy. But this afternoon is very pleasant. O I thought of the soldiers that had to be on guard such stormy days and nights. But that is their lot & they will have to put up with it. But I hope these dark days will soon be over & the brave defenders of our Country be returned home in safety.

"I have received two letters from Rob since the battle. He said the bullets flew thick as hail around him & a cannon ball hit right beside. says he 'I wonder how I escaped.' There was 29 killed in his Regt & I do not know how many wounded. Before the battle 5 or 6 fellows deserted. I do not know who they were but from what I can learn I think they were some of those drunk fellows that were on the cars with us going to Steubenville camp. Rob said nothing about them, but Major Pearce told someone in Cadiz. He gave no names but intamated rather strongly that it were some of them I knew, that such were afraid of bullets although they talked as though they were afraid of nothing, but such mens conduct tells plainly what they are. But enough of that.

"Ellen Mitchell and I were at Unionvale last week. We stopped at Croskeys for Ann. I got to see that new barn but Ellen said she was looking at John [Croskey] all the time. that she never thought of the barn. Was not that a pity, I know you will say it was?

"Lizzie Hervey was married last Thursday. I heard his name but disremember it now but its no difference he is a married man anyhow. They say he is too old to go to war. She was very thoughtful. When she was getting a man in war times she thought she would get one they could not take from her.

"There was a singing at Irish Ridge last Thurs night. there was not many there nor was the singing worth much except some that got beaux it no doubt paid them very well. Grays two girls [Thompson's sisters] were there and their Cousin Miss Laura Black. Wm. Oglevee went with Amanda Gray, James McFadden with Mag and Mr. Heron with Miss Black. no doubt it paid them what do you say about it? There is one tonight at Science Hill. Oh Frank if you wre here I would go but as you are not I shall stay at home. Oh I had almost forgot to tell you about the drafted men. I saw them leave Cadiz, some of them the madest fellows you ever saw but Uncle Sam make his boys do as he tells them.

"Some 50 or 75 have got substitutes. Oh I would be a substitute for no man if I were they but the 'fools are not all dead yet.' Oh I am so sorry Bingham is not elected. I don't know what will become of our land when those traitors get in office. but I hope the war will be over before they get the power. I saw Charly Warfel the next day after he heard Bingham was defeated he put me in mind of a fish out of water he hated it so bad. But never mind said he I hope our boys will get home before another year & then we will show them what we will do. they thought it was something great because they beat us but I know if our boys had been at home they would not. O Uncles raised their barn last thurs & Mr. Warfel his machine shop last Saturday. Susan McCullough was at Uncles last week. She told me when I wrote to send her best respects. Well I will have to close please excuse careless bad writing & remember me soon with another letter. For the present Adieu. Your Friend, Nannie D. Mit. I am a going to send that photograph."

In it she stood beside the most elaborate setting in Davis' studio, a fluted pillar with a drapery, set on a pedestal; her image did not match its elegance. Her calm expression and pose expressed the plain dignity she sought; her dress and figure showed the work she had done herself to attain it. Her dress was a solid dark satinette, with huge crocheted buttons from neck to hem, the bodice reinforced by gathers above the pleated skirt which rumpled to the floor, not in the stylish figure created by corset and hoopskirt. Her dark hair was drawn straight back from its center part. Her narrow white collar emphasized her sturdy neck; and the white undersleeves gathered at her wrists, her very large hands, one curled at her side, the other draped over a book.

Chapter 10

Reapers in Motion

In jubilation, Editor Allen headed the *Sentinel*'s election results with a large print of his party symbol, a strutting cock, and crowed, "Come Out, Old Fellow! First Appearance since '56! Bingham Defeated! Glory Enough For A Thousand Years!" Below, he printed an advertising block to illustrate "Democratic Reaper in Motion! The Abolitionists 'Cut All To Pieces!' A Glorious Harvest!!" White had surpassed Bingham in Tuscarawas County by 1,177 votes, in Belmont by 1,077, in Noble by 300. Bingham had won in Harrison by only 196 votes and in White's Guernsey by a mere 85. White had a majority in the District of 2,273, whereas the previous year it had given conjoined Republican and Union Party candidates a 1,600 vote victory.

In the Harrison votes for all state and county offices, Republicans fell from an average majority of 560 last year to under half that, at 269. Across Ohio, the Union Party and Republicans lost; five others besides Bingham were turned out of Congress, and only Ashley of Toledo was reelected. Fourteen of Ohio's nineteen districts chose Democratic congressmen. In Indiana and Pennsylvania, Democratic tickets also won (*CDS* 22 O).

By Bingham's later account, he had been gerrymandered out of office, when the Union Party Ohio legislators the previous year revamped the district of his home county. Certainly Clement Vallandigham was gerrymandered to defeat, as he carried his old counties and lost due to the added one. The redistricting does not explain Bingham's defeat, however, because support for him sank drastically even in his home county, and he lost others he before had won, and as the Union Party candidate. Moreover, Bingham had recently canvased the new district, rallying recruits for its military committees, winning the gratitude of these varied political leaders, and drawing audiences to his speeches.

Since then, in the past month, men had turned against Bingham, as Patrick of the *Tuscarawas Advocate* explained, because of the Emancipation Proclamation and draft, and the fact that "people were tired of the war" (*CDS* 22 O). Suddenly its reality had come home. Battles at Antietam, Perryville, and Corinth, Mississippi, brought mourning to the neighborhoods, and no crippling defeat to the rebel armies; voters spurned Bingham to condemn the war. The campaigns had no issue other than Bingham's support for the war and the emancipation bills to prosecute it. The Democratic papers printed not one positive comment about their candidate White. They even confirmed the opposition's charges that White advocated slavery, and had shunned his own Methodist minister for writing and speaking against it.

In Bingham's 1860 election, by contrast, he had gathered the overwhelming approval of voters. The divided Democrats had not even placed a candidate against him. Their district convention decided that no one could satisfy both their Breckinridge and Douglas camps, and a campaign against Bingham was not worth the rancor it would raise among themselves. They privately advocated the Independent candidate George Wells, who represented the moderate party of the South, the Constitutional Union (Beauregard *Bingham* 53). Bingham won the district with over 64 percent of the vote. In Harrison, he defeated Wells nearly two to one, and he took 6.6 percent more of the votes in his contest than Lincoln did in his.

In 1862 Harrison men consistently voted straight party tickets in all but the congressional and neglected coroner's races. Total voting for other state and local offices varied merely within 7 votes. Four of the five state contests elicited the same 1,572 votes for Democrats. Total voting in the congressional race rose, from 1860's 3,064, to

3,386; but this was almost 50 fewer votes than men cast in most other contests. Notably, this was the number of Republican voters who, in the "abusive tactics" of this bitter election, were "induced to erase Bingham's name from their ticket" (*CR* 22 O). In further subtraction, Bingham's 2,035 supporters of 1860 shrank to 1,791. And those who voted against him swelled from Wells's 1,029 to White's 1,595.

Many voters, by Editor Hatton's account, had reacted to the "great excitement" of the draft, which they blamed on Union/Republican officials; but his primary explanation of the defeat was the absence of the soldiers, three-fourths of whom he accredited Republicans or Union Democrats who would have supported Bingham. This theory is not demonstrable, even in Harrison County. Assuming the county population had not mushroomed in the past two years (and it had declined by 1,005 in the ten years previous), if the lack of soldiers' votes so altered the election, voting totals should clearly show this effect; but they do not. The difference between the highest voting totals of 1860 and 1862 is only 236, and the addition of 80 percent of these votes would not have compensated for the voters who registered their desertion of Bingham. Furthermore, nearly this number of drafted men had left and could not vote in 1862; and most of them were Democrats.

In 1860 the Democratic Presidential candidates had outpolled Lincoln in four townships, with the Breckinridge voters in Athens and Archer, and the Douglas men in German and Rumley; there Bingham had also lost, narrowly in Athens and Archer, but by a 20 percent margin in the others. Unsurprisingly, in 1862 Bingham fell in these townships even harder; Archer rejected him nearly two to one, with over 66 percent of the votes for White. And four other townships, making eight of the fifteen, turned against Bingham: the central ones of Greene and Stock, where about 30 percent of 1860's vote had gone to Breckinridge; and the western ones of Moorefield and Monroe, where 41 and 23 percent had supported Douglas. Where Monroe in 1860, moreover, had given Democrats under 30 percent of Presidential ballots, it devoted over 55 percent to White. Bingham's share of the congressional vote fell from 1860's in every single township, most drastically where the moderate Democrats who before had not opposed him now voted to turn him out. In Freeport township, only 28 had voted for Wells, but 90 voted for White, giving him 45 percent of the ballots. In Washington only 14 had voted for Wells; 71 came out for White. And everywhere Bingham had enjoyed favor that gave him 60 to 91 percent of the vote, he declined by over 10 percent. In Cadiz township, his 75 percent share shrank to 62 percent.

In the final analysis, White's election showed that the consensus supporting the President and the war had broken.

The *Sentinel* in these weeks published several long doggerels exulting at Bingham's defeat, including "The Burial of Hon. John" and, "from the Budget Box of the Cadiz Literary Junto, John A. Bingham's Lament, by Phelix": "I've tried to spout ye eloquence, / On nigger and his wool; / But now I've learned some sense, / I'll be no more a fool...(5

N, 29 O). A young Cadiz schoolmaster claimed the credit for Phelix's "scurrilous piece," shocking some, because the genteel James Cady had charge of the public school which Bingham's own young daughter attended (*CR* 15 N).

Currently, Cady and the other "Scientific" teachers undertook a new project. On 11 Oct., they met in the town of New Market to form the "Teachers' Scientific Circle," with the purposes of improving their knowledge, testing different modes of instruction, and advancing education. They elected Center chairman, Sector secretary, Tangent reporter, Quadrant treasurer, and Diameter critic. The actual names of members were listed in a notice for a subsequent Cadiz meeting: D. S. Coultrap, R. C. Brown, A. Miller, M. B. Adams, J. Cady, Jos. Lee, and M. K. Turner (*CDS* 29 O, 10 D). The Scientific Circle emerged at a time propitious for their ambitions. With Franklin College having emptied into the army, and many members of the Literary Junto now in service, the Scientifics had a clear stage. And with the election apparently reversing the abolition "rebholeushion," as tab. had caricatured it, the way seemed open for their own reforms. The first of these had a certain political intent. The Circle's first business was Tangent's proposed resolution that "every teacher should thoroughly understand the principles of civil government" and instruct pupils in these; it was accepted. Thereby, most of the current Democratic agenda could enter the Circle's "educational or scientific business." And the first topics for discussion at their Cadiz meeting were the Government and Democracy.

The tenor of their other concerns was more creative. They were iconoclasts, had an earnest aim of creating practical foundations and uses for education, and attempted science from the grass roots. But since they disdained both the constraining systems of the textbooks and empirical study, they often labored diligently over blind spots — as in the Circle's second-accepted project of finding a formula that would predict livestock weight from mere dimensions.

The third proposal probably came from tab.: "to give a practical illustration of a new method of teaching the subject of definitions by synonyms." Finally, Sine furnished the question whether "established usage" should always provide the "standard of grammatical accuracy." Here tab. and Sine posed issues of significance to the English language as it was developing in the nation's West and being formed — or not — by school instruction. Both their proposals took the pragmatic approach that characterizes progressive educational reform in America. With a brief contexting, we can empathize with tab.'s evident frustration in delivering standard vocabulary lessons to his pupils, especially since he himself found the available grammar texts an unscientific "humbub." And we may ask, as Sine implied, whether tab. was not justified in employing *humbub* rather than either the established *humbug* or *hubbub* which he alloyed in his coinage.

The old method of teaching definitions was firmly entrenched in grammar, which was encased in Latin models. An 1832 reviser of *Murray's English Grammar* addressed his subject as Cae-sar had the wild land of Gaul, by writing "Grammar is divided into four parts": orthography (spelling), etymology (definitions), syntax (word order), and prosody (poetics). "Etymology teaches to class words according to their use in language," that is, grammatical function, "and shows their various changes, and deviations" (Benedict 14). Both the grammar texts and the dictionaries of antebellum America insisted on strict grammatical labeling of words and formal, categorical definitions. With etymologies they traced correct meanings to roots, and disallowed deviations in usage. In one of William Grimshaw's many dictionaries, for example, the 1835 *Ladies' Lexicon*, *fix* is a verb meaning "to make firm," and any use of it to mean *to repair, to prepare,* or *a predicament* represents a commonly spoken error (77). Among these dictionaries, moreover, there was an ongoing "war" — the subject of a classic study by Eva Mae Burkett — of competition between followers of Noah Webster's lexicography and opponents of his practices; and none had prevailed as a standard for guidance. While the language burgeoned and changed in the American expansion, the lexicographers retained the methods of Samuel Johnson and other English writers, and recorded the words being added to the language without finding, or agreeing on, new strategies to explain and regulate their usage. Of the lexicographers, the makers of school dictionaries most apprehended the problems faced by tab., and they tried experiments for teaching children such as illustration by example or analogies, but none had been successful (Burkett 6, 65, 75).

The Ohio region's settlement by recent immigrants and its relatively democratic society accelerated divergences from the standards which grammar texts tried to uphold. Speech in the countryside, as a reader can see it recorded in private letters, preserved pronunciations and words (as *a-going* and many verb forms) from the usages of Scots-Irish settlers, and the marketplace jargon of rural trade. Rather than being restricted to casual communication among the unschooled, when the area gained access through railroad and newspapers to the language of the East, and when public education taught correct English, the colloquialisms rose into local writing and publications, mostly where they added accent and color. The invective language in the newspapers often relied on phrasing that would not pass a grammarian's parsing ("John A. Bingham *don't want* the Union restored today") for emphasis and tone. Correct English was too "polite" for these writers. Sine, it seems, recognized the need to justify such effective flexibility, beyond rigid rules. As for tab. and his definition by synonyms, he too anticipated a change to come: Noble Butler's 1846 *Introductory Lessons*, for instance, presented words within strict grammatical classes, but his 1873 *School Reader* cited the vocabulary words of each reading lesson without listing the part of speech, simply defining them, most often merely with a synonym.

While the Scientific Circle plotted their progress, signs of new prosperity arose in Cadiz, whereas many parts of the nation, Hatton noted, suffered an economic depression from the war. Successful men, probably enjoying the increasing fruits of the wool trade, were building new shops and houses. H.S. McFadden had erected one of the largest structures in town to house his family and business rooms. Banker M. J. Brown was putting up a handsome residence near Mr. Dewey's. James Bullock had a new house, whose front was "decidedly the neatest in town," attesting to the "taste and mechanical genius" of its carpenter Thomas McCreary. More "specimens of architecture" seemed in the offing; and Charles Warfel was constructing a two-story frame building across from the depot in which to run a steam engine and planing works, the town's first machine shop for finishing lumber into window sashes, moldings, and trims (*CR* 5 N). "The General" ventured this enterprise after several other attempts had failed, and when the business of his grain mill and sawmill in Charlestown must have fallen low, with the departure of most of the nearby laborers and carpenters to the army.

Among the houses recently built was Josiah M. Estep's, an ornamented brick set back from Steubenville Street in a small lawn. In October, however, Estep was not enjoying the gracious life it projected, nor receiving congratulations on his party's success in the election. Instead, he was besieged by rumored accusation that when he as Commissioner accompanied the drafted men to Camp Zanesville, he extorted money from them, by charging them $5 for passes out of camp and more lucrative schemes. He issued a defense — which provides details of the substitute process. Estep claimed that his official pay ended upon reaching camp, but he remained there at his own expense because the men who had brought substitutes needed him to prepare and oversee their paperwork. These documents had to ensure the substitute was "properly bound, and accepted by the Colonel in lieu of" the drafted man, before the latter was safe in paying his substitute. In addition, he needed his discharge papers properly endorsed by the colonel. Some men, Estep recounted, were so in haste to leave camp that they entrusted their money for the substitutes, along with their paperwork, to him. He was fully occupied for four days and some nights with this business; and no one at all paid him for his services (*CR* 22 O). Thus the temper of the men who had vowed to "wade in blood" had not abated; those who escaped came home to vent their spleen on Estep.

Among the opposite party, vilifications shrilled. "Lawyer Shotwell, the Harrison county *Bloodhound*, is still on our trail," Hatton cried, "pursuing us with the vindictiveness of a devil incarnate." Shotwell blamed the shrinkage in the county vote for Republicans on Hatton's Republican ticket, despite Bingham's greater losses elsewhere on the Union one, and entertained citizens in the streets, shops, and public offices with his abuse of Hatton. "He has nothing better to do," Hatton complained, while he himself had no time to spare from work to follow "that political *giant*" around to refute the charges of "the crafty, vindictive Shotwell — a man who has not [enough] true friends in the county to bury him, if he were to die tomorrow" (22 O).

Far different from this wishful vision was the actual scene of the funeral of Col. George Webster. All public business in Steubenville stopped, flags dropped to half-mast, and a large concourse of city and country people gathered at his late residence on 4th Street. The ceremony at 1 P.M. led by Rev. C.C. Beatty was unusually impressive. At 2, the military escort arrived with the remains of Col. Webster, and placed his coffin on the hearse. The procession that followed him to his grave was a fourth-mile long, in this order: Military, Masons, Clergy, Members of the Bar, Odd Fellows, Temple of Honor, Firemen, Public Schools, and Citizens. Webster's minister, of the 2nd Presbyterian Church, gave the graveside prayer. Thus Col. Webster, "a sacrifice to the accursed Rebellion," went to "a patriot's reward" (*CR* 22 O).

The *Sentinel*'s foreman Wm. H. Arnold wrote an obituary for Enoch Conaway, son of Charles of Archer township. "Intelligent, warm hearted, generous and good-natured," he had not hesitated to serve his government. He was advancing on the enemy when "pierced through the breast by a rebel bullet." Now he lay under the sod of Kentucky, and Arnold pictured his cold, lowly bed with the aid of Collins' famous "How sleep the brave" ode of 1746, proceeding to quote its "When Spring, with dewy fingers cold, / Returns to deck their hallowed mold, / She there shall dress a sweeter sod / Than Fancy's feet have ever trod" (29 O).

A letter from the 43rd Ohio at Corinth, Miss., told of their losses in the battle — 30 dead, 70 wounded. Their Colonel, Adjutant, and Capt. J. M. Spangler of Belmont County were killed. Capt. Sanford Timmons wrote that, in his Co. C, W. W. Leggett, Jacob Benedick, and Thomas Crumley were dead, eight others wounded (*CR* 22 O).

Sanford Timmons himself had been wounded in the foot, and like officers from the other embattled regiments, he returned home to recuperate. Major Pearce of the 98th was in town, awaiting exchange, and Capt. Norris, limping on his wounded calf. The 30th's survivors of Antietam brought welcome tidings. Their regiment had returned to Western Virginia, a region of less danger. They expected their Captain Cunningham soon to be promoted, as Col. Ewing had been. The wounded Sgt. John Fogle had a promise of promotion. Lt. E. Heddington, whose horse had been shot from under him, arrived in town on Friday, and after the Sabbath evening service at the Methodist Church, he was married to Miss Sallie J. Laizure before a large congregation. Capt. John Brown brought home a tale that topped Major Pearce's surrender to Gen. Polk. At Antietam he was captured and taken to prison in Richmond, where a furor arose which reached the *Richmond Dispatch* that John was a son of the Harpers Ferry insurrectionist, and had recently raised a company from Ohio with the purpose of avenging his late father; under this supposition that paper called for an immediate trial, which would put a quick end to a second John Brown. Fortunately, he was found not to deserve this infamy, and he was paroled (*CR* 22 O, 29 O).

The 74th regiment was yet in Nashville, and enduring the lack of supplies Bragg's army had seized, "subsisting principally by foraging." On daily expeditions they went out in the countryside with one or two hundred wagons, to gather up corn. Rebel forces impeded their harvesting by felling trees across the roads and attacking their loaded wagontrain (*CR* 29 O).

For families of common soldiers in the 98th, news of them was sparse. And the swelling castigations of Gen. Buell labeled the battle they had fought and the entire campaign of circuitous marches a disastrous waste, leading to the one satisfaction that Buell had now been removed from command (*CR* 5 N). Families who had cheered their boys and men off to glory could take little consolation in this verdict. But at least they had no experience that could portend to them the aftermath still to come, as the grim reaper found a ripe field.

Chapter 11

The Cedars of Lebanon, Kentucky

From similar beginnings, Cadiz and Lebanon became very different societies in ways pertinent to the Civil War, and for reasons dating to near their origins, since neither received a later great influx, and the 1860 censuses of both their counties abound with the same family names as their early settlers'. Like Cadiz, Lebanon became the county seat of an agricultural county. In 1860, it had 953 residents, to Cadiz's 1,168; its county 12,593 to Harrison's 19,129, with 36.3 people per square mile to Harrison's 47.7. Like Harrison, Marion County was created by a division of an original larger county — Washington, in 1834.

All three of Lebanon's early historians identified its founders as Scots-Irish descendants of the Covenanters, the same people who largely settled the Cadiz area. Two were associated by marriage or descent with McElroys, whose family tradition claimed their ancestors participated in establishing the Solemn League and Covenant. In the 1700s they immigrated to Pennsylvania, then about 1760 to Campbell County, Virginia (Knott iv), the frontier fringe in the southern foothills of the Blue Ridge. Their next move took them to another fringe, the last pocket available of the Kentucky Bluegrass, the farthest southwest extent and poorer land, bordered by shale hills and high knobs of the Pennyroyal Plateau. In 1789, they joined "a colony of Scotch-Irish Presbyterians from Campbell County" who crossed the mountains and became the first settlers near a creek where they built their log church, on the site that in 1813 became the village of Lebanon (Knott, History of Presbyterian Church 7, 15). A grove of juniper trees there which the settlers called "cedars" brought forth the name from Psalms, for the place where "the righteous shall flourish ... like a cedar in Lebanon" (Ps. 92:12). They renamed the creek, so when they walked over it on a plank to church, they crossed over Jordan.

At some point in these migrations, any connection to the Covenanting sects disappeared. Charles A. Johnston, in his Lebanon recollections, recounted that his grandfather Johnston, of a Pennsylvania family, "was a Seceder but he got back in the kirk all right." By his account, the 1730 founder of the Seceders himself, one Ebenezer Erskine, had returned to the Established Church of Scotland (53, 55).

The proclivity for dispute which typifies Covenanters in all historical accounts did not characterize social intercourse in the Lebanon area. One sure sign is their lack, despite other cultural advancements, of need and support for local newspapers, in which to conduct controversies. Whereas Cadiz had a newspaper continuously from 1816, and a second one, the *Sentinel*, from 1832 (McGavran 38), in Lebanon one appeared, the first in its county, only in the early 1850s; and it was politically neutral (Knott 73-74). Another indication of the cordiality and cooperation around Lebanon is the thriving there of Roman Catholics, as well as Baptists.

The Scots-Irish had moved to the region when other families were arriving, 1789 to 1791, from the "Maryland Catholic Diaspora." These were small farmers who had fallen into debt and followed neighbors who had settled the better Bluegrass land northward, around Bardstown. They included Abells, Spaldings, Hamiltons, Mudds, and Mattinglys (T. Spalding 163-65). Among them was Benedict Spalding, who had owned Maryland plantations, had twelve indentured servants and ten slaves, and "rapidly acquired slaves and a very large tract of land of approximately 2,000 acres" (H. Spalding 1-4).

The first settlers appreciated and adopted others' arts and customs. The young people of Lebanon joined in celebrations of May-day, for instance, with a procession to a bower in the woods to enthrone a queen. The Presbyterians, like the other congregations, built a church of fine architectural design, with a towering spire and twelve smaller spires on its walls, the interior completely frescoed (Johnston 73-74, 50-51).

Charles Johnston as a boy watched the bricks being made and burned on the church lot, by slaves of the Presbyterian members. Of the early settlers' families, two McElroys had held five and six slaves in Campbell County in 1787, but the Ray family, none. By 1799 in Kentucky, James McElroy had come to own 1,050 acres and 26 slaves; Nicholas Ray 1,094 acres and 10 slaves; Benjamin Ray 880 acres but no slaves (Washington County Tax List).

The settlers early established an economy that could take advantage of the nearby Rolling Fork, which in high waters would carry flatboats into the Salt River, thus to the Ohio. Their land grew corn and flax, amply fed hogs, and pastured horses. They soon built distilleries to turn surplus corn into whiskey, the excess of which went to Natchez and New Orleans, along with surplus bacon and flax seed. They also had hogs and horses to drive south overland, for sale from Georgia to Mississippi (Knott 27-29).

The corn and hog farms of Marion County did not demand the extensive, and brutal, labor of the hemp fields in other Bluegrass plantation areas. The proportion of the population in slavery barely increased from the 25.9 percent of Washington County in 1799 to the 28 percent of Marion in 1860, when, by contrast, nearly 50 percent of the residents of Woodford, Bourbon, and Fayette counties were slaves (Lucas xx). Marion slaveholders were relatively humane in their treatment, Johnston claimed, especially in selling no slaves except the persistently unruly, and so were "'slave poor'"; selling them, moreover, required sending them down the rivers — the threat of which terrified a slave into obedience — and was not profitable. One man of Lebanon, whom Johnston named, made a business of trading in slaves, and was socially disapproved for it (112-13); this man had not acquired notable wealth — by 1860.

Many settlers' families, on the other hand, remained small farmers who worked their own land. Financially, they were comparable, on the 1860 census, to middling farmers in Harrison County. Three Kirks, for instance, a family who had not owned slaves in 1799 or 1810, had real estate worth $7,720, $6,560, $6,000, like Rudolf Mitchell's $7,000; these Kirks had personal property of $2,664, $6,800, $3,000, to Rudolf's $1,000. Moreover, some descendants of early slaveholders had become small farmers of lesser wealth than the Kirks, such as Leonard Hamilton and two Abells of 1860. Marion County, however, had more numerous wealthier farmers; at least four owned real estate of $30,000-40,000, and one far more. By contrast, the richest farmer on Irish Ridge, Samuel Cochran, had $17,000 in real estate; and in Greene Township, Isaac Holmes $19,000; their personal property of $3,000 and $6,000 was far surpassed by those of $12,000, $21,000, $30,000, and $30,000 in Marion County. Harrison had one very rich gentleman farmer, who was also a

financier; Walter B. Beebe owned $75,000 in real and $15,000 in personal property. Marion farmer Foster Ray had $120,000 and $100,000.

To estimate the differences in the wealth the Marion and Harrison settler families had acquired by 1860, and distributed among their members, I have compared 39 households of 11 family names from both. The Marion families appeared on 1799 and 1810 censuses, and exclude the rich Foster Ray. The Harrison families are those of old land-owning families: Cochran, Dickerson, Gray, Grove, Haverfield, Hines, Holmes, Kyle, McFadden, Mitchell, and Oglevee. The Marion descendants varied widely in wealth, from one Knott with real estate of $100, personal property of $150, to the average of seven Spaldings' worth at $13,114 and $20,200. The average value of the 39 households among 11 families was $10,510 real and $11,449 personal property. The Harrison family averages ranged from the $2,500 real estate between the two Kyles, and $363 in personal property per each of four Hines, to the $14,250 real-estate average of two Cochrans and $2,740 personal-property average of six McFaddens. Overall, the average among the 39 property owners was $6,065 in real estate and $1,439 in personal property. Thus the Marion County households had average real estate holdings worth 173 percent of those of Harrison ones, and average personal property 796 percent of the Harrisons'.

The ordinary craftsmen in the towns were financially equivalent, ranging from no ownership to something like Frank Grove's real estate worth $1,700 and personal $500. But in Lebanon a different system overrode them; there "master" carpenters, cabinetmakers, and others had made five to six times as much as those who worked alone; a plasterer of near Frank's age, for instance, with two apprentice plasterers and a carpenter under his roof, had over $17,000. The Cadiz *Sentinel*'s Charles N. Allen, 35, termed himself a "Master Printer" and had an apprentice of 15 in his house; Allen owned no real estate, but $3,000 in personal property. Richard Hatton, 52, had $3,000 real, $2,000 personal property.

The professional men in each town ranged widely in wealth, from the mere $200 apiece of Cadiz attorney John S. Pearce and his father, Dr. John Pearce, to the $40,000/$2,000 of Cadiz lawyer Josiah Scott, the $18,200/$20,000 of Lebanon lawyer James M. Fogle, and the $15,750/$48,000 of Lebanon physician Michael S. Shuck. Attorney Stewart Beebe Shotwell was doing well, at 40, having $14,000 real, $8,000 personal property. John A. Bingham, 44, had $6,000 real and $2,000 personal property.

In Lebanon, one of the Rays was a banker, with $38,000/$22,000. Even considering the larger size and population of Harrison County, it had surpassingly enriched its bankers and brokers. Five of them were wealthy men. Robert Lyons, 56, had $7,000/$20,000; Rezin Welch, 65, $3,000/$26,000; William Hogg, 39, $27,000/$14,500; Chauncey Dewey, 64, $30,000/$30,000; and Joseph S. Thomas, 42, with his wife and children, a total of $37,500/$75,000.

The wealthy families of these counties had quite different lifestyles. The Thomas family, with six children aged 19 to 1, kept the most elaborate household staff in Cadiz: two white girls as maids, of 17 and 14, the latter born in Scotland, and a black man, 21, born in Ohio, as servant. By contrast, families of the Lebanon area, in addition to the slaves they maintained, hosted nuns from Ireland, priests from Germany, and governesses from Italy.

Lebanon, like Cadiz, had a branch railroad; but whereas the Harrisonians perennially complained and despaired of their Indian-trail roads, impassable for weeks when snow turned to mud, the Marionites had cooperated to build good macadam turnpikes in the several directions of their trade. Knott claimed that Marion County was foremost in the entire state in its proportion of fine roads (32).

When war began, these roads invited armies to Lebanon. Early on, Confederates came to seize the locomotive and cars. Soon the other side arrived. Union Brig.-General George H. Thomas in the fall of 1861 brought troops for training on his estate near Lebanon (Knott 54). The women of town, of both Union and secessionist sympathies, joined in making pies they sold in town and in camp, profitably amused that the 14th Ohio fellows would gobble six pies seriatim. The tinsmith shop of Charles Johnston's father became a factory for the little sheet-iron "damp stoves" soldiers wanted to buy for their tents. The music hall in the third story of Dr. Shuck's elegant building with a cast-iron front on Main Street had entertainment six nights a week; there girls were charmed by shiny braid and buttons; and in the parlors of fine families, young ladies sang and played their pianos for admiring officers. Altogether, Lebanon was a "gay and lively town" that fall; and the citizens parted as friends with Thomas' soldiers when they marched out, on their way to drive the rebels from south-central Kentucky, which they did at the battle of Mill Springs, in January 1862 (Johnston 102-104).

Then the town and post sat guarded by fifty-some soldiers, no more than a skirmish for John Hunt Morgan and his battalion of cavalry on their July expedition into Kentucky, when they killed two of the home-guards, burned all military supplies on the rail branch, and rode on north. The Federals thereupon returned to Lebanon to fortify it, and only then did a strain commence in the local hospitality. Colonel Dumont and his Indiana troops tore up the streets and made the entire town a fortress. They ditched the berm on either edge of the street to a moat, and threw up breastworks to make a maze of barricades against any traffic. Atop the music hall they built an observation post. The citizens were in effect garrisoned, in a potential "death pen," since an enemy on any of the knobs to the south with a few cannon "could have knocked the town into atoms, without the least danger to themselves." Morgan's raiders had ridden through town with less damage and danger than these industrious defenders brought; but so, Lebanon sweated out the summer (Knott 55).

The invasion by Bragg's army in September brought, in effect, liberation. The Indiana infantry departed, Louisiana cavalry arrived, a native son Confederate surgeon took charge, the hated breastworks were leveled, town and countryside resumed their commerce. The dashing gentlemen of Louisiana seemed a decided improvement in military soci-

ety, and the only privations were a lapse of mail service and newspapers. The news came from the cavalry, that the Confederate armies were daily trouncing the invading North, from Maryland throughout Kentucky. After several weeks of these accounts which confirmed their own situation, citizens were generally convinced they were securely lodged in the Confederacy. Then the cavalry delivered the *coup de grace* to Union sympathies, in hundreds of printed copies of the Emancipation Proclamation which omitted the President's provision for slave-holding Union states. Within a week, the Confederates raised a new company of cavalry in the area (Johnston 106). The Proclamation seemed to people first incredible, then shocking, as they had believed Lincoln had no intention to interfere with slavery and no power to do so. This, then, was the mood of Lebanon on 5 October, when the Confederates rode away, on their route to Perryville (Knott 56).

A few days later, the Union army returned in a cavalcade of soldiers who had been maimed at Perryville. Here on the rail branch would be the area hospital headquarters — when doctors and supplies could arrive — and depot for corpses. The boys' schoolhouse, the churches, and the music hall soon filled with the wounded. Johnston helped Union boys up the stairs to the music hall, and he recalled one barely older than he who had been shot through the jaw, so that his tongue was cut in half: "The wound had never been dressed and not even 'tied up,'" yet he "seemed pert as a cricket" (108).

Both Union and Confederate wounded arrived in Lebanon, and their prognosis was grim. William P. Baas, M.D., has estimated the causes of the deaths resulting from wounds at Perryville, which surged every few days through October, continued every day until late December, and ended only in June 1863. Those who survived to be evacuated to Lebanon did not have the severe head, chest, and abdominal damage that killed soldiers within 24–36 hours. They began to suffer from bacterial infections of their wounds — with fever, loss of fluids, and kidney failure — and died massively on 15 Oct., a week after their battle. After this, delayed infections brought pneumonia, peritonitis, blood clots, and organ failures; then those who could not eat or digest began to die of starvation; at month's end, gangrene, organ damage from fever, and internal bleeding began to take their toll.

The lack of wound hygiene was particularly acute at Lebanon, because it had a crucial shortage of the basic element which at the time could aid the wounded soldier, that which Wesley Poulson applied to his "shivered" leg: water. The area had been in drought for months, and "Lebanon was, possibly, the worst watered town in Kentucky," where three-fourths of the town wells were dry in droughts, and outside town were only two springs (Johnston 93). The lethal spread of infection from wound to wound by the sponges, as the water in basins was not changed, frequent in military hospitals, must have devastatingly afflicted patients in Lebanon. Moreover, the sparsity of water created unhealthful conditions for all visiting soldiers, and spawned epidemic diseases such as typhoid fever, which caused many deaths that are not statistically attributed

to the battle, but resulted from the emergencies it brought.

After a forty-mile trek from Crab Orchard, and over three weeks without tents, McCook's corps neared Lebanon, where, along with the wounded, new recruits had been shipped. McCook's men had to lie on the bank of the Rolling Fork for water. Many, if not most, of these soldiers had lost their knapsacks and other equipment, when Confederates captured their baggage at Perryville; they posed a threat to any property in their reach, and to most of Lebanon they currently represented an invading enemy. The 98th Ohio arrived in Lebanon on 25 Oct. to guard it, defending property while their comrades endured privations.

From Robert Mitchell to his brother Hugh: "Lebanon Oct the 28th 1862, Dear Brother, I seat myself to let yo know I am well at preasant this very nice day since the snowstorm last night. it frose very hard. I am provose guard in the town today. we have to stop ever soldier we see in the town and put them in the guard house. There wase some very near frose the night of the snow storm but I slept worm. I was in a tent I was guarding some tents and we put up and slep in it all night. there is only 50 men in since the fight there was 8 or 10 of them since thc fight and there is som 8 wonded and some sick. Tom Kyle is a geting better. I herd one died since the fight and Robert Hagan he was woned in the foot and mortified. I have seen lots of towns since I left home and seen the elephond to. [The *elephant* was a metaphor for any tremendous thing.] Bill McBride is good soldier for he faut well. we got hour male today. Lebanon is an ugly place. the guard will not allow them to sel whiky a jot and they not allow a soldier to be in town [unless] he has a pas from the General. When the guard get them without they [put] them in the Gail until they [are sent] out where there Regt is. we sent of on the cars abou 300 or 400 prisoners yesterday to Louisville. they very heurd the most of them has no shoes on there feat a tol. we have not got hor tents yet but wil get them before long. we exbect a bare of pants....

"I told yo to send me a pare of boots and I want to get them made hight in the legs. Thomps Gray and I are to send for a box and he is going to send for some dryed frute and a can of cheres and a pair of buxcin Gluves and bair of socks and I want yo to but some of the same things to. I want yo to put a pin cosin and fine comb. nothing more at presant. write soon. Robert Mitchell"

From Robert to Nancy, 31 Oct.: "Dear Sister, I seate my self to write yo a fiew lines to let yo i am well at presant. I recived yor leter with 50ct in it yesterday. I have gust come of Co. Drill. Leftenant Carson is well again he was left at Danvill sick. John Miler is sick but he is a geting beter. I got them $10 yo sent last we. The setler fetched it from louisville for me. we have been on provoose guard for the weak. Me and Tomps Gray was plased at a privat house to keep them from burning his fence. i liked it first rate for he had to board us and we got to sleep in a bed. Know i will let yo know somthng about the fight...."

Robert's needs for a pin cushion, clothes, and fine comb suggest the tattered, dirty, probably lousy appearance of these soldiers to Lebanon. They did not resemble the fine figures who had

been cheered out of Cadiz and Covington: they never again would. James Moore of Robert's company, then 19, who served to the war's end and was absent from service only once, when sick in an army hospital, recalled that except for his hospital stay, "he did not have his clothes once off a single night" (Beers).

In disposition, however, these young men were yet far from hardened soldiers. Despite their losses — by Kennon's account, of the 989 men who left Camp Steubenville, 675 had gone into the battle, and one-third, 225, were killed or wounded — they had more respect and pity than animosity for their enemies. They were talking with a large number of rebel prisoners, many from "a Mississippi and Alabama regiment with whom the 98th Ohio did the principal part of her fighting," who were astonished to learn the 98th was only six weeks in service, and who remarked they found kinder treatment from their captors than their own army. Kennon added, "Some very sorrowful and yet amusing things occur. A dozen or so of our wounded boys and as many wounded Rebels were talking together about the battle. One of our boys, who had his left arm amputated just below the elbow, was sitting on a blanket before the fire, looking feeble but in good spirits and evidently rapidly improving. On his right sat a Rebel boy — who had been wounded in the same fight, — they looked very much alike — about the same size — and his arm had been amputated — left arm — at as near as possible the same place. He looked well also. Those two boys were talking together about the fight, and wondering if it might not be possible that *each of them*

had shot the other? At last says the little secesh boy, 'If I did shoot you, I am very
sorry for it.' Our boy said, '*Well*, I hope I
didn't shoot you." Those boys became
very intimate, and I saw them walking
over camp together a number of times,
not only apparently, but *certainly* upon
most intimate and friendly terms. Such is
war — or rather one of the incidents connected with it. You wouldn't believe — in
looking at a lot of our boys and Rebels
sitting down together, talking in the most
friendly manner — that two weeks ago
they were trying their best to kill each
other. These boys would not do so to-day,
when the blood is cool, but when the
fierce fever of excitement and battle runs
the pulse up to fever heat, who can tell
what either party would do?"

Moreover, in regard to the issue of
slaves, whom they were now first en-
countering, an uncertainty and attitude
of negotiation prevailed: "We have in
our tent *just now* a secesh Colonel prisoner, and a negro woman — slave — from
Alabama, who was brought to this town
from Alabama by the Colonel of the 10th
Indiana. The darkey was abandoned
here, and the Indiana Regiment has gone
off. — She wants to be free. She wants to
get clear of the Slave States. We have no
power over it, and if a proper claimant
makes a requisition by civil authority
she will at once be delivered up. That her
uneasiness is great you can readily imagine. — I have just been talking to the
Colonel (secesh) about it, and asked him
what had better be done about it, (he is
from North Carolina). He says to hold
on to her. But that, perhaps,…is looking to his own personal interest. I can't
tell what will become of the woman" (*BC*
13 N).

Chapter 12

Cumberland, Maryland: "The Wild Romantic Scenes"

The 126th Ohio were in the Allegheny Mountains in Cumberland, Maryland, "now encamped in Sibley tents on the east side of town, on a hillside, from which we have a full view of the city," Thomas H. Smith, 1st Lieutenant of McCready's Co. H, wrote the *CR* on 30 Oct.: "The Potomac river and the Mountains on the north, south and west covered with dense forests [in autumn foliage], arrayed in the most beautiful attire, presenting one of the grandest scenes I ever beheld." He reported the regiment's officers at Camp McCook: "B[enjamin]. F. Smith, of pipe-smoking notoriety, is our Colonel. His conduct at Shilo, as well as Gain's Mill, Malvern Hill, and the last bloody battle at Bull Run "showed" doubt that he is a brave man, and a cool and skilled commander." "W[illiam]. H. Harlan, formerly a Captain in the 30th O.V.I, from Jefferson co., O., is our Lieut. Col. He has the grit and capability…. Aaron Ebright, a civilian of Lancaster co., O., is our Major. He as yet is inexperienced

(save a little drill he got at home) and as yet is not a military man." Dr. William Estep of Belmont was the "very attentive and efficient" surgeon, and, from Jefferson, Alexander Patterson Quarter Master, Lewis Sutherland Adjutant, and the Rev. John K. Andrews Chaplain, appreciated for his "brief, appropriate, earnest and eloquent" exercises. The 126th had met only the 4th Maryland regiment and 6th Maryland battery at Cumberland, but expected more troops to arrive, and soon "join in the onward march to Richmond." Rebel cavalry were raiding within twenty miles of Cumberland, however; and its site amid the mountains was as strategic as beautiful, the narrow passageway of the railroad and National Road, the head of the Chesapeake and Ohio Canal. Smith observed, "There are a great many secesh here. They think the proclamation is an awful thing, and will eventually ruin the country. The loyal people and the soldiers so far as I have learned hail it with gladness" (*CR* 5 N).

Moses Conaway, McCready's 2nd Sergeant, described the scene of "confusion" in his large crowded tent, which made it no place to win a "literary reputation." Some were joking and plaguing others who attempted serious pursuits, "low, earnest conversation" and reading the Bible or the news, which included secesh papers that provoked noisy arguments. The regiment's health was not good, for reasons unknown, but was fortunate in contrast to others', in which "friend after friend falls, and have fallen, neath the unhallowed juggernaut of the rebellion, whose wheels are steeped in *crime*, and bathed in the blood ... while enemies at home, as well as in the South, wood up the flames of the infernal enginry of treason and tyranny...." Conaway lengthily defended the army's record and propounded the need to overthrow every system that stood "in the way of the re-establishment of the Government"; he closed with a vow that the mountains would "re-echo, with the thunder of the canons of thy liberators" (to J. B. Conaway, *CR* 3 D).

James W. Oglevee wrote on 4 Nov.: "Miss Nancy, I received yours of the 27th Oct. in do course of time.... We have changed our place of rendezvous again. Surely we have no perminant resting place but liable at any moment to be called away to the battlefield to engage in fiery combat perhaps some to fall & return to mother earth again. yet such is war & war will continue so long as sin exists....

"The morning [of the trip] was quite frosty cool but I being one of the fortunate ones in receiving an overcoat (as there was only forty distributed among each company) so I felt pretty comfortable notwithstanding the cold. I seated my self in the dore of the car in order that I might see what could be seen but could not see much except heigh hills & rocky mounds. We arrived here after a ride of about 20 hours. This trip was not near so hard as the one from Steubenville to Parkersburg. this is by far the nicest camp we have been in yet. If I had time I would like to set here & write you a great long letter to discribe to you as well as I could the wild romantic scenes by which I am surrounded. but ... time will not permit me to do so....

"Surely this war is a terrible thing & I do hope that this accursed rebellion will soon scease & we all permitted to return home to enjoy the liberty which we have gon forth to defend.

"In reply to your question (whether Lizzie Kyle would have had an escort from the Irish Ridge singing) I would inform you that it always takes two to make a bargan & fer me to say that it would have been different I might tell a fib & you know that I oppose all such practices.

"The 98 Regt is not here nor I suppose it will not be. I received a letter from Finley last night written on the 28th. He was then at Lebanon Ky & he thought they would remain there perhaps all winter.

"Mr. E. L. Hargrave sends his best respects.... Tell Matt to write to me as I know she has more time than I & I will endeavor to answer.... Please write soon. So good by. J. W. Oglevee"

From Frank P. Grove, Camp Mc-Cook, 9 Nov.: "Miss N. D. Mitchell, Dear friend, I take my seat by the side of a cracker box this morning for the purpose of collecting a few of my wandering thoughts to convey them to you by means of pen ink & paper. Ought we not be thankful that tho we are seperated by hills and even mountains, yet through this medium we have the pleasure of conveying our thoughts to each other. When we view the starry heavens and meditate upon them how strange it appears that we can look at the same stars, and the same moon that lights your path in your walks at night lights the Soldiers path as they wearily walk their beat round the Campground. I often think of those things. But all this is but a strong evidence of an oaver ruling Providence which I trust will protect me from the arrow that flies by day and the pestilence that walketh in darkness secretly.

"Nan this is Sabbath day. if I ware at home I would not do this. but I don't know that it is any harm under the circumstances…. Except my thanks for that photograph it looks as natural as life. If the Rebs ever caches me that will be the last thing that I will give up. It is the only likeness of any kind that I have with me. John Mitchell come pretty nigh getting to see it. he saw me pull it out of the letter he said he knew who it was, but he was not close enough to recognize it. I made him believe it belonged to another fellow, that he had Just gave it to me to look at.

"Well Nancy I have had a spell of the Jaundice was in the Hospital one week…. Oh Nan I wonder if those folks that went to Cocherens from the singing had as high a time as we had the night we ware there. James Oglevee and I was talking a short time ago about that memorable night. you will observe that every young man that was thare that night is now in the army except one that is William Oglevee. Oh if we could Just take a look in to futurity and see what another year will bring forth. Well Nancy I don't want you to stay home on my account if you would enjoy yourself better than you could with me. have you seen anything of Mr. Roberts since the raising at your Uncles. I expect he will attend the singings on Shortcreek, this winter. What kind of weather have you back thare. we have had some winter here this two or three days it commenced snowing on Friday. Saturday morning the snow was about 2 inches deep — it has been snowing a little occasionally ever since. It is right cold standing out of doors those mornings eating breakfast. The cooking all has to be done out of doors rain or shine. We have canvass tents to stay in this cold weather. They are round run up to a point like a haystack and have a stove in the center. Sometimes I sleep warm enough & sometimes I am cold. We have some straw throwed in our tents on the ground for us to ly on. We don't drill any scarcely since the weather has got bad. Thare is a great many of our Reg't sick the most of them has the Jaundice. I have heard it said that dirty liveing is the cause of Jaundice. I think this goes to prove it. I think I have eat my peck of dirt. But enough of that. When have you heard from Robert. I wrote a letter to him last week but have not rec'd an answer yet.

"Has Jim Oglevee ever writen you a letter. if he has not he is slighting you for I think he must have writen to nearly all the girls of his acquaintance in Cadiz Shortcreek & Green townships….

"We drawed our dress coates last week we have got all our cloths more I think than we can carry conveniently. You ought to see us dressed up you would think we ware all officers all we want is the shoulder straps.

"Nan we have the nicest little Colonel. he still smokes his pipe. I don't know whether it is the same pipe he smoked at the battle of Shilo or not....

"What kind of a Schoolteacher have you got this winter — Do you intend going to school this winter — Do you have preaching regularly since Mc-Cready left. do you ever go to prayer meeting any these times. I would like to be thare some night but we have lots of prayers in Camp we have prayers in our tent night and morning. But I will stop writeing for the present lest I weary your patience. Please write again. Fare well for the present. Your friend & well wisher, F. P. Grove"

From Nancy D. Mitchell to Frank P. Grove, 12 Nov.: "Kind Friend, Your letter of the 9th of this month came to hand last night and its contents perused with intense interest and pleasure as all your productions are, and I hope I may long be cheered by the epistles of your mind & pen....

"I was much pleased to hear that you have got well again and are able to be in camp again & hope that from henceforth you may be blessed with that best of earthly blessings — Health. We had stormy weather here last Friday night & Saturday....

"Oh! Frank I am here alone. They are all gone. How glad would I be if your welcome foot steps were this moment heard. But Oh! why entertain such thoughts as these. It can not be so now.

The future alone can tell when it will be so if ever. How I long for the bright Angel of Peace to revisit again this once favored land. But it is a picture our imagination cannot draw. However we trust the nation will soon emerge from the calamity & take her position for the protection of human liberty & her people become God fearing and loving.

"We have had Preaching since Mr. McCready left every Sabbath except one that being the first Sabbath after he had gone. We had a first rate preacher last Sabbath (Jas. Sankey was his name) the forenoon he preached from Exodus 33rd Chap 14th verse 'My presence shall go with thee & I will give thee rest' & the afternoon from Malachi Third Chap 9th verse 'Ye are cursed with a curse; for ye have robbed me even this whole nation.' No doubt some will say he preached a 'Political Sermon.' But let 'Rebel Sympathizers' say what they may he found it in the Bible. And also he read a letter from Mr. McCready addressed to the Congregation. It was enough to melt an Iron heart to sympathy."

[McCready's letter treated the issue of slavery:

"Your pulpit was not silent in regard to those sins which have convulsed the land.... Seven years ago, when thousands of statesmen and divines, who are now with it, were against it, it preached what it preaches to-day.... To these truths, which I have preached to you, dear brethren, if I fall in this struggle, I am a martyr. But for their influence, I had not been here.... But you and I had raised up a standard for God's truth. We stood up for its divinity. We talked — the time came to act. God demanded sacrifices in its behalf. The clergy of the

South had shown how much they were willing to dare for this error — this great self-evident lie — this blot upon civilization — this outrage upon all religion and all virtue. God put the question to us: Were we willing to do and dare as much for truth, for liberty, for country? What could I reply? I may fall! your beloved sons and brothers may fall! Be it so. Our testimony in behalf of God's truth is not lost. You will reap the benefits of it in future years" (Wishart 226)].

"I had a letter from Rob last night…. He said the time of the battle he thought they were trying to fool them as they had done so often before 'But after a while I heard the cannon roar and saw plenty of Rebles' said he. Oh but I would like to see him. I am afraid he is a bad boy. Capt Norris is in Cadiz now but intends going back to his Regt in a few days. Well Frank I was at a singing at Irish Ridge last Monday night. it was about like all the singings they have there — a large crowd but not much of a singing. McConnell tryed to get a school but could not get one. I am very well satisfied he did not.

"I have received two letters from J. W. Oglevee but have not answered the last one. I must do so this evening. You wanted to know if I have seen Mr. Roberts since Uncles raising? Yes I saw him at church one day. You say you expect he will attend the singings on Short-creek this winter. he may attend the singings at Science Hill if he thinks Emaline Holmes would be their.

"Oh I forgot to tell you who had escorts home from the singing Monday night.

"Your brother went with Mat Mitchell. Wm. Harrison with E[liza]. J.

Ritchey. John Slemmons with Ruth Ritchey. John Dickerson with Amanda McCoy. A. S. Porter went with a Miss Dickerson I am not acquainted with her & W. Barricklow intended to go with Bel Ritchey. But could not find her. I heard him ask James McFadden if he saw anything of his girl. Wasn't that a pity?

"I go to prayer meeting whenever the weather will permit. I see some vacant seats there but I hope the ones that have left them may be returned home to occupy them again but if God has otherwise ordered may I meet them on that happy shore. Where farewells are unknown and Parting words are never spoken. Some of the drafted men have come home on furlough. I don't know how many. Sam Dickerson and McCoy (I forget his first name) came home yesterday. They have to leave to go to the 43rd Regt. Dickerson tried to get in Norris or Cunningham's Co. but could not. I do not know the reason for neather of the Co. are full.

"Rebekah Welling is to get married next week to a Mr. McCoy. he lives near Columbus is quite wealthy & has six children. may long life and prosperity attend the happy twain.

"We have a very good schoolteacher this winter. I have not gone any yet but intend to start in about two weeks. Whether I shall learn any I do not know but at any rate I intend to try. Oh! this unfortunate war that has caused so many acheing hearts & languid hours, if it was only over: how cheerfully could go through any task still I am reminded of that verse 'The darkest shadows of the night are just before the morning.'

"Warfels girls get along teaching very well. They have 74 [?] scholars enrolled. Charles Parrish is getting bet-ter slowly he has had a rather serious time.

"Oh I had almost forgotten to tell that Robert Peacock is sentenced to be shot next Friday for deserting unless the President sees fit to pardon him. Oh! what an unfortunate man. But I must close thanking you for your kind let-ter…. Your Humble Friend & well wish-er, Nannie D."

Robert Peacock of Irish Ridge had enlisted with the "Cadiz Guards" in April 1861 among the three-month vol-unteers. After discharge from the 13th O.V.I., he joined Capt. Cunningham's company of the 30th, which had recent-ly met its first battles. His sentence for desertion may have been a rumor, since President Lincoln had just issued an order that he would not pardon desert-ers, yet Robert Peacock did not go be-fore the firing squad. He continued serv-ing with the 30th. If he was sentenced for desertion, on the other hand, his life and service may have continued through intervention by John A. Bingham.

Frank P. Grove from Camp McCook to Nancy, 26 Nov.: "Dear Friend, It is a pleasure to me that I enjoy the privilege of addressing you this morning. Yours of the 12th inst came to hand in due time & the contents as carefully perused as though it was sacred words. It is a plea-sure to me to write to one that is punc-tual in answering as you are…. I wrote a letter to Ellen Mitchell by her own re-quesst and she never answered it. I don't know what is the reason unless she has so much writeing to do till Gabrial [Hol-land] that she has not time. But I ought to have told you that I am enjoying my usual health. John Mitchell has been ex-cused from duty for a couple of weeks on account of haveing a sore finger. [This note of suspicion marks the outset of soldiers' opinions that Nancy's cousin was a malingerer. And if John had been commanding respect as 3rd Sergeant, his company would have been more careful in their gossip about his sister.]

"Well Nancy this day is a little stormy it is snowing some. how I would enjoy myself if I could step in this morn-ing and spend the day with you. I think I could talk right straight along all day. this is just the kind of a day that I like to sit in the house & talk to the girls but I am affraid I will not enjoy that privilege soon for I have bid adieu to my native home till the sun of peace dispells this dark cloud of rebellion and smiles again upon us. I was on patroll guard in town last night consequently I am excmpt from drill this forenoon. But the Regi-ment is out on Battallion drill. they are practising firing. they are fairly makeing the ground shake. we have been practis-ing firing for the last three days, making bayonet charges &c."

[Instruction in maneuvers with the bayonet, according to army manuals, commenced only after soldiers had pro-ceeded through all the drills of march-ing and firing; so McCready's men were newly attempting these exercises. They did not even receive knapsacks until 22 Nov., Frank's diary noted, and first drilled with these burdens on their backs the next day.

Frank became fond of bayonet drill. The lessons in the art of fencing with musket and bayonet resembled instruc-tion in ballet, certainly a challenge to the minister and his men who did not know a ballroom or waltz. McCready had received and inscribed his *Manual of Bayonet Exercise* on 5 Sept., a translation by George B. McClellan of the French treatise by Gomard. The Thirty Radical Movements to be attained, with each repeated until mastered, are perplexing from even the first lesson: for The Right Volt, "Face square to the right by turning on the toes of the left foot, and describing *to the left*, a quarter of a circle with the right foot"; for The Left Rear Volt, "Face to the rear by turning on the toes of the left foot, and describing, *by the front*, a half circle with the right foot — Fig. 8" (31-32). The illustrations of motions compounded their foreign character, with four mustachioed, wasp-waisted soldiers in tiny, pointy-toed slippers, posed amid a debris of unidentified shoeprints. Such was the introduction to the pirouettes and jetés required for "Blows With The Butt" and "Blow parried by tierce-sixte."]

"Nancy I heard that Will [his brother] had Mat Mitchell out at Londonderry. Dan Tidrick says it is reported that they are going to git married. I dont think it is so (do you). The Guernsey County boys say that [Sgt.] Tom McKiney fooled Mat Mitchell. You know my sentiments about Will going with Mat. She is a cousin of yours too. perhaps I ought not to talk this way, but I am making a confidential friend of you. If I thought she was half as good a girl as her cousin Nan I would not say a word but enought of that, but I would like if you would tell me whether you think thare is anything of it or not.

"…We sent away 9 rebble prisoners to Camp chase to day. I had a long talk with them last night. They talk a good deal like we do. They say they wish the

war was oaver. for they never want to be in another fight nor see another battlefield. They tell some horrible tales about the great slaughter before Richmond, at Sharpsburgh & others. I think they tell the truth too for they tell of the horrible slaughter on both sides. They say they got the worst of the battle. One of them told me he saw dead men lying with thair arms clasped round each other in death. he said he saw eight hundred & twenty eight of our men lying dead in one heap. that was at the battle of Richmond — our men had caried them back as they retreated but finally had to abandon them and they fell into the hands of the enemy. They complain on thair officers as we do of ours on account of bad treatment & bad management. they say the war is kept up by politicle aspirants & speculators and that the war will never be settled by fighting. but I dont think so. I think we can whip them. they say McClellan was a good General. they said they thought they had him surrounded at Richmond so that he could not git out but when they went to take him he was not thare. But I am well satisfied that he is removed, ain't you? …Please write soon for I allways look anxiously for an answer. Yours in love, F. P. Grove"

Nancy to Frank, 2 December: "My noble Friend, The agreeable news of your health and welfare, which was received not long since, gave me inexpressable pleasure, and I now sit down to pen to you a few of my scattering thoughts.

"I was indeed happy to learn that you were still at Cumberland — that you have not had to face the cannons mouth, nor witness the horrors of a gory battle-field. The 98th Regt has gone from Lebanon Ky. It is said their destination is in Tennessee. they thought they would get to stay there all winter. Truly they have no abiding place. Mr. Sloan of Harrisville was at Lebanon when they left. He said the boys threw down their guns and told the Colonel they were ready to go but he might take care of the guns. So the Col went & got wagons and hauled their guns & knapsacks and part of the men. They would likely ride time about. How far these wagons will go with them I do not know but I suppose not very far. He (Sloan) said they were going to stay a few days in Columbia Ky some 50 or 60 miles from Lebanon and the wagons will likely go no farther. Capt Norris left Cadiz last Saturday morn for to join his Regt. He told Pap that Ase Glaisner & Moffat [two young men of Irish Ridge who evidently deserted before the battle of Perryville and came home] said they were going with him but he (Norris) said he was afraid they would back out. Ase did not go for he was married the same night to Miss Sarah Brown. Oh don't you think she was a fool for marrying such a villain as he?"

[Several Brown families, their elders born in Ireland, were Irish Ridge farmers, but they probably did not oversee Sarah's courtship. In 1860 she was living with the wealthier farm family of Henry Boyles, just outside Cadiz near the Beebe and Dewey estates, along with a younger girl domestic and Thomas Crumley, farmhand, from another Ridge family. The placement of girls in domestic service in such families appears meant for their advantage, gaining wider acquaintances and opportunities nearer town, as well as earnings. A daughter of

the Glazeners clearly bettered her circumstances by residing as a domestic with the Stewart Beebe Shotwell family, instead of the crowded home of a farm laborer. The "hired girl" lived much as a member of the family, like the farmhand who lived and worked there until he could establish his own farm. The association of Sarah Brown and Thomas Crumley at the Boyles' suggests a possible reason for her unwise marriage; Thomas, an early volunteer, was among the dead of the 43rd Ohio at Corinth, Miss.; and Sarah may have been his bereaved sweetheart. The marriage license of Asa and Sarah E. was issued 29 Nov., "on oath of Glazener." They were married the next day at a travelers' inn on the Wheeling road, by a bootmaker of Harrisville who was also a Justice of the Peace (*CR* 10 D, Jarvis). After the wedding jaunt, Sarah was to see very little of her groom. He returned to his regiment, but then deserted for the second time, on 20 Jan. (Ohio A. G., *Roll of Deserters* 148). Then, according to a letter from late in the war, Asa became a bounty jumper, joining units to collect bounties, and deserting.]

"Whether Moffat went I did not hear but Norris told them they could do as they pleased about going and when he went back he was going to report them & it might cost them their lives. Ira Dickerson [probable sunstroke victim] was at home last week. I have not heard whether he has gone back or not. He looks very badly."

[In the following, Nancy names Francis Patton, Frank's nephew; Samuel Kyle, his brother-in-law; and Thomas Kyle, the young private who had tried to steal the farmer's peaches and turkey in

Louisville, and received an arm wound at Perryville.]

"Oh! Frank. Your good mother is here she says Francis was at town and Samuel Kyle told him his brother Tommie was dead. His nurse sent a dispatch that he was dying and shortly after they got another dispatch that he was dead. Kate told me last Sabbath that her father had been to see him — that he was getting along very well although he had several bones taken out. I think that his death has been from some other cause. But he is no more. he is sleeping his last long dreamless sleep

'Soldier rest, thy warfare or'e,

Sleep the sleep, that knows not breaking,

Dream of battle fields no more,

Days of danger — nights of waking.'"

[Tommie Kyle had received the most advanced care possible, being moved to an army hospital in Cincinnati. There the surgeons tried a new procedure, intending to save his arm, "excision and resection." They cut out the damaged section of bone and rejoined the limb, so the arm would be shortened but retain a hand. Some doctors were reporting excellent results with excision; others predicted these reattached forearms would atrophy or dangle useless — if the patient recovered from the effects of the two sawings. In Union surgery throughout the war, where bones were injured, mortality following excision and resection amounted to 28 percent, more than the 26 percent for sheer amputations, far over the 18 percent when surgeons did not apply their saws. Too, soldiers who had surgery over 48 hours after wounds died at fully twice the rate of those operated on more promptly

(Denney 100-102). The Kyle family no doubt had been assured Tommie's arm was saved, and were shocked when he lost his life on 30 November.]

"Pap has suffered greatly for 4 or 5 days with a catarrh on his hand. He has not slept if any for 2 nights. Tom Shirie has been here for several days helping to build a sheep house — and your brother Will also is here but he has gone this evening to help Uncles to thrash.

"Well Frank about Will and Mat going to get married I dont believe a word of it. Will offered to bet five dollars with me to day that they would never be married. I did not bet becaus I do not think he wants her. I knew McKinnie fooled her or least I thought he did for I was told they were engaged to be married. Oh I was at a singing at Science Hill last night-week and Bill Oglevee got with Mat about half-way home and came in and stayed with her and you had better think Ellen and I put them through. Whenever we would open the door Bill would jump and run and try catch us — finally he succeeded in getting us and I wished it wasn't me for he was a little mad, I believe and he did not care how rough he used us.

"Oh Frank Mr Ury cant get any body to build his house. He has been after Tom Shirie time and again but cannot get him. It is a pity of the old man but he hates the 'Naggars' as he calls them so bad that its not much different if he don't succeed in getting a white man to build it.

"Well you wanted to know what I think about the war if it will be over soon....

"I am so glad they have removed those traitors McClellen and Buell and I hope our Country will prosper by their removel. Oh! it is a shame to honor such men. Yet the Democrats thought there never was such a General as McClellen. Yea! they gave him the name of a *great man.* But '*Tis a matter most absurd to call a villain great.'* As for Buell he ought to be shot, for the way he acted at the battle of Chaplain Hill. They say he could have taken or scattered the whole of Braggs army. How many lives ushered into Eternity perhaps unprepared while if he had done his duty it might not have been.

"Charles Parrish is no better and I am afraid will never be any better. I suppose you have heard before that Johnson Hammond [of Norris' Company] is at home sick. They think he will not recover. Nathan Haverfield will arive home this week so I hear. Oh! Frank I would like to see you and have a long familiar chat with you. I dreampt the other night that you were home; but I awoke and lo it was a dream. Still I hope I may yet enjoy the reality of my dream.

"Ellen Mitchell has written to you this week and I reckon she has told you all the news and mine will not be of much account. I don't want you to take any more excuses about not writing good letters for you are as good a correspondent as ever I want to get letters from. But I am afraid you will never read this and I had better quit…. Ever your Friend, Nannie M."

In Cumberland, Capt. McCready began writing letters to Editor Hatton: "Dear Sir: …The *Republican* is a welcome guest to Camp. We scan the pages of the home papers closely, and find many an item of interest that we would overlook at home…. The Post Master

told me the other day that over twenty-five thousand letters had been received by the 126th Regiment since he took charge of the mail, which was about two months ago. So we have some good friends at home who care for us if we are soldier boys. And from the way the boys improve the spare hours I think we have paid back our correspondence with interest. Our friends will be pleased to learn that the boys from the neighborhood of Cadiz are well in my Company, and so far as I know throughout the Regiment. A couple of the members of my company, I am sorry to say, are sick…. It is a singular fact that short as our moves have been, … the men have to undergo a sort of acclimation. At each place too sickness assumed a peculiar type. At Steubenville, Diarrhoea was the trouble. At Parkersburg the tendency was to Ague with Diarrhoea. In Cumberland if a man were sick you might be almost sure he had Typhoid fever or Jaundice, or a kind of mixed form of disease combining the symptoms of both…. The first death in the Regt. occurred night before last at 8 o'clock, and in our company I am sorry to say. Our second Lieutenant, W. H. Nargney [pronounced Narney] died of Typhoid fever. He brought into our company a fine squad of men from Tuscarawas county, and though he came among us a stranger he and his men, by their kindness of heart and manly deportment soon won our esteem so that our intercourse was most pleasant. Poor fellow! he had but few days of health — he was seldom able to drill, but did all he could…. The corpse was taken home on the cars at six next morning. The company followed his remains to the depot in silence. It was not yet light. The half hour yet remaining was spent in appropriate religious services, conducted by the Chaplain. All things considered the funeral was peculiarly solemn and impressive. May the solemn lesson be blessed to us who survive! Our Reg't has been greatly favored in every respect. It is well clothed, well fed and has been fortunate above its fellows in escaping hardships. It is becoming well drilled.

"The boys enjoy themselves first rate. The other day the Colonel concluded to vary the afternoon drill somewhat. Orders were issued for us to go out without arms. He had provided a football. The game opened with a shout, as if we were charging on a brigade of Rebels. Only about five minutes sufficed to kick the breath out of the ball to the evident chagrin of a whole Regiment of men, some of whom are not last years children anyhow. [These hundreds of men played a version of Gaelic football, in which teams vie in kicking a round ball toward their goals as in soccer, using hard kicks rather than dribbling.]

"But the Colonel was not to be beat that way. Richmond must be taken at whatever expense. He sent for an india-rubber ball. Yesterday the forces were marshalled again in a large field. The right wing under Col. Harlan.—The left under Major Ebright. The left wing (which includes Co. H) was victorious in two hotly contested engagements. I must do the Col. and Major the justice to say that they were at all times in the thickest of the fight. Their horses were foaming with sweat when the game was over. My congregation would think me crazy if they saw me running, trying to kick a football. I wont say that I kicked it, but if I did not, the reason is I could not get in reach of it.

"Well, such a thing occasionally acts like a charm upon the spirits of the men....

"But one thing I must not forget.... We want a drummer and fifer, and fifteen or sixteen men. We would of course prefer a good drummer and fifer, but if they are only midling good they can soon learn, and for this, boys of from 14 to 18 would be preferred if they are rugged and have the consent of their parents or guardians.... Yours, J. S. McCready" (*CR* 10 D)

The musician he enlisted on 15 December did not come from a Harrison County family. Timothy Lemanskey, 13, was probably an adventuresome boy from Cumberland.

Chapter 13

"A School of Crime and Sin"

Winter and war cast a pall on the Ohio hills. The snows began early, with over three inches on 25 Oct., bringing farmers extra work of sheltering and feeding sheep, with sons and farmhands absent. News of their soldiers was increasingly dismal. W. B. Kirk, Captain of Co. B, 126th, was reported so ill in Cumberland with typhoid that little hope was held for his recovery (*CDS* 26 N). He did survive, but with impaired health. Moses Cannon, at home in New Athens on leave from Capt. Hanna's company of the 69th in Nashville, reported that the 12 hospitals there had 2,300 soldier patients, and "but few recoveries of hospital inmates," with an average of 10 dying each day. Many physicians were "ignorant and brutal Doctors," guilty of "criminal negligence" and "*quackery* of the most shameless kind" (*CR* 10 D). Capt. Albion W. Bostwick of the 74th, son-in-law of Editor Hatton, came home 1 Dec., having resigned after suffering from typhoid fever for six weeks. The trip from Nashville spurred the disease, and in his father Judge Bostwick's house he quickly sank.

According to the *Sentinel*, Bostwick unwisely postponed his preparation for death, and only in his last few days became concerned about his soul and the afterlife, praying for forgiveness. His wife of seven years was left a widow on 10 Dec., and also childless; their one son had burned to death a year earlier. Bostwick had served a year in the Mexican War, taking part in the march to Vera Cruz; thereafter he became a telegraph operator, until in the previous January he raised Co. G. in the county (*CDS* 17 D, *CR* 24 D).

The funeral bell tolled through the streets as the Kyles took Tommie to his grave. That night the wagoner of his company, John Penn, 43, arrived in a coffin from Lebanon, dead of a "recent injury" (*CR* 10 D), perhaps when he guarded the baggage at Perryville, in a area the enemy shelled. He left a poor widow and three school-age children. On 15 Dec., Oliver Randals, 19, "loved by all who knew him," wounded at Perryville, was returned to his home in Shortcreek township: "May he rest in peace in the quiet graveyard where oft his childhood steps have wandered, where no cannon's roar can be heard, and where man 'sleeps the sweet, long sleep'" (*CR* 24 D).

Another of Co. C, Thomas J. Stringer, 19, had died of his knee wound; and William Heberling, 23, of his fractured femur, among seventeen of the 98th dead in the hospitals of Perryville from "amputated left thigh," "wound through right breast," "wound right side," "wound followed by typhoid fever," "arm amputated, died of erisipelas"— acute strep infection (*CR* 26 N).

Col. Poorman sent from Lebanon, 13 Nov., to the *Belmont Chronicle* "a gloomy picture for friends" but "a truer record of bravery of the Reg't...than the fulsome flattery of newspaper correspondents, or the too often unmerited praise of official reports."

	Officers	*Enlisted Men*
Present for duty	17	462
Present sick	5	117
Absent sick	1	103
Absent wounded	2	123
Killed in battle	1	30
Died of wounds	1	30
Paroled prisoners mortally wounded		27
Absent on duty	16	30
Absent without leave	2	15
Died of disease		9
Discharged		9
Deserted		13
Total	30	959

...This fearful reduction...is attributed to the very heavy duty performed...and the miserable water we have been compelled to use in our marches through this State.

"Nearly all the absent sick were left in Louisville after our forced march from the Kentucky River..." (*CR* 26 N).

On 19 Nov. Poorman reported that the eleven hospitals in Lebanon had all been filled to capacity until two days before, when the number of sick began to decrease due to medical management by the "Angels of Mercy": "Woman, whose God-like tellings of mercy and sympathy lead her wherever there is sorrow or suffering, is at work, and by her presence, her ingenuity and energy is alleviating the sorrow and suffering of the poor, afflicted, heart-sick soldier; and doing more for his recovery by her kind words and gentle treatment, than all medical skill in the universe could accomplish." Among these "good Samaritans" were "the wife of Hon. R. P. Spaulding and Mrs.— Ray, who have taken upon themselves the general supervision of all the hospitals in the place; and so effectually are they performing the arduous duties they have imposed upon themselves, that there is scarcely a sick soldier" not daily visited by them. "Ordering here a nurse, there a stove, another place a change of clothing etc., speaking as they go encouraging words to all, and threatening nurses and attendants with dismissal if they neglect their duty" (*CR* 26 N).

The 98th also needed provisions. Dried fruit and butter were first collected at the house of Mrs. Dr. McBean. Meanwhile, Capt. John Norris asked for clothing for each man of his company — a woolen undershirt, two pairs of woolen socks, and mittens, the "mitts" to have one finger, for the trigger finger (*CDS* 19 N). By November's end, women of the town and vicinity organized themselves into a Soldier's Aid Society, to raise items for sick and disabled soldiers. They met in the grand-jury room of the courthouse on Thursdays from nine in the morning until ten at night. They collected woolen shirts, drawers, and socks, and canned and dried fruits; in December they sent three boxes of fruit to Dr. Sharp in Columbia, Ky., and then began filling boxes to send to the wounded of the Battle of Fredericksburg. The secretary of this Soldiers', or Ladies Aid Society was Martha B. O. Thomas, wife of the wealthy banker (*CR* 26 N, 10 D, 24 D).

A letter from Capt. Butts at Columbia noted that his health had been very poor for two months, but was improving a little. "War is destructive in every sense of the word. Though there is far too much immorality in our regiment, yet compared with some others which have been no longer in the service the 98th is saintly. It is only a child in profanity and vice; but a disregard of God's law is too general in the army....The lamented Col. Webster in all his deportment was eminently moral and exemplary. Of Col. Poorman I need only say that so far as his authority and influence extend, they are good. We are learning to love him, and no man in the army takes better care of his men. He is a model soldier."

In the battle at Perryville, "Not one of my Company run, no not one. Lieuts. Lacey and McCullough manifested the greatest bravery and did their duty nobly and well. We were under fire about five hours, and were closely engaged one and one-half to two hours, during which time we were exposed to murderous fire. The balls flew like hail. The boom of artillery — the rattle of musketry — the bursting of shell, and the whistling bullets commingled with the shrieks of the wounded, and the moans of the dying"; yet they had but one thought, except of home and heaven, Butts wrote, "to defeat the enemy." The former Methodist preacher testified to his own unnatural, or supernatural, first experience of battle: "For myself I may say that I never enjoyed more of God's presence than on that field."

Butts proceeded to the financial plight of his men, many of whom had not received the promised $25 bounty from their township and support for their families. Franklin township in particular had defaulted. (Cadiz and Greene townships had begun paying, from pledges, $14 a month to the wife of a volunteer, plus $1 for each child under 14 [*CR* 10 D]). Some men at home, according to Butts, had pledged but then refused to pay. "I now notify such whining sycophants and canting hypocrites, that until their honor is redeemed, I shall have no faith in their professions of manhood, patriotism or religion." And "when we return home those who have refused to pay the pittances they subscribed need look for no favors at the hands of these volunteers."

"The President's proclamation meets with near universal favor with the army because they want to suppress the rebellion. Southern men can leave their plantations and farms in the hands of slaves to fight for rebellion, and the money from their farm crops goes to rebellion" (*CR* 17 D).

Letters from area soldiers became important — and controversial — social and political documents in the crucial debate over the Emancipation Proclamation. Two letters published in the *CR* on 26 November, from "I. R. J." of the

43rd Ohio exemplify this. One can attribute many of the subsequent condemnations of army morality and veracity, which rose locally after these letters appeared, to the threat such testimony posed to popular assumptions that slavery was a benign institution. Written from near Corinth, Miss., on 8 Nov., I. R. J.'s letters addressed the stereotypes of slavery and fears of emancipation held by people he knew at home. He finally, specifically and dramatically, skewered the basic racial rationale for slavery.

No I. R. J. appears on the 43rd O.V.I. roster; the initials are most likely a misreading of Samuel R. Johnson's of Co. C, first led by Moses Urquhart, at this time under Capt. Sanford Timmons; or Townsend R. Jones's of Co. B.

The soldiers favored the Proclamation, he wrote; many who a year prior had been "conservative" now even advocated arming blacks and fomenting insurrection; the fortifications that saved them in the last battles were built by negroes; and another battle seemed near. Every regiment also had hired negro cooks, paying $10 to $18 a month. They came voluntarily within the lines. "With regard to the contrabands, so far as I can learn, they are waiting, like Micawber, for 'something to turn up' in order that they may leave the plantations and attach themselves to the army. I believe if our army were to pass through the South and leave the negroes to themselves the President's Proclamation would hardly be necessary — nine-tenths of all the slaves would take refuge with the army. Negroes know more about what is going on than is commonly believed. I talked to one not long since who had traveled from the interior of Mississippi. I asked him how long he had waited for the approach of our army. He said more than a year. I asked him if the slaves of that vicinity expected to be free. He replied that if our army would go down there every slave would leave the plantations. Many would have come with him, but had not the courage to brave the perils of the journey, and run the risk of being caught and severely punished, or sent further south.

"We have slaves from Alabama, Mississippi, Tennessee, Kentucky, and Arkansas. All tell the same tale. The slaves are ripe for revolution — all they want is a leader. They are too ignorant, the circle of communication too narrow, for them to do much unaided, but, with the help of our army to set the revolution in motion, it would soon gather strength and increase in velocity until it would acquire a momentum that would be beyond the power of the Southern Confederacy to check. All this would be done with scarcely an effort on our part.

"A negro preaches at the contraband headquarters every Sabbath. Almost all the blacks attend regularly, and are orderly and attentive. Of course the preaching is not very elegant....The speaker will talk incessantly from 10 A.M till 2 P.M., and be listened to attentively during the four hours. One thing is certain — the negroes are very tractable, and under proper influence, would soon be capable of taking care of themselves. Many of them are really shrewd, with all their ignorance.

"The great hue and cry raised by doughfaces about the effect of turning the slaves loose upon the community is without reason. If the slaves are all as capable of taking care of themselves as those I have seen, they will get along anywhere.

"There are more white slaves in the South than is generally supposed. There are two slave boys in our regiment as white as I am — not a kink in their hair. Their mother is here also; she is almost white. The master is the father to one of the boys, the master's son father to the other, and yet this mother and her two sons were to be sold South when they made their escape to our army. They lived near Rienzi. How any reasonable man could uphold such a system is beyond my comprehension. I. R. J." (*CR* 26 N)

Thus "doughfaces" at home who had sent off soldiers simply to restore law and order were confronted with testimony that they had raised revolutionists. Among their political opposites, also, rose fears of their own army. The country's "public safety is imminently threatened" by our "use of a military power of proportions so gigantic that no nation ever permitted the existence of such without more or less risk to the people who employed it." This alarm sounded in the abolitionist Robert Dale Owen's letter to President Lincoln urging him to enact the Emancipation Proclamation swiftly, not only for human justice, but also because of increasing public opinion that the army should seize control of the government and remove all of Lincoln's cabinet who favored emancipation (*CR* 5 N). The growing fear of the army prodded Hatton to print, a month later, a column recounting the "vast" armies in ancient history and the Bible — a lame response to the threat posed by the millions presently in arms (*CR* 3 D).

There was more to Col. Christian Poorman's *Chronicle* letters than Hatton printed, and it fueled an attack which the Democratic presses of the area mounted against the army, becoming the barrage the *Sentinel* reprinted from the *Newark Advocate*. "The War and Its Effects on Morality in the Army" began, "To a very large extent, the mischief-making portion of the American clergy are responsible for the state of feeling which gave rise to the existing war. It is well, therefore, that these 'unworthy ambassadors of Christ' should have their attention called occasionally to the state of morals associated with the war which they have had so large a share in begetting. To this end, we give the following." What followed was a General Order from Virginia of 1 Nov. regarding the taking of private property by soldiers; it came from Poorman to the *Chronicle*, thence to the *Sentinel*, the *Advocate*, and back. Poorman was quoted: "It is astonishing how soon men forget all the moral lessons of their youth, and leave behind them the practice of honesty, when they are separated from home and in the army. *I fear more for the future of the country from the fearful increase of dishonesty engaged and cultivated in our own army, than I do from the success of the rebellion.* There are hundreds, yea thousands of men in the army who would have scorned the thought of doing a dishonest act, or taking what was not their own, who will appropriate to their own use the property of others, intrude upon the sanctity of private dwellings, destroy what they cannot use, and insult or abuse anyone who will remonstrate or attempt to interfere." Such was the fate of morals in the army, the *Advocate* commented, as pictured by a *Republican Editor* commanding a regiment; so, "the parents of the country can see what a school of crime and sin their sons have been called to enter because the Republican preachers and politicians refused to allow the Union to be saved by a peaceful adjustment of the country's troubles" (*CDS* 3 D).

From the beginning of December, the *Sentinel* filled with outright attacks on Republicans for starting the war and the administration for pursuing it, with the results of 300,000 men killed, 5 thousand millions of property destroyed, freedom of speech abolished, writ of Habeas Corpus suspended, public debt of over 2,000,000,000, Negroes "fattened" at an expense of $100 million per year. A reprinted ballad called for "Poor old Father Abraham" to resign (3 D). Lincoln's Message to Congress, with his proposals of gradual emancipation extending to the year 1900, compensation to loyal slaveholders, colonization of emancipated slaves in Africa, but permanent freedom for all slaves given liberty by the chances of war, only further exacerbated Democratic dudgeon. Allen pronounced the Message proof that this was a party war, which he now denounced: "When the war was first inaugurated, we were laboring under the impression that the Administration was only making it a war for the restoration of the Union and the preservation of the Constitution. With that understanding we gave our influence and our means towards assisting the Administration in its prosecution...." Lincoln's only objects now appeared the freeing of all negroes and obtaining fat contracts for his par-

tisans. Allen took his stand: "For our part we shall have nothing to do with sustaining an Administration" with such aims; "we are done with either talking for or sustaining such an Administration in its present outrageous prosecution of the war. That's all" (*CDS* 10 D).

The Democrats began circulating a new petition, urging the men of every township to sign it, for a law to prevent immigration and settlement of blacks into Ohio: "Let all who are opposed to Ohio becoming flooded with negroes be active in this matter..." (*CDS* 10 D). At the same time, the Democrats took to a curious denial that slavery had anything to do with the war at hand. Allen reprinted a gem of their logic in an attack on the administration and "The Abolition Pulpit Slang-whangers" with this rebuttal from the *Cincinnati Enquirer*: "If slavery is the cause of the war, so is property the cause of theft" (*CDS* 17 D).

Allen's diatribes broke into racist virulence. The *Cadiz Republican*, following Cady's verse burlesque of Bingham, had printed a long one of "Joseph W. White's Congratulations to this Friends," by "Tobay True," including these lines:

And although the land to its center was
    shaken,
Every Democrat would save his bacon
And nary a copperhead'ld venture to go
To embrace in death the cowardly foe.
For when they'd hear the rattle of bullets
Away they'd run like long-legged pullets.
So they were exceedingly wise you see,
When they staid at home and voted for
    me [*CR* 3 D].

In reply, Allen charged that Hatton "saw that he must do something to match Cady's poetry. For this purpose, he gets a nigger, who signs herself 'Topay,' to write a political effusion....It is about such a piece of poetry as a nigger, whether white or black would write," "nigger slang poetry" for Hatton's "nigger paper" (*CDS* 10 D). The female labeling of the versifier suggests that she was Malinda Warfel.

John A. Bingham had returned to Washington for his lame-duck session, and prominently spoken for admission of the "so-called State of West Virginia," which both House and Senate subsequently approved. It was another unconstitutional revolution, Allen charged; the legislature of Virginia had not consented, and the body meeting in Wheeling did not represent its state; so the Congress continued to dissolve the Union. Allen soon added to his rant that the new state "that Bingham was so anxious for its admission into the Union, and thus divide States without their consent, is composed principally of stupendous rocks and barren mountains. Yet that God-forsaken place will be entitled to just as many votes" in the Senate as Ohio (*CDS* 17 D, 24 D).

The Teachers' Scientific Circle met in Cadiz and amended their constitution to admit all ladies who attended to full membership, and also to exempt them from any expenses. They voted to accept proposals to exhibit the "blunders" of Ray's arithmetic textbook and Town's definitions in his *Spelling and Grammar*, and to consider "Should punctuation be taught as an art, or as depending upon elocutionary principles?" "Why was the line dividing the hemisphere placed 20 degrees west of Greenwich?" "How may the approximate weight of livestock be determined by their dimensions?" and "Should the teacher understand and instruct pupils in civil government?" On the last matter, they agreed on the need for correct principles and then discussed practical methods. Tangent argued for "agitation" of the issue: "Agitation could work wonders" and had "abolitionized" the formerly abolition-hating people of the North; textbooks on *this* subject were needed (*CDS* 3 D).

On Saturday night 6 Dec., the Scientifics ventured out to observe a total eclipse of the moon. They recorded and reported the exact minutes from midnight until four that they studied the passage of darkness through the heavens (*CDS* 10 D).

Meanwhile, a horrendous event in Cadiz challenged social trust in a fundamental custom of family and economic life. The following condensation of the *Cadiz Republican's* report retains some of its choked syntax: **Another Horrible Tragedy! Two Young Girls Brutally Murdered.** The atrocious deed, perpetrated without the slightest cause, is allied with feeling such a shuddering sense of the brutality of man, and chills the blood as it courses through the veins to even think of so horrible an affair. Our village was thrown into an excitement probably never committed before, that unauthorized violence coupled with one of the most cold blooded murders had been committed that was ever recorded in the annals of crime.

Early Friday morning, Mr. T. J. Kirk, living a few rods east of town, took his wife and two small boys to visit friends, leaving daughters Alice and Amy, 15 and 11 years, and Miss Naomi Knight, an adopted child of 18 years, together with a hired man of 22 years, Henry Riquartz, who appeared a very trusty, quiet young man. But how grating to the sensibilities when innocent children become victims of misplaced confidence!

Alice went to the dentist and returned in the afternoon. The plates on the table showed the three had been to dinner, but no one seemed about. She called and looked in the barn for them before Riquartz came from a chamber room and answered he knew nothing of the girls. Near night, Alice was going to search for the girls, when Riquartz said he had seen them coming, so she should prepare supper. She put on her bonnet to go and meet them. Riquartz seized her by the throat and strangled her unconscious. When conscious, she found her hands tied together behind her back and her feet bound. The villain remarked he did not desire to murder her, but only to place her so she could not alarm neighbors until he killed himself, and that the other girls would never come back, and he bid her goodbye and left the house.

Soon after, a neighbor woman came to Kirk's on an errand. She discovered Alice and freed her. The two went to the village to alarm people. About 5:30, people arrived and found Riquartz suspended in the barn, having hanged himself. About 7:00 the girls were found dead in the granary, the villain apparently having accomplished his hellish purposes and then brutally strangled the innocent girls. Leather cords were tightly drawn around their necks, their faces swollen, eyes protruding from the sockets. Probably only *he* ate from the three plates *after* killing them (*CDS* 3 D).

The shock of this crime doubtless ended the customary trusting welcome of a poor youth, even a stranger, into the home as a hired man, a welcome that had granted him a place in the family and a start in society.

Chapter 14

Christmas and
New Year's Greetings

As Christmas approached, Ferguson's Confectionary advertised common and fancy candies on hand, almonds, filberts, Cream and Pea nuts, figs, dates, French currants, Western Reserve and English cheeses, cinnamon, ginger, allspice, cigars, snuff, pickles, pepper sauce, visiting cards and envelopes, watch chains, and toys "of all descriptions" (*CDS* 26 N). As the day neared, Ferguson added oysters to his stock; John Beall's Book and Drug Store had presents ready; and Barrett and Quest offered jewelry from an elegant gold watch down to a dime breast-pin (*CDS*, *CR* 24 D). But the dreads of the war framed anticipations; a little girl reflected, "Everyone must die except God and Santa Claus" (*CR* 26 N).

The first reports from Fredericksburg, Va., depicted a successful attack on Lee's army; gradually the news came of the "terrible disaster" in which "we were butchered" in charges at the stone wall. The effects of war reached Ohio as every train through Columbus came "freight-ed with coffins containing the bodies of dead soldiers being brought home to their friends.—As many as sixteen coffins are on one train. The tears of mothers, widows, sisters and orphans are watering the whole North, and the blood of their fathers, husbands, sons and brothers are making red the land of the South—all as appears to give freedom to the negro, and gratify abolitionism" (*CDS* 24 D).

The holidays nonetheless brought pleasures. The frosted snow invited sledriding down the hills, and careening through the winding lanes on horse-drawn sleighs. On Christmas Eve at a "grand festival" of the Cadiz Presbyterian Sunday School the children and choir sang "Joy to the World," "The Sunday School Army," and other hymns; after prayer and an address, they distributed gifts from "the Christmas Tree" (*CDS* 24 D).

The *Sentinel* provided a disquisition into Genesis which was sure to enliven some family gatherings: "A Difficult

Question Answered. Can anybody tell why, when Eve was manufactured from one of Adam's ribs, a hired girl was not made to wait on her? We can, easy!" The answer amusingly reflected life in homes and villages, including the men's political preoccupation: "Because Adam never came whining to Eve with a ragged stocking to be darned, a collar string to be sewed, or a glove to be mended, 'right away, quick now!' Because he never read the newspapers until the sun had got down behind the palm trees and stretching himself, yawned out, 'Ain't supper most ready, my dear?'

"Not he. He made the fire, and hung on the kettle himself, we'll venture, and pulled the radishes, and peeled the onions, and did everything else that he ought to do! He fed the chickens, and milked the cows, and looked after the pigs himself. He never brought half a dozen friends to dinner when Eve hadn't any pomegranates.... He never stayed out till 11 o'clock to a war meeting hurrahing for the out candidate, and then scold because poor Eve was crying inside the gates.... He never played billiards, or drove fast horses, or choked Eve with cigar smoke. He never loafed around the groceries while solitary Eve was rocking little Cain's cradle at home. — In short he did not think she was especially created for the purpose of waiting on him, and wasn't under the impression that it disgraced a man to lighten his wife's cares a little.

"That's the reason that Eve did not need a hired girl, and we wish it was the reason none of her descendants did!" (24 D).

Withal Allen's politicking and brashness, at home he no doubt shared his wife's cares. He and Elizabeth had an infant daughter, Virginia, after their one other child, Teresa, had died in 1857, aged five.

This Christmas, the presents many families anxiously awaited were their soldiers' letters. The 98th had been struck by an epidemic of measles — a disease more dangerous for adults, more often bringing convulsions, pneumonia, or inflammation of the brain. The men lying in the cold along Big Russell Creek near Columbia, Ky., lacked any of the care their homes would have given them. Robert Mitchell fell so ill that he desperately wanted his father to come to him, and could not write. He begged Thompson Gray, who was sick himself, to write Rudolf urging him to rush to Kentucky. Rudolf, though, was disabled by the running sore on his hand; on 17 December Nancy penned the family's reply to Thompson with their regret and worry for Robert. Thus the letter that came on Christmas Eve was welcome: "Dear Sister ... i am well at present. Bill McBride is with us now. Gray is able to go about again. his speach is com back to him again. he came down from town to day. we have had nice weather for a week but is a going to snow i gues today. i have not been well for a weeke or 2 but am well again. hour Company is a recruting up some. i hurd that Roberson Christy is a going to get maried. i reckon he will bugey ride some then and get vinegar to drink. [The bridegroom would be abducted by his friends, displayed to the neighborhood in a wheelbarrow or child's buggy, and forced to drink vinegar, in this shivaree.]

"we have got winter quarters up. we split out slab of poplar and set one end in the ground and put hour tent over it and got some stone and built Chimey. it minds me of home. we think that we will be home again the first of May. John Miller is sick but not bad. There 12 in our house now since McBride came. we get fresh beef to eate potatoes and beans and rice and cofee. yo ma send me as many boxes as yo please. i can eate them. we have a great time a talking about home at nights. i reckon Hugh has to work since paps hand got sore. hour cap [Norris] got back on last friday. he gave me them postage last night. Ase Glasoner came to. he has to walk the mark now.

"we have had no drill since came to this camp. when we first cam we was handy to town. we have moved back further in to a woods. wel i guess i told yo all the news. nothing more at preasant but i want yo to write oftener so write soon. Robert Mitchell tel ever body to wrte to me"

Some of the sick in Robert's regiment had left. Sgt. Hugh Russell of his company, and Lts. Lacey and McCullough of Butts's came home in bad health. Corp. Wm. Pittenger was back in Cadiz, explaining that he had been afflicted with rheumatism during his tour in Kentucky, and was home to recover (*CR* 12-24, 12-17). He may have taken this retreat without leave, since subsequently his rank was reduced to that of private.

It might be "interesting if not consoling" to the absent-without-leave, Col. Poorman advised, that at the bi-monthly muster for pay on 31 Dec. they would be marked "deserters" and their pay stopped.

Christmas Day, Poorman reported, brought pleasant weather and many boxes of treats for the 98th from friends at home (*CR* 14 Ja 1863). Other regiments in the area were not so fortunate. On Christmas Eve, Morgan and his cavalry seized a huge Union sutler wagon bearing Christmas boxes, and paused in their current raid for a party. The next day Morgan moved north, to destroy the railroad which supplied the Federal forces and depot at Nashville. On Christmas Day, regiments such as the 98th began moving to chase or block Morgan (Brewer 133, 139). By 29 Dec., the 98th had moved to Campbellsville, but sent its sick back to Lebanon; these included Robert and Thompson (*CR* 14 Ja). Morgan continued his raid until 5 Jan., burning railroad trestles, capturing Federal troops, threatening Lebanon, while eight Union regiments and a cavalry pursued him (Brewer 174).

In another Christmas letter, Nancy found unfamiliar greenery. From F. P. Grove, North Mountain, Va., 15 Dec.: "Dear Nancy, Owing to our recent movement I have neglected answering your letter.... [We have] our tents pitched in the woods at the foot of North Mountain & close to north mountain station on the railroad. This is the place whare Jackson crossed with his army when he made the raid into Maryland & Pennsylvania about the time of the Antietam fight in September last. this is about 25 miles this side of Harpers ferry. The railroad track was all toren up along here on down to Harpers ferry. The ties piled up & burned & the railes heated and bent. The road is repaired this far and the hands are still at work. They don't even stop on sabbath. Sabbath morning the hands ware driven in by the Rebles. They ware sent out again & one company of our Regt. sent along to guard them. Thare was about 500 Rebel cavalry at Martynsburgh about 7 miles from here day before yesterday. Thare was six companies of cavilry some artillary & part of our Regt. went down thare today to rout them. it is said thare is some Rebel Infantry about 8 miles from here. Thare are two Regiments of Infantry here. One Battery of artillary and 8 or 10 Companies of Cavilry & we are expecting more today.

"I like this plaice verry well only water is verry scarce & bad. we can hardly git a drink & they have to take the horses about 2 miles to water. This is a fine looking country east of us on till the blue ridge which we can see from here. The valley of Verginia lies before us with the Potomac river running through it about 2 miles from here. Calvin Haverfield & I took a stroll today up to the Summit of North mountain. it is verry steep & rocky some places we had to git down on our hands & knees and crawl up. when we got up thare we could see all oaver the country & I don't know but allmost to Richmond. I plucked some pine and a laurel leaf off the top of the mountain which I intend to send to you.

"The boys are all well & in good spirits. I like soldiering verry well, but still if the war was oaver I would verry willingly go home, and the firs place I would go after I got home would be to your house. This is beatifull weather it puts me in mind of last fall when the sawmill was at your house. *Oh* the pleasant times we had then. I went down to see the sawmill but I had another object in view. If you had not been thare I would not have cared so much about the sawmill. I see round your house in my imagination every day. *my heart is thare.* I hope my imaginations will be realised but it is uncertain for I don't know what day I may have to face the enemy.

"…Lieut. Hammond has resigned and gone home. I suppose he thought he was gitting a little too close to the enemy….

"Oh I must tell you I heard a secesh letter read, that a young Lady wrote to her beau in the army. it was picked up in Camp after a battle. I never heard such a letter in my life. I did not think any girl would write the like to a Gent. [Frank was unconversant with the florid language in the French romances read by chaperoned Southern young ladies, and used innocently by them.] But you need not be affraid of anyone gitting your letters for I sent what old letters I had home in a box that I sent with orders for them to be put in my trunk. Those that I git after this I intend to destroy the name so that if any one gits them they won't know who they are from. you need not think strange if you do not git letters so regular after this for I expect we will move often…. But be shure and write…. Your true Friend, Frank"

Nancy replied to Frank on 27 Dec.: "My beloved Friend … Nothing to me is more delightful in this world than a *true friend* that is wise and good, that kindly receives & returns my affection. Nothing would be more distressing to me than the loss of such a friend

'Oh dark indeed would be this world
Did we not sometimes find
The best of all Earth's fairy gifts
A true and kindred mind.
And though we only meet to part

Yet pleasant thoughts remain
To cheer our onward path when time
Has strewn that path with pain'

"Since I wrote to you last we have had some very cold weather. Last week it snowed considerable & was quite cold….

"The Methodists at Dickerson Church are having a revival. It commenced this day one week ago. how long it will continue I do not know but likely for another week. And by the way I must tell you that I was there last night. I expect I would not have been there if Hugh & Jennie had not coaxed me to go with them. However I think I am none the worse for going. Next in order will be to tell you who went to the 'mourners bench'—Caroline McBride (I suppose you know her?) Sarah A Johnson Lucinda Dickerson Mary McCoy and a Mr. Ennis were the ones that were at the bench last night. I heard someone say that they had been there for 3 or 4 nights previous and I think they went away from it last night unconverted. But I suppose they will persevere until they get converted.

"Our school was out Wend. last but will commence on Monday again. I wish our vacation was longer for I do not like to go very well. I doubt not but I would like to go well enough if it was not for the War and my friends that are engaged in this bloody struggle. I feel so disappointed about Burnside being repulsed at Fredericksburg, for I thought from what I heard that the victory would be ours. But ah! no! from what I can learn our loss was 15000 and likely greater. It seems so hard that so many noble lives must be ushered into Eternity and noth-ing gained. But someone has said 'the darkest shadows of the night are just before the morning,' and I fondly hope that these dark days in our countrys history are but the prelude of brighter ones.

"How sad to know that we have so many traitors in the North. Abram Holmes [of the 52nd, captured and paroled] told Mr. McFarland the other day 'that nothing but his gray hairs saved his life' and also that the President and his Cabinet were traitors. He and Taylor [Capt. James Taylor Holmes, also captured] have been exchanged and will have to leave in a few days for to join their Regt which is now at Nashville Tenn.

"I heard that Mr. McFarland was going to report him to his Colonel and likely he will give him a *Dishonorable Discharge*. I hope he will for a man as he (Holmes) ought to be treated as a 'Rebel.' Yes worse than a Rebel. [Abram in fact was promoted to Lieutenant.]

"Oh! Frank a Gent told me the other day that you and Maggie Braden have a notion to hitch together when the war is over (I suppose he ment get married). as boys are scarce I had better not tell his name. Oh! yes Ellen Mitchell told me to ask you if you would like to have a *pull*. she said if you did just come for she was ready any time. Nan and Mat are going to teach school in Londonderry this winter. Nan wrote Mat said she did not like to go. The reason is I reckon that her heart is here. As for Nan I guess she would as leave be there….

"Will Oglevee has been sick for two weeks and does not appear to mend any. The doctor says his Liver and Stomache are out of order. I think he has not been well since he went with Mat. I expect she squeezed him so hard that she mashed his Liver and Stomache together....

"Your Brother Will arrived on Christmas day. he had a bad cold but is getting better.... I remain Your true friend, Nannie"

Christmas for Capt. McCready was a day of reflections, some of which he wrote from Martinsburg, Virginia, to the people at home, via the *Cadiz Republican*: "a most beautiful Christmas morning as I ever saw I think. No frost of any consequence & day soft & balmy as a Mayday. Indeed, we have had no winter yet.

"But as I sit down to write, the thought rises, and not without a tinge of sadness I confess, how changed our circumstances are since last Christmas. Then we ate our Christmas dinners at home with our good wives and mothers and fathers and sisters and brothers and chatted with them at our own firesides. How gladly we would take the chat today without the dinner! But ... We are away down here in a strange land, strangers and pilgrims sojourning in tabernacles *like* if not *with* Abraham, Isaac and Jacob, with sentinels pacing around us with slow and solemn tread.

"And God only knows what changes another Christmas will bring.... But 'Heaven from all creatures hides the book of fate' [Pope]. And far be it from me to lift the veil that hides the future if I could. 'Sufficient unto the day is the evil thereof,' especially when it is said 'as thy day so shall thy strength be,' and 'I will never leave thee, no I will never forsake thee.' There is more of consolation in these words of God to those who take them to heart than there would be in a knowledge of the future could we obtain it. That would not suit us.— Some things

which are to befal us would cause us more pain in the prospect than they will in realization. It is kind in God to hide the future that we may enjoy the present. Hence, God never gave the greatest inspired Prophet a minute insight into his own future as relates to the present life. But because another Christmas will bring great changes — because ere that some of us may be some sleeping the sleep that knows no waking on dreary battlefield or in the cemetery of some Hospital, or may have to pass through scenes which will blanch the hardest cheek and appal the stoutest heart, shall we sit down in despondency and cry about it? ... 'Take no thought for the morrow for the morrow will take thought for the things of itself.'

"What a day Christmas used to be in our boyish days! How long it seemed to be coming? The week or two before it seemed so long. Visions of roast beef and Turkey, and pudding and crulls & all manner of curious things rose up in my imagination.— Work was laid aside. It was too bad to have to chop a stick of wood. Long before day all was astir. A big wood fire soon filled the house with light and heat. And as one after another gathered around it merry voices rang out 'my christmas box,' 'my christmas gift.' By and by breakfast came. But the great effort was reserved for dinner. Our good mother [who had died in 1851, while he was a student at Franklin College] donned her best cap, put on another dress and a clean white apron and looked so kind and pretty. Our brothers and sisters looked glad and laughed and jumped and hopped about, cutting up all manner of antics. Father seemed to think there was a good deal of nonsense about the whole thing, but yielded so far as to get out the razor and shave, and condescended to crack a joke occasionally with the children as if he'd kind of half become a child himself again. The best of the larder was on the table that day, though may be not a soul present but ourselves. That was the mystery. How we wondered that Mother went to so much trouble for us children. At night the big Bible was brought out, an appropriate psalm was sung and chapter read, God was thanked so earnestly for letting us live to another Christmas, and for giving us such a happy day, and we were all fervently commended to His kind care for another year. Thus came and went our Christmas 'long, long ago.' That was the Christmas *that was Christmas.*

"Well, may our dear friends enjoy a happy Christmas at home today, and think of us not forgetting us, especially in the closing exercise of prayer and thanksgiving at their evening altars!— And may God so order that we shall spend our next Christmas at our homes with those we love!

"…We have now entered the celebrated valley of the Shenandoah. On the North lies the range called North Mountain. On the east about twenty miles, and over the blue mountains of Md, lies the bloody field of 'Antietam,' and a little farther on, 'South Mountain.' On the South Harpersferry. Down this beautiful valley Banks retreated; across it the rebel forces marched in great numbers to Antietam….

"On every hand we come across Jackson's old camps. He seems to have had his seat here. Like another old gentleman we read about [the devil in Job

1:6-7], he seems to delight in walking to and fro and going up and down in this valley. Nor is this strange when we reflect that the valley is very beautiful and romantic, and that further, here he is in the house of his friends.

"I have already said this is a very productive Valley. The soil is limestone, and those rocks are so abundant as to be quite sufficient to fence it, I should judge. Indeed, there are miles of the finest stone fences here that I ever saw; owing no doubt to the scarcity of timber as well as the abundance of stone. The timber found in the valley and on the mountain sides is more like timber of Ohio than any we have seen on this side of the Ohio river. The only peculiarity about it is, that the forest, no matter what other trees they contain, are sprinkled with the inevitable pine. The only home tree I miss is the beautiful sugar [maple] tree. I don't know when I have seen a sugar tree.— The Shenandoah Valley at this point is about 12 miles wide, and level, but somewhat rolling like the prairies of the West are said to be. Its length I have no means of knowing. There is one peculiarity about it — that is its fixed rocks. The stranger will soon observe that almost everywhere great chains or fences of limestone rock, of God's making, consisting of rocks rising up edgewise apparently, and so ragged or jagged as to make you wonder what would become of you if you should be thrown from a horse or in some way fell upon them. Those chains much resembling a stone fence at a little distance are often from six to ten feet high, ordinarily from two to four, and from four to eight feet through, and what is most singular run almost perfectly straight from North to South, and to the distance of forty rods, or a mile often. Often these chains are so close together that a small field will contain three or four of them running across it, and the ground is cultivated between them, some fields contain none of them, and some are entirely marred with them — rising above the ground like the back-bone of as many huge sea monsters. The inhabitants of the valley seem to have been generally wealthy, and slaveholders prior to the rebellion, and are therefore, generally secessionists.

"The Union people here have been hardly [severely] dealt with by the rebels — their farms have been desolated, and themselves forced to flee or join the rebel army. — Indeed you can tell a rebel or loyal farm as you travel along the road. If you see the barn-yard full of fowls, and the stock yard full of stock, and the fields abounding with cattle and horses, you may set that farmer down for a rebel. And after all the lying [lies] about the depredations of Union soldiers, if you find a farm waste and desolate, you may conclude it is a Union man's. This valley is full of grain. Yes, while we are living on hard bread and three year old pickled 'flitch,'…here are thousands of bushels of wheat in the stack yards of Rebels which we are protecting for Jackson. And with all the strategy of our wiseacres he will have it yet before spring.

"How strange a thing this rebellion is! It was not waged against oppression nor in behalf of any species of liberty. It was the rising of a people against their own Government, and one too which they had administered. It was born in injustice, has been nourished by falsehood, and is sustained by a baseless currency. But the rebels have faith in it. And what is currency any how? Among savages, chips and beads and pebbles are money.

"When here, Jackson's men had plenty of money, and scattered it with a lavish hand…. We may laugh at the idea of a currency without a basis; but their finances have not given way under it. We may deride their naked and barefooted Regiments but they have astonished Europe with the terror of their arms. Besides all stories of bare feet and starvation are three-fourths lies….

"There seems to be more loyalty in the city of Martinsburgh than in any other town we have come to, though it is in this rebel valley. It was cheering to us, who had not been greeted with a smile, hardly, since we left our own Ohio, to receive so many congratulations. — The doors and porticoes were full, on each side of the streets, of persons who really looked pleased that we had come. Occasionally, it is true, we came to a house with the doors shut and all dark looking, except at some obscure window where you would see a little corner of the blind pulled back and owlish eyes peering…. 'Hurrah for the Union soldiers!' shouted crowds of little boys from every corner, while ladies, old and young, and men and boys waved us welcome as we passed. The old 'Star Spangled banner' waved from one upper window. You ought to have heard the shout that rent the air as each company came in sight of it. What strange creatures we are! How the sight of that old flag sacred to the honor of our country, or the sound of 'the Star Spangled Banner,' under such circumstances, thrills our whole being! In the cemetery here, lie a score or more of Union soldiers and at their feet as many rebels. The rebel graves lie rough and neglected just as they were left by those who buried them. On the other hand, the Union graves have been filled up and smoothed and moss planted over them by Union ladies. From these circumstances, I infer that there is more Union sentiment here than we have found in any similar town before.

"I cannot account for this ... Unionism except from the fact that the people seem to be generally poor. But few hold slaves and they have seen all their public buildings — their pride — laid in the dust by rebel hands. The destruction of the rail road and rail road buildings is complete. They were destroyed by Jackson's command. He was present in person to see that it was thoroughly done. A Union man told me it was but the work of a few hours. They ran to it with rails, poles and crowbars, turned the whole track up-side down, piled up the ties and laid the rails over them and set them on fire. Of course the rails as they were heated bent to the ground with their own weight....

"Yesterday I had the pleasure of visiting for the first time some rebel prisoners. About 25 were brought in, from Western Virginia. They are well clad. Their uniforms, though coarse, are superior, for warmth and service to ours. They are greatly superior in color to our dark blue cloths. Everybody who has hunted squirrels knows that if there is a black squirrel in the woods you will see it, while a grey one, by being so much like the trees and leaves in color escapes from notice. God has made many animals grey for protection purposes — as

the squirrel, rabbit, coon, deer, partridge, pheasant, &c — If I mistake not the color of their uniforms in the fog and smoke of battle render them a far less conspicuous mark than we are. Battles, therefore, other things being equal will be attended with greater loss of life on our part than on theirs. Some of them seemed quite intelligent men.

"Of course the great subject came up and we talked freely and kindly. I asked them what they were fighting for. They said because we were taking their slaves from them. I told them this was a consequence of the war, not the cause of it, for we had not meddled with their slaves till they had fired on the flag at Sumpter. They admitted it.

"They asked me what we were fighting for? I told them for the preservation of our government and, for aught I knew, our liberties and all we hold dear. For if the principle of State sovereignty were once admitted, it would rend in pieces all governments, even the confederacy itself. They admitted it would. I said slavery was the cause of the war. They said it was. — I told them I was in favor of its destruction for that reason. Well, they said, we could not whip them. They said we had good fighters and so had they, and we could not whip them nor could they whip us. They wished we had peace — said that we would have peace by the first of March. I told him if so it would be by whipping of the southern Confederacy and that I would not be surprised if we would not have peace till march a year on any other conditions than the submission of the south. He said that there would be peace as soon as Mr. Lincoln's Administration ended — that the results of the late elections had shown that. I ask democrats to think of this — that they are giving life and hope to the rebels who are killing their sons.

"I told him he misread those elections. That there were two parties in the north. One who thought the government was to be preserved by war, the other that it was to be preserved by compromise — but both agreeing that the Government must and shall be preserved. The Democrats thought the war might have been prevented and could be ended by compromise and the Government preserved. In this they were and are mistaken, for an indispensable condition of peace with Jeff. Davis must be the recognition of Southern Independence. That the Democrats when they found this out would prefer war to the last. I hope I did not misrepresent them. J. S. McCready" (*CR* 14 Ja 1863).

On New Year's Day, McCready composed his private thoughts in his diary. His four months in the army seemed "'months of mercy to me. During that time I have been fit for duty, except about two weeks. My wife, in the providence of God, was permitted to visit me and remain almost a month. Our fare has been good and our marches easy. My sick brother has gone home. In a religious point of view, my lot has not been quite so pleasant. Still I have been preserved from bringing disgrace upon the cause of God by any irregularity in my walk, and I hope I enjoy the favor of my God. Imperfect as I am, I greatly desire to say: "Above all things thy face, Lord, seek, will I." And now I would desire, above all things, God's blessing upon myself, and wife, and friends....

"'I, therefore, J. S. McCready, on this first of January, 1863, in the presence of God and his holy angels, in this my tent, alone, so far as this world is concerned, do again, as I have often done before, give myself, my wife, and all I have to God, and do this day avouch the Lord to be my God in Christ. And I solemnly swear with uplifted hand to be on the Lord's side, his Spirit assisting me, to be faithful to his cause, to live in his fear, and to make him my reliance in those dangers and trials of which I have reason to expect this year to be fruitful. So help me God, Father, Son, and Spirit, to keep this bond for Christ's sake, whereunto I do this day affix my hand and seal. J. S. McCready'" (Wishart 228-9).

In Cadiz, New Year's greetings appeared in the newspapers' traditional Carriers' Addresses, long verses summarizing the year, composed by the "printers' devils," apprentices who delivered papers and expected a tip on this occasion. The *Sentinel*'s included lines on Antietam:

Amid the fierce combattant's yell,
GEORGE and DUFFIELD foremost fell,
And with no home friends standing
  'round,
Their blood oozed out on the ground.

It satirized Republicans of the nation, state, and district:

We snatched the laurel from
  Bingham's brow
And a *White* man represents us now;

and complimented the local scene and citizens:

We have parsons and squires to join us
  together,

And doctors to dose us when under the
    weather,
We've tailors to clothe us, and lawyers to
    cheat,
And Ferguson always has something to
    eat;
We've mechanics and tradesmen and
    horse jockeys, too,
And gravediggers to bury us when we
    drop through.
The ladies, God bless 'em, last but not
    least
Upon your sweet smiles I hope soon to
    feast,
And when I'm increased in good looks
    and strength,

With an overcoat tail of *orthodox* length;
When my head is farther removed from
    the ground,
You may expect the devil to be "shinin'
    around."

    It closed with an appeal for a quarter tip and a thank-you:

May a fat Turkey grace your holiday
    revel,
Is the kind wish of GEORGE
    HOWARD, the DEVIL.

Chapter 15

"War Is a Lottery"*

After Christmas, the Cadiz Guards and two other companies from the county marched out of Nashville with Rosecrans' army, and thirty miles southeast through rain and mud to Stones River outside Murfreesboro, where Bragg's army lay. They met the enemy's cannonfire on 30 December. As dawn crept into the fog on New Year's Eve, the 13th with Col. Joseph G. Hawkins stood guard just west of the river, in the left wing of the army under Maj. Gen Thomas Crittenden, in the division commanded by Brig. Gen. Horatio P. Van Cleve, and brigade of Col. James Fyffe. Across the railroad and pike, Co. K of the 69th and Co. G of the 74th were among Maj. Gen. George H. Thomas' center force, in the division of Brig. Gen. James Negley. The 69th with Col. William B. Cassilly belonged to the brigade of Col. Timothy Stanley. The 74th with Col. Granville Moody were in the brigade of Col. John F. Miller. These men awaited orders to attack. Beyond them stretched the lines of Maj. Gen. Alexander McCook's right

wing, expecting merely to hold in place.

Before the fog lifted, Bragg launched charges designed to collapse Rosecran's army and cut if off from ammunition and retreat. He surprised McCook's right wing with rapid flank attacks of cavalry, artillery, and the infantries of Hardee and Polk. McCook's line began to fall back like a clockhand, while Gen. Sheridan's division tried to hold the right center of the Union position. Meanwhile, Bragg focused a frontal attack on the ammunition train on the pike, and also dashed one or two thousand cavalry upon McCook's supply train two and a half miles in his rear, which a brigade from Crittenden's left wing raced to defend, but was able to rescue only two wagons and some mules (*OR* Walker 1.20.1.441). Rosecrans' army was in peril; and it had to maneuver lines under fire on broken ground through stands of bushy cedars, which isolated commanders and units and brought threatening confusions.

The 13th returned from outpost duty at 8 A.M., and soon started off with

*"*War is a lottery in which every customer may expect to draw a sword*" (CR 28 Ja).

the brigade and battery to cross Stones River; shortly, they got orders to turn around and double-quick a mile, to the pike where rebel cavalry had captured a squadron of mounted guards and were hauling off the supply train, impeded only by the deep mud. Most of the brigade came up in line in a cornfield left of the pike (*OR* Fyffe 597), the 13th on its right end, across the pike. Union cavalry then charged at the enemy, and the battery found good position to fire on them, driving them off. The 13th moved forward, about 10 A.M., to the woods beyond the cornfield, which the rebels had left (*OR* Jarvis 603). At this time the division commander Van Cleve ordered the brigade to form in two lines on the right of the division, and to advance alongside the brigade of Col. Harker on their right (Fyffe). The 59th Ohio and 44th Indiana became the first line, with the 13th Ohio and 86th Indiana, to its right, the second. They moved down the slope right of the pike, on ground so uneven and dense in cedar the men could not see to keep their lines, across an open field, and into the next woods. The 13th, in the second line, twenty yards behind the first, lay down behind a fence edging the cedars (Jarvis).

During this advance, they passed Col. Harker's brigade, and Col. Fyffe observed that it did not move, while in front of him and outflanking him on the right, the enemy approached in great force. Fyffe tried to summon Harker with three messages, and rode to Van Cleve with his alarm; returning, he found his front line under attack and Harker's 65th Ohio arisen in the field on his right flank and firing; but summar-

ily the 65th marched back to Harker's line (Fyffe). Before Fyffe could get another regiment to aid him, his first line was overwhelmed and trampling over the prostrate second. As the 13th stood to fire with their Col. Hawkins' encouragement to stay cool and aim low, he was shot down; soon they were nearly surrounded (Jarvis).

They retreated to the crest of the cedar ridge, where the brigade resisted repeated charges, again endured flank attacks on both sides when regiments beside them withdrew, and finally drove the enemy down the slope and across the field, cheering as they charged (Fyffe). Here ended the day's fighting for the Cadiz Guards, and their cheer. One wrote in a private letter on 5 Jan., "Our regiment was in the hottest of the battle. Our company, when the battle commenced, numbered thirty-three in all. In the first day's fight Joseph Moody and B. F. Bell were killed, five wounded and thirteen missing, supposed to be captured, as we were driven back with great slaughter. Lieutenant Fox had his thigh bone broken, and has since died." Sergeant Frank Mealy had the severe wound of a broken ankle bone, Joseph Ferrell, one in the thigh; Edward Horner, through the shoulder; Owen T. Jenkins, in the leg; Augustus McElvaine, in the ankle. The writer noted that his haversack was shot off his shoulder, and concluded with this summary: "We lost our Colonel, greatly to our sorrow. Our regiment was driven into a slaughter pen in the first day's fight, through the miserable blunder of our division General, Van Cleave. He allowed the enemy to flank us, putting us between a galling cross-fire" (*CDS* 21 Ja).

The 69th and 74th regiments in Negley's division of Thomas' center force were similarly buffeted as McCook's men were swept off their right and then Sheridan's retreated, out of ammunition. By 11 A.M. Negley's cannon had fired all available shells, the batteries' horses were maimed, his regiments had but few of their sixty cartridges remaining, the enemy had fresh troops charging on three sides and others marching into the cedars behind his position, and he was cut off from his superiors and the ammunition train. His men had to charge in order to retreat (*OR* Negley 407-8).

Meanwhile, the 69th floundered. Besides Captain Hanna's Co. K in this regiment, a squad under Lt. Hoffman in Co. I were Harrison County sons. Their lines and movements faltered, and one described their day's embarrassment: "The men are much mortified at the conduct of their Colonel and Lieutenant Colonel during the thickest of the fight. The former was stupidly, beastly drunk, and the latter was absent as usual" (*CDS* 21 Ja). The brigade commander Col. Stanley had discovered Col. Cassilly's flagrant drunkenness early in the action, "ordered him to the rear in arrest, and placed Major Hickcox in command, who soon after was injured by the concussion of a shell, … and thus the regiment was left without a commander" — because the senior captain like the Lt. Col. was absent with a skirmisher detachment — until later Stanley put Captain Putnam in charge (*OR* Stanley 421). Lt. Col. Elliott returned only at 5 P.M.; he reported simply orderly advances and retreats, and "many killed and wounded" in this fight (*OR* 430); but none of Hanna's Harrison men were injured (*CDS* 21 Ja).

The thirty-eight of the regiment who were missing on 4 Jan., however, probably were captured on this day, when they were unable to fight effectively (*OR* Stanley 422-23).

The captain of Co. G. in the 74th had been the late Albion Bostwick; it was now commanded by Lt. T. L. McIlravy, who wrote to "Friend Allen" on 10 Jan.: "We remained still until the rebels drove back Gen. McCook on our right. Then heavy cannonading commenced all along the lines. The artillery that the 7th brigade supported ran out of ammunition. The brigade stood up to it like brave men, never flinching, but alas, the rebels were rather too strong for us at that point, so we were ordered to retreat. This we did through a dense thicket of Cedars, the rebels after us yelling 'Bull Run,' 'Bull Run.' But the run soon changed when we got out of the thicket, so that our men could see the Stars and Stripes. They soon were rallied and fit for duty, except some stragglers that broke for Nashville. — Then came our time to cheer. The rebels fell on our right and left as we threwed their ranks in confusion, and they were forced to retreat as best they could. Night came on, and all was quiet once more. We then built small fires, made some coffee, and eat a few 'hard tacks,' and retired to our muddy couches, for it had rained the principal part of the day. The next morning we were aroused by the roaring of cannon and the rattling of musketry. We were soon under arms and ready to meet the foe, being anxious to put an end to the contest, and rest our wearied limbs in this desolated and uninhabited town, called 'Murfreesboro.' The cannonading soon ceased and nothing of importance transpired through the day except some heavy skirmishing along the lines. Night again came on, and all was still. So we spent our New Year's day" (28 Ja).

That day the left wing division of Van Cleve, who had been wounded, moved east under command by Col. Beatty. They passed the cannon guarding the ford, crossed Stones River, climbed the high bank, and ranged across an open ridge (Fyffe 598-99). The 13th became the front of the extreme left of these lines (Jarvis 604). Enemy skirmishers engaged theirs from early on the following day, and about 3 P.M. a massive attack began, by the Confederate forces of Generals Cheatham and Hanson (*OR* Moody 440), aimed at Beatty's right near the river and the ford which led to the rear of Rosecrans' army, which was already under rebel cannonfire on its front. The attack rapidly rolled up the troops it targeted. The 13th and Beatty's left lines stood at a diagonal to this devastating charge and fired on it obliquely and freely, until a rebel battery came up to blast them directly with shrapnel. They drew back 300 yards and stood again, but again faced the mangling iron and lead of the battery, which had taken their place. They were ordered back across the river (Jarvis 604). Two more of Capt. Carnahan's company were now missing, leaving only thirteen of the thirty-three who had come to the battlefield (*CDS* 21 Ja).

As they retreated across the ford and the rebels converged on it, however, another force emerged. Negley's division, including the 69th and 74th, had been alerted that afternoon to the threat of the attack, and waited behind the batteries overlooking the ford. After their

comrades climbed to pass through them, under fire, they moved at the enemy charges and returned their blasts, stalling them on the opposite river bank. At this success, they charged to a rail fence by the river, where they met barrages from two rebel batteries as well as rifles, and fired with such a fury the enemy began to back off. Here the brigade leader Col. Miller ordered a charge across the river; they splashed through the water and bullets from front and right, and continued this charge, despite Miller's receipt of two orders that he should retire, up the steep wooded bank, across the cornfield where Beatty's men had fallen, and up to the woods that held an enemy battery of four cannon, which they captured. At this point it was nearly dark, and in this fight of about an hour they had fired nearly all their sixty cartridges. The 69th and 74th were among the troops most credited with bravery (*OR* Miller 432, 434-35). For those who had felt "mortified" two days prior, and mocked with "Bull Run!" this reverse was welcome; as McIlravy described it, "we drove the rebels howling before us."

None of Hoffman's squad in the 69th had been injured, but four of the Harrison men in K, including Zenas Poulson, were wounded. In the 74th, eight had wounds: M. K. McFadden, Theodore Liggett, Leander Baker, John Handy, in the leg; Clark Mansfield, ankle; Abraham Dennis, arm; Wm. Chambers, elbow; and Hiram Cox, mouth. "None of these wounds are supposed to be dangerous," McIlravy reported; but of course they were.

Rosecrans' army suffered 13,000 casualties at Stones River, near the cost of

Fredericksburg; but Bragg's, which retreated on 3 Jan., lost about the same number. This battle was accurately, sadly summarized by the letter-writer of the Cadiz Guards: "The fight was terrific — the slaughter dreadful. Both sides were badly used up, though of course our papers will claim it as a victory. The real truth is, we have nothing to exult over. Our army was in the hottest place it has ever been" (*CDS* 21 Ja).

Meanwhile, the soldiers of the 98th who were able for duty chased Morgan's cavalry as they left Kentucky after destroying bridges in the army's supply line; and the sick were unwelcome visitors in Lebanon. Samuel Thompson Gray wrote to Nancy on 5 Jan. from Hospital No. 5 in Lebanon: "Friend Nan, Yours of the 17th of last month came to hand in due time and the contents were devoured with eagerness and gratitude for to a sick man away from home nothing is so cheering as to receive good, friendly, cheerful news from friends at home. And permit me to congratulate you on the interesting and fluent manner in which you penned it. While you continue to write such letters I would desire to remain a correspondent. But the next time you are not through when one sheet is full please fill another one or two.

"...Robert received a letter from home yesterday. From him I learn that you have severe cold in Ohio and good sleighing. I always did like snow this time a year, but I presume it is a fine thing for us soldiers that the snow and frost is and has been light; however the boys will not suffer much while Kentucky has rails or wood that will burn. [Not again would they guard fences while their friends froze in the snow. The farm fences around Lebanon had also recently fueled bonfires with which Morgan's men fooled the garrison to fear a huge army surrounded the town.]

"I saw Robert this morning and find that he is improving quite rapidly. I think he will be able to join the Reg't in a week or ten days. When I wrote to your Father to come to him I did not altogether approve of it but I did it at his urgent request. My own health is very poor. I do not suffer much except from weakness. But it seems that I can gain no strength since I had the measles, whether it is from their effects or not that I remain so weak I am not able to say. I intend making an effort to get a furlough and get home to recruit my health....

"I regret very much to hear of your Father's affliction and hope it may not cripple as long as you anticipate.

"The Misses Warfels will begin to think School Teaching is not so pleasant a profession as they had anticipated. I still wish them success. I was sorry to hear of the affliction in Oglevee's family. Fin is also much afflicted but it is [in his] mind. He is one of the sickest boys in the company — that is, sick of the war. And I tell you if he was at home free he would be about the last man to enlist.

"All the boys who were able to march are at Campbellsville. Their tents, knapsacks, &c. are here yet, but will be moved up this afternoon or tomorrow. They have doubtless had a rough, tiresome march in pursuit of Morgan....

"The news from Tennessee are glorious today. I hope it may not turn out like the Burnsides' victory which you chronicled in your last. It seems strange that the hosts of Rebeldom cannot be driven from in front of our Capital. Surely there is something wrong in our officers in that region. I believe that if Richmond was once in our hands they would be ready to sue for peace but until that time the prospect of a settlement is very slim indeed.— The cars have just whistled — Well I went down town to see if the box came, but no, but then they say Louisville is full of boxes for Lebanon. So I suppose it will come soon.

[What Thompson described next represented a war-time change in Lebanon. The hopes of Southerners for success of the Confederacy had risen high; the nation in general expected European recognition of it soon, which would end the Union blockade of the South or threaten Lincoln with another, foreign war. The Deep South's plantation owners foresaw expansion, and were investing in slaves, driving up prices, presenting the "slave-poor" farmers such as Lebanon's with an economic opportunity. The local slave-trader became extremely wealthy, as the 1870 census shows.] "Nan, when down town I saw the disgusting sight of a negro sale. Yes human beings created by God in his own image bid off for the mere pittance of $500. When I left a fine, intelligent mulatto girl was placed upon the block. Twas to me the most barbarous spectacle I ever saw. May God hasten the day when our country shall be rid of all such remnants of the dark ages!...

"Yesterday three men in this hospital passed away from the scenes of earth to those of other climes, but where. The day of the Lord alone will reveal. I know nothing of their lives. But as they passed away I could not but think what a happy hour if they are only prepared but if not Oh! what a moment? They were all insensible. It is a notorious fact that more soldiers are killed by strong medicine than by disease or sword and I verily believe than by both together.

"The citizens here have no sympathy with us or at least they never exhibit any. One solitary Lady (blessed angel) is all that ever visits the hospitals or brings any relief to the sick in this large town. Many a poor soldier's life might be saved here if we could only get proper food. Our nourishment here is very good for convalescent men such as your brother and myself but for a right sick man it is very unsuitable indeed.

"I presume Robert has informed you that Lieut. Saunders met with a sad defeat the other night in the breaking of his arm. [In the pursuit of Morgan, he was riding in a wagon which overturned, throwing him down a fifty-foot bluff (*CDS* 21 Ja).] He expects to get a furlough…. As ever your sincere friend, S. T. Gray"

The 98th's officers in poor health began resigning; Captain Butts and Adjutant Kennon left the army for home. Sick and wounded enlisted men who could travel got leaves, and some others left without them. In mid-January, John S. Pearce was in Cadiz "looking up stragglers." He had been exchanged and promoted Lt. Col, while staying in Columbus. More of the regiment came to the county depots; Allen adopted a formula for his notices, as that "Nelson Birney, son of John Birney, Esq., of Washington township" "was bro't home a corpse a few days since" (*CDS* 21 Ja, 28 Ja).

Chapter 16

Orations of the Nation: The War Debate That Heralded the Gettysburg Address

January of 1863 brought the dramatic declaration of opposition to the war which forged the Copperhead movement to rivet the North's attention, including President Lincoln's, and certainly Harrison County's. As John A. Bingham returned to Washington for his lame-duck session in the House, his long-time mutual antagonist from the Dayton, Ohio, district, now also a lame duck, was crafting his design to end the war. Clement L. Vallandigham had lately become a national figure. In December he had addressed a rally organized by the Wood brothers, who were powers in the *New York News* and New York politics; he had won Fernando Wood's confidence "as a statesman and prophet" to oppose Lincoln and the war (Klement 120). On 22 Dec., Vallandigham had introduced in the House a resolution, which the Republicans tabled, but the Democratic newspapers published,

along with Vallandigham's proposal to debate it: that the House call for "an immediate cessation of hostilities" leading "to the speedy final settlement of the unhappy controversies which brought this unnecessary and injurious civil war" through cooperation of Congress "with the Executive and the States for restoration of the Union by such explicit and most solemn amendment and provisions for the Constitution as may be found necessary for securing the rights of the several States and sections within the Union under the Constitution" (*CDS* 7 Ja 1863).

Vallandigham spent the holidays in Washington, preparing an oration to deliver in the House, and alerted some colleagues and reporters it was coming (Klement 123). His timing was thoroughly propitious. The Union effort was not only failing in arms, but also staggering in debt and fear of European intervention, and veering near a semantic abyss, a void in which the appeals and arguments that had rallied money and men for a war to defend the Union were collapsing.

In the war of words, Vallandigham's oration and Bingham's speech in rebuttal were prime, mercurial occasions. Both were summarized in detail in newspapers, or printed entirely, as in the newspapers of Bingham's home town; Vallandigham's was published in five-cent pamphlets which "sold like hotcakes" (Klement 128) and supplied C. N. Allen's copy. These orations constituted one of the "Great Debates in American History" excerpted in the twelve-volume 1913 selection of these by the eminent scholar Marion Mills Miller, who, moreover, pointed out that Bingham's "theme … received simpler and briefer but even more effective treatment by the President a few months later"—in the Gettysburg Address (Miller 6: 276). Both orations contained more of the raw material than Miller noted, moreover, for Lincoln's "refounding" of the nation in the "intellectual revolution," as Garry Wills terms it, and "clever assault on the constitutional past" in his "fateful 272 words" (Wills 39-40).

It was oratorical ability that had made Bingham successful as Lincoln's point-man on the House floor. The most active member of the Judiciary Committee, he introduced key war measures and managed the bills through debate; frequently he made the long arguments which drove, or tired, Representatives to a vote. He was, in sales terms, a "closer." Bingham in December delivered the argument for a bill which incensed conservatives, and severely tested general

credibility of Lincoln as an upholder of the Union and Constitution—the admission of West Virginia as a state. Bingham's speech, printed in his home newspaper on 7 January, showed how far-stretched and contorted logic had to become, to advance the government's cause. Bingham used the precedent of states having been organized in territories; but he could not claim Virginia's constitutional rights were not violated; rather, he inserted a contradictory, transcending law: a "great principle of self-preservation, to the transcendent law of nature and nature's God, which declares that the safety and happiness of society are the objects at which all political institutions aim, and to which all such institutions must be sacrificed." Answering an objection, Bingham divorced the disloyal citizens from the state: "But, sir, the majority of the people of any State are not the State when they organize treason against the Government.... Now, sir, I beg leave to ask, can the minority of the people of a State, by the act of a State, by the act of a majority committing treason, and taking up arms against the Federal Government, be stripped of their right within the State of protection...? ...I repeat where the majority become rebels in arms, the minority are the State." Bingham spoke on about the relation of the Emancipation Proclamation to the "new State of Virginia" until the Speaker closed debate, a vote was called, and the bill passed, 96 to 55 (*CR* 7 Ja).

This argument was, of course, logical and consistent with Lincoln's concept that the states "*could* not" secede, the Union remained unbroken, and the South had raised a "civil insurrection" rather than a foreign power (Wills 133). The opposite terminology and perception of the war, however, as presented in Vallandigham's resolution, constituted the standard popular description, according to which Bingham presented a ridiculous doctrine that "the *States* are in rebellion, and therefore have committed *felo de se*" (suicide); thus Ohio Rep. Samuel S. Cox castigated Bingham's "crazed speculations" in interpreting the significance of his and other Republicans' election defeats. The "people" had protested the conversion of a war "to overthrow the organization of the Southern confederacy" into one "to overthrow State constitutions" and "defeat the cause of the nation, by making the old Union impossible" — in plans for emancipation (speech 15 Dec. 1862, *CDS* 7 Ja).

In arguments for emancipation, too, Bingham shared Lincoln's fundamental belief which he would implant in the Gettysburg Address, that the Declaration of Independence was "the founding document" of the nation, with its equality overriding the rights to property, including slaves, that the Constitution had guaranteed (Wills 144-5). But the two differed here in substance and style, in ways that made Bingham the superb orator, Lincoln the consummate President. Bingham, from his entrance to the House in 1854, had opposed the spread and enforcement of slavery on the bases also of the "due process" clause of the Bill of Rights, Constitutional clauses and judicial opinions, the Northwest Ordinance, and natural law (Beauregard 26, 28, 30-1). These gave him the resources and versatility of an able expositor and debater, a nimble orator.

The "Cicero of the House" also used a full range of oral style, from sarcasm to florid fervor, and his extemporaneous speaking impressed listeners with its intense sincerity (Beauregard 12); but Bingham's speeches could be accused of misquotation, slipperiness, and torrential rhetoric which did not fix a point of permanence. To modern readers, like Vallandigham's biographer, they can appear "disorganized discourse" (Klement 133). By contrast, Lincoln played close to the vest, deliberated privately in writing, and wrote the concise document that revolutionized literary style (Wills 162, 148) from oral oration to Emersonian text.

Lincoln himself, significantly, planted the kernels of the January orations in the House. The centerpiece of his Annual Message to Congress on 1 Dec. 1862, between his factual account of foreign and domestic problems and his proposal of Constitutional amendments which would provide for gradual, compensated emancipation, portrayed the country's essential and necessary unity as geographical: "A nation may be said to consist of its territory, its people, and its laws. The territory is the only part which is of certain durable. 'One generation passeth away, and another generation cometh, but the earth abideth forever'" (Ecclesiastes 1:4). Lincoln quoted from his First Inaugural Address to insist on the impossibility of severing the country's sections, since no natural boundary existed, and at length he delineated the crucial connection of the interior region with the Mississippi Valley. In concluding, Lincoln urged people to remember they had vowed to save the Union, with words the Gettysburg

Address would echo ironically: "The world will not forget that we say this" (Lincoln 8: 112-16, 131).

Lincoln's theme of the nation's indivisibility brought him his only approving reference in the 15 Dec. address of the House by Cox, who dismissed Lincoln's emancipation proposals as "simple Mother Goose melodies." Cox's long speech, widely published, produced background material for the orators who followed him. It was composed by the rules of the text most often taught in schools, and followed the classic arrangement given in Hugh Blair's *Rhetoric*. Cox's exordium exalted the people's will as the necessary director of any administration. His division contrasted the radical and conservative political aims. His narration accounted the expenses and youths dead from the war and blamed these on the radicals. His arguments proposed a return to McClellan's leadership of the army in a "civilized" war, which would respect the rights of citizens organized in resistance as though they were a foreign nation; and urged consideration of means of compromise and foreign mediation to end hostilities.

Herein, Cox posed as a rumor a question that would reverberate in the later debate, and Copperhead movement: Was it true that the President was advised that the South would return to the Union, if certain conditions were offered them? Cox's "pathetic part" followed arguments, in accord with Blair's scheme of parts — a negative part heaping blame on House Republicans, and a positive part identifying the unity of nationality as "the unforced and spontaneous union of inclinations among a people," and quoting the Bible. His peroration appealed to the compromising spirit of Christian brotherhood. (*CDS* 7 Ja).

On 9 Jan., Norton of Missouri promoted the Democrats' cause in a speech condemning the Republican party for causing the war, and calling for the disbanding of both armies and for a national convention to amend the Constitution to "settle the dispute." Bingham replied to Norton, with a thrust that bared the peril of the President; he lambasted the Democrats for offering amendments and so deserting their slogan "the Constitution as it is," while he ignored the fact of Lincoln's recent proposal of amendments.

In this debate, Bingham demonstrated the style and substance of his oratory. He first scored an amusing point of rhetorical ethos. With his audience well aware of Blair's proscriptions against written-out oration — "a Discourse read, is far inferior to an Oration spoken" (Blair 2: 226, 236-7) — and of Bingham's own reliance on notes only, he chided Norton for written preparation: "If [his utterances] had sprung hot from the brain of the gentleman by reason of any sudden excitement of passion, I could possibly find some palliation for them, though sudden excitement could not possibly furnish occasion or excuse for his speech; but when he has conned it all over in the privacy of his chamber, when he has reduced it deliberately to manuscript and comes here and reads it deliberately in the hearing of the representatives of the people, it is fit that it should be denounced as unfit to be uttered by a representative of the people...."

Bingham's defense of the legitimacy of the Republican party was then quickly interrupted by Biddle of Pennsylvania, who interjected George Washington's warning against "sectional parties." Bingham answered with one of his characteristic nimble springs between colloquial fulmination and grandiloquence: "Talk to me of a sectional party! Talk to me about Washington's views on sectional parties! We are walking in his footsteps, and but following his great example when we enact, as a Republican organization, that by the supreme law of the land the vast territories of the Republic, the heritage of the nation, capable of furnishing homes for one hundred million freemen, shall not be blasted by the manacled footsteps of the bondman.... Go read the act of 1789."

Biddle protested that Bingham cited not the Constitution, but rather the prior Articles of Confederation. Bingham replied, quoting Chief Justice Taney, with a lengthy, intricate tracing of the substance of the Articles to preservation in the 1789 Northwest Ordinance and the fifth and sixth amendments. This argument typified Bingham's longstanding position, and its convolutions show why Bingham's reasonings could not easily convert prejudiced listeners — or readers — from a simplistic stand on the Constitution's language.

Bingham's extemporaneous style, moreover, and reputation as "Cicero of the House" had both strengths and liabilities. Opponents could dismiss his arguments, as Cox of Ohio did his tracing of national freedom: "I dislike to interrupt the gentleman in such a splendid torrent of eloquence, but...." Bingham also drew laughter, which could abet or undercut his persuasion, when he brought a lofty discourse to land suddenly in a flat-footed platitude. After Cox asked whether Bingham's recent defeat did not result from his belonging to a "sectional party," Bingham ended his lengthy defense, "Let the gentleman put that in his pipe and smoke it." Castigating the Democrats for trying to amend the Constitution in January 1861 instead of quelling the rebellion, Bingham brought forth the following: "When now you shout the Constitution as it is, you have stolen our thunder, gentlemen. [Laughter]

"A Voice: Not all of it."

In the reply to Biddle, Bingham then proceeded to attack Vallandigham's 1861 proposed amendments specifically; Cox objected to his interpretation that these provided for secession; and Bingham called for Vallandigham's exact articles to be appended to his remarks. Bingham was laying a trap for Vallandigham, which had some immediate success, for both Cox and Holman responded by absolving House Democrats from Vallandigham's 1861 proposal (CR 4 F). The trap, however, cut off Lincoln's new boots of amendments, and it was too complex and legalistic to operate among a public disillusioned with the war and supporting Vallandigham's ascension. The "Cicero of the House" could preach, argue to judges, and elicit knee-slapping cheers from Ohio farmers; but his old-fashioned oratory now faced a challenge beyond its range.

In his 14 Jan. speech, Vallandigham amalgamated and extended the appeals in Lincoln's and Cox's addresses, but he modulated them to a new ethos. Vallandigham's mission and impact here elevated his speech far above mere political rhetoric. Throughout prior history, as Barnet Baskerville explains in *The People's Voice*, "the orator was chief among American folk heroes" and oratory shaped public affairs in ways that have evaded historians' accounts. This tradition radically altered — during the war, according to Garry Wills, because of the Gettysburg Address — or after the war, according to Baskerville, when crucial issues subsided, and an oratory of "Obfuscation and Diversion" replaced antebellum "Artistic Expression." In the earlier role of the orator, he had to know and *feel* the ideals of the society he addressed: "Cognizant of what his age would have him be, he must accommodate to (while attempting to influence) the tastes, values, and expectations of those to whom he speaks." Thus, the "orator is at once engine and mirror; not only can he provide the impetus toward what he feels should be, he can also reflect (often unconsciously) what is" (Baskerville 2-3, 5).

Vallandigham positioned himself as mirror and engine, but he sought to revise the mode of transmission to present himself as the new model orator, and thus heroic leader, by largely desisting from poetic "eloquence," the artistic expression pre-Civil War audiences had always required of an orator (Baskerville 83). Vallandigham bared himself of most trappings of eloquence — of literary and histrionic effects — to present himself in a unity of substance and style as the new "practical statesman" needed by the nation. In so doing, he also denied himself the protective excuses carried by attempts at eloquence.

His exordium announced his purpose, with "much plainness of speech" to "consider the STATE OF THE UNION" and the duty of every citizen in the present crisis of "Revolution." He then began a narration of the outbreak of the war, making Republicans the antagonists and the President's attempt to defend forts in the "seceded States" the first martial act; he described the "hurricane" surge of war fervor in the North and West, with persecutions and mob rule, then Executive tyranny, and Congressional submission to it (Vallandigham *Globe* 54). In this opening, Vallandigham applied the inductive method which Blair termed "analytic" and "very artful" in addressing prejudiced hearers who must be led to the truth in steps (Blair 1: 403).

With a transitional question asking, "Can any man to-day see the end" of this war, Vallandigham turned to a second, longer narration, of his consistent objection over the years to abolition, coercion of the South, and the war. He led up to a paean to his honest stand on his convictions, which he attributed to his knowledge of history and human nature, in defying the "madness" that had pressed for war. He had "appealed to TIME," and right nobly had "the Avenger" justified him. In two meta-phors Vallandigham lyricized his purity of soul: he would rather his "right arm were plucked from its socket" and cast into hell than desert his principles; he blessed God "that not the smell of so much as one drop" of war blood stained his garments (Vallandigham *Globe* 54). Vallandigham placed this self-assertion, within Blair's arrangement, as a central part of his narration, making himself his subject along with the State of the Union, a coordinate in contrast to it. He also appealed to the "passions" of his audience; here, he began to depart from Blair's rules, and apply principles from the less classical, more pragmatic rhetoric of Campbell. Campbell's textbook emphasized passions as indispensable for any persuasion toward action, and basic among them the "one main engine by which the orator operates" on emotions — sympathy with him (Campbell in Golden 210, 224-5). Vallandigham observed Campbell's advice to the letter, in averring his honesty, asserting his intellectual and moral character, and then, after a denunciation of the "delusion" of trying to preserve the Union by war, defending himself from possible criticism of his votes for payment of soldiers. Vallandigham quoted Calhoun's explanations of his actions during the Mexican War, which Calhoun opposed, to justify himself — and also elevate himself, to stand upon the testimony of the great statesman of South Carolina. This rhetorical alliance projected Vallandigham's intent to speak for the nation as a whole, and from the principles of Southern statesmen to which, his speech would argue, the nation should revert.

Returning to the State of the Union, Vallandigham's narration charged into his first forthright argument, that all possible resources had been thrown to the war and it was a failure in every regard. With a litany of facts and figures he indicted the government, coming to this climax: "War for the Union was abandoned; war for the negro openly begun…. With what success? Let the dead at Fredericksburg and Vicksburg answer." This argument forcibly laid out what was apparently true: obviously the terms of the war had changed, and victory was following the

Southern army. So it had the aim of the first of Blair's distinct classes of arguments — truth — Blair's other types being directed toward moral rightness or else profitable interest (Blair 2: 405). Blair's first rule for arrangement was to avoid blending arguments of separate classes; furthermore, he warned that pathetic address while demonstrating truth was absurd (Blair 2: 405, 411). But Vallandigham could not forbear moral denunciation even amid this, his strongest material argument; sneering at the label "rebels," he pronounced the nation's forefathers and George Washington rebels, and denounced their present "imbecile" descendants (Vallandigham *Globe* 54). Here he risked the personal ethos he had asserted, and contradicted his previously stated respect for those who had honestly supported the war.

This and all of his long subsequent arguments — of the geographical and cultural interdependence of the nation which made unity inevitable, of the need to accept and protect slavery, of the merits of a cease-fire, withdrawal of troops, and pursuit of mediated compromise — appealed in plain language to current common sense vision and practicality. What Vallandigham said — except about slavery — has much truth in the light of history: the war could not settle the States' Rights issues which produced it, nor sectional and racial antagonisms; and only long cooperative intercourse, after passions cooled and grass grew on the battlefields, would restore unity. He made, moreover, telling points, arguing, for instance, that "practical recognition" of the government in Richmond would merely acknowledge its factual existence, as a surgeon in splinting a fractured limb admits it is broken; and, as for punishing the seceders, we would not hang them all whether the war ended in fifty years, or tomorrow (Vallandigham *Globe* 59).

Most of these arguments violated Blair's rule against blended arguments, as they mixed moral truth and duty with the personal and social profitable interest of white men. But here Vallandigham was mirroring the thinking of a popular audience, and in all ways using the rhetorical principles of Campbell which overrode Blair's strictures. Campbell emphasized common sense as the basis of moral logic, and self-interest in consequences as one of the strongest passions by which a speaker could move hearers, far stronger than sympathy with others; moreover, such a pleading constituted, for him, "a species of reasoning" (Campbell in Golden 177, 220-1). For Campbell, a speaker's persuasion of the immediate audience furnished both the aim and test of arguments. For Blair also, persuasion was the purpose of oration, but conviction, based on clear, reasoned argument, had to be its basis (Blair 2: 247). If hearers and readers applied Blair's rules, they would judge Vallandigham critically.

Vallandigham's arguments, however, rested upon his Campbellian establishment of audience sympathy and admiration for his honesty, knowledge, and practicality; and his "pathetic part" which followed, forming his peroration, defied Blair's warning against Ciceronian self-ostentation (Blair 2: 206). Vallandigham projected a poignant image of himself; he recalled "the day-dream" of his boyhood to celebrate the nation's one-hundredth birthday "as orator of the day"—a "vision" lingering, he said,

before his eyes, in which he yet had hope. To a skeptical view, Vallandigham inflated his presumed ethos to a bubble, and provided a symbol of his egotistical blindness to the nation's present and coming sufferings.

In closing, Vallandigham gave a summarizing call to action which linked his cease-fire propositions to the beginning of reunion, and posed the alternative of revolution and bloodshed worse than the Reign of Terror in France.

Vallandigham was halfway through his speech, according to the Cincinnati *Gazette*'s reporter, when Bingham began to make notes for his reply (*CR* 21 Ja). He rose to challenge this "prepared denunciation of the war" and the President; he did not follow Vallandigham's arrangement of issues, but rather organized a discourse that followed Blair's rules to such an extent that one can view this debate as a contest between the rhetoric of Blair and that of Campbell which equipped Vallandigham. Bingham first challenged Vallandigham on the "truth of history" he had claimed to represent, and explicated the Buchanan administration's policy of "no coercion" which let insurrection flourish in 1861. Then he argued the Constitutional duty of the President and Congress to preserve the country, and depicted Vallandigham's anti-coercion position as a surrender to the rebellion. Bingham next defended President Lincoln's call for troops as his duty, and contrasted Vallandigham's position.

In this beginning, and at key points throughout, Bingham credited Vallandigham with the stature of a rival to Lincoln, an acknowledgment of his ethos as the Democrats' new statesman.

His arguments against Vallandigham rose gradually from a material examination of Vallandigham's truth and logic to a ferocious prosecution of his possible treason; in this climactic, Blairian arrangement, Bingham inflated Vallandigham's self-importance until his overblown role carried dangerous liabilities. Within and beyond these arguments, Bingham skewered images Vallandigham had used, converting them to an opposite purpose. The first, and last, were the graves and blood of war. In a sarcastic aside, Bingham alluded to Vallandigham's invocation of the Fredericksburg graves "with so much tenderness"; quickly, he deemed Vallandigham and his cohorts "not clear of the blood shed in this war." Thereupon Bingham reduced Vallandigham's speech to two disjunctive propositions: Vallandigham presumed that peaceful reunion would readily follow a cessation of the war, yet he assumed "that secession is a constitutional right," even "justified by the great example of the fathers of the Republic" — whom Vallandigham had termed rebels.

As Bingham launched into Vallandigham's 1861 proposed amendment that would create sections of the country which could protect their states from federal intrusion, or legalize their secession, he discounted the whole body of Vallandigham's geographical discourse by agreeing with him, on nature's design for one people's common heritage, and then setting Vallandigham's sectional proposal at odds with it. Vallandigham had stepped into this trap by renewing his call "to give to each section the power to protect itself within the Union" (Vallandigham *Globe* 59).

Bingham's next charge against Vallandigham, however, was a conflation without literal basis. Vallandigham had called for "an armistice — no formal treaty," but "informal, practical recognition" of and mediated negotiations with Richmond, and possibly a national convention to resolve the conflicting issues after a new President had been elected. Bingham charged him with proposing a "final treaty of peace" with the rebels and demanded to know under what authority he could assure they would reunite. Other than false accusation, there are two ways of understanding Bingham's charge. Vallandigham had argued for *de facto* recognition, and so his armistice would be a *de facto* treaty. Second, Vallandigham's assumption of eventual reunion could scarcely be heard without recollection of the rumor Cox had asserted, that the President had received an offer from the Southern states to reunite under certain conditions, and of Cox's proposal of negotiations as among separate warring nations (*CDS* 7 Ja). Bingham elevated Vallandigham to privileged responsibility for a proffer from the South. He posed an either/or, whether Vallandigham promised reunion as simply his own speculation, or whether he had private information from the rebellion leaders. Vallandigham disdained to answer, sustaining his statesmanly authority, but allowing the inference that it rested on Southern communication, that he spoke as a "mouthpiece" for Jefferson Davis.

Bingham had dissected Vallandigham's speech into its classes under Blair's rules; and only near closing did he address its appeal to interest which Vallandigham had interwoven.

He castigated the premise of the argument that the Northwest must ally itself with the South, if New England pursued war, as a base assumption that the Northwest had a craven "mercenary spirit."

Bingham, however, granted "the effect of such an appeal" for peace to the people who treasured their sons and wanted them home. He did not, he could not, argue that the war served their present interest. Instead, he began a peroration glorifying future interest: "the great question of to-day is, shall the Republic live? Any sacrifice of blood ... is not too great to be made" to "maintain intact" the inherited Constitution. Bingham did not stop here, did not choose this summation as the strength of his case on which it should rest (Blair 2: 425). He doubtless apprehended that no logical dissection of Vallandigham could cut off his pragmatic attraction of a war-sick, non-abolitionist public majority; and he knew his own standard, the Constitution intact, had become untenable in a defense of Lincoln and war. At this point Bingham cast aside logic and practical sense, and brought from far afield an appeal to pathos and to a rarefied, remote ethos. In it he defied Campbell's warning against rhetorical passions which "deject the mind," such as sorrow and humility, also Campbell's criticism of analogy (Golden 148, 190), and moreover he ignored Blair's strictures against comparisons or addresses to the imagination in any pathetic part (Blair 2: 419). I infer, therefore, that he had not preconceived this peroration as a response to Vallandigham's speech: he could not have anticipated the condemnatory images of graves and blood it would bring;

and, if he sought a testimony justifying war to counter Vallandigham's historical survey, Bingham could have made a more judicious choice than the Crimean War. The "quotation" to which he led did not come from any major statesman, but probably from some writer and publication he had recently read which was obscure then and now, perhaps shared with his wife; I have not been able to find its source.

Bingham alluded to the "triumphs" and "compensations" of the Crimean War, for England — where that war was condemned as a shameful, bungled waste — and drew this "beautiful manifestation": "Go follow Florence Nightingale as she walked beneath the frowning walls of Sevastopol by her gentle chariots soothing the suffering, and by her divine words cheering the dying, illustrating to all by her beautiful life and her heroic sacrifice the significance of that new revelation, 'the pure in heart shall see God.'"

Yet, Bingham continued, men of England asked, what had they gained by this war? He posed the answer in a quotation from "one of her most gifted sons": "Go ask those who have suffered most from the war, to whom it has changed forever the beauty of heart and the imagery of heaven, those who will never more see the sun rise without first thinking what graves it gilded behind the earth's dark line in the Crimea, those who will never more see the crocus bloom in spring without first thinking what dust it is that feeds the wild flowers of Balaklava; and they will answer you, though it be with stifled utterance, we would not, even to bring back again our honored dead, wash away that blood from England's breastplate.' May like answer be given when this war is ended" (*CR* 11 F).

So Bingham consecrated the soldiers' blood which Vallandigham had scorned. Too, he implicitly invoked and eulogized women's selfless sacrifices to the war, and empathetically painted their mourning, and that of men of sensibility, as a dignified, destined, near-desirable, new "beauty of heart." However farfetched it was, this analogical elegy carried the passion of the orator who had impelled his neighbors' sons into battle, and many to their graves. It deeply moved Bingham's audience. The Cincinnati *Gazette* correspondent telegraphed that Bingham "concluded by a beautiful reference to the British sentiment on the Crimean war." He summarized the quotation, including the blood on the breastplate, and recorded the "Loud applause in the galleries and on the floor" (*CR* 21 Ja).

Thus, ten months before Lincoln's Gettysburg Address, Bingham pronounced its encapsulation of the nation's war in the form of elegy.

Chapter 17

Peace Clarions, Threnodies, and Wolf Calls

Vallandigham's speech, according to the *Sentinel*, delivered the "verdict" of all intelligent Americans (28 Ja). Accompanying its publication was a call from "MANY CITIZENS" to a "MASS MEETING OF THE DEMOCRACY" to oppose the "conspiracy" which promoted war, to "arrest" the wicked projects of their "rulers," and to demand "laws such as will command the voluntary respect of the governed," with the vow never to assist in compelling people of any state "to obey laws through constraint" (*CDS* 4 F). When the promised "distinguished speakers" were secured, the mass meeting was set for 7 March, to bring none other than Dr. Edson Olds of Lancaster, who had been imprisoned for allegedly interfering with recruiting, then released (*CDS* 24 D 1862), and Rep. George L. Converse of Columbus.

So Democrats began to rally voters to Vallandigham's peace platform, and to organize for township elections in April that would "crush" local Republicans. They expected the state would attempt another draft in the spring, which people would now refuse to support, especially since they perceived that half of all men sent to the army soon fell prey to bullets or diseases (*CDS* 11 F). In their first township rally, "the unflinching Democracy of old Athens" was to convene at Stumptown on Saturday, 21 Feb. (*CDS* 18 F). Thus arose to local prominence an Athens township hamlet and its "squire." Stumptown sat on a crossroads a few miles west of New Athens. Its name derided its settlers' disinclination to clear the ground when they chopped the forest for their fields. In 1862, Matthew H. Phillips owned 141 acres nearby; J. H. Phillips, 90 acres adjoining these (Jarvis).

Some Democrats flinched from the clarion call. Their reply questioned the absence of names, including the elected party committee, from the mass meeting call: it "savors of usurpation," and "*insinuations* implied in it, smell mightily of treason — and a covert desire to stir up civil strife in our own midst." Reflecting the threatening echoes of the call in neighborhood conversation, these writers reminded that they had families to protect, and were concerned "to keep away the waves of civil war from our own doors." They did not believe the government endangered their liberties so that "manly *resistance*" was necessary: "We live beside Republican neighbors, — we discuss freely, yet courteously, our differences, and neither of us are under any necessity of carrying revolvers from apprehension of danger from one another." They did not want to follow "men who in their *greedy desire for position and place*" would sacrifice civility. Furthermore, they believed "in the omnipotency of law — and need[ed] not to be taught, by the sophistries of an antiquated Athens township 'squire'—*nor* the special pleadings of an *unfledged* village lawyer [Philip Donahue had written the call], that laws must have the *voluntary* respect of all before they can operate." The "self-styled leaders" needed not "prepare revolvers and hot coffee for MANY CITIZEN DEMOCRATS" (*CR* 18 F).

This letter of the "Citizen Democrats," Allen charged, was "fishy," not one any "natural gentleman" would write, more likely Hatton's "dictator," Lewis Lewton. Allen filled his issue with reports of widespread enthusiastic support for Vallandigham, and soldiers' letters from Columbiana County opposing the war and emancipation (18 F). Then, in answer to Hatton's and others' speculation that the party leader who had recruited soldiers would not ally with Phillips and Donahue, Allen revealed that "Mr. Estep is the person that invited Dr. Olds to come to Cadiz and address the Democracy." Quoting a New

York article on the popularity of the name "Copperhead," Allen added, "Copperhead, then, let it be! It's a very expressive designation" (25 F).

The extent to which the county Democrats moved to the Copperhead stand became clear in a second letter from the "Citizen Democrat" dissenters, protesting they were being "sold out" to "the mad, wild, ultra and treasonable vagaries of the Athens township Incubus," and had "privately and *quietly* concluded" that they should form a third party rather than be the "tail end" of Phillips' and his "'spiritual friends' of Stumptown" (*CR* 4 Mr). The latter title alluded to a rumor that the Stumptown rally had been headily fueled by whiskey.

The Stumptown event seemed to its participants "the largest and best township meeting we ever attended," drawing nearly every Athens Democrat, adopting all the resolutions "with great unanimity," including the last one, to gather there again at Hilton's Blacksmith shop at 8:30 A.M. on 7 March and ride together to Cadiz for the mass meeting (*CDS* 25 F). James Crossam presided, Matthew Phillips was secretary, and Philip Donahue was orator and author of the resolutions. These stridently declared Vallandigham's themes, including prediction that a separation of states would bring all those in connection with the Mississippi River to union with the South, and pledge that "any peaceable way of settling our present difficulties would be preferable to a continuance of this war" (*CR* 4 Mr).

Its costs mounted. While sick soldiers like Robert Mitchell and Thompson Gray came home on furloughs, their comrades who remained in the hospitals were dying in the horrible suffering of typhoid fever — vomiting, raving, hiccuping from hemorrhaging mouths (*CR* 24 Mr, *Ladies'* 17). On Valentine's Day, Bill McBride, an "intelligent, industrious young man" (*CDS* 25 F), Robert's corporal who had fought well, died in a Louisville hospital. Josiah E. Thomas, 20, expired in a hospital across the Ohio River; and Marshall Martin, 44, head of a family in Moorefield, died upriver at Gallipolis.

Col. Poorman came home because of illness in his family, and buried a son (*CR*, *CDS* 4 F).

Meanwhile, their regiment moved to join Rosecrans' army in Tennessee. They left Capt. Butts in a Louisville hospital, and rode a steamship down the Ohio two days, then up the Cumberland River. One of Butts' men, Harrison N. Carver, took up the role of military correspondent, with some flourish. The first day up the Cumberland provided him only a crooked stream with mats of cane and reed to describe. Near Dover, Tennessee, however, "the banks of the river grew more romantic; rugged cliffs, rising to the height of 200 feet seeming to push the chafing waters to the more yielding banks beyond. But instead of associating the idea of their's being the homes of timid rabbits or crafty foxes or forest minstrels, flocks of loathsome buzzards were hovering over them. I would not advise a student of aesthetics to take a trip up the Cumberland in February." They passed burning bales of hay, then a boat with crowded decks, afire, and came under Fort Donelson: "by the dim moon-light could be seen circling the brow of the hill, the earthworks to which the Rebels would retreat

when the fire of the gunboats grew too hot for them." While gazing at the fort Grant's army had captured after a bitter battle the previous February, they heard cannon booming upriver; they soon learned that Forrest's cavalry had attacked the post at Dover; and they were put ashore to bury the enemy dead.

When they reached Nashville, more men went into the hospital with typhoid fever, including Lt. McCullough. The regiment had only 287 present. Some, however, like five of Co. F, were on "French furlough" — gone "to see their mamas" (*CR* 25 F).

The 30th had left Virginia on a journey of three weeks, to the swamps of the Mississippi opposite Vicksburg. The first morning there they were put to work in the canal Grant hoped would circumvent the city's blockading cannon. They labored day and night in the deep swamp water "until there was but 337 men for duty," then were relieved. Sgt. McIlravy had much company in calling this canal a "hoax" which they might "dig and dig, and still the Mississippi will go its way rejoicing and still run past Vicksburgh" (*CR* 25 F).

The Cadiz Guards of the 13th who had been captured at Stones River began to come home — Harris Hatton, William Host, and James Hanna — the last with a discharge; he had survived about sixteen battles and skirmishes, and two imprisonments in Richmond. "We're pleased he has been discharged," Allen commented, "and wish we could say the same of every other man now in the army" (25 F). Those wounded at Stones River were dying, like J. B. Dysert, whose former fellow students at Franklin College elegized him in a Tribute (*CR* 18 F).

Coffins arrived from the 126th at Martinsburg. The tenor of Capt. Mc-Cready's letters became his meditation upon death and graves. He, Chaplain Andrews, and Lt. McKinney had visited the battlefield of Antietam, and found a wounded soldier near the Dunker Church to guide them: "the Church is shattered greatly, and here are graves scattered about, and yonder is a tree with eight or ten bullet marks on it, there is another shattered with a cannon ball, and another... — oh, more than you can count, several have been cut off, and the fence is riddled with bullet holes, but still I had expected to see destruction more complete.... But as I began to look more closely the terrible truth began to be realized.

"I observed no marks on the ground of bursting shells or balls as I had expected. They have all been obliterated if they existed. But though load after load of relics has been hauled off, the ground is still strewn with torn hats and caps, broken canteens and cartridge boxes and haversacks. Balls and shells and pieces of shell have all been carried off. Of course, occasional ones will be found for centuries.

"Graves are scattered about much as they fell, I suppose — over two or three farms, one here, two or three in another spot, and five, ten, fifty or five hundred in another place. Rebel graves are without marks of any kind. Union graves are all marked with head boards, with the names of Regiment and State of the soldier penciled upon them....The Union soldiers are generally buried in single graves. Sometimes where our dead were very numerous, a ditch was dug wide enough to place the bodies cross-wise; and they were laid in one deep, each marked by a headboard as above. Where the rebel dead were very numerous, a ditch was dug capable of holding three hundred, and they were buried five deep, or in a 'windrow' as the soldiers call it. There are quite a number of these 'windrows'.... Every day people are coming, looking up their dead, and removing them home. In one view this is nonsense. The dead will sleep as sweetly, and the voice of the Arch-Angel and the trump of God wake them as certainly here as elsewhere. It don't matter where our dust reposes. But wherever the Bible doctrine of the resurrection prevails a decent care is taken of the dead, and far be it from me to fault the beautiful custom. I don't know but I would say with Jacob, 'carry me to the cave of Macpelah' [Genesis 49: 29] and let me sleep with those I love. These graves will be plowed over and obliterated in a year or two."

McCready complained of the failure at home to support the soldiers' families: "When we were trying to raise volunteers, it was no unusual thing for the rich who would not go themselves, to get round the poor man and urge him to go, and leave a wife and two or three babes who had nothing between them and poverty, but the strong arm and warm heart of the husband and father. More than once I heard ... 'we will see your *family* cared for.'...As far as I can learn, not *five dollars* have been expended for the support of needy families represented in my company.... A man told me his wife had received three dollars, and was told that she would get no more. A boy lying in the Hospital dangerously ill, called me to him, and with evident concern told me his mother, a widow, a helpless family all dependent on him for support, ... had never received a dollar.—I went through the company.... Now these men have not been paid for three months... The Government won't pay them, and the people won't support their families....

"We have a great deal of sickness in camp now. A young man, of company K, is just now dead with Typhoid fever. J. S. McCready" (*CR* 18 F).

For families dependent on their soldiers, life was harsh; for all, it was expensive. Prices had increased 50 to 200 percent. Ordinary foodstuffs and once-cheap clothing rose out of reach for common people. Previously, the *New Lisbon Patriot* pointed out, a man could buy a shirt for 30¢, less than one-third of a day's wages; now muslin itself cost 40¢ a yard! The *Patriot* blamed all this inflation on plans to free the slaves (*CDS* 25 F).

Army privates were to be paid $11 a month, corporals $13 (Le Grand 62), far less than a laborer would bring to a family. Some comparison of the support soldiers' pay furnished their families— when they were paid— can be made from the deposit of Capt. Norris' company pay in the Harrison Branch Bank, for their families. Received near the second week of February, it must represent the visit from the paymaster which Col. Poorman had anticipated for 31 Dec. Some forty-five of Co. C sent home $2,200, about $49 per family. At $1 per day, this sum would near the wages of a six-day-a-week laborer for two months; but the February deposit brought Co. C's families their first money since early fall. Co. F had sent to the bank only $1,335 for their families (*CR* 11 F). When sol-

diers' families were not supported by the townships, their welfare was in jeopardy.

A far different financial concern emerged along with the Copperhead movement. An informative and artful letter in both newspapers delivered it, in a voice not elsewhere published, but one so well-known its author needed not supply his name, no more than he advertised his business — the most powerful factor in the economy. This wool-broker relished his reputation for crafty hard-bargaining. Most likely he was William Hogg, whose son, Charles Mather Hogg, would dominate area wool trade well into the next century, and set in Cadiz a lifestyle of baronial splendor.

"To the Wool Growers of Harrison County" from "one of your old friends" began with an astute overview: "You have nearly 175,000 sheep in this county — or more — worth probably not far from $1,000,000." You have learned your business from "doubtful and interested sources or by long and costly experience," he continued; and in this process "many of you were '*fleeced*' by some of our not over honest tribe." Two seasons ago, a "howl" created a panic so that you disposed of your wool for "a trifling consideration to some of our agents and speculators." "Some of us now, in dark dens, are doubtless manufacturing a panic for next summer's wool harvest, as we did in '61, when the war the very cause which should have driven prices up, was alleged by us as a reason why they should come down. The cry of peace (and we hope it a true one) will be the next panic cry, but not until there be a reduction in prices generally should it be suffered to operate on wool. While woolen fabrics have usually remained at uniform prices, that of the raw material has been constantly fluctuating — making your business a precarious and uncertain one.... Woolen goods have now advanced many per cent. So should the wool...."

From this argument, the broker urged the farmers at once to form a new organization among themselves, a county wool-growers' association: "Every class must take care of itself — for the golden age of honor has not yet arrived." Combined, "you can compel buyers to do you justice, for your wool must be had." He challenged the farmers to organize. Then he warned, "But if you choose to go on as you have been going why do so — and if you again find among your flocks and fleeces any of us you need not blame your old and inveterate foe. WOLF"

Chapter 18

Martinsburg, Virginia, and Its Symbols

Throughout the war, Martinsburg was yet part of Virginia. Established for the seat of Berkeley County around 1773, it stood on a broad rise at the head of the Shenandoah Valley, about ten miles south and east of the winding Potomac River, and twenty miles north of the oldest Valley town of Winchester. Here Revolutionary War veterans built homes, and Quakers, Scots-Irish, and Germans. At least one of these families emigrated from Martinsburg to Cadiz, about 1812, that of Charles and Susanna Timmons and their seven children (Hanna).

A crossroads on the routes of early settlers, a grain mill and market center for farmers, and, since 1842, an industrial railroad site, Martinsburg had the diverse appearance of a junction in society. It had, and has, barefaced wooden rectangles like most houses and stores then in Cadiz, but also handsome old mansions crafted from the local buff limestone, and numerous brick homes in Greek Revival architecture. The communal buildings graced utility with im-pressive charm. The limestone jail rose three stories high, and imposed on the street the round tower of a castle fortress (Wood 18-19). The brick Market House built in 1846-47 asserted its centrality in Gothic Revival style, opening to the streets in large round arches, illuminating the second-story lodge halls for the Masons and Odd Fellows with grand pointed-arch windows, capping its corner with a pinnacled tower. The Presbyterian Church was a full Greek Revival temple. The Catholic Church had been built over a period of fifteen years in Romanesque Revival style (*Historic Properties*).

The 126th O.V.I. had set up their tents in a field west of town on 23 December, according to Frank Grove's diary. Five days later, they were joined by the 106th New York Regiment, under Col. Edward P. James. On 10 January, during a snow and rain storm, Capt. McCready described for the *CR* his tour: "A few days ago I took a ramble round the town and through the Cemetery to

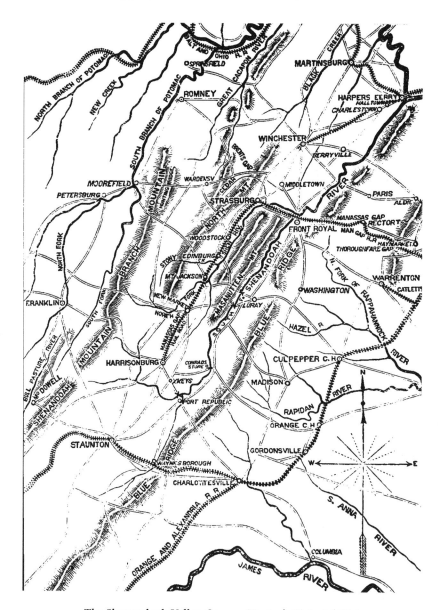

The Shenandoah Valley. Source: *Harper's Pictorial History.*

see the sights. The general appearance of Martinsburgh would indicate at present that its inhabitants are generally in moderate circumstances. On the South side of it evidently live the aristocracy and the rebels, as a matter of course. There are some fine residences in this part of the town. Here resides Mrs. Faulkner and family, wife and daughters of Charles J. Faulkner who has figured so conspicuously as rebel Minister to France. [President Buchanan appointed Faulkner, and Lincoln replaced him in 1861. McCready told the following rumor of his whereabouts with some irony, but the reality had more, as

Martinsburg, Virginia, in 1861. Courtesy of the Berkeley County Historical Society, Martinsburg, West Virginia.

Faulkner during the war was an aide to Stonewall Jackson (Cheeseman 47).] He is at present (it is reported) living with his daughter in Accomac county, in retirement, a lonely exile, and no doubt sick of rebellion. He bought a large lot of shot and powder before leaving, and told the people that he was going to Accomac to hunt. He said that from early youth he had been passionately fond of hunting, but owing to his constant press of business he had never had leisure to indulge his passion. It is probable he is not otherwise engaged at present. His residence is a splendid one, I could see in passing it. [The stone walls of this estate, "Boydville," surround a rolling lawn, brick-walled gardens, numerous outbuildings that include a law office and ice house, and a Georgian mansion with a 120-foot frontage, comprising a central section of nine rooms and center hall and two wings, one for the nursery, the other for kitchen and servants. Built before 1820 by Gen. Elisha Boyd, who served in the Virginia legislature and the War of 1812, and had the "lucrative" position of Commonwealth's attorney for the county for forty years, Boydville was inherited by the youngest daughter Mary, who had married Faulkner, a Martinsburg native and representative in the Virginia legislature, and, later, in Congress (Cheeseman 45-46). The splendor of this estate did not deter our Cadiz minister, or particularly invite his attention; he sought an interview with its resident, which would surely have been a conversation of interest to us, and to Stonewall Jackson.] I had intended calling, but understand Mrs. Faulkner was not at home; Faulkner is a shrewd man. The citizens call him 'the fox.' His wife is said to be a very ordinary woman intellectually. — She plays Union now since the Federals have the control, and treats the Union soldiers with great consideration it is said. Of course, this is a part of the scene she is acting. Who believes she is loyal, or her daughters either? Yet she is away (perhaps to see her husband) by permission of the authorities. But she is the wife of C. J. Faulkner, one of the leading demon spirits of this rebellion! It is also rumored that her husband has been guaranteed protection if he would return upon his parole of honor. Why is not the property of such rebels at once confiscated? And why are they not hung to the limb of a tree as fast as we get our hands on them? We Yankees are a disgustingly polite people. We still lick the foot that has been kicking us for twenty years.

"By the way, I have not found that in his southern breed of people yet, about which we have read so much in days of yore — I mean 'the chivalry,' the 'F. F. V.'s [first families of Virginia], before whom our politicians have so long stood hat in hand trembling like so many slaves. Nor do I expect to. They are like the big wood breed of Indians we read about, which are so magnanimous, so disinterested, and so heroic that the brightest examples on record in the annals of christian and pagan heroism fail before them. As there was a Pocahontas among the Indian women, however, so there may be noble spirits involved in this rebellion or reared in the South. But it is all a mistake that the Yankees suffer in comparison with the South. In religion, in morals, in patriotism, in education. In true high tone gentility the Yankees are their superiors — in arms their equals.

"In my rambles I visited the Cemetery. It is a beautiful spot in the same direction from town that the Cemetery at Cadiz is, and much resembling it in the general lie of the ground, though somewhat more rolling. [He visited Green Hill, east of town like the new Cadiz cemetery; but it is laid out on its hill in an elaborate symmetry of concentric circles, around a central landscaped circle and chapel.] It has been the burying ground for 10 or 12 years for a city of four thousand inhabitants, and of course is much better cared for. A family living on the one corner of it has the care of it…. The first and greatest object of interest to me was the graves of Union soldiers. They sleep on the west corner next town in a row, their feet to the East, according to the manner of burial of our fathers, time immemorial indicating their belief in the coming of the savior to raise the dead at the last day. They number in all forty graves, all marked with nice little head and foot boards. Only three of them have any names upon them.— These are A. Bachelor, Co. D, H. Botham and I. Van Metre, Co. B, 65th Illinois Infantry. The graves have been nicely dressed up and leveled on their top so as to make room for planting two rows of moss, from head to foot.— This moss is of a kind I have never seen before, it remains uninjured throughout the coldest weather, and soon spreads so as to make the whole grave one green matt. Upon asking the sexton's wife, who was so kind as to care thus for the poor Union soldiers' graves? She pointed me to her daughter and another young lady, and said they and about a dozen other young ladies did it. Of course I thanked them in behalf of myself, my fellow sol-diers and the friends of the deceased. May God render *their* memorial everlasting, and may their death beds be peaceful and happy for the kindness they have shown to these poor strangers in their sickness and death! The following are all the names to be found: Lieut. S. J. Jones, Co. A, 13th Ala, Charles Bryant, N.C. Regt., P. Gwin, S.C., D. Right, Oct. 13, 1862. Death is the great pacifier. These sons of America rushed to arms, those from the distant south to assail, those from the great west to defend the flag of our fathers. Animated by these respective purposes they meet on this blood ground deadly enemies, though personally never having heard of each other, and bearing each other no ill will.— But their hostility has ceased. They sleep peacefully in this plat — more fortunate perhaps if prepared to die than their fellows in getting away so soon. They know which side is right in this struggle. And the day is coming when the highest tribunal in the universe will decide this question in the face of assembled worlds, and when we will make inquisition for blood at some bodies hands. And wo to those men at whose door it is laid!

"A person is struck in passing among the graves here as well as in every Cemetery with the bad taste exhibited in many of the inscriptions, as well as bad grammar. It is best as a general rule simply to inscribe the dates of birth, death and the age, and if anything else is desired, let it be some appropriate sentence from the Bible, brief and well chosen. I had intended giving a couple of verses of doggerel which I copied from one stone, but will not take time to do so. Were such an inscription on the grave of a friend of mine I would have it obliterated.

"In some cases singularly good taste is exhibited. Some Inscriptions evidently written by the same hand were singularly simple and beautiful, in my opinion. They are as follows: Rosana Doll, aged 43 years. '*Her faith and hope, under severe protracted bodily suffering, endured to the end.*' What a volume is couched in this sentiment! … Happy family if this is a true record! Whoever wrote these inscriptions understood the Christian religion, and, in my opinion, had exquisite taste…. The health of the Regiment is good, I may say, though … the measels have broken out among us. Geo. Jones, Samuel Love, Hugh R. Thompson and Solomon Little have them — of my company…. They are quartered in a church, have their beds in the pews, two pews being put together for each bed. The house is very comfortable. The danger consists in exposure after having the measels. They are a dangerous thing for the soldier to have. He needs to be at the fireside at home and to have a kind cautious mother's care. I will have the boys cared for as well as I can….

"One of our company cooks — a contraband — was taken from us the other day. He belonged to a rebel by the name of Stuart. Stuart came to Camp and saw his negro. Whether he said anything to our field officers on the subject or not I don't know. But the boys manifested their disgust by throwing stones after him and shouting as he passed out of the lines. The next, however, he came back with a squad of Cavalry when we were out on dress-parade. Went to the Lieutenant Colonel, told him that he had authority from Colonel McReynolds [Andrew T.

McReynolds, 1st New York Cavalry] to take the negro and pointed to the Cavalry of which the Colonel is in command. The Lieutenant Colonel supposing all was right, of course told him to proceed. — At this point I came into Camp and supposing that the troops had the authority of those named above and that it was useless to resist, sent the negro word to run for his life. But the poor, timid creature only ran over into the next regiment encamped beside us and entered a tent. That Regiment was out on dress parade too and had no time to think. The slave-catchers pursued him, dragged him out of his tent, put him on a horse and galloped off. — You have seen the hawk dart down upon a chicken and have heard its piercing screams as it was borne off in the talons of its cruel foe, until they died away and its head dropped. How indignant and sorry you felt. What our feelings were you may imagine them when we saw this cold hearted villain carry off the helpless, unoffending victim of his avarice, whose labor and intellect he has stolen, as well as the labor of his mother before him. 'Now,' said several of the boys, 'I wish I was at home.' The democrats were as mad as the republicans. Some of them would have shot him if I had let them. 'Now,' says the Chaplain, 'I am sick.' Another told me he could not eat. I told him I felt like eating bones and all. Ah, we are at school here. We have seen in a mild way the cursed root of all our troubles. What mean these blood-stained battle-fields in all thy borders, Old Virginia, in which flow rivers of blood, Northern and Southern, in a common stream. This! 'Behold the cries of the oppressed have entered into the ear of the Lord of Sabaoth.'…

"After the colored man was gone,

we discovered that it was a complete imposition practiced upon us by about a dozen of the N. Y. Cavalry in connection with Stuart, for which they were no doubt well paid, and that Colonel McReynolds was ignorant of the matter. He promised to have the guilty perpetrators punished if he could discover them. Whether he succeeded I have not heard. I told him to inform his men that if another such attempt was made I would empty their saddles for them. He said I would have done right had I done so....

"But the Devil in this case, as he often does, over shot the mark. It has roused the indignation of the whole Regiment and the adjoining New York Regiment too and shown to our officers the state of feeling on this subject. It has revealed the path for us to pursue in the future. Colonel McReynolds told me his way of doing. When a man came to his tent at North Mountain, a few days ago, and said: 'Colonel I want your authority to take this nigger back to Maryland.' 'Let go that man's neck,' said the Colonel, 'before you speak to me. That is no way to catch a man.' He let go. 'Now,' says the Colonel, 'what do you want?' He repeated his request. 'Well,' said the Colonel, 'we soldiers have nothing to do with the Colored man.' (which by the way was not correct) 'if he wants to go with you you can take him if not it is not our lookout.' The negro, turning on his heel, said: 'Massa, me not dun want to go.' The Slave-holder stepped off amid the shouts of the soldiers. The next negro whose master comes won't want to leave us either, I expect, and if his master touches him we will arrest him as a disturber of the peace.

"I am sorry for the colored man, but seeing he was taken back I am glad I saw it. I shall not soon forget the horrible sight, for which some people have such a taste, nor my feelings in seeing it. I have learned something. As I told the Chaplain, I wanted to see the Devil once in his lair. 'But,' said he, 'I don't like to see him eating the lambs.' But thank God the jaws of the lion are broken, the prey taken from the mighty and three millions of captives delivered, so far as our Government is concerned. J. S. McCready, Capt. Co. 'H'" (*CR* 28 Ja).

This camp had "lots of music," because the New York regiment had a "splendid brass band," Frank Grove wrote Nancy. The 126th soon started its own; on 2 Feb. Frank recorded, "Today I received the Symbols and became a member of the Brass Band." The soldiers went in great numbers to dances held for them in town; Frank tried to attend one on New Year's night, "but when I got allmost thare I saw thare was a fuss kicked up thare was a crowd in the street trying to break in & some one in the inside was shooting out of the window at them to keep them back so I thought that was not the place for me."

Capt. McCready soon entered Martinsburg society as the minister at a wedding. "The preachers here are secesh. And this couple, a few drops of the old Revolutionary blood coursing in their veins, said they would not be married by a rebel if they never should be married. The Chaplain being away they sent for me." He described the wedding of Henry Gettle and Lucinda Virginia Drake, on the evening of 5 Feb.: "It may be interesting to a portion of my readers to state farther that the bride was dressed in white — 'white,' what says some one. That's too deep a question for me. [This Victorian fashion was too impractical and pretentious for the Ohioans; however, it surprised and pleased G. A. Custer, who remarked on the "pure white" worn by a Virginia bride and bridesmaid in 1862, and their unsurpassed beauty, in a letter to his sister (Whittaker 127).] The entertainment consisted of three kinds of beautiful cake and a little wine. The couple and guests looked cheerful and happy, and I am sure I wish the choicest of heavens blessings to rest upon them…. How strange and beautiful an institution marriage is, bringing into the closest relationship, confidence and intimacy two strangers perchance, and binding their hearts together with cords of love strong as death! It is a relic of paradise. It and the sabbath are twin sisters of innocence, and trace their origin back to Eden…. Much of the misery in this world results from … insincerity and infidelity in this relation. But far more than counterbalancing all this is the happiness resulting from it, to those who enter into it in the fear of God" (*CR* 25 F).

The Symbols in the Grass

Picket duty in snowstorms and exposure to the weather and germs in the camp quickly crippled the regiment. By the end of January, Surgeon Estep's sick list had "a daily average of one hundred and sixty-five cases, made up of Catarrhal, Typhoid Fever, Measles, Mumps, Small Pox and Sporadic cases…. We have to accommodate this large number in our regimental tents,

one small brick church and a new frame house that I seized and appropriated as Hospitals. And all the Government has supplied me with as bedding is twenty blankets, yet by confiscation and donations received, have cared for sixty-five cases — several others are in private houses…. Many of the delicacies and necessities for the sick have been freely furnished by the whole-souled, soldier-loving, loyal and angelic ladies of this place, for which they have my warmest thanks. What we most need is bedding, such as ticks for straw, pillow slips, blankets, sheets, comforts, old worn out shirts and sheets … and delicacies for the sick" (*CDS* 4 F). Later, Dr. Estep thanked the Cadiz Soldiers' Aid Society for 2 woolen shirts, 4 pairs socks, 4 white blankets, 2 carpet blankets, 1 coverlet, pillow ticks, and dried apples (*CR* 25 F).

Writing to Robert Mitchell, whose health was improving at home, on 6 Feb. Frank Grove observed, "Thare is a great many of our Regt sick and a good many dieing. John Mitchell has got his discharge papers from the Doctor, I suppose. He will not be here long after he gits them signed. He looks bad but I think if he gits home he will git better. Thare is a great many being discharged from the Regt…. Samuel Hines is sick. I think he will have to be discharged…. We don't drill any this bad weather. We have got about through all the drill. I like the bayonet drill the best."

Samuel Hines described his illness in replying to a letter from his cousin Nancy on 8 Feb.: "i hant bin well for some time i hav had a bad cold and i got so bad that i coodent eat eny thing for about to weaks. i got vary pore…. this is a bad plase to get sick. a man hast to lay in theas hard tents or go to the hospitle and Dont like to go to one of them. it is sutchey bad smeling plase. a Man wood get sicker theare then in the tent. i will hav a bad cof all the time when i lay down. i cof right smart…. thare is to hundred and fifty ant abel for duty. thare is fifteen died in the regment. thare has bin to in our Company. the names of them was William Toole and Harvy Watson. Thay ar sent hom…. well Nancy i will try and bee a good boy as long as i am in the army. i wont gambel or drink whiskey aney strong drink. Thare is some very bad men in the reg. Thay dont care for nothing. i hope i may bee at home before long when i can dwel in peace at home."

These men had no money to spend on whiskey or healthful provisions. They were anxiously awaiting a visit from the pay master, McCready reported, and all had been borrowing from each other, dividing up "the last half dime, the last apple, or the last loaf." They would not be paid until 28 March, when Frank received five months' pay, of $71.50. On 19 Feb. the company's circumstances were "gloomy": "Our sick list numbers *thirty-three* today, thirty the day before…. several of these are in delicate health, one in immediate danger. Yesterday we buried one of our boys — John Gibbons. He died a few minutes after 12 on sabbath. — Poor fellow! he was a pleasant boy of 19, raised in Tuscarawas county. His father is living and he greatly desired to see him before he would die. But though I telegraphed he did not come. John was of a quiet turn, was always pleasant, always at the post of duty, willing to do his part. I hope he is infinitely better off than with us. But he will be

missed here, and no doubt missed at his father's fireside at home. His usual answer when asked how he was, was 'O pretty well' and that even when it took two or three breaths to express it. May God comfort his bereaved relatives and make the stroke profitable to them and to us!

"In regard to the Hospital arrangements I would not wish to deceive the people at home…. of course the nurse who has twenty sick to wait on cannot minister to them with a wife's or mother's or sister's care, who can sit by the bed side and whisper kind sweet soft words of sympathy. But as far as I can judge the sick are kindly cared for. The nurses seem kind, attentive and efficient. The Doctors (there are three of them for the Regiment) are a busy set of men and for aught I know skillful medical men…. And there is one thing for which I will praise them, and that is their willingness, to lay aside for the moment everything, that we may pray with and for the sick…. But the Measles Hospital has been too much crowded. I requested and obtained leave to get my convalescent sick out to private houses. A convalescent Hospital has been opened which will enlarge the room and separate the convalescent from the dying….

"There is but *one* thing of which I can make any complaint…. A soldier may be at the point of death and his discharge paper may be sent off and his discharge morally certain and yet *he cannot get home.* A man's family may be dying and it may be evident that his services will not be needed for a month, but he cannot get home. Let me give a few cases which actually occurred, as a specimen. A man's hand was wounded so as to disable him for weeks. He got word that his wife was dying. He could not get away.— Another got a furlough asking in the name of the Surgeon that he get leave *to go home to die*. He could not get it. A Captain got word that his children were sick and his wife going to die. He could not get home a day.— Now this is both wicked and foolish…. See its effects. It keeps soldiers here to die, who, could they get home to sit among their friends, eat at their own tables, and drink out of their own fountains, might get well…. Also it involves useless expense — in subsistence and medical stores. It promotes sickness by crowding so many together. It promotes desertion the very thing it was intended to prevent. Are there not hundreds at home now? Will the people arrest them and send them back? …The people don't think they did much harm in going home any way they could when there was no way they could get home honorable. Another thing, it is diminishing our army unnecessarily.— What is its effect but this? The Surgeon often cannot decide certain whether a man will die or live. Two ways are open for him, either to err on the side of mercy and discharge the man, or keep him until he dies to see whether he is entitled to a discharge. The Surgeon and company officers are apt to choose the former alternative and in this way a great many are discharged who will get well. If these doubtful cases could get leave to go home, many of them would return in the Spring and do good service…. J. S. McCready" (*CR* 25 F).

At the end of February, John L. Mitchell deserted. Frank revealed this in a letter to Nancy on 24 Feb., among other observations: "Oh Nan you just ought to hear the Union Women here telling about what hard times they had when the Rebels was here. Some of them hid thair men up the chimney to keep the Rebels from gitting them. Well Nancy I suppose robert will be going back to the army before long. I expect you will be as sorry to see him go as you ware the first time. that is the objection I have to going home, parting with friends & loved ones when the time comes to start back. Well Nan I suppose from your letter a good many of the girls will be married before I git back. When Warfels leaves Charlestown [Charles Warfel was building a house in Cadiz] the town will be allmoast broke up for want of girls. Well I suppose Ellen Mitchell has had a new beau. I wonder if Gabriel has quit blowing. did you see anything of John Mitchell. he is missing from here. Thare is a heap of sickness here yet & thare is a death allmost every day. I don't think any of our Regt has the smallpox now. but it is said some of the New York regt has them. Well I heard that Bill McBride is dead. I was sorry to hear of his death. but so it is. Do you have preaching regular. I often think of the pleasant times we used to have rideing from Church together. do you remember the time you got throwed off your horse comeing from Church, right thare by whare the darkies lives. Oh I ammagine I see you yet."

The 126th's chaplain was composing verses, in his moments away from the sick and dying. As soon as large hospital tents arrived for the camp and were supplied with cots and invalids, a vision struck: the grass began to grow inside most curiously. By midmonth, thick grass rose to the beds where the fevered lay, and it flourished as never on the farm. The blanched and crimsoned faces stared across a sea of brilliant green. One sick soldier whispered, "Chaplain, I have been thinking about this grass. It's a strange place for it to grow." The providence of this grass was a mystery, compounded by its springing from earth torn and packed in the fall by Stonewall Jackson's camp upon it. The Rev. J. K. Andrews in ferment began a poem he titled "The Sick Soldier's Talk with the Grass Growing in the Hospital":

Strangely out of time and place!
How came you here?
Why thus appear?
Come you forth to chide and blame,
Crimson mortal cheek with shame,
Or bring you cheer?

Winter's scepter rules the hour;
Fierce winds blow,
The drifting snow
Wildly careers. E'en the ground
Lies ice-locked close around
Where now you grow.
....

Fragile, tender, beauteous thing!
Encircled so
By scenes of woe;
Tainted by the fevered breath;
Tortured by the moan of death;
Yet still you grow.
Not the hard and heavy tread
Of foeman's foot
That crushed your root;
Not the winter's killing breath
Wilts, or blights, or dooms to death,
Your tender shoot.

Higher, stronger, still you grow;
As though the while
Ye would beguile
Thoughts away from piteous moans,

Sickening sights, and dying groans,
By life's sweet smile.

Hast thou, stranger, tongue and message?
Then speak, for lo!
My soul would know
From thee, prophet thou, or preacher,
Heavenly, or earthly teacher,
Why all this woe?
Sufferer, I have a message,
Hear it thou; 'Tis heaven's presage
Both you, and I
Are doomed to die
And lowly lie.
Yet when life's o'er,
And I'm no more,
You, immortal shall survive.
On, still on, the soul must live
    Forevermore.
....

Soldier! wan, and wasted now,
Death-dew gathering on the brow,
Catch these whispers soft and low:
....

You *die* to *save*—
Save a periled nation's life,
End a nation's bloody strife,
And free the slave.
Patriot! Listen! I've for thee
Gladdening words of prophesy.
As in the dust
By foeman crushed,
Downtrodden, I
Did helpless lie,
And yet not die;
With sickening moans,
And dying groans,
And fevered breath,
And taint of death
Poisoning the air;
Green, fresh and fair
Before your eyes
You see me rise….(Andrews)

On 27 February his versification of "All this wailing," "Baptism of fire," and "Springing germs of liberty" ended. The poem had 169 lines. Too many — but only four apiece for the men of his reg-iment dead and dying in Martinsburg. Less than a couplet each for them and the others so broken in health they had to be discharged.

Chapter 19

Spring Returns

Discharged from the Martinsburg hospital, the sick James Oglevee came home on 7 March, as the rutted roads vanished in a driving snow storm (*CR* 11 Mr). This was the day for the "Grand Rally"; the "roads, like the abolition party, were in a horrible condition; and, as if in conspiracy with the storm-king, no trains were run on the Cadiz Branch until late in the afternoon, on account of the bursting of a flue of the locomotive early in the morning." Yet the "Gallant Democracy" picked their paths from the Stumptown blacksmith shop and elsewhere, into Cadiz. Their celebrated guests Dr. Olds and Mr. Converse, however, were stranded at the Junction, until some German township Democrats found them and promptly "went to work, got a hand car, and by hard untiring effort" pumped the miles up the grade to deliver them to the anticipated momentous occasion (*CDS* 11 Mr).

At one o'clock the bell called the men — nearly a thousand, according to C. N. Allen — to the courthouse. It "filled to overflowing, and hundreds went away unable to gain admittance";

the "jam inside ... was awful." James B. Jamison, chairman of the Central Committee, announced their purposes of organizing for the spring and fall elections, and hearing their speakers. Allen, Josiah Estep, Philip Donahue, Allen Maxwell, and Barrack Oglevee were appointed a Committee on Resolutions. Dr. Olds then spoke for two hours with "resistless force of logic" to "deafening shouts of applause" and cheers that "almost lifted the roof." He "held the immense audience spell-bound with an irresistible array of facts, convicting the party in power of a premeditated attack on the American Union" and making a "powerful and heart-touching appeal for peace" (*CDS* 11 Mr). Clearly, Olds echoed the House oration of Vallandigham, who now was running for fall election to the powerful, pivotal position of Governor of Ohio.

After Olds's address, Allen read thirteen resolutions from his committee. These also digested Vallandigham's peace proposals, except that they called for a national convention soon; and they distilled some significant phrasings.

They condemned secession but asserted that states could not be coerced, whose "people are the supreme power," superior to any of government. They attacked usurpations of liberties and vowed that "only State authority" could preserve them — meaning that a Governor Vallandigham should overrule federal laws and edicts, including military orders. Other resolutions pronounced abolitionism "moral treason," the Emancipation Proclamation unconstitutional, the new Conscription Bill a "subversive" act which the state should "resist"; they disallowed any war settlement separating Ohio from the Mississippi Valley states. The "vast audience" adopted all the resolutions "without a single dissenting voice." They moved to send their resolutions to newspapers in Cadiz, also St. Clairsville, New Philadelphia, Guernsey County, Columbus, and Cincinnati (*CDS* 11 Mr).

Mr. Converse then attacked the new Conscription Bill in a "telling speech," despite his bad cold — no doubt worsened by his hand-car ride through the snow storm. His topic did not require much oratory, however. This bill ordered all males between 20 and 45, white and black, to enroll for the draft, exempted no one for religious reasons, and threatened anyone who resisted or advised others to avoid military service with a $500 fine and two years in prison. Soldiers absent from duty had to return by 1 April, or be punished for desertion. Families or friends who harbored deserters faced fines of $500 and from six months to two years in prison. Further, provost marshals were being sent to arrest deserters wherever they could find them, and send them to the nearest mil-

itary post (*CR, CDS* 4 Mr, 11 Mr, 18 Mr). The family of John L. Mitchell and many others would soon be lawbreakers.

Two days before the rally, a different danger had appeared to Allen, when the editorial offices of Samuel Medary at the Columbus *Crisis* were wrecked by a mob of about 200 soldiers and citizens. Medary was away at the time (*CDS* 11 Mr). Allen blamed abolitionist incitement, and grew fearful of his own such emergency; probably to protect his establishment he moved it this month to a prominent location, one door west of Hogg's storeroom on Main Street, opposite Lemmon's tavern, a frame building formerly the residence of William Hogg, which Allen purchased (*CDS, CR* 1 Ap). Into it Allen likely moved with his family, and remained day and night to guard his office and presses. If so, his wife endured pitiable hours overhead the banging presses.

The *CR* contradicted Allen's account of the rally, claiming it drew only two or three hundred men, they did not all agree with the resolutions, which were Donahue's, and several fistfights broke out. Subsequently, though, Hatton granted the rally's general amity, in contrasting it with one held the day before it in Canton. There, no public hall would admit Olds and Converse, they made their speeches in the street, and a large-scale fistfight ended the meeting (*CR* 11 Mr, 18 Mr).

Hatton's criticism of the rally showed "his natural habit — lying," Allen replied, beginning a lengthy attack. The party leaders supported the peace platform, and Estep had helped write the resolutions, in his own office the night before the meeting. Allen himself had favored the war until the Emancipation Proclamation; and after it he ceased to support Lincoln or the war. Hatton could call him "traitor," "butternut," or any other name, so long as it wasn't "Abolitionist" (*CDS* 18 Mr, 25 Mr).

In regard to the racial bigotry at the core of this political shift — and also some of Allen's charges that Hatton had discouraged army recruitment — one of its odd manifestations first appeared the week after the rally, when with blackened faces the "Union Minstrels" gave a "concert" in the courthouse to benefit the Soldiers' Aid Society, performing several plays with music to provide "a hearty laugh." The 15¢ tickets sold so well for their Thursday night show that they repeated it on Friday (*CDS* 18 Mr). The eight "Ethiopian Minstrels" raised $30 (*CR* 1 Ap, 15 Ap). One of them was Charles P. Dewey, who had been in the 30th Ohio from 1 March 1862 until discharged after Antietam, and his travels may have acquainted him with the shows he and his friends imported to Cadiz. He likely was one of the boys who had been "run off" to the army according to a Hatton editorial the week of his enlistment, a piece Allen now copied in charging Hatton had defamed recruiting officers: "We have had in our midst, for some two months, a couple of MILITARY LOAFERS, from Captain Cunningham's company, who have ... induc[ed] boys to violate their engagements, and leave their homes and employment contrary to the wishes of their parents; and they have succeeded in clandestinely running off some three or four boys from this place in a mean, underhanded and dishonorable way. The boys, we understand, were sworn in SE-CRETLY by Lieut. John Brown..." (*CDS* 1 Ap). The son of banker Chauncey Dewey was not one of Hatton's printers, however, as Allen implied.

Allen also claimed Hatton had unpatriotically opposed and then ended his son's service. The Hattons had had other reasons for objecting: Benjamin Franklin Hatton (Benjamin in the 1860 census, Frank thereafter) was only fifteen when he ran away from home to become the drummer boy for his brother-in-law's company of the 74th (*DAB*). His discharge in July from Nashville occurred among ten from his company by the surgeons, and two deaths from disease; so illness likely effected it.

During March, Allen's paper accused Hatton of all kinds of lies and crookedness, to which Hatton gave this answer: "Charley Allen is evidently the *biggest liar* and the *greatest blackguard* to be found outside of *perdition*. We mean politically, of course; for, aside from politics, he is rather a clever kind of fellow. But, politically, there is nothing too mean for him to descend to" (*CR* 1 Ap). Allen's and his cohorts' primary rants against emancipation had such a political motive; and, to incite fears of inundation by freed slaves, they spouted propaganda with stereotypes that belied their own personal knowledge. Allen's racist diatribes were lies about people who were his neighbors. A glimpse at the editors' immediate neighborhoods in the 1860 census shows that both were well acquainted with respectable black families who had established themselves through long and self-sponsored migrations.

Allen's house sat just outside the village limits at township #218. At #219 lived John Ward, 61, his wife, a seamstress daughter, and a child. At #220 was Robert Fife, a farmhand, his wife, both 20, and a baby. At #221 lived Lot Willis, 37, a black barber born in Virginia, listing $400 in real and $1,000 in personal property. With him lived six Willis children, all born in Ohio, and all over four in age attending school. Also residing with Willis were Fleming Peterson, 16, a black barber born in Ohio; Rezree Lawrence, 17, a black farmhand attending school, born in Ohio; Frances West, 16, a black domestic born in Virginia; and Sally Gasing, 60, mulatto, born in Virginia.

The abolitionist Hatton had similar neighbors. His house was #7 in the village. #5 housed Susan Johnson, a mulatto washerwoman born in Virginia and her five children: William and Walker were both 14, Catherine, 7, born in Virginia; Frances and Laura were younger and born in Ohio; all these children over four in age were attending school. With Susan Johnson also lived Sarah Mason, 16, born in Virginia and attending school. At #6 lived James Coursey, 36, a black laborer born in Ohio with $50 in personal property; his wife Chloe, born in Virginia; and three young children, with the oldest, Anne, 5, in school.

Therefore the racist calumnies Allen published grossly misrepresented people whom he knew.

The political excitement of March included the rumored arrival of secret societies bent on threats and violence. Hatton published a report that Olds and Converse were organizers of the "Knights of the Golden Circle"; he subsequently declared this secret society was established in the county, and plotting

the "downfall of the government" (18 Mr). An opposing group arose in local chapters of the National Union Association, first formed in the courthouse 14 March, the Laceyville schoolhouse two days later, then elsewhere (CR 11 Mr, 18 Mr). In one denunciation of this "secret military organization," Allen warned that its scheduled speaker, Lewis Lewton, was "better suited to blackguarding and slandering decent and respectable young ladies than he is to make political speeches" (18 Mr).

The heavy ammunition used by both camps came in reports and letters of soldiers. One of Norris' men in the 98th wrote that his company, including its Democrats, favored military service, of any kind, for blacks: "so let Charley [Allen] quit howling that the soldiers are opposed to the negroes being put in the service; for it is false, and … slanders the soldiers…" (CR 4 Mr). The 126th in Martinsburg sent both papers resolutions opposing the new Democratic positions (CR 4 Mr). Allen refused to print these and alleged the men had been ordered to vote for them (CR 11 Mr). The *Sentinel* returned fire with a reprinted letter from the 37th Ohio opposite Vicksburg which complained the soldiers were "treated like dogs" and asserted the war was clearly futile. A letter from an unnamed soldier in Capt. Voorhee's Co., 126th, castigated the abolitionists of his regiment, and the war: "This is nothing but a cursed negro war…. They say there is going to be another draft, but I don't want to see another man come out of Ohio" (18 Mr).

The soldiers' views were considered so significant that Democrats launched letters to influence them. From near

Murfreesboro on 13 March, Capt. T. C. McIlravy, 74th, reported receiving some which he knew "from the slang, have been gotten up by rebel sympathizers." Such writers, he warned in a sulfurous local reference, "had better go and stick their heads in some coal bank" instead of "lighting up their secesh gas and trying to spread it" among the troops, who would deem it a duty to return and "blot out any black-mouthed secesh, or quell any meeting composed of such." McIlravy soon provided a mild foretaste, when on 27 March he attended a School Exhibition in Cadiz, rose at its close, and called on Philip Donahue to answer whether anyone in the county opposed suppressing the rebellion. The audience asked Donahue to speak, "but he stood *pale* and *speechless*" (*CR* 1 Ap).

Soldiers writing to Hatton began to threaten violence. One of Voorhee's reported, "You ought to hear the boys swear when they get the Cadiz *Sentinel*"; they wanted to return home and "*hang the Peace cowards*" (11 Mr). From Capt. Hanna's Co., 69th, G. W. Brown, a Democrat, declared that Allen, Donahue, and Phillips should "stretch hemp," and that soldiers in his corps despised such men more than the "rankest rebel in the Southern army" (18 Mr).

How adamant such threats were, people at home could not know; but they could not expect soldiers to return unchanged. Some came back outlaws, like the former Steubenville attorney caught and sentenced there this month for horse-stealing. Capt. Wm. Simpson claimed to have lost his mind in the Battle of Wilson's Creek, Missouri, in August 1861, after which he wandered through Virginia and worked in a Balti-

more saloon, before coming to his old neighborhood and joining "an organized band of horse thieves." He received five years at hard labor (*CDS* 25 Mr).

Soldiers' homecomings, on the other hand, could be cruel receptions. Wesley S. Poulson, discharged from the Perryville hospital, in Cincinnati was "hopping away from the [railroad] cars with one leg" when a man accosted him: "That's what you get by freeing the d — d niggers. You'd better staid at home." Scant respect would greet Capt. Butts when he came home from the hospital and army; he was widely derided for mistreating his men, not permitting them "as much privilege as other Captains did their men," Poulson explained, to confiscate "apples, peaches, chickens, geese, turkeys, pigs, sheep" along their way (*CR* 4 Mr).

As furloughs ended for the convalescing soldiers of the 98th, and toleration for desertions, the news of the army they would rejoin in Tennessee was not inviting. About twenty-five miles south of Nashville, five regiments had been "cut to pieces" by the enemy, and four regiments mostly captured (*CDS*, *CR* 11 Mr).

From Martinsburg arrived more corpses — from Capt. Voorhee's company, Thomas McClain of North township and John Cole of Rumley — more sick and deserters, but no pay for families. Capt. McCready again complained of the townships' lack of support, concluding with an extract from a wife's letter: "'Dear husband — xxx I wish you were home. I think more long to see you than any one else. I am trying very hard to learn to write so that I can write letters to you. I am trying this winter to live better than I used to. I have joined Church. I want you to live better too. Your baby can walk some. I have not got the children baptized yet but will as soon as I can take them out. I have seen more trouble and hardships this winter than ever I did before. Mrs. ___ wont rent the house to me this summer. I dont know what I'll do.' I asked him why she could not get the house again. He said because they could not get money to pay the rent…. Those who know say they are very poor…. Her husband is a good soldier. His neighbors promised to support his wife. But all I will add is that she shall have a house if we should have to sell ours. J. S. McCready" (*CR* 11 Mr).

During the stormy month, the regiment moved its camp a short distance to improve health, according to Frank Grove's diary; and on 17 March a teacher came to give the new band its first lesson. Disease and desertion continued to preoccupy them. Samuel Hines wrote to Nancy on 27 March: "i hope John will soon get well a gane. i hav got the sore throat prety bad. i was in the Convalesont hospitle for five weeaks…. i coodent hardly eat aney thing…. thay poot me on guard yesterday and then i got it a gane as bad as ever…. thare was to in our Company Dissorted and has gon home. some whar els thay got a pass to go after some sassefrack and thay Dident return…. i hope that thay may get home safe to for if thay ar brot back thay will bee punished prety bad for runing of…. well i will bee a good boy and i will go to Church evry Day."

Sick soldiers returning home brought with them the pestilences of camps and hospitals. From this time forward, illness and deaths in their neigh-borhoods increased dramatically. On Irish Ridge, old Samuel McFadden (Irish) was dying in the horrors of typhoid fever. The chronic and seasonal illnesses which people usually weathered, moreover, were aggravated by the stress of worry and care for their soldiers. Eliza Ann Oglevee, mother of James, Finley, and Hugh, was dying of her consumption at age fifty-four (*CR* 8 Ap).

This season also brought farm families their most intensive day and night labor, as they had to assist the ewes giving birth, and their lambs. As "Wolf" attested, the farmers were extending their flocks to even higher numbers, so they had many novice, nervous mothers to attend. They had fewer hands than ever for this lambing; all had long work managing births, warming lambs, getting them to breathe and suckle, and caring for the orphans (Parker 156, 162, 171, 185).

Yet the farmers flocked to campaign joustings. The county's schoolhouses rang with more competing speeches and cheers. John A. Bingham came home and joined Union meetings at the courthouse, with Philip Donahue present as a reporter (*CR* 15 Ap). Allen was too busy to attend. In the moving of his office, his foreman, Wm. H. Arnold, had two fingers "mashed," so Allen had to set type and work the press himself, while Arnold edited the issue. Allen alleged that Arnold demonstrated such editorial ability that henceforth he would be the Associate Editor. Under Arnold, however, the paper filled with European news, a tale of sailors' adventures, and a romance. The touts of Vallandigham shrank, and editorials omitted the hate-mongering epithets of Allen's polemic flair (8 Ap, 15 Ap, 22 Ap,

29 Ap). Meanwhile, Donahue supplied the *Sentinel* with a fulsome Vallandigham campaign in his letters.

The sharp division in the county emerged in the voting on 6 April. Archer, Athens, German, Moorefield, Rumley, and Stock townships gave peace Democrats victories; Cadiz, Franklin, Greene, North, Nottingham, Shortcreek, and Washington elected the Union ticket. In Cadiz township, Republicans James H. Haverfield and Joseph Sharon and Union Democrat John C. Jamison became trustees, defeating James B. Jamison, John M. Ritchey, and Robert Cochran. The counties of the area also disagreed: Belmont, Carroll, and Tuscarawas went Democratic, Guernsey was mixed, and Jefferson chose Union candidates (*CR* 8 Ap, *CDS* 15 Ap).

The larger campaigns raged on. On 11 April, Bingham defended the Conscription Act before the Union Association (*CR* 15 Ap). In reporting the speech as "Looker On," Donahue charged Bingham with urging his partisans "to dish out our [Democratic] presses in the streets" if they continued to oppose the Administration; "He also declares that every man who dares speak thus, should be made feel that in doing so he is perilling his life." Donahue urged the county's Democrats to be "willing and READY to risk your lives in defense" of your rights; "then make all NEEDFUL preparations": "Let us be ready, at a moment's warning, to avenge ourselves upon any man who dares follow the instructions of this disturber of the peace of society" (*CDS* 15 Ap).

Soon the Democratic presses of Ohio had picked up Donahue's "quotation"; the Mt. Vernon *Banner* labeled Bingham a "'crack-brained Abolitionist'" whose "'head should be shaved and a poultice of ice applied to his fevered brain'" (*CDS* 29 Ap). Donahue expanded his charge against Bingham, which Hatton termed false, as he went "from schoolhouse to schoolhouse advising resistance to the draft." Donahue also, allegedly, proclaimed that if the Conscription Act were enforced, "John A. Bingham's house would be laid in ashes"; and urged Democrats "to go armed, all the time" (*CR* 22 Ap, 6 My).

Another local orator arose. William A. Pittenger, released from the 98th, addressed the Union Association echoing Bingham: "Shall this nation live or shall it die?" and "The voice from the shade of the august and honored dead, whose hallowed graves are filled with sacrifice for the Union..." (*CR* 22 Ap). With eulogy, Pittenger had recent experience. "Pitt" wrote the death notice of his friend James M. Crawford, 98th, who had died in Franklin, Tenn., on 18 March of typhoid fever: "Yea, CRAWFORD is dead. His spirit has taken flight within the veil, and soared to a clime far above.... As a soldier he was true, brave and faithful...." Pittenger also helped compose the Junto Literary Society's tribute to Crawford, a former member (*CR* 1 Ap, 8 Ap).

Crawford's death in its details, however, had not resembled the valiant warrior's which Pittenger tended to glorify. Capt. Norris wrote to James' father that James had requested that no guns be fired over his grave, meaning no military recognition. Norris had had no instructions to send his body home, so had buried him in two woolen blankets and a heavy coffin in case his father could come to remove him (*CDS* 1 Ap). This brief letter bore the grim reality.

At April's end, the peace campaign was going full tilt, with the sharp, express charge against the President that he had in December received an offer of peace from Richmond. In New York, Fernando Wood announced to a meeting that he had the "documents to PROVE" it, and did not publish them only because of a promise made to a "high government official"—who was, by another account, the President himself. Vallandigham in his Ohio speeches testified that this letter existed, a proposal of reunion and peace which Lincoln had immediately rejected, to which he responded by sending 20,000 Union soldiers to their deaths at Fredericksburg. The stage was set for Ohio's Democratic Rally on 1 May in Mt. Vernon, with speeches by Vallandigham, Medary, and others—"an array of talent" (*CDS* 22 Ap).

At last the long winter's drenches had retreated; new grass shimmered on the hills, orchards and woods bloomed, and the lanes invited young men to hire a team and buggy and take a "festive damsel" for a drive (*CDS, CR* 22 Ap). The courtship season featured jokes about daughters "*pressed* into the *infantry* service," recalcitrant old bachelors, and "lucifer matches" made at the altar. It inspired pranks: the published marriage notices of three couples were discovered to be some rascal's forgeries to embarrass them (*CR* 22 Ap, 29 Ap). Cadiz was musically prepared for it, as shown by a list Hatton gave in reply to the *Carrolton Courier*'s brag that its town, with ten pianos, was unequaled: Cadiz had over thirty pianos; five

melodeons; one brass band; one band of Ethiopian minstrels; innumerable guitars, bass viols, banjos, tambourines, and castanets; one church organ; and several church choirs (15 Ap).

For at least one young woman, thoughts of romance stirred mourning, and L. F. of the Rumley village of Jefferson published her "Lines written on the Death of C. L. Duffield" (30th, shot at Antietam): "…O! 'tis hard to give thee up, / One as talented, kind, and young… / Yet I wait in patient sadness, / To join thee in a fairer clime" (*CR* 15 Ap). L. F. was probably Lydia Ferguson; she never did marry.

The wartime situation of another woman emboldened her to venture to speak not only publicly, but also for pay. Mrs. Buckley, whose husband was in the army, had the justifying aim of supporting herself and her children. First she spoke at the courthouse on Temperance, and proved herself "a *good* talker." She offered another free afternoon lecture for ladies only, in the Masonic Hall, and proposed a series of eight talks, with a charge of one dollar each, if ladies would subscribe. Her daring subject would be Physiology. The prejudice against such a project was clear in the recommendation to attend: "It is always better to *hear*, before we condemn." For her independent, self-reliant character, and undoubted understanding of her subject, she deserved patronage (*CR* 15 Ap).

In the cheery light of spring, two young men recently returned from dismal war scenes decided to set out after brighter ones. Thomas H. Smith, McCready's 1st Lieutenant, had resigned in mid-March and arrived home in bad health; a few weeks later he had a commission to recruit the county's first company of cavalry, along with James W. Hanna, who had survived numerous battles and trips to Southern prisons (*CR* 1 Ap, 15 Ap).

Nancy Mitchell found a newly romantic temper in a letter of 9 April from Frank: "I have not fallen in love with any of the Ladies here yet. I have not made up acquaintance with any of them yet, neither do I expect to. For

What are years when absent from thee
What are winning smiles to me,
What are others thoughts & feelings
I care not for aught but thee

"Thare is a great many dances in town here. Some of the boys go, but I have never been at any of them yet.... Thare was a dance in town last night. Thare was a row kicked up & they have a parsel of the boys in the guardhouse today....

"John Mitchell sent for his Millitary clothes. I put them up in a box & Dan Tidrick expressed them home to him. I sent a picture with a company record on it to David Braden with orders to have it framed. It would be worthwhile for you to stop & see it someday. you could see all our officers' names & what position they hold in the Company, who died and who was discharged &c.

[This finely engraved and colored print portrayed female figures of war, peace, and liberty, around two inset battle scenes, above the list of McCready's men. It would be the most elegant picture in many neighborhood homes; Nancy and her cousins would often see it displayed, bearing the record of "3rd Sergeant John L. Mitchell — Deserted."]

"I dont know whether they are going to send for John Mitchell or not. but if they dont he will be caught after while for thare will be Officers round thare afterwhile gathering up deserters. [By month's end, two of Capt. Lyons' Company were in Cadiz looking for deserters (*CR* 29 Ap).] John ought to have went to Columbus before the first of April & I think he could have got a discharge but it would not be safe to go now. Nancy this is a beautiful morning...."

Chapter 20

A Marching Band in the Virginia Mountains

The last week of April, while the Army of the Potomac moved to attack Lee's outnumbered army near Chancellorsville, rebel forces dashed through the mountains in a plan to clear northwestern Virginia of federal control all the way to the Ohio River (*OR* Jones 1.25.1.119). Their progress threatened the capture of all the guard posts, destruction of the crucial B & O railroad bridges, and invasion even of Wheeling. As they advanced they cut telegraph wires, commandeered fresh horses, and quickly made widespread conquest and wreckage, while officials from Cincinnati to Baltimore flurried after information and troops to intercept them. The Union commanders of regiments scattered in the region raced them to this place and that which anticipated attack; they ordered gunboats upriver, on 29 April, to defend Wheeling and Parkersburg; and one colonel became excited to the extent that he stayed in Clarksburg and burned a bridge to its east "in a causeless panic," when he should have

had his troops ten miles east of that, to protect the central rail juncture at Grafton (*OR* 1.25.2.298-9).

The invaders started from the Shenandoah Valley on 20 April. Gen. J. D. Imboden with over 3,300 men, 700 of them mounted, and a battery crossed into the Greenbrier Valley and turned north. Brig. Gen. William E. Jones with 3,000 cavalry headed northwest through the mountains; on 25 April he was reported only twenty miles from the important rail and military depot at New Creek, a town now named Keyser. That night, Col. B. F. Smith was ordered to take the 126th Ohio and Maulsby's battery (6th Virginia, Co. C, under Capt. Thomas A. Maulsby) to New Creek to defend it (*OR* 1.25.1.252-3; 2.34; 2.252).

Names of towns, counties, and other places in this region have changed, but it remains a remote and spectacularly scenic area in the steep mountain ranges and creek valleys with the rushing headwaters of the Potomac. The B & O followed the North Branch of the

Potomac River southwest from Cumberland, Maryland, through these mountains and found rare level space for storehouses at the head of New Creek and its valley, between Knobley Mountain and the Eastern Front Ridge of the Allegheny Mountains. About twenty miles south of the depot town is a pass through the mountain to the east, so narrow the cascading stream which carved it nearly fills the long chasm between the towering rock cliffs. Not a likely avenue for an invasion, Greenland Gap was thought by Gen. Jones to be unguarded until the head of his 1,500 advance cavalry exited into the strait of the valley. There a company of fifty from the 23rd Illinois ("Irish Brigade") and thirty others of the 14th (West) Virginia had scouted the oncoming force and barricaded themselves in a large log church and two log cabins in the cavalry's path. As Jones' men galloped from the Gap, the guards opened fire, and withstood charges from the multiplying enemy, refusing to surrender, until nightfall four hours later, when axes hacked at the windows, torches lit the roof, and a powder keg waited beneath the floor. They became captives bound for the Richmond prison (*OR* Jones 1.25.1.114; Wallace, 108-9; Herbert, 124).

The next day, 26 April, more of Jones' cavalry took the scenic ride through the Gap, while the 126th jolted up the rails to New Creek.

Capt. McCready did not set out to fight the rebels in eagerness, or other martial mood. His thoughts, as he recorded them on 9 May, were still much more those of a minister than a military man: "We took the cars about 6 o'clock A.M. Our Sabbath day was of course gone in a great measure — that beautiful relic of Eden's bliss, and earnest of that rest which remaineth for the people of God in Heaven, which the soldier needs to counteract the demoralising influences of camp life. A person could not read in a small print Bible, owing to the motion of the cars. — all we could do was to lift our eyes to the hills whence cometh our aid occasionally, and try to sleep away the time. We landed at this place around sundown, slept in some soldiers' barracks and the next morning took up our march back into the mountains to 'Greenland Gap,' as a certain pass or opening in the mountains through which the rebels had entered Western Virginia is called, or at least a part of them. Our design was to intercept them if they attempted to return through it or to attack them if we could find them. We went fourteen miles the first day and encamped near night very tired. We arose at three the next morning and marched the other seven miles [to the Gap] against 3 o'clock. It was our first march and went hard. — About noon we marched eight miles farther up to the top of the mountains in the northwest corner of Hardy [now Grant] county. [They followed Jones' cavalry on the Northwestern pike over Allegheny Mountain to Camp Storm, which was a guard post on the Stony River, near a pike junction.] Here we remained quietly until the evening of the President's fast (Thursday) when we were notified that the rebels were approaching with a heavy force and we were ordered to send out a force and blockade the road with fallen trees and to erect breastworks for our defense.

[Jones and Imboden by 30 April had overrun posts from Oakland, Md., to Fairmont, W.Va. Gen. B. F. Kelley at New Creek anticipated a combined attack there over the Northwestern road, and ordered Col. Smith and the 126th to blockade it for miles between Stony River and the North Branch of the Potomac (*OR* Schenck 1.25.2.317).] "The field in which we were encamped was soon full of fallen timber. Never did I see so much work done in so short a time. Whole trees were rolled about like little things. In an hour formidable fortifications were constructed which would have greatly increased our defensive power. And from the cheerful air of the officers and men I have no doubt our regiment would have fought its full weight against any force however great. But it proved a false rumor. On Saturday evening we received orders to be ready at 4 o'clock in the morning to march to New Creek — another Sabbath march! It came. We started. The men were glad to return to civilization — they marched fast [in the valley west of Allegheny Mountain]. We could march better than at first. We were getting used to it. At 12 o'clock we had marched twelve miles. We stopped for dinner. A message met us. We were ordered to turn back and take the road [over the mountain] to Greenland gap once more. Wearied and footsore and above all disgusted with what we believed and what turned out to be nonsense we reached our old camp in the pass, having marched 25 miles that day — a pretty good Sabbath day's journey truly! After remaining there until Thursday, and it raining most of that time terribly, we started at 3 o'clock P.M. and reached here yesterday.... Our campaign turned out as I expected — a bootless one — like all

the Sabbath ones have turned out. I can say as David did 'I know it.' I remembered Bull Run and Ball's Bluff and Winchester and Pea Ridge and Pittsburg Landing and the late expedition against Charleston, which sailed on Sabbath, and possibly the late repulse on the Rappahannock [at Chancellorsville] for aught I know. I hear God speaking in these events with an emphasis which should impress the heart of every general in the land, 'Remember the Sabbath day to keep it holy.'...

"There is much beautiful mountain scenery to be found among them that richly repays the traveler for his painful climbing. [The present-day road from Greenland Gap up Allegheny Mountain, now the site of the village of Mt. Storm, has over six and one-half miles of 9 percent grade.] The top of the mountain on which we encamped and which I suppose is a fine representation of the Alleghenies, generally is too cold for wheat and corn, but produces abundantly of oats, rye and buckwheat. It is mostly owned by persons who live in the valleys below and who keep it for grazing. It abounds with brooks and streams which are said to contain an abundance of species of fish called 'Mountain Trout.' Eels are said to be plenty also. The top and sides of the mountains are covered with beautiful sugar camps.— They have had an excellent season for making sugar and have it in great abundance. They do not seem to understand how to 'sift it off' as we used to say but have it in large cakes which they sold cheap to the boys. Most of them said they never got a good fill of sugar before. But they got it that time. The only kind of bread in general use among them is rye bread. Occasionally we boarded out for a few meals for a charge. One family only charged us a dime a meal. From 10 to 20 cents was the usual price. They keep liquor in almost every house and a good rifle gun and one or two large dogs. Half the men I conversed with and some of them old men too, swear. I frequently heard the father *swear* as he nursed one little child and had three or four and his wife sitting beside him. They have a good peach, apple and rye country and no market for these things and they 'still' them and make liquor to keep them from going to loss.— Hence every here and there you come across a 'still house.' They are just about where our fore-fathers were fifty years ago, on the temperance question, but infinitely below them in religion, morality, education and general information. About half are loyal and *they are loyal*. There are Union families the men of which have not slept in their houses for months until we went up there. They were glad to see us. One woman, a genuine one, where I had got my breakfast, and was very kind, the morning before we started, asked me when we were going away. I told her, in two or three days. 'That soon!' she said. 'Ah, then the trouble will begin again. The men will have to go to the woods.'

"Churches are very scarce and school houses as scarce — religion and education here as elsewhere go hand in hand and one is at about the same level as the other — and the ebb of both is low. Ah this war is to reach far beyond our pen in its results, as one hundred years to come it will show up in these wild mountains [in improvements]. My letter is too long but I am not done talking yet. It was at Greenland Gap that a smart battle was fought between about 80 Federal soldiers under Capt. Wallace and the present invading rebel force under Gen. Jones. Our boys found quite an abundance of trophies in the shape of Revolvers, Sabers &c. Capt. Wallace and his men fought with such desperate valor as to damp the ardor of the whole rebel force which must have amounted to from fifteen hundred to three thousand. Our men took possession of a Church which they held from about 2 o'clock P.M. till 8 or 9 o'clock, against the furious assault of so many men.— Then they were only driven from it by the rebels setting fire to it. Even then they held it until the roof began to fall it, then they threw their guns and ammunition into the fire and stepped out. They lost two men killed and four wounded. The rebel loss was at least eight killed and about fifty wounded, including Colonel Delaney whose arm was shattered near the shoulder. The Union and Rebel dead are buried together. I visited the graves." He recorded the inscriptions of verses over the burials of two unnamed Federal soldiers who had died on 28 April, and the names on the rebel graves: Spencer, Co. E 1st Md. cavalry; Kennedy Grogan, Baltimore; Clinton Fletcher, Co. A 7th Va. cavalry; Samuel Dorsey, Sykesville, Md.; Robt. Carsille, Co. B Md. cavalry.; Thomas Brook, Shenandoah Co., Va.; and Lorenza Don Ahoi, Co. K 7th Va., who received this inscription:

Friends and physicians could not save,
My mortal body from the grave,
Nor cap the grave confines me here,
When Christ invites me to appear.

"A number of Regiments of [Confederate] Cavalry are going towards Wheeling. I don't know their destination.... A soldier by the name of

William French was brought in from Greenland Gap this morning dead. Either he had shot himself or his comrades had shot him. They were out on picket and had whiskey with them. This is the old story. Another victim to drink.

"I forgot to mention that among the rebel wounded at Greenland Gap is a young men, about 19 years of age, whose right arm is shattered with a ball, near the shoulder, but is doing well. He inquired if I was acquainted about Morristown Ohio—said his name was Charles Holmes, and that Wm. Lion, near Morristown, was married to his aunt. He will not fight any more in the Rebel ranks, for some time. Yours truly, J.S. McCready" (*CR* 20 My).

In their first pursuit of the enemy, through the mountains, the regiment marched prepared to fight, carrying no knapsacks, as Frank Grove wrote to Nancy on 13 May—yet the band lugged their horns, drums, and cymbals! "After a few days of hard marching we found it was no use for Infantry to run over these mountains after cavilry perticularly when they have two days start of us. So we returned to this place on last Friday after being out 11 days without tents having nothing with us but our blankets and it rained allmost half the time. I tell you Nancy we had pretty hard times. Some days we marched as high as 30 miles. part of the time we marched along the Creek. The streams ware high & we had to wade them often. One night we did not camp till after dark, then we camped in the creek bottom whare the ground was so wet we had to lay railes down to lye on. But notwithstanding our hardships we had some fun too. For thare is some of the queerest looking people amongst the mountains ever you saw. Some of them has been living thare all thare lives & don't know what County they live in. The Brass Band was a great curiosity to them. Verry few had ever heard a Band. Oh if you had just seen them running fit to break their necks to hear it.

[As Frank turned to a fond remembrance of Nancy, his favor tactlessly placed her among "the queerest looking people"; but doubtless he saw a resemblance stemming from a common ancestry.] "I stopped at a house one day & bought a pie. Thare was a Girl brought them out to me and Oh, Nan, she put me so much in mind of you I could not help but Just stand & look at her. It done me good to see her. It was on Sabbath day. That is the best day to march here, for that is the day they visit in the Mountains & they always have lots of pies baked....

"Oh Nan, I know that Mat [Mitchell] and Wilkins boys & Dan Tidrick have been sparing at each other for some time. They ware in the same tent with me & I could hear them talking. I don't know exactly how it started, but I think it started from something Dan wrote to some person last winter when Mat was in Londonderry & she got to hear it. But I won't let on to them that I know anything about it.... Well Nancy as it is your request I will destroy your letters after this. I have sent the most of them home. But I lapped them up in paper & sealed them up with orders for Will to put them in my trunk. So I don't think thare is any danger of any one reading them. But I will burn the rest of them altho I hate to see them burn....

Nothing more. But remain your Friend untill *Death*. Yours Truely, *Frank*"

The rebel forces took a southern route in returning to Lee's army. The delay at Greenland Gap, and rains and deep mud, had precluded a conquest of northwestern Virginia. They had, however, destroyed sixteen rail bridges; captured two trains and 500 prisoners; burned all the federal oil supplies near Parkersburg; and seized over 4,000 cattle, along with horses, wagons, and guns worth hundreds of thousands of dollars, for their army (*OR* 1.25.1.115-20, 104).

Chapter 21

May: A Mob in the Streets

The "Rebel Invasion of Western Virginia" excited fright in the Ohio Valley as far north as Pittsburgh. Wheeling's officials declared themselves helpless. If the rebels and the gunboats came, they would sit in a crossfire. The "reliable accounts" of the first week of May numbered the cavalry raiding Morgantown at 20,000 (*CR* 6 My). In Cadiz, the Union League appointed themselves "Home Guards," and called members to drill at the courthouse. These assemblies drew the Democratic editor's ridicule of warmongering cowards in the "League with Hell," and probably raised his fear (*CDS* 29 Ap). Allen felt certain his office and presses were about to be attacked by a mob.

What happened when the "mobbing" came was disputed, as usual, in differing accounts; Allen's issue with a three-column report does not survive, but the *Cadiz Republican* summarized it.

He anticipated a night-time assault, and gathered friends to keep watch with him and guard his office. This party in Hogg's former parlor were "armed to the teeth," and their presence itself aroused excitement in the town for several nights (*CR* 6 My). Then late Thursday night, a gang of men roamed through the streets, and approached the office, firing several "horse pistols." Allen's bastion returned fire, and the mob fled. His defenders alone, by his account, drove off the assailants and saved his property from destruction. Leading Cadiz Republicans instigated this attack, he charged; and even the constables knew of the plot and did nothing to protect him. Allen did not name or number the mob, although he claimed he knew most of its participants, and returned soldiers were among them. He alleged the specific instigators to be Bingham and Hatton (*CR* 13 My).

According to Hatton, the event amounted to a prank inspired by Allen's nightly fortifications: "some disorderly boys ... paraded in the streets, after all orderly citizens were in bed, and fired pistols in the air for sport; and several pistols, it is said, were fired from the office by those guarding it; but with no intentions, we presume, on either side, of hurting anybody." He added that

Allen would have been justified in killing anyone who tried to break into his office (6 My). This story simply confirmed Hatton's wide reputation, Allen retorted, as the "most natural liar" ever known; Hatton's office had been busy at a late hour and "used as a headquarters by some of the persons who engaged in the mob"; among it, the "nearest to a boy, and a very mean and contemptible sneaking one at that … was one of Mr. Hatton's employees." The next morning, furthermore, Hatton had come uptown especially early, anticipating the sight of the *Sentinel* presses "dished out into the street" (13 My). This quarrel extended in mudslinging charges that Allen had set fire to his printing office in Tuscarawas County; that Hatton had been "thrashed in the streets" of Carrollton for lying about its citizens; that he had been sued in Guernsey County for selling pigs fed on oil-cakes instead of corn (*CR* 20 My, *CDS* 27 My).

Meanwhile, serious plots of subversion grew. Soldiers were receiving letters, as Barrett Dickerson of the 63rd reported to his uncle Joseph, "urging the boys to desert, and come home. They say they are going to resist the draft and all the boys that can get home they will see that they shall not be brought back again" to the army (*CR* 6 My).

In view of such efforts, Gen. Burnside, military commander of the Dept. of Ohio, had issued an order 13 April that citizens who aided the country's enemies in any way, or habitually declared sympathy for them, would be tried as traitors or spies (*CR* 6 My). The prominent offender was Vallandigham, who continued his campaign speeches against the President and the war. On the Fast Day

Lincoln had declared, Vallandigham denounced him on the statehouse steps, reiterating that Lincoln had rejected a peace proposal. At the rally in Mt. Vernon on 1 May, Vallandigham further specified this charge, and urged resistance to the Conscription Law (*CR* 13 My, *CDS* 20 My). An army captain took notes; and on 5 May a number of Burnside's soldiers came to Vallandigham's house at 3 A.M. and hurried him to military prison in Cincinnati, before a mob assembled and burned the Unionist *Journal* office and five stores. The Dayton *Empire*, which had called for an uprising against military rules through "blood and carnage" was banned from publishing (*CR* 13 My).

Vallandigham himself was undaunted. He wrote an address to the Democracy of Ohio from prison assuring them his only offense was in his political opinions, his arrest was illegal, and time would vindicate him (*CDS* 13 My). At his court-martial, he rejected the aid of his three attorneys, cross-examined witnesses himself, and called none of his own (*CDS* 20 My). The one charge on which he was not convicted involved his allegations of Lincoln's rejection of a peace proposal.

By this time, the press of the South, it seems, had removed this count from serious consideration, by treating it with scorn and avowals of uncompromising resolve for an independent Confederacy (*CDS* 20 My). The hopes Vallandigham had raised for an immediate truce dimmed. His followers continued his campaign for Governor, nevertheless, with Vallandigham as their martyred great statesman, persecuted by abolitionists (*CDS* 20 My). His sentence to prison for the war's duration was changed by the President to transportation into Gen. Bragg's lines in Tennessee, a journey he began on 22 May (*CR* 27 My).

The arrest inspired opponents of the *Sentinel* to send copies of its issues along with "lying misrepresentations to Gen. Burnside, to induce that officer to arrest us, and close our office." When Burnside did not pounce, Allen's enemies circulated a petition for pledges to cut off all business with the paper and its patrons. They used "taunts, threats and jeers" to compel signatures; but acquired only eight (*CDS*, *CR* 20 My). Allen had taken caution, however; at month's end he reprinted a rejoicing welcome of Gen. Burnside's intent to allow published discussion of governmental policy in the tone of cool reflection and loyalty, without disparagement of the army or invective (27 My).

Philip Donahue stayed at the front. Ridiculing Union Association speeches, he attacked the "disastrous" notion of J. V. Lee "that practically the administration was the government," and the insane wickedness in Bingham's idea that the present strife would bring a lasting peace to the country (*CDS* 13 My). Bingham, by Hatton's account, elicited tears as he "painted" the rebellion's effects; then "every muscle became rigid" as he spoke of local treachery. One of his themes gave a counterpoint to the Democrats' motto of the people's sovereignty which would be distilled in the Gettysburg Address: the government "is in and with the people" (*CR* 13 My).

In fact, the Union's war seemed the failure Vallandigham had declared it. During May the "GLORIOUS NEWS"

of great victory at Chancellorsville gradually changed to reports of retreats with "appalling losses," over 11,000 casualties (*CR*, *CDS*, 6-27 My).

Wounded soldiers returned to find troubles at home. John Handy of Archer township, "a poor man with a wife and two small children," had joined Bostwick's company of the 74th. Wounded in the leg at Stones River, he was released from the hospital in mid-May, permanently disabled. At home he heard that a prominent man who had urged him to join the army had come to his house the past summer and "grossly and basely" propositioned his wife. The next week, Handy rode into Cadiz; he was sitting on his horse in front of Atkinson's store, talking with friends, when along came the offender, attorney Lewis Lewton, "and reached out his hand to shake hands with him. Handy told him he would not shake hands with as mean a man as he was ... and then raising a small cane that he walks with, drew off and hit Lewton in the head. Lewton then picked up a stone or brick and throwed it at Handy. Handy then got off his horse, and was making at Lewton to again strike him, when some of the bystanders interfered.... Lewton then went before Justice Howard, and entered complaint...." Handy was fined $5, an apparently outrageous injustice to him (*CDS* 27 My).

Lewton claimed he had been wronged: "In offering to Mrs. Handy to see that she should be properly supported in the absence of her husband, I certainly intended nothing more than a kindness to her; and it was only through the malice of a personal enemy of mine who accidentally learned from her the offer I had made, that a false construction was put upon it..." (*CDS* 3 Je). As a member of the military committee during recruitment, Lewton could have made this offer innocently; and the *Sentinel's* earlier snipe at him for indecent conduct toward young women implies a political plot which preyed upon the Handys as well.

May-days brought happier meetings. To John C. Jamison's farm, several farmers brought their prize bucks, worth $70 to $300, for a shearing contest. Jamison's sheared over 21 pounds; A. H. Carnahan's, John Conwell's, and John Haverfield's, 14 to 15 (*CR* 6 My). Later, John C. Jamison, James Love, and other county wool-growers met in Cadiz to form the association "WOLF" had proposed. They resolved to work for a uniform price of $1 per pound this season, and appointed a committee, which included C. M. Hogg, to confer with wool-growers in other sections. They also discussed a current issue, a growing "revolt [in the East] against the time-honored custom of washing sheep" before shearing. They resolved to "agitate this question until we abolish the washing of sheep" (*CR* 20 My). This choice of rhetoric, by men politically divided, suggests the Association took up their common purpose in high humor, no doubt cheered by fellowship with their "old enemy WOLF."

The end of May brought more mourning to Irish Ridge and Charlestown. On 23 May James Oglevee died of consumption. His death notice appeared with a feminine pseudonym, written most likely by Malinda Warfel. He had entered Franklin College to prepare for the ministry, "but he felt that his country needed him" and enlisted despite chronic illness. His discharge came too late, when "seeds of disease ... were already fast ripening for the harvest of death, and he was but coming home to die; and though we shudder as we think of him, in the pride of his young manhood, shut down beneath the darkness of the coffin lid forever; yet we sorrow not as those who have no hope.... Sleep on, faithful soldier; calmly and well, in thy narrow grave, till the resurrection morn.... 'Green be the turf above thee, / Friend of my better days...'" (*CR* 3 Je).

Capt. McCready wrote regretfully of James' enlistment, which he had tried to discourage. James had concealed his "poor hollow breast" from the Surgeon at Camp Steubenville by throwing out his chest. "The service seemed to agree with him and he became fleshy.... But about the 20th of December we got our knapsacks. The first day's drill with them brought on hemorage of the lungs, and from that time he went down..." (*CR* 17 Je).

Chapter 22

Mudsills Amid the Tennessee Chivalry

As spring came to Middle Tennessee, Rosecrans' army were yet guarding Nashville with its hospitals full of soldiers. Southeast of it, the men of the 13th, 69th, and 74th Ohio patrolled the ground of their last battle, near Murfreesboro. The 98th and 52nd picketed a small outpost about eighteen miles south of Nashville, at the town of Franklin. Bragg's army waited twenty-four miles south of them along the Duck River, and his famously effective cavalries of Wharton, Forrest, Wheeler, and Van Dorn made frequent attacks and captures of men and supplies, while Morgan's riders freely raided Kentucky.

Franklin was about the size of Cadiz, but looked far different. On broad streets, houses from cottages to mansions sat in the midst of gardens, graced with porches, balconies, and galleries featuring columns of all types. The business houses were not dark board flats, but handsome buildings of cherry-red brick. The cotton store rose behind four great columns to a pedimental roof. The

courthouse was no steepled squat cube, but a comparatively vast temple with a woodwork frieze and four cast-iron columns with trumpet capitals of the new Egyptian mode. Business and leisure in this graceful town, however, had halted. Most of the men had left it to join Bragg's army and his cavalries, who were revered here as "the chivalry," and many buildings were empty and wrecked.

Today in Franklin one hears many a tourist castigate the depredations by the "mercenaries" of the Union army. Among those "mudsills" were the former farmboys and schoolteachers of the 98th; they did ruin much in the area. How they became capable of deliberate destruction emerges from their experience of their spring in Tennessee, in which encounters with both the residents and the "chivalry" changed their attitudes.

The land itself differed from what the soldiers had seen in Ohio and Kentucky. By comparison, Franklin sat in a great wealth. The knolls and sweeping

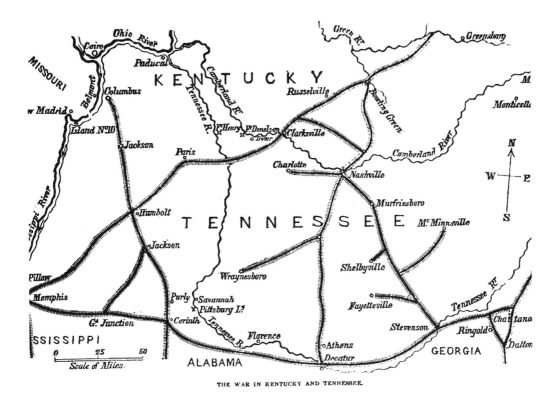

Middle Tennessee in the war. Source: *Harper's Pictorial History.*

valleys of Williamson County in the limestone basin of the Cumberland River had deep, rich soil and a climate favorable for raising swine and sheep, and crops including cotton. In the 1860 census, the farms had a per acre value of $61, far above the $44 of Harrison farmlands. Many were large plantations, as 44 farms contained between 500 and 1,000 acres; and 5 had over 1,000. Only 6 counties of the 84 in Tennessee had more numerous large farms. In slaveholding also Williamson County resembled cotton-producing counties to its west; only 7 Tennessee counties had more slaveowners than its 1,207; only 5 counties held more than its 12,367 slaves, who outnumbered its 11,415 white and 45 free colored residents.

The Ohio soldiers perceived Franklin as the home of a rich, landed aristocracy, with partial accuracy. Of 693 households of the town and suburbs in 1860, 463 — two-thirds — were headed by farmers. Four of them held over $200,000 in assets, nine had over $100,000, and 28 percent in all had over $10,000. Relatively few, only 43, were middling farmers like Rudolf Mitchell. On the other hand, 169 held assets under $5,000; and 115 farmers owned no property at all, so were tenant farmers. Thus 61 percent of the white farmers were poor workingmen.

The unanimity of zeal for the Confederacy and its army did not stem directly from personal property interests, nor from a long-standing drive toward secession. In 1860 Williamson County had decidedly favored preservation of the Union, and cast nearly twice as many votes for Bell as for Breckinridge. Their newspaper later deplored the secessionist moves of South Carolina's people as unreasonable and presumptuous (*Goodspeed* 798). Only after Fort Sumpter did the society move toward Confederate identification, but then rapidly, and as a whole. The county's thirty surviving Confederate veterans who responded to the Tennessee Civil War Veterans Questionnaires in 1915 and 1922 represented all economic ranges. Thirteen came from families who owned 300 and more acres. Twelve had parents who owned 160 or fewer acres; one's father owned town property. Four were sons of tenant farmers. Over one-third of the families of these Confederate soldiers had not been slaveowners (*Dyer*).

Many workingmen had departed for the Southern army along with the gentlemen farmers; and their families stayed on when the Union regiments arrived, while those with resources elsewhere left. The remnant united in admiration of the "chivalry," and scorn for soldiers who shoveled and chopped to fortify the town. Early in their service in Tennessee, the 98th met a work of Bragg's cavalry which riveted their ideas of it and the citizenry. Pickets south of Franklin had been attacked, and a brigade under Col. John Coburn, 33rd Indiana, marched out to find the enemy. On 4 March Coburn's 1,845 men skirmished with some of Van Dorn's cavalry about six miles down the pike toward Spring Hill, and pushed them south. The next day Coburn's regiments drove the enemy back again, into a pass through wooded knobs; they attacked into a set trap, with batteries and about 7,500 of Van Dorn's men hidden in the woods. While Coburn's men fought these, Forrest's cavalry came up in their rear, and only some 400 escaped. About 48 were killed (*OR* 1.23.1. Rosecrans 73-47; Gilbert 75-76; Jordan 81, 84; Coburn 91).

Later, the 98th went out to identify the dead. Norris' Sgt. John W. Simmons recounted the experience within an impassioned letter to Cadiz friends, denouncing the anti-war activity at home: "If those furious and frantic peace men could see and hear as we can, and know the sentiments of the people of the South, and witness the hatred that even the smallest child has for a 'Yankee,' as they call us all. If they had to bear the scoffs and sneers showered upon us by all, old and young, ... they would vanish all such vague and foolish ideas of reinstating the Union by an honorable compromise for the present, at least....

"I find that confiscating the Negroes touches them in the right place. They all begin to think that they will have to raise their 'Bread' by the sweat of their brows, and become white laborers and 'mudsills.' From this neighborhood every available man has gone into the rebel service, and few are left to till the soil but 'Negroes.' Take those negroes away from them, and their means of support is cut off....

"They dare not force their negroes to fight, or put arms in their hands.... It would be just what the Negroes would desire themselves, and the moment they received their arms from their masters would be the death knell of slavery and the slaveholder, for they could and would liberate themselves. They flock by hundreds to our lines, and desire nothing but to be armed and let loose, and I tell you what, I sometimes feel it would be a blessing to this country, and to the civilized world to let them loose, that the bloody scoundrels who strip our dead might be totally exterminated, root and branch. For in the engagement between the rebels and Col. Colburn, they striped our men of every stitch of clothing, dug a shallow hole and covered them up. A force was raising them and recognizing the dead in order to bury them, so that their friends could find them, when uncovering them they were found entirely striped of everything. I witnessed this myself with my own eyes, or I could not have believed it. I suppose that Donahue and Phillips rejoice in their heart of hearts, when these bloody scoundrels obtain a victory over us, and chuckle over the *chivalry* of their Southern brethren.

"...I can't help expressing my feelings when writing about those fiendish Devils, who sneakingly and cowardly *butcher* and *murder* loyal men, and still boast of their chivalry. Ever since I beheld our comrades in the battle of Spring Hill, striped of their clothing and mercilessly thrown in a hole stark naked, silent witness of their extreme degradation, I have had the Devil in me, larger than seven black cats. I have no mercy for them nor for their sympathising friends in the North..." (*CR* 8 Ap).

Letters from Murfreesboro brought similar threats against the rebel sympathizers at home, as one of the 13th reported; descriptions of the unplanted Tennessee fields, their laborers taken south by slaveowners or working for the Union army, and a scarcity of food; accounts of waiting for the chivalry and standing picket in the danger from bushwackers nearby, as those of the 69th wrote (*CR* 15 F, 29 Ap, 20 My).

From Nashville, Benjamin Russell related a poignant instance of the Copperhead campaign among the troops: "One of our boys got a letter the other day ... and someone asked him what was the matter?— The answer was that his father had stabbed him in the back. His father had turned to be a rebel. The poor fellow almost cried about it; but he ... sat down and wrote his father an answer ... telling him that would be his last letter home, and that he need never expect to see him again" (*CR* 29 Ap).

The 98th continued to shrink. Lt. Col. John Pearce yet waited for exchange, in Columbus, and there he and his wife now mourned their infant son, nearly their "idol" (*CDS* 1 Ap). Lt. Saunders' broken arm did not mend, and he resigned, disabled (*CR* 6 My). Sgt. Samuel McKinney was promoted to 2nd Lieutenant, but on the same day he died in Franklin. In April the regiment had 224 cases of sickness, many of fevers, including typhoid. Surgeon West preferred to keep the sick in the regiment's hospital tents, rather than send them to Nashville: "when we send a man to general hospital we never see him again." Samuel Batten from Freeport died there on 30 April (*CDS* 20 My).

Meanwhile, Bragg's cavalries rode around them. On 10 April Van Dorn and Forrest with about 9,000 men advanced on Granger's 5,194 infantry at Franklin. Receiving a panic-struck wire of attack from a post six miles north, Granger sent his 2,728 cavalry there. The subsequent fighting at Franklin comprised for

Granger a map of his position's perils; afterwards, he would drastically reconfigure the landscape.

At this time, the fort his men were building was not finished, nor any outerwork begun. It sat across the winding Harpeth River from Franklin, on the north river bluff forty feet above the town plateau. The headquarters and camps were nearby it. The bridges in the area had been destroyed, but a pontoon bridge near headquarters and a rail bridge crossed to the Franklin outskirts. The river ran about three feet deep in a sharp ravine, but had numerous fords for riders. Its constraints and delays to infantry movements made surveillance of the area and reliance on the fort crucial. The fort oversaw all approaches except where some houses blocked the view, but only to the high knobs two miles south. All of Franklin literally lay under the gun, for the fort mainly embraced two 24-pound siege guns.

On 10 April, the very air of Franklin rose to favor Van Dorn and Forrest. Its dust, and that from the oncoming hooves, blew in the wind directly into eyes at the fort; even through field glasses, they could not distinguish horsemen from fences a mile distant. Headquarters' first notice of the enemy came in the noise of gunfire that forced the pickets' withdrawal to the south edge of Franklin where the 40th Ohio were on guard; this regiment held off the cavalry until it ran out of cartridges, then retreated through the streets, pursued by Mississippi riders. From the fort, the siege guns and two other cannon opened fire; soon the town sat under a crossfire from them and the guns of a rebel battery. Most of the cavalry, however, took the cover of woods along the Harpeth and advanced out of the way of the siege guns. Granger hatched a plan to trap them, by sending infantry to attack from a ford in their rear while his main force marched over the pontoon bridge to confront them. His regiments, though, could not move fast enough from their scattered guard posts to the bridge; and the rear attack began prematurely, without reinforcements; so the cavalry turned on it successfully, then, near evening, spurred away from Granger's marchers (*OR* 1.23.1. Granger 222-7).

The guardians of Franklin began working day and night on entrenchments and fortifications, ringing it with such military refinements as abatises, imprisoning the residents in their privations. Robert Mitchell, weakened by fever, wrote to Nancy from a hospital tent on 7 May, "we are a cutting all the timber around here so we can have fare site of the rebles. we have a good fort her as good as fort Donilson for i seen it as I came up the river…. the people is very bad of in this [town] for wood. they cant get out side of the picket for it. they wont let them out for they are all secesh."

The 98th had moved to a plantation just south of town, where Thompson Gray wrote to Nancy on 8 May: "Kind Friend, … No doubt you have heard ere this that we were not engaged in that battle and also that we only missed it by being relieved from picket duty four hours previous to the attack. Since then we have had a scout after the Rebs starting at half past one in the morning, marching out eight miles into the enemies country, capturing a few Rebs and returning to camp again ten A.M. without breakfast. Our reg't. was in front.

Company C marched as skirmishers five miles.... I was pained to hear that my very valued friend James Oglevee was likely so near the end of his mortal career and I am happy to hear since that he is now improving with a prospect of getting up again. I doubt not that James has set his house in order and that [he] is prepared when called hence to go to Christ which is far better.... Life is sweet to all of us. Yet I believe a great part of our love for it arises from the fact that we never feel full assurance that as soon as we shake off this mortal coil we will be transported to a heaven of bliss at God's right hand. I do not think anyone has perfect happiness here and did they feel assured that such happiness awaited

them beyond the grave I believe that we would all be impatient to depart.... It has been very painful to us to hear and know that disease was so prevalent in the Society of home and friends, those whom we hold most near and dear yet we would not murmur knowing that it is the chastisements of him who chastises in mercy and for our good. Since leaving home I have learned that an Uncle and a Cousin have been called upon to try the realities of the spirit world. The latter was in the army near Vicksburg. But thank God they each gave reasonable evidence that our loss was their Eternal gain....

"I suppose Amanda [his sister] is still prospering finely in teaching the young Ideas to shoot *deceitfully*.... I

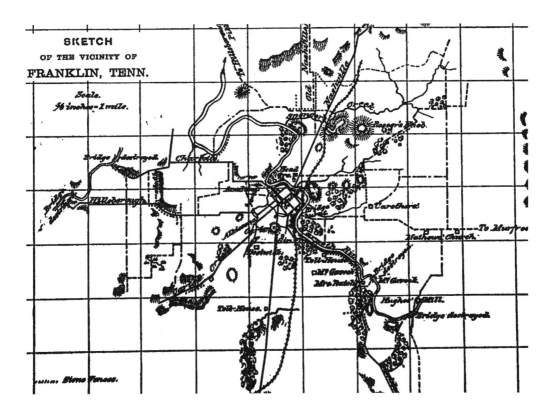

Franklin, Tennessee, in 1863 with Union Headquarters and the nearby fort. Source: *Official Records* 1.23.1.225.

think Kerrs girls will have their hands full. But I wish them success 'especially' '*Agnes.*' I fear you and Mary Dickerson have been taking my name in vain and passing jokes at my expense. one thing is sure if she fell in love with me (as you term it) She is the first lady that ever was so simple. Though of course I feel flattered by it yet I can not promise that it will ever add to her popularity. But I guess you were joking. I will decline to give my views at this time in regard to the wisdom of soldiers marrying Southern Belles. But one thing I will say. If the gals in Virginia are so good looking as here the sooner you get *Frank* back the safer you will be. I think I shall settle here in *Tenn.* (the garden of the world) when the war is over. I will not promise to marry a Southern Belle however as I do not *know* that i can *get one.*

"Two days ago we received marching orders and started with the expectation of going to Columbia in search of our enemies. But after crossing the [Harpeth] river and marching out the Lewisburg pike about a mile we encamped and went to cutting timber. Our camp is in one of the finest groves I have ever seen on the plantation of one *Col.* McGavran. In this same grove a dinner was given to Ex. *Pres.* Buchanan by the Citizens of Tennessee. The purpose to which it is now applied is certainly the more beneficial to the country of the two. About one mile of his very fine board fence has come over to camp for protection. Fin O. [Oglevee] and I were over to look at his garden &c yesterday. peas and strawberries in blossom, Tomatoes nearly so, roses in bloom &c &c were object of our admiration. I have seen as finely ornamented grounds in

Ohio and Kentucky but never on so extensive a scale. His negro quarters are very good but all vacated, He having sent his slaves to a sugar plantation he owns in Louisiana."

This large plantation belonged to John McGavock, who in 1860 lived there with his wife and three young children. He was one of the richest men in the area; and "Carnton," named for the place in Ireland the McGavocks had left for Virginia, had a magnificent mansion that now is meticulously restored. Inside and out, it remarkably displays the Franklin taste for columns. The large center hall, for instance, has an arch resting on pillars that are fluted in spirals; wallpaper, hand-painted in France, lines it with a colonnade, traced with gold filigree. Throughout, images of the temples of the ancient world are harmoniously gathered into the Southern family home, like an inheritance.

The full effects of the fatigue duties around Franklin were reported home on 26 May by Nathan M. Purviance, of Norris' company: "All the hilltops, in the vicinity north of the village, have been made to rise higher by our persevering labors until fortifications are now about completed that seem almost impregnable…. The ground that we are now encamped on was, on our arrival here, covered with valuable timber, with here and there grand and costly buildings all under fences in good repair; but now the timber is fallen and destroyed; the fences are gone; the buildings are either burned down or torn down and instead of all these you can only see the huge embankments of our earthworks looming up upon every side. Were a costly mansion standing upon an elevation of ground and that elevation deemed a suitable place to fortify, a torch applied to it would soon remove it and within twenty-four hours it would puzzle its former occupant to find where it stood. Were boards needed to make our bunks or floor our tents or for any other purpose we were not long in repairing to any residence of some 'old secesh' and pouncing upon his fences, out houses, or dwelling, if necessary; there would be such a hammering and rattling and pounding and knocking as has not been heard since the building of Noah's ark. Were a piece of valuable timber supposed to obstruct the range of our guns, a thousand or two stalwart men would be detailed every day until it was felled. Were bricks needed to build fortifications or ovens or something else, the walls of some 'secesh house' would amply supply us…. Such are the rules of war and such is but a hint of the destruction of property and desolation of country where armies are stationed.— Rebel prisoners, passing through here en route to Nashville, and who have lived here or been here before the rebellion, declare they would not have recognized the place…."

Purviance criticized the peace campaign at home; all the rebel prisoners he had met — and the witnesses of their ruined homes — vowed they would never submit to a compromise (*CR* 10 Je).

For these soldiers, the war had now outstripped political debate on its causes, and become itself the cause, with its own momentum and "rules." The Ohio soldiers who had guarded Kentucky fences while their comrades lay in the snow now took vengeful jubilation in torching "secesh" houses. Tennesseeans who had taken up arms thinking to protect their homes saw them obliterated, and rejoined their fight of defiance.

The trophies were not those of honor won, but of humiliation inflicted. One memorial very bitter for the 98th emerged here on a hilltop east of Murfreesboro. On 20 March Col. Albert S. Hall of the 105th Ohio and 1,300 infantry were encircled by about 2,250 of Morgan's cavalry, but fended them off in five hours of fighting; Morgan was wounded and left sixty-three men dead or dying on the hill (*OR* 1.23.1. Hall 155, 157). Found among them was a trophy from the Battle of Perryville — the revolver which had belonged to the late Col. George Webster, evidently passed through Bragg's cavalries as a prize. Their capture of it substantiates accounts that he was at the front when he fell. From the hands of the enemy, though, the gun shamed the failure of the former "Webster Guards." It was sent by the army to Webster's widow in Steubenville (*CDS* 29 Ap).

Chapter 23

June: Butternuts and Black Soldiers

A cool, dry June brought the most luscious strawberries in memory, and a berry festival supper at the courthouse, which raised $125 for soldiers' aid (*CR* 10 Je, 24 Je). All month, however, the air swirled dark and shrill with swarms of locusts, until the branches of young trees shriveled and drooped as though under a heavy frost, and no remedy availed (*CDS* 10 Je, 1 Jl). The plague of illnesses spread also. Capt. McCready compared it to the epidemic his regiment had suffered at Martinsburg, and observed that almost every soldier there was troubled by the dangerous sickness of a friend at home (*CR* 17 Je).

Sheep shearing continued nevertheless, and rancorous meetings. The Democrats convened in the courthouse yard on 6 June to choose delegates for the state meeting that would nominate the candidate for governor. Philip Donahue proposed an amendment instructing them to vote for Vallandigham. A debate ensued, in which Billy Paterson praised Vallandigham in a drunken speech, so

the *Cadiz Republican's* new local editor Frank Hatton reported, which Donahue commended, while slandering the army. At this, the 98th's disabled William Saunders, a Democrat, "asked to be allowed to correct him, but whenever the Lieut. attempted to speak the crowd"—most lying on the ground—"would raise their snakish heads and offer him all kinds of insults…. They hooted him down, but not before he told them he bade such Democracy farewell." Donahue then spoke on, vowing that if drafted he would become rebellious; and his amendment passed unanimously (*CR*, *CDS* 10 Je).

Vallandigham's supporters, far from daunted, took steam from his arrest, trial, and banishment. Around fifty delegates, granted half-fare by the railroad, boarded the train to Columbus to be among the reputed 50,000 who nominated Vallandigham and demanded that the President restore him to Ohio. Their purpose, as Allen summarized it, was an honorable peace restoring the nation

(10 Je, 17 Je). They now argued that Vallandigham at his "Inquisition" had proposed to *prove* that offers of peaceful compromise had been offered by the South, which Lincoln rejected, but the military court denied him opportunity (*CDS* 24 Je).

The Democrats' efforts to retrieve Vallandigham led to large demonstrations in Ohio and elsewhere, and an envoy Committee of 19 from the state convention who met with the President and demanded the candidate's return. Lincoln agreed to release him to them on the condition that they granted the government's right to put down rebellion — which they rejected as unjust and irrelevant (*CDS* 8 Jl). It was scarcely irrelevant, while many were publicly threatening to rebel against conscription laws.

Locally, the Vallandigham campaign drew prominent men. Contrary to the frequent generalization that Ohio "butternuts" were subsistence farmers with Virginia ties who resented economic or governmental powers, here wealthy farmers and a financier stepped onto the platform. The county's Democratic Committee became Allen, Donahue, Henry Boyles, Samuel Cochran, and Walter Beebe. Their county ticket featured five men from different northern and western townships, and for prosecuting attorney none other than the absent John S. Pearce, Lt. Col. of the 98th. The state senatorial convention for Harrison and Belmont chose Asa Holmes to chair and nominated Donahue their candidate by acclamation (*CDS* 15 Jl). In Greene township, Thomas Mitchell was among the Democratic Club members condemning the Emancipation Proclamation and endorsing Vallandigham (*CDS* 1 Jl).

After his hoot-down at the courthouse, Saunders promptly went over to the Union Party, whose convention 13 June appointed him a delegate along with John C. Jamison, S. B. Shotwell, Lewis Lewton, Capt. John Castill, John Oglevee, Thomas Grove, Richard Hatton, and others. A motion passed recommending John A. Bingham as their first choice for governor (*CR* 17 Je); beyond that, the group had difficulty assembling the united front they proclaimed. Shotwell wanted delegates to include a man from each of the old parties in every township; John Bargar told him it could not be done in his home, Stock, for every Democrat there was a Copperhead (*CDS* 17 Je). The convention made at least one appointment of a delegate, Walter Jamison, who repudiated it and averred his continuance with the Democrats (*CR, CDS* 24 Je).

A Union Association began in Stock, with difficulties. At their first meeting they found themselves locked out of the schoolhouse by opponents. The next week, 27 June, they went to Dog Run schoolhouse, the only district where a few would defend Union principles, but where copperheads interrupted the meeting often with "low slang and hellish groans" (*CR* 1 Jl).

The Cadiz Unionists themselves were divided by renewed attacks on Hatton by Shotwell, who had gotten the governor's appointment to chair the County Military Committee, and Hatton's removal. Shotwell revived an old threat that McConnell would paint his store with a sign denouncing Hatton (*CDS* 10 Je, 24 Je).

Most Union meetings in the countryside were opportunities for Lt. Thomas Smith to recruit young men for the new cavalry company, and for William Pittenger to expand his patriotic oratory. Pittenger waxed for an hour at Grape Vine Hollow schoolhouse, and in nights following at Harrisville, Moorefield, and Deersville (*CR* 3 Je). Some hearers began to request that he get "Bingham to write another speech for him" (*CDS* 24 Je).

The Deersville meeting broke up in a fight. One or more young men came wearing breastpins in the form of butternut symbols, and controversy over these erupted to the swearing, yelling, and fisticuffs of a riot that defied the village officers. One man, who had come from his barn with his wool shears in hand, and defended a butternut-bearer, was hit with a club before the pin or pins were put away, and the fight ended. No one was recruited for the cavalry (*CR* 17 Je, *CDS* 24 Je).

Just to the south in Belmont County, a meeting provoked violence. On 2 July, the Democrats were convening in St. Clairsville, and eighteen of them set out from Morristown on the omnibus of Frank Simpson. As it drove through Lloydsville, Alfred Nichols stepped into the road, stopped the coach, and threatened to fight. He retreated from Simpson's invitation, the coach went on, but during the day Nichols summoned about fifteen friends, armed them, "and actually procured a SWIVEL and planted it in his yard so as to command the road." When the omnibus reappeared, Nichols fired his cannon. The charge flew over the reined-up horses and severed tree limbs. The twenty passengers

rushed to capture the cannon, but did not. One gun was fired, and Simpson was shot through the arm. Some of the Democrats threatened to come back at night and burn out the "Abolition hole." Then they returned to Morristown, where Dr. Jones rode to St. Clairsville to alert the sheriff. He also telegraphed authorities in Wheeling urging that U. S. troops be sent into the battle begun by Lloydsville. The Democratic St. Clairsville *Gazette* warned that presenting any troops into Ohio would bring bloodshed. Whether or not armed violence was incipient in the political meetings, it was assumed as a threat; the Democrats at their St. Clairsville convention, the *Chronicle* claimed, carried numerous pistols in hand and in pockets (*CDS* 15 Jl, 22 Jl).

In the middle of June, Cadiz witnessed a transformative gathering, but seemingly with little comprehension. "We noticed some fifteen negro recruits drilling on the street on last Monday under the command of a colored man who has been in the rebel army since the out-break of the rebellion until the battle of Perryville. He ran off from them during that battle and came into our lines. He went with Capt. Norris to Franklin, Tenn., and came from that place to this for the purpose of enlisting [soldiers]. These recruits, we understand, are for a Massachusetts regiment; they were a hearty set of men, and will, no doubt, do the butternuts of the southern army a great deal of damage" (*CR* 17 Je). Four were from Cadiz, the rest from Georgetown; they expected to leave within the week (*CDS* 17 Je).

The recruiter was one of the former slaves and servants of officers in Bragg's army whom men of the 98th described in letters. Clearly they had furnished him with directions and introductions to sponsor his leadership of African-American men from their home area into the war. Gov. Tod had just issued the first call for Ohio men of color to enlist in the already-organized Massachusetts regiment, and publicized their destination as Hilton Head Island, South Carolina (*CR* 27 My). The next week, twenty-one or -two volunteers, likely organized by the recruiter, came into Cadiz from the neighborhood south of Athens township, around Barnesville in Belmont County, to board the branch train—"stout, hardy looking, orderly men" (*CR* 3 Je).

By this time, the 54th Massachusetts regiment (of the film *Glory*) had filled, so these men were destined into the 55th. In a regimental roster which listed the 55th's homes, neither Cadiz nor Georgetown appears, but the roster was not compiled until 1868. One from Cadiz may have been Nimrod Brooks, whom the *Roster of Union Soldiers* lists in Co. G of the 55th, who is buried in the Cadiz cemetery with a headstone of the 1st U.S. Colored Infantry. Nineteen men from the villages in western Belmont enrolled in Co. F: John D. Wood, 28, and William Thomas, 18, from Flushing; John Carter, 23, and Daniel A. Paine, 25, from Belmont; Jasper Haddox, 29, Thornton Hurley and Joseph H. Hurley, both 23, from Summertown (Somerton); and, from Barnesville, Isaac Edwards, 23; Anthony Freeman, 23; William Mabra, 35; four Petersons, being David S., 23; Marcus, 29; Joseph H., 24; and Ferdinand, 22; William F. Robinson, 18; two Shipps, being John H.,

20; and James, 26; Caswell Samson, 22; and Joseph Wilson, 25. From the town of Yorkville, on the river, came Thomas Hill, 25. In addition, four of Co. F enrolled from the Short Creek area east of Cadiz and Georgetown, listing the village as Mt. Pleasant, in Jefferson County: Nelson Champ, 19; brothers David U. King, 23, and Jonathan King, 26; and Abraham Stewart, 20. These men were all termed farmers, except for Mabra, an engineer (Fox 130-32).

Columbiana County sent to the 55th Richard M. White, 22, a Salem teacher who became the Commissary Sergeant.

Only six of these men—Mabra, the Petersons and Ships—from two Belmont townships, could I identify in the 1860 census. I located numerous other names of 55th volunteers, in this and another area in central Ohio, who were Ohio-born and not noted on the census as being other than white; it can be inferred that many were so assimilated that a census taker assumed they were white, making them eligible to vote; yet they joined the 55th.

These men knowingly faced greater dangers than whites in volunteering. If captured, they would not be paroled or imprisoned like white soldiers, but rather executed or enslaved, according to official threats from the South (Fox 6). They left the protected freedom of Ohio to fight in the most hostile region of the South. In joining the 55th, they placed themselves among many who had escaped from slavery; one-fourth of the 980 enlisted men on the 1868 roster reported they had been slaves. Those of mixed race became a minority, to the 550 "pure blacks" (Fox 110).

This regiment was probably the most national in the army. Its commissioned officers were white New England men, several Harvard-educated. The enlisted men had birthplaces in seventeen northern states and nine southern ones, and also drew sixty-eight men from disputed Kentucky. In proportion, however, Ohio-born men were greatest: 222, or 22.7 percent (Fox 112).

Upon first reaching camp in Massachusetts, these men of widely varied origin, experience, and social status united in creating their own tradition. After the first night roll-call of the first squad to arrive, in "a striking and unusual scene," one man "stepped from the ranks and made a simple and appropriate prayer, and the whole squad joined in singing one of their peculiar hymns." Each company continued this practice, and the "really fine singing" in the evenings attracted many visitors to the camp. The men formed several glee clubs; and "one remarkably good one, mostly from Company F," gave a concert in Dedham before they left on 21 July. During training camp seventeen men took lessons and became the regiment's band, which played on their departing march through Boston (Fox 4).

The June recruitment in Harrison, Jefferson, and Belmont counties obviously proved successful: at the beginning of August, Ohio's premier African-American recruiter came to the same area. O. S. B. Wall was a black merchant of Oberlin who had raised forty-eight men to become the core of Ohio volunteers in the 54th Massachusetts (Moebs 482, 511). At the beginning of August, he enrolled Jefferson County men in the 5th Regiment, U. S. Colored Troops: Peter Bates, 22; Joseph Carter, 19; Benjamin F. Fletcher, 25; Samuel Jordan, 19; and John M. Miller, 20. On 14 August in Harrison County, Wall recruited Thomas R. H. Johnson, age 22, and Albert Swayne, 22. The 1860 census found Albert Swayne in Cadiz, and listed him as black and a barber, born in Ohio, living with Rebecca, 40, a black domestic born in Ohio with $100 in real estate, and four younger children.

O. S. B. Wall enrolled men in Belmont County during the first two weeks of September. They included Joseph Brannam, 21; George W. Cany (elsewhere listed as Curry), 20; John Ley, 44 (or John Lee, 20); Arthur I. Myers, 23; Lucius Steward, 35; and Oscar Winters, 18. These men entered Co. D of the 5th (Ohio A. G., *Muster Roll, 5th Regiment*).

Two men from Guernsey County entered Company A of the 5th: Timothy Early, 40, on 29 June; and David Getson, 28, on 29 July (Ohio A.G, *Civil War Muster Rolls*).

Two different muster rolls for the 5th kept by Ohio, where the regiment was formed, listed men differently — only one of the difficulties in identifying African-American volunteers. During the summer of 1863, and afterwards, they joined other regiments of the U.S.C.T.; and for most, rosters do not exist, only individual muster sheets which are indexed by the regiment and soldier's name within it, in the National Archives in Washington.

These muster sheets recorded birthplaces of the volunteers, often more specifically than the census; the muster rolls thus can furnish valuable evidence. They show, for instance, that the early migration route across the mountains from Virginia to Ohio had continued. Nelson Champ, 19, of Mt. Pleasant, in the 55th Mass., for instance, gave his birthplace as Loudon County, Va. A volunteer from Georgetown, enlisting in the 4th U.S.C.I. in 1864, also gave Loudon County as his place of birth. In scanning approximately one-third of the 4th's muster roll sheets, I noted Loudon County to be the Virginia birthplace most numerously listed by volunteers in Belmont, Athens, Ross, and Pickaway counties, that is, across southern Ohio.

Thus one can find a thorough study of the societies in which many African Americans lived before coming to Ohio in Brenda E. Stevenson's social history of Loudon County, *Life in Black and White: Family and Community in the Slave South* (1996). Loudon held great plantations of the Lee and other patrician Virginia families. It also bordered the fordable Potomac River near the National road from Baltimore through the Cumberland Gap of Maryland, into Pennsylvania, and Ohio; and in its western hills lived many Quakers actively opposed to slavery. Very likely, it was an African-American family from Loudon who in 1813 joined the Quaker wagon train on which the family of William Cooper Howells came to Ohio. This migration continued, and furnished many soldiers who returned to Virginia to fight.

Chapter 24

Under Fire in Tennessee, Mississippi, Virginia

Shelbyville, Tennessee

In Tennessee in early June, most of the troops and cavalry moved out of Franklin and east to Triune, on the pike to Shelbyville, the fortified center of Bragg's army which guarded his supply base southeast of it in Tullahoma. This advance of Granger's men initiated Gen. Rosecrans' plan to draw Bragg's attention and cavalry to this area with a feint attack, while the mass of Rosecrans' men at Murfreesboro would sweep east and south around Bragg's flank to his rear. For the plot to work, Granger's force, which now was designated the Reserve Corps, had to make a show of considerable threat (*OR* 1.23.1. Rosecrans 404); it contained under 18,000 men present for duty, however, including the garrison left at Franklin; and these decoys were launched in the midst of Bragg's cavalries over 14,000 strong and at Polk's larger corps (*OR* 1.23.1.410, 585).

The feint quickly enticed Bragg's cavalry, who on 4 June attacked Franklin, then turned on the men at Triune. There Robert Mitchell contended with the dangers and his lingering illness by taking out his pen, on 6 June: "Dear Sister ... I am some better than I was. there was a fight at franklin yesterday evening there was some hevy canonading until dark but we hear this morning that the rebles got whipt.... Gray has gon on picket to day. there was some fireing on picket last night. rite here is where the batle of stone river comenced. there is bulet holes in the trees.... We are 4 miles from the river. we are camp on a rich man farm. he ones 2000 acher land the nisest house I ever seen and we are burning up all his rails and he is an old reble. there is know body living in the town it is the county seat."

Lt. Col. John Pearce had recently rejoined the regiment, and Robert's worries increased. On 10 June he wrote, "Dear Sister I seat my self to wrte you a fiew ben that you dont wrte me any. I see that you wrte to Gray once and while. he left his leter out one day and sean come

218

from you. the little dog spill my ink well. wel the cavelry had a little fight here yesterday. the rebles kild two of hour men and tuck a noyer prisoner. hour Regt was ordered out in front they went out on the double quick but the rebles was gon. there were cavelry runing all the time.... Col porman is a going to resign and think Pirce will to. he no better than wooden man. he cant drill a regt. the rebls would take us al prisoners. I dont feal so well to day. I have the hedach and am very weake yet and cold and chily. I have not got a letter from you for 2 weaks and I think is time you was a writing and tel me all the news. this is the hardest place ever was yet. we cant get any lite bred and we have to eat crackers and sow belley.... I will close til get a leter from you. Robert Mitchell"

The next day brought another attack, and shellfire on the camp. Robert's next letters recounted, "the boyes said they felt worse than they did at peryville," and "there was 7 or 8 shell hit in hour camp but there was not very many of them busted but it would make us dod[ge] when they woud whistle over hour head."

Thompson Gray composed a philosophical mood on 16 June: "Friend Nan, ... Just think tis already ten months since I bid farewell to the quiet and endearing scenes of home and the grave oft honored walls of Old Franklin's care for the trying scenes and stern realities of the soldier. And yet it seems but yesterday. And yet how much history fond memory draws forth from the impress of the soul as a record of the scenes and changes of that short time. Whatever our ... circumstances in future life the record of this short life spent in the cause of

human liberty will ne'er be effaced from our memories, but rather when in after years the spark of life wanes low then will these reminiscences shine brighter and be imprinted deeper than ever. And then will we thank God that we have been permitted to pass through all these hardships for the sake of Liberty and free and Christian institutions of our great and noble country. But oh how remarkable and sad the changes that those ten months have brought with them. from over nine hundred men disease and death have reduced to little over one third that number of substantial men. [Another of his company was about to expire; John Pennock of Irish Ridge died in an Ohio camp hospital after a long sickness, with his sisters and brothers at his side (*CDS* 8 Jl).] Our brave, humane & Christian commander Col. Webster fills an honored grave, while many of our Company officers have from one cause or another passed away from among us.

"And now to still add another sad one to the list. Our gallant and loved Colonel has resigned and is now (this morning) about starting for his home in St. Clairsville. How we will miss him. Were it not for the stern realities of the battlefield we might spare him. But we have little confidence in Col. Pearce anywhere & much less on the Battlefield. With Poorman as our leader we feared nothing, for we knew he would never desert us. I think he might have remained with us but he has thought differently. One thing he goes in a good cause viz: To fight Traitors at home. May God speed him!...

"Since coming here we have had some skirmishing & one day the Rebs had the impudence to plant a battery in sight of our camp and threw some shells among us which by the way came close enough to make us think they might come closer. If they had burst I have no doubt some of us would have been hurt....

"The decease of friend Oglevee was not unexpected to me.... Bell Birney too has left this world and no doubt gone to the Christian's reward. such are the uncertainties of life. Many are passing the portals of Death & Oh how many pass away without one ray of hope.

"Oh may you nor I never be called upon to mourn the loss of a relative who gives no evidence of hope beyond the grave.

"I was a little surprised to hear that J. L. [Nancy's cousin John Mitchell] was so ill with little prospect of ever being better. I had thought that perhaps he would get better when the spring returned with its reviving heat. But from your letter I presume that the allwise disposer of all things has ordered otherwise. I was pleased to hear that Kerr's girls are doing so well at Science Hill [school].... I dont know why you should charge us who say we are going to live in the south in coming years with being influenced by the charms of some fair lady unless perchance you think no northerner could be persuaded to leave the wintry and half barren north for the bright, genial, sunny south. For my part should I conclude to make my home in Tennessee, t'would be thousands of miles nearer home than I had formerly anticipated though it was not the attractions of the fair sex that had formed my motives for a home on some foreign shore.

"Well you desire to know something of Eliza Richey's letter. In the first place when there last winter Eliza asked me to write to them when I returned to camp. On account of my former rather intimate relations with the family I assented. Though with a determination that if they scented theirs with Copperheadism I would resent it as an insult. after arriving I wrote a letter to the three girls and mailed it to Eliza & of course I hinted a little of my detestation of Copperheads. She answered it kindly but did not ask me to write again. for which I am not caring.

"But she never said a word about *val*, Charlie or any of the Copperheads.... I think their impudence in putting down Lieut Saunders is the boldest thing I have ever known done in Cadiz & the best thing they could do to secure the ill will of this company. Each soldier considers it as an insult to himself & were we there we would have told them so to their sorrow....

"I see by the papers that Bill Pittenger who was discharged from our company, has become quite a stump speaker. If the people of our county thought no more of him than Company C does he would have small audience. Who wrote the obituary of J W Oglevee? some of us think it was Lind Warfle.... Good bye, Thomps"

The next moves of the regiment were described by John Erwin of Co. F: "On the morning of June 23rd Gen. Granger's force left Triune, Tenn., and marched in an easterly direction over a rough and almost uninhabited portion of country. The day was hot and sultry, and had not our road lay through an almost unbroken cedar forest, during the heat of the day, we must have suffered with it.

"About 6 o'clock in the evening we crossed a branch of Stone River and camped near Salem, a small place, 5 miles from Murfreesboro. Our camp was in a large open field. Next day it was raining. Orders were given to pack our knapsacks and tents, and send all baggage to Murfreesboro, with those who were not able for hard service. [Robert was among these; he had to walk to the convalescent camp.]

"We left camp about 2 o'clock P.M., and taking a south easterly course, we marched over roads and through fields rendered almost impassable by the heavy and continuous rain. By one o'clock that night we had marched 8 miles.

"Brisk cannonading had been going on in our front during the afternoon. At night the heavens were lit up by the burning of the town of Middleton which had been captured by our cavalry. It continued to rain all night. We camped about 1 o'clock at night about two miles from the Murfreesboro pike. A fire of rails was soon built and tins of coffee were made and meat roasted and eaten soldier style. Then lying down on some rails and covering up with our gum blankets slept soundly till morning.

"Next morning we moved forward through mud and water to the pike, which we struck about 8½ miles from Murfreesboro, and where C. L. Vallandigham was given into the hands of his *southern brethren*. We encamped during the remainder of that day, the next and the day following till noon, during which time it scarcely ceased raining long enough to dry our damp clothes. After filling haversacks with provisions, about noon on the 27th Gen. Granger's force moved forward for the purpose of taking Guy's Gap, distant 7 or 8 miles. The day was warm and rainy, yet the men moved forward cheerfully. Our cavalry commenced skirmishing soon after leaving camp and drove them by a succession of charges — giving them time to fire an occasional shot from their artillery, which did us no harm. The infantry occupied Guy's Gap about 5 o'clock, P.M., where it camped for the night. The cavalry had passed forward to Shelbyville and captured two pieces of artillery on the public square and one in the bridge across Duck River, and 480 prisoners, including 30 officers.

"Such was the confusion with which they [the enemy, driven out of entrenchments on the north side of the Duck] left that many of them were drowned in attempting to swim across the river. A large quantity of fire-arms were thrown into the river in order to prevent capture, many of which have since been taken out. Our loss was small. The cavalry was commanded by Gen. Stanley.

"We lay in camp till noon the next day, when orders were received to march back to our previous camping ground. The evening was very warm, we camped near sun-down on the same ground we had previously occupied.— Here we remained till next day at noon, and replenished our haversacks. About 2 P.M. we again started toward Shelbyville in one of the heaviest rains I have witnessed for a long time. We marched 14 miles, that evening, by a little after dark, which is acknowledged to be rather the fastest marching the 98th has ever done yet. I did not hear of a single man straggling from the regiment. The regiment in front [despite] knowing that we had the name of being good on a march, led out. But experience taught them it was useless to attempt anything of that kind. It is a great deal harder to march in the rear of a large body of troops than in the front. Those in front can move forward at pleasure, while those in the rear must halt every time a battery wagon or anything of that kind stops and then move in double quick in order to make up the lost space.

"We camped in sight of the recently evacuated rebel works which consisted of a line of rifle pits and forts of small magnitude from one bend of Duck River to the other. Had they been well manned, it would have cost a good many lives to have taken them. The line of rifle pits are about 3 miles north of Shelbyville....

"Next day we camped in the vicinity of Shelbyville, which is 25 miles from Murfreesboro. Many of us witnessed a scene that day which we will long remember. It made a deep impression on our minds, and sent a thrill of joy through all our hearts.

"A band had halted in front of a neat, rustic, country home, and just as our regiment was passing the house an old lady, so enfeebled by years that she could scarcely walk, came out, unfolded the 'Stars and Stripes' to float in the summer breeze. The band struck up the tune called 'The Star Spangled Banner.' The scene was so touching, so simple, so sublime, that I could scarcely refrain from tears.

"We are now camped in the suburbs of the town. It is, without exception, I believe, one of the most loyal places in Tennessee. It is situated in a beautiful country, well watered and good

land. There is a spring not more than 150 yards from the public square that affords water enough, now, to keep a saw mill in constant motion. The ravages of war have made sad havoc with the commercial interests of the place. Its best buildings have been used as quarters for men, and when one became so filthy it could no longer be used another was occupied.

"Refugees [Unionist citizens] are coming in by hundreds as are also deserters from Bragg's army. Tennessee rebel soldiers that have deserted told me that whole regiments of them had sworn that if compelled to leave Tennessee they would throw down their arms and go home, and it seems they are doing it pretty generally. Alabamians say that when they get into their native State they will throw down their arms and go home" (*CR* 22 Jl).

Local soldiers who advanced in the left wing of Rosecrans' army gave similar reports of deserting rebel soldiers. The 69th and 74th, in Gen. Thomas' 14th Corps, had left Murfreesboro on 24 June to press through Hoover's Gap toward Beech Grove, and on to Manchester and Tullahoma. The 13th remained to guard Murfreesboro (*OR* 1.23.1.412, 415); but W. H. Host accompanied Gen. Crittenden's 21st Corps headquarters, and wrote from Manchester that the fight at Hoover's Gap had lasted four hours, and now deserters were coming in and asking not to be exchanged (*CR* 22 Jl). From the 74th, A. Giles described hundreds of "voluntary prisoners," who no longer taunted "we will not be troubled long by your presence here," as they had when they claimed that anti-war activity would soon call the Union soldiers home (*CR* 29 Jl).

Erwin recounted a celebration in Shelbyville: "The 4th of July passed off quietly and appropriately. An address was delivered and the Declaration of 1776 read by a refugee from this place named Cooper. It was listened to attentively by a large crowd of soldiers and citizens, male and female, who felt that his words were words of burning truth....

"I herewith send you a copy of the [Shelbyville] *Rebel*. I expect if we could get a copy of to-day's paper the leading editorial would have a different tune" (*CR* 7-22).

The striking contrast between welcoming Shelbyville and scornful Franklin can be only partly explained by differences in their adjoining areas. Bedford County shared the rich soil of Williamson, and its early landgrants also brought North Carolina veterans of the Revolutionary War (Goodspeed 862-63). By the 1860 census, these counties numbered similar populations, but their proportions differed. Bedford had 14,788 white residents, to Williamson's 11,415; and only 6,744 slaves rather than 12,367. Bedford had the same number, 5, of plantations over 1,000 acres; but 28 as against 44 owners of 500 to 1,000 acres, and a preponderance of middle-rank farmers owning from 20 to 500 acres. Only 4 people, far from 25, held more than 50 slaves.

Bedford's agriculture represented farm rather than plantation production — less than 10 percent of either the tobacco or cotton of Williamson. More of its land was being farmed, and much less lay unbroken, yet the value of its farms was only $38 per acre, far under the $61 in Williamson with its cash-pro-

ducing plantations. The distribution of land and wealth in Bedford, thus, was wider and more vested in middle-class farmers.

Bedford like Williamson had voted against secession as the rebellion began, but when the Union and Confederate armies called for men, Bedford's went to both sides almost equally (Goodspeed 872). The county held strongly divided loyalties in the war; the basis of their division, like Williamson's unanimity, was not obvious socioeconomic interest. The twenty-five Confederate veterans from Bedford who replied to the Dyer questionnaire (no Federals responded) also represented the full range of their society. To Dyer's questions about slaveowners' idleness, discrimination against poor whites, and political domination, however, the Bedford veterans gave more forthright critical answers. Whereas Williamson men generally claimed that all white men performed and respected manual labor, and no differences separated slaveowners from others, poorer Bedford men described nonworking, discriminating slaveowners (1:299; 4:1559; 4:1775). These Confederates perceived less solidarity in white society, and were not defenders of the aristocracy.

What galvanized Middle Tennessee whites of all classes to the Confederate cause, according to Stephen V. Ash's study, was an ideology valuing a hierarchical, patriarchal society with slavery as its foundation, a unifying racial identification, and a fear of slave revolts (40, 49-50). Williamson County evidently so united; but in racial population and wealth it was less typical of Middle Tennessee than Bedford. In another regard, however, related to perceptions which formulate ideology, Williamson did more typify the rural counties of Middle Tennessee. Franklin from 1820 had one, and only one, newspaper, one "authority on Democratic doctrines." Shelbyville from at least 1836 had two (Goodspeed 804, 876-77). Of twenty-six other counties of the region in the Goodspeed histories, only one, Murfreesboro's Rutherford, had consistent antebellum publication of two politically divergent newspapers. Two competing newspapers either signify, or create, a culture of more diverse views and values than one of idealistic conformity.

As the 98th Ohio took renewed hope and cheer in Shelbyville, their new leader drew inspiration to begin winning their respect. John S. Pearce declined his home Democrats' nomination for the office of prosecuting attorney. He wrote to Hatton, "I want no office — I would rather be a private in my regiment than to resign and accept one — men are needed.... I want all to know that I have no sympathy with Vallandigham or his platform — the soldiers, are almost, if not entirely, a unite upon this thing — We must fight — we can end the war in no other way" (*CR* 29 Jl).

Vicksburg

Cadiz's David Cunningham was now Major of the 30th Ohio (*CDS* 20 My), who had marched eighty-five miles in three days from Grand Gulf to the outskirts of Vicksburg on 18 May. In Ewing's brigade of Sherman's corps, they joined Grant's army on the northern end of their crescent encasement of the city and its entrenched defenders. The enemy forts and rifle pits overlooked steep ravines that were tangled with felled timber; one of the few inroads, the Graveyard Road, with an enemy bastion on it, seemed to invite attack (*OR* 1.24.1.257, 169-71). On 19 May, the 30th followed Ewing's other three regiments in a charge which partly neared the entrenchments before drawing back. Nine of the 30th took wounds (*OR* 1.24.2.159).

On 22 May a volunteer storming party ran the narrow deep road toward the bastion, with the 30th close behind. They rushed halfway up the ridge, until stalled by double-rank firing from two sides, and the bodies of the dead and wounded in their path: "The second company forced its way over the remains of the first, a third over those of the preceding, but their perseverance served only further to encumber the impassable way" (*OR* 1.24.1. Ewing 281-82). A captain of the 30th and 5 others were killed; 6 officers and 37 men, wounded; 2, captured (*OR* 1.24.2.163).

The enemy works withstood attacks elsewhere, and Sherman's men moved toward them underground by digging mines, while overhead the artillery dueled.

Families at home could scarcely imagine their soldiers' scenes in the siege. When they read an eyewitness account, it was rapt in fantastic spectacle. A *Cleveland Herald* reporter climbed a parapet in moonlight and glimpsed the spires of the courthouse and two churches yet standing. "The mortars are playing to-night, and they are well worth seeing.... Suddenly up shoots a flash of light, and in a moment the ponderous shell, with its fuse glowing and sparkling, rises slowly from behind the bluffs; up, up, it goes, as though mounting to the zenith; over it comes toward us, down through its flights trajectory into the city, and explode[s] with a shock that jars the ground for miles. There are women and tender children where those shells fall, but war is war."

Sherman's "eight-inch monsters" were "grumbling" on his right, McPherson's guns blasting nearby, and other batteries preparing to open at midnight: "music to your heart's content." He visited the trenches, and entered mines where the soldiers, filthy and soaked in sweat, dug with picks day and night by dim candlelight in the stifling tunnels. In the moonlight again, he saw the advance pickets lying on the ground, and rebel pickets not many steps beyond. Between them, covering the hillside, appeared the "little gray mounds" of those who had "climbed the parapet and rolled back into eternity" (*CR* 8 Jl).

Explosions from the mines opened some forts to charges, but hand-grenade fights repulsed them. At last on 4 July, after forty-two days of fighting, Vicksburg was surrendered. The soldiers of both sides emerged from trenches and viewed the numbers of the other with amazement; from some small enemy forts came 100 men, all looking like miners. The nearly 30,000 new prisoners got respectful treatment, and Union soldiers gave them coffee, which they had not drunk in a year (*CDS* 15 Jl).

Martinsburg

Capt. McCready was yet the pastor of his congregation at home. He had offered to resign, lest without a minister the church should wane; but it voted to keep him in charge (*CR* 17 Je). Some members may have approved this measure to keep him away, however; events of the coming election would reveal that many had become strongly opposed to him and the war (Hanna 152).

His ministry at Martinsburg continued with the marriages of two of its daughters to soldiers: Margaret Barnes to Thomas McLane of Co. D, 126th; and Lucy Donelly to Wesley H. Taylor of the 106th New York (*CDS* 24 Je).

His men enjoyed the town's hospitality and visitors from home. On 10 June, Frank Grove wrote in his diary, "We attended a School Picnic. Had Dinner & Supper & a pleasant time in General. The Band had Just got thair new Uniform & attracted considerable attention." Three days later he was glad to greet his mother and sister Emily, whose son was his nephew and comrade Frank McNary. He noted also, "Great excitement a attack expected."

Not everyone was surprised. For the previous two weeks or more, McCready recollected on 29 June, "an impression seemed to prevail among the citizens that the rebels were going to clear out the valley. I do not know that the soldiers paid much attention to it. The prevailing opinion seemed to be that we could whip them if they came — that is, the soldiers thought so, or a good many of them, but not so the citizens."

Twenty miles south in the Shenandoah Valley, three Union brigades guarded Winchester. They frequently encountered rebel cavalry raiders in the area, and Gen. Milroy assumed the skirmishing with his outposts all this Saturday threatened only an assault which his men and forts could withstand. In the evening, however, he realized that the enemy gathered before him comprised Ewell's whole corps, the late Stonewall Jackson's. At the same time, Milroy's superiors learned Lee's entire army were crossing the Blue Ridge bound for Winchester; the prompt telegram ordering Milroy to evacuate could not reach him because the wire between Winchester and Martinsburg had already been cut (*OR* 1.27.2. Holt 190-91). Headquarters meanwhile expressed Brig. Gen. Daniel Tyler and two staff from Baltimore to take command of Col. B. F. Smith's men at Martinsburg and aid Milroy's retreat. When Tyler arrived the next morning, though, he found Smith preparing for action and left him in charge (*OR* 1.27.2. Tyler 16).

During Saturday Col. Smith ordered the 106th N.Y. back to town from their station at North Mountain (*OR* 1.27.2. James 40). Then his forces, as McCready wrote, "consisted of the 126th O.V.I., not over five hundred strong, (for two companies [A and I] were away on detached duty) the 106th N.Y., not over six hundred strong (for two companies of it were taken prisoners in the former raid under Imboden) about eighty Cavalry and a Battery of six guns (6 pounders) under Capt. Maulsby with one hundred and fifty men. Our force did not exceed from 1,200 to 1,400 men; still, as we had never been in a larger army, we felt that we were pretty strong and counted more on the damage our six little guns, under the brave Maulsby, would do than more experienced soldiers would have counted on twenty such guns doing. Our tents were struck and all our camp equipage boxed and loaded in our wagons on Saturday by

order from headquarters and we were ordered to be ready to march at a moment's notice and were marched out a little distance after dark, to meet the enemy, but word coming that we need not expect him till morning, we were ordered back to camp, and slept peacefully. The next morning (Sabbath, the 14th) we rose early, loaded up and again got ready for obeying any order. About 11 o'-clock we were ordered out toward Winchester and took our position behind some stone fences about half a mile from town. Soon the skirmishing began sharply and was kept up all day. Sometimes it would die away, then it would revive, and so rapidly would it become that you would suppose the battle was fairly begun.—These skirmishes, however, which precede a battle, are rather harmless affairs. It was thought that two or three rebels were killed, during the day, but they kept at long range.

"Our position was changed, during the day, to a more elevated one, to prevent being flanked." They moved to the ridge east of town which held the cemetery McCready had contemplated months earlier. Behind this graveyard, roads forked to Potomac River crossings north at Williamsport and east at Shepherdstown.

About an hour after Smith's men moved, an envoy carrying a flag of truce brought him a message from Brig. Gen. A. G. Jenkins of the rebel cavalry, demanding the surrender of Martinsburg. Jenkins threatened to shell the town in an hour if Smith did not comply, and warned him to alert the citizens to leave it. Smith replied that he would not surrender, but would notify the townspeople of Jenkins' threats (*OR* 1.27.2. Tyler 17). Smith told

Jenkins "to shell away, as fast as he pleased," as McCready expressed it: "We hardly believed he had any artillery."

From the edge of the cemetery, "the surrounding country, for the most part, could be seen. A squad of rebel officers, I suppose, were seen all afternoon off, out of range, watching us. Every now and then an immense cloud of dust would rise, ominously in the South showing that something was going on. In the meantime, the men and officers were perfectly calm — too calm, perhaps — and watching, with apparently careless interest, all the movements taking place, and discussing them in all their probable bearings. Among the men and line officers there was no other idea than that we were to fight a battle and perhaps the prevailing feeling was a desire that it should begin, and end, at once; all suspense. We would have preferred it had it been another day than Sabbath, but we were on the defensive and not the assailants. About an hour before sun-down it was whispered among the company officers that we were not going to hold the place — that we were far out-numbered — that they had from ten to fifteen thousand...."

"The only object of our commander was to post pone the attack until we could escape under cover of night. — The Sun was fast sinking in the west when their line of battle came into full view. It was but too evident that we had to contend on unequal terms. — Their line of battle must have been near two miles long — long enough to make three or four times round us. — They must have numbered from eight to fifteen thousand. Our artillery opened upon their line — with what effect I could not tell,

except that ... it silenced their unearthly yells very quickly.

"Our forces were ordered to move off the field. Soon after the enemy's artillery opened upon us and the shells and balls and pieces of rail road iron flew thick and fast over and among us but, by a miracle of Providence, none of us were struck, though they seemed to graze the whole line sometimes."

"they opened two Batteries on us all at once," Frank wrote to Nancy. "Thair Cavilry & Infantry making a charge on our Skermishers at the same time. Our Battery replied vigerously but our forces being poasted on a hill in an open field fully exposed to the enemies fire, thair forces not being in range of our musketry & finding they ware comeing with overwhelming numbers we thought it best to retreat. I tell you the shot shell & railroad iron flew amongst us & oaver us moast fearfully. Oh if you had just seen me dodge. and I tell you it took dodgeing to keep out of the way of them shells & cannon balls for they come so fast and tore up the ground all round me."

The sudden barrage concentrated on Smith's men the missiles from as many as thirty cannon, and the retreat started in turmoil. Rebel cavalry in force were already charging through the streets of Martinsburg as Smith's few tried to stall them, and had occupied the road north to Williamsport, the route taken earlier by the wagon train. On that road, the 126th's Co. I was surrounded and captured as they tried to retreat from the blockhouse at Opequon Creek. Smith led the two regiments east on the Shepherdsville road; but after he left, strangely, Gen. Tyler took command of the four guns of Maulsby's battery yet on the field, ordered their men to fire before retreating, and did not direct them to the Shepherdsville road. They took the northern road, were captured, but escaped, losing their artillery.

The court of inquiry which later investigated found many discrepancies between Tyler's and Smith's accounts of the day, with Tyler more to blame for the results of having two commanding officers on the field at once; Tyler, it concluded, should have taken charge as according to his orders.

The direction from Gen. Tyler which the 126th received in its first contest argued an opposite verdict. Its leader Lt. Col. Harlan testified that "the general ordered him at one time to open fire upon his own skirmishers." Harlan had placed them himself, but could not convince Tyler they were his men; so he disobeyed Tyler's order (*OR* 1.27.2. Smith 38-39; Holt 198-201).

During the day, Gen. Tyler did more communicating on the telegraph wires to his superiors than with Col. Smith and his troops. At eight in the morning, he wired Baltimore headquarters that the enemy was but three miles distant; at ten, he wired that Ewell's entire corps were at Winchester (*OR* 1.27.2.33); at eleven, he learned the enemy had captured the outpost eight miles away; at twelve, he notified Smith a retreat would be necessary, sometime later; only after this did Tyler inquire after the rail engines and cars he assumed would carry the retreat to Harpers Ferry, and find none available (*OR* 1.27.2.17-18). He returned to the telegraph, to issue more vagaries. At three, he wired headquarters and President Lincoln that Gen. Milroy was "in a

tight place"—"it is neck or nothing." With perfect obfuscation he relayed, "We are besieged here; have had a little skirmish. I imagine our rebel friends are waiting for grub and artillery" (*OR* 1.27.2.174). At seven, he wired the President that the retreat would start at nightfall for Williamsport, eliciting the immediate exasperated retort "If you are besieged, how do you dispatch me? Why did you not leave before being besieged? A. Lincoln." At this time the line was cut, during an hour and a half of cannonfire (*OR* 1.27.3.109).

Considering the bizarre vacillations of Tyler and the obtuseness of Smith, who thought all day that Tyler was merely visiting him on an inspection, it is probably just as well they did not recognize their emergency as the enemy encircled them. Only by a desperate run into a very dark night, their men evaded the capture which 4,000 of Winchester's troops suffered. The escape seemed to McCready "a signal mercy from Divine Providence," and "all reflecting men in the Regiment ... so regard it." The enemy had already cleared guards from the area they crossed; Co. A had been posted five miles east, and shelled out while Martinsburg was attacked. The forced march reached the Potomac and forded it about one in the morning, then took the canal path along the bank ten miles south, and climbed the thousand-foot Maryland Heights across the river from Harpers Ferry, arriving at ten o'-clock, exhausted, McCready noted.

Frank felt "Uneasy about Mother to know what became of her."

Lee's whole army visibly followed them through the Shepherdstown ford into Maryland in the next days; and the fortifications on Maryland Heights, guarding the arsenal, storehouses, and rails below, could not withstand an attack. Gen. Tyler took charge and began extensive works (*OR* 1.27.2. Tyler 21-4). Frank chronicled: "June 16th Rebels repoarted intrenching East of Maryland Heights. 6 oc. Troops falling into line & intrenching & digging rifle pits. An attack expected. lying in line of battle all day. Today Mr. Clark came in & repoarted Mother to be at a house 3 miles from town on the Williamsport road. June the 21. Sabbath ... Nothing spacial going on but digging Rifle pits & mounting guns and makeing fortifications of different kinds. Have to git up every morning at 3 Oclock and stand in line of Battle along the trenches till daylight. Enemy encamped up the Valley about 10 miles. June 28th. Sabbath ... Enemy moving towards Pennsylvania. General Hooker was here yesterday & ordered all the forces away from here but Hallock ordered him to hoald the place."

"I think we ought to have went," he wrote Nancy the next day, "he needs all the men he can get. Thare will be some hard fighting in Maryland & Pennsylvania before long."

The regiment had made its first acquaintance with discipline — and lingo — in the general army, which brought McCready's comment on 29 June. They had arguments whether the move from Martinsburg constituted a "retreat," "change of base," or "reconnoissance in force to the rear," debates which made him laugh and provided "an example of the way in which even calamities are warded off by the human mind and even turned into sport. If they draw meat, for example, in which there happens to be some occu-

pants of another species, you will hear them 'driving it' up and placing a guard around it to keep it from moving off. The other day they drew some crackers of a suspicious character, and grave discussions were held as to how they would prevent them from running off during the night. It was suggested that the box be strapped down, that it be 'bucked and gagged,'...This sarcasm is a powerful weapon in the hands of the soldier. He dare not grumble audibly. It might be construed into mutiny and punished. He dare not even argue his case with a supercilious and dogmatic officer. But what punishment can reach the good humored sarcasm of a regiment of men and what officer is brazen enough to face the gibes of ten thousand men, who can mimick his voice, his every word and jesture! In this way a man is sometimes able to 'see himself as others see him'" (*CR* 15 Jl).

On 29 June, Hooker had been replaced by Meade, Tyler by Maj. Gen. French, and the men on Maryland Heights ordered to join Meade's forces. Some remained behind to finish and guard the evacuation, including Col. Smith's men, who "were under excellent discipline, and perfectly reliable" (*OR* 1.27.1. French 488).

McCready described the waste: "The forts were demolished. — As much as could be hauled to the canal during two days and nights by a great number of teams was removed. But dozens of barrels of Molasses were poured out, dozens of barrels of sugar, salt and ground coffee were torn to pieces and scattered. Car loads of ammunition burnt, hundreds of guns broken. A box of ammunition accidentally exploded, killing nine and wounding seventeen.

"It was confidently expected we would be attacked in leaving or on our way.— The rebel trains were making unusual speed in passing on our right, owing to the battle at Gettysburg (of which we knew nothing.) Rebel cavalry had driven in our pickets. Our communication had been cut off. We took the canal about 11 o'clock at night and started in a train of about twenty-seven boats" (*CR* 12 Ag).

They rode perched on the wooden covers of the barges on this dangerous trip, "under armes nearly all the time," Frank recorded, for four days and nights, and reached Washington on 4 July, where sickened men went to hospitals and the rest boarded railroad cars to join Meade's army in its march after Lee's.

Chapter 25

Morgan's Raid
and the Soldiers

A year after the great harmonious gathering in the oak grove, Cadiz had no celebration of this Fourth of July. In the entire county, there was only one observance, in New Market; and the *Sentinel* advised shunning its "political" talk (*CR* 1 Jl).

That Saturday afternoon in Cadiz township, all able men of 18 to 45 years had orders from the trustees to report to militia meetings: in town, at John Minteer's farm on the Cambridge road, or at Alexander Henderson's on Deersville road. They had ignored recent calls from the governor to enlist for six months of militia service, and from the county military committee of Obadiah Slemmons, John C. Jamison, Charles Warfel, J. M. Paul, and S. B. Shotwell; but as Lee's army overran Pennsylvania, Gov. Tod's warnings that the Ohio border faced invasion raised alarm. The *Sentinel* advised, "You had better meet the enemy at the river than at your own doors" (*CR, CDS* 24 Je, 1 Jl).

The first militia business was, of course, elections. In the Cadiz district they became Capt. Thomas H. Smith, 1st Lt. Pat Haverfield, and 2nd Lt. Martin Jamison. Smith, formerly McCready's 1st Lt., had decided not to leave with the cavalry company he had recruited. Haverfield, a 126th sutler along with Sam Ferguson, had lost most of his merchandise in Martinsburg (*CDS* 24 Je). Officers from the Cambridge road district were L. Lawrence, M. McAdams, and S. Dickerson; from the Deersville, G. L. Haverfield, N. Haverfield, and D. Hines. Brilles the clothier advertised his readiness to provide their uniforms on short order. Not a day should be lost in fitting up the militia, Hatton urged, in view of the low water in the Ohio. Allen, amid his columns pressing Vallandigham's campaign, urged "every Democrat to prepare himself to defend our own soil and homes," although remaining opposed to "a war for Abolitionism" (*CR, CDS* 8 Jl).

Invasion did approach, not from the east but the west. Morgan's cavalry, reported 5,000 strong, entered Indiana and burned Salem 11 July, and soon rode into Ohio (*CDS* 15 Jl). Rumors soon abounded placing Morgan at such disparate sites as near Cincinnati or Parkersburg. His men were said to be pillaging whole neighborhoods, stealing money, jewelry, silver spoons, ladies' kid gloves, silk hose, and ribbons, and shooting a man who refused to act as their guide (*CDS* 22 Jl, *CR* 29 Jl).

The first Harrison Countians whom Morgan neared were its cavalry company. This "brave and jolly" crew under James W. Hanna, most from Cadiz, named themselves the "Rocky Mountain Cavalry." They included George C. Finney and James Thompson from Hatton's office; they were bound for Fort Laramie in the Idaho Territory. Frank Hatton boasted, "if they ever come in contact with the 'big injuns' they will quickly learn them the art of 'skedaddling'" (*CR* 24 Je). On their first ride, from Columbus to Cincinnati, they found other opponents. On 13 July, they camped near London, fed themselves and their horses, and went into town. There, probably in a tavern, some butternuts "raised a fuss with some of our boys which resulted in the cracking of several of these rascals," Finney reported; after most of the boys had left the place, a butternut hit Sgt. Sellers in the head with a rock, severely hurting him. On 15 July they neared Waynesville, south of Dayton, and heard that Morgan's raiders were in front of them. The captain went to the telegraph office to investigate, learned that Morgan was twenty-eight miles away, and wired his colonel for advice on proceeding. The reply with the colonel's name ordered

them onward, but the captain "suspicioned the genuineness of this dispatch and retreated"; indeed, Morgan had possession of the wires. That night they rode four miles back "to a thick woods where we lay so still that Morgan would not have found us had he come that way. We were not armed except by sabres."

When they emerged and journeyed on through the country Morgan had passed, all its good horses, harness, and carriages had been looted (*CR* 29 Jl). Morgan and his actual 2,000 raiders by this time were crossing the regions of Chillicothe and Athens on their way to a ford of the Ohio near Pomeroy, with about 8,000 troops in pursuit. On 19 July at Bluffington Island, Morgan's men found themselves nearly surrounded; 700 were captured, but the general led 1,100 to escape through a hidden ravine and start a grueling, desperate ride north through the hills. On 23 July he had 600 men in the saddle when he entered Guernsey County and struck the National Road toward the shallows near Wheeling (Keller 145, 168, 178, 206-7).

That Thursday evening, a dispatch from Cambridge told a Cadiz resident Morgan's whereabouts. The townspeople took no serious alarm, confident Morgan would stay on the direct, paved pike to the river rather than climb north on the steep, winding roads through their county. They called a meeting, nevertheless, to consider what measures they could take if he approached. At it, attention evidently fastened on the banks and private monies in town that Morgan could rob. With this thought arose a conviction that Morgan would directly bring a raid and ruin, unless they could defend the town, and realization of their unpreparedness. Their militia had officers, but no muskets or ammunition. They decided the military committee should telegraph the governor for 500 arms and 40 rounds for each. Then they delegated scouts to ride out toward Cambridge and south toward the National Road to learn Morgan's next moves.

On Friday morning the governor promised to send the arms that day. By noon several hundred men from the townships around Cadiz came in, on horse and on foot, some bringing their small-bore squirrel rifles. Then scouts rode in with the news that Morgan's band had burned Campbell's Station and passed Washington in Guernsey, and had turned onto the road to Cadiz, which they could reach by night. Messengers went out to the distant townships, summoning their men to the town's defense. Meanwhile, it was learned that the train could not bring the arms until after six o'clock. Without them, no resistance to Morgan's raiders seemed possible, and some citizens began taking away their horses and valuables, while other families fled (*CR* 29 Jl).

Morgan rode through Londonderry and Smyrna, into the valley of Big Stillwater creek, as two Cadiz men, M. J. Brown and John Robinson, "driving a spirited team, rushed through" Moorefield to scout the rebel route. An hour later they returned to the hilltop village, "furiously driving Jehu like," calling that Morgan would shortly appear. Very soon, smoke rose from the covered bridge over Big Stillwater; moments later, from that on Little Stillwater a half-mile from town.

The Moorefield men rushed to hide their horses in the deep hollows around,

and their treasures in "the most unthought of places"; women and children ran "hither and thither with their trinkets trying to find some very secure place"; and several "would-be Generals on horseback" rode the village street "giving spicy directions as to what others should do, or where to go. A thing they soon found out when the advance guard of Morgan's force came galloping into town, putting them to flight, and quite an exciting race occurred though our street accompanied with the Rebel yell, 'Halt, Halt!'" A few "generals" escaped by "some exceedingly fast riding." The others lost their horses.

Soon the street, stables, and every vacated house were occupied by Morgan's men, who "freely solicited every house for provisions of every kind; some of them exhibiting abnormal appetites for pound cake and preserves." After consuming the village's prepared foods, they rested nonchalantly, although the cavalry pursuing them were only three miles behind. Morgan himself took a nap on the parlor bed in Mills' Hotel, his bodyguards sitting on chairs around him reading their collection of newspapers. When he awoke, he took a leisurely stroll up the street alone, and then the raiders rode on, taking with them several "escorts drafted into service as guides" (McGavran 52-54).

The village's Presbyterian minister was a Franklin College graduate who had preached against slavery for many years; fearing he would be captured or killed by Morgan, the Rev. Thomas R. Crawford had retreated to the graveyard grove of his Nottingham Church, two miles past town on the Cadiz road. There the rebels loomed only twenty feet from his hiding place, and he apprehended the greater danger of appearing a spy than an abolitionist; but the raiders were pressed onward before they discovered him (Beauregard, *Franklin* 84).

News came to Cadiz about three o'clock that Morgan was at Moorefield, and fears rose. More men were assembling from the outlying townships, but few bringing any weapons. In all, about 1,000 men stood ready, bearing only "200 to 300 squirrel rifles in their hands." The military committee proceeded with the customary preliminary to any action, however; they appointed officers — in sufficient variety for a brigade in a besieged garrison. S. W. Bostwick, father of the late Capt. Albion, became "commandant of all the forces; Chas. Warfel, Col.; Thos. C. Rowles, Lieut. Col.; O. Slemmons, Major; Robt. Wilkin, Capt. of the colored troops; D. B. Welch, Quartermaster; K. W. Kinsey, Commissary of Subsistence, and Joseph Sharon, Provost Marshall of Cadiz Post" (*CR* 12 Ag). The officers reflect the breadth of the men who assembled, with attorneys Bostwick and Sharon; Wilkin, from an old Washington township farm family; and sufficient African Americans to form a company.

Morgan now veered from the main road, probably to elude the cavalry behind him and avoid any possible confrontation ahead at the bridges over Brushy Fork. Near Rankin's church he turned east onto lanes to Stumptown and New Athens. Whether the fame of the forge of the peace-militants drew him, or his Moorefield escorts guided him there for safe passage, history does not record, nor any momentous greeting among the stumps. But New Athens, as Morgan headed across the hills,

had no doubt its cradledom of abolitionism formed Morgan's particular target. The citizens took added fright that his Masonic sword was coming for vengeance on their historic opposition to secret societies. They expected the preachers, professors, and few remaining men students would be slaughtered; the women, especially the college students, raped; the village, burned to the ground. Many men hid themselves in undignified places, and the students gathered in a prayer meeting (Beauregard, *Franklin* 85).

The thousand men in Cadiz organized into companies, each with officers. About six in the evening, the guns and cartridges rolled into the depot, and D. B. Welch began distributing them, a process that occupied two hours. At nine o'clock, the new militia stood in formation; Judge Bostwick marched them to the fairgrounds; there they fortified themselves with refreshments prepared by the town women, and waited for orders.

Two miles west of New Athens, Morgan's riders turned north again, onto the road to Cadiz (*CR* 29 Jl). By this time it was night, and the cavalry behind him under Col. Shackelford had stopped in Moorefield; its women had to cook new dinners for them, and were serving food past midnight (McGavran 54). As Morgan headed up Irish Ridge, he had no force threatening his rear, and he seemed bound for Cadiz and its banks. Two miles north of New Athens, he changed course. His reason, according to the Cadiz militiamen, was fear of the mighty defense they had mounted. Considering Morgan's experience with Ohio citizenry on his romp across the state, however, it is unlikely that any excited rumors in Athens township convinced him that a group of sufficient number, arms, and discipline awaited him whom his crack cavalry would not immediately disperse. Word of 500 government arms, moreover, in hands that had never drilled with or fired them, would have beckoned Morgan's expertise at a rout and trophy seizure. Withal its lack of skills, though, the new militia did invest itself with every military trapping available, and one can guess the "camp" at the fairgrounds soon lit with campfires. Mounting the ridge four to five miles south, Morgan's men would have seen these blazes like signs of a regiment of regulars. At this point, they turned onto lanes east across the ridge toward Georgetown, which sat on the road to Wheeling; they stopped for the night on W. W. Dickerson's farm (*CR* 29 Jl).

The militia learned of the changed route at one in the morning. Although its charge from the governor was simply to "retard Morgan's progress," the 800 with guns set out at two to find him (*CR* 12 Ag). They hastened seven miles out the Plank Road, an old Indian trail whose precipitous sharp bends on the rocky hills and wendings through Short Creek vales were laid with boards, and halted in the narrow hollow just out of sight of Georgetown. Scouts went forth to learn whether Morgan was there, or had passed through. It was dark and foggy in the dales of Little Short Creek; some scouts came back uncertain, and others did not return. So Thomas Smith, acting adjutant, wearing his uniform, went down the road into Georgetown. There he was told that Morgan had not come, and four scouts had gone out the Athens road, whom he could quickly

find: "I thought, as any other man would, that I could advance with proper safety, at least until I could come up with them (the scouts). I never overtook them. They had gone off the road to partake of refreshments, and instead of informing me of that fact I was permitted to ride on until I suppose I was two and a half or three miles from Georgetown. I rode on until I arrived at the top of a hill intending to return as soon as I had proceeded that far. At this point I observed six horsemen coming towards me. They were dressed in citizens clothes. No two of them were dressed alike.— It was not quite daylight and I must confess I was at a loss to know whether they were our men or not.— I soon observed that they were armed principally with carbines and concluded that they were actually rebels. I observed here that a large column of horsemen was just out of camp coming in the direction of Georgetown. I about-faced and used every exertion to get my horse to use his utmost speed. I had neither whip nor spur and the horse being more anxious for company than I, was rather slow about getting away. The six horsemen whom I had observed put spurs to their horses and cried halt. I paid no attention.... I still disobeyed and finally got my horse to lope, when I looked around and found that they (all six) were about 13 or 20 feet in the rear of me with aimed pieces exclaiming halt by g — d or you're a dead man. What must I do in this case? Must I rush madly on when I knew I must be caught and probably shot? I, for one, deemed discretion the better part of valor in that case, and surrendered.... The chief of the squad asked me where I came from, what I was doing there and what that sword was hanging by my side for. I replied that I came from Georgetown, that I was riding for information and that I was acting Adjutant of the Militia. I could not have denied being on military duty for the fact of having a sword by my side would have belied me.... I was sent to the head of the column, under guard, and introduced to Major Steele, who commanded the advance, when the following dialogue took place:

STEELE: What time did the militia leave Cadiz?

SMITH: Do not remember exactly but think it was about midnight.

STEELE: Where is the militia now?

Smith: Between Cadiz and Georgetown.

STEELE: I am aware of that fact but where are they now?

SMITH: Cannot tell. I left them between Cadiz and Georgetown.

STEELE: I want you to tell the truth in the matter for if your statements differ materially from the statements of others whom we made captive I will have you shot.

SMITH: I will tell you the truth and nothing more."

In answering Steele, Smith reported the militia had 800 to 900 men, 500 armed with Springfield muskets and the rest with squirrel rifles, a few horsemen, and no artillery.

"After this conversation we observed some militia coming up the road, when Steele said to me, you must not say a word or make any signs to them.— One of the militia was John Haverfield, who lives near Cadiz. These men, after a while, stopped, reversed steam and went the other way as fast as they could with the rebs after them. One David Harrison was caught and, I was informed, told that if he led them into danger he would be the first man they would shoot."

By this time the militia had learned Morgan's cavalry were coming down the road from Stumptown. They marched to a hill just west of Georgetown which overlooked the road in the narrow valley. In the ranks was Frank Hatton, who recounted, "We had not been stationed here long until two of our scouts came dashing down the Stumptown road, pursued and fired on by five of the enemy's scouts, one of whom [rode on and] was captured in Georgetown.— Our scouts reported the enemy advancing. The men were immediately formed in line of battle and placed in position, anxiously awaiting the approach of the enemy, who were reported at John Hanna's. While in this position we were seen by the enemy's scouts who reported back.... [The main force] immediately retreated back to the forks of the road a short distance west of Hanna's house where they took up the road which strikes the Plank Road about a mile west of Harrisville" (CR 29 Jl).

As they backtracked, Morgan's men rode into the sights of Shackleford's cavalry and battery, whose cannon shelled them, wounding two (CR 12 Ag). They dashed up the detour lane, among them, Thomas Smith: "Steele says to me, 'I thought you had no artillery?' I remarked that it was not ours unless it had been brought up since I left the Regiment. The column then moved rapidly on leaving Georgetown on the left. This rapid movement continued pretty nearly the whole of the time.... After riding sometime in front Gen. Morgan ordered that I be brought back to the middle of the column where he appeared to remain most of the time. I approached him and gave the usual salute which he very respectfully acknowledged and remarked that the boys were a little suspicious of me and that he would have to treat me as a prisoner of war. He then asked me about the forces at Wheeling and Wellsville and also about the stage of water at these places. I told him that I knew nothing of the forces at either of these places. He doubted my word.... He stated further that he intended to cross the river that night or have a d—d big fight."

The militia ran after them, by its official account: "Gen'l Bostwick ordered our force through Georgetown by the Plank Road in the direction of Harrisville (our men moving at double-quick)" up the high hill to the junction "which intersects the Harrisville and N Athens road (the road by which the enemy had to pass) about two miles distant, at which point we hoped to intercept them. Our front arrived at this point, just a few moments after the enemy's rear had passed fleeing at great speed." The militia pursued them, "thinking they would halt to pillage," Frank Hatton wrote; however, "They were pressed so hard by the Militia that they were unable to do any harm in Harrisville, more than the gobbling up of twenty-seven Union cavalry, belonging to the 4th Virginia, and the capturing of twenty-five or thirty horses from the residents."

Morgan was merely ten minutes ahead of the militia, but it was seven in the morning, and "at Harrisville the good citizens had all kinds of eatables ready for them. Having had nothing to eat since the night before, the men were somewhat hungry, and partook of a hearty breakfast, for which they were all very thankful to the citizens of that place. Leaving Harrisville we pursued Morgan down Long Run, supposing that it was his intention to strike the Ohio river at Warrenton [at the mouth of Short Creek], and knowing that if he did attempt to cross at that place and was forced to fall back we would be able to cut off his retreat. The men marched as fast as they possibly could, but, owing to the roughness of the road over which they had to travel, their progress was somewhat impeded.

"Along the route, Morgan stripped the country of all the horses which were close to the road, leaving his broken down ones in exchange.

"The Militia pursued him closely until we came to the forks of the Smithfield and Long Run roads, where we learned from our scouts that the scouts of the enemy had ascertained that there was considerable of a force stationed at Warrenton to dispute their approach. Consequently the rebels left the Long Run Road at this point and moved in the direction of Smithfield, Jefferson county."

It then appeared that Morgan would try to cross the river at Wellsburg. Judge Bostwick plotted another interception; he marched the militia to Warrenton and intended to take them upriver on the railroad. They arrived in Warrenton at two in the afternoon, having marched in twelve hours twenty-five or thirty-two miles, by differing accounts. There a Pennsylvania militia regiment had orders to ride north, and the Harrisonians remained to defend Warrenton. On Sunday morning, Morgan was reported surrounded at Fishing Creek in Jefferson County, and the militia marched toward Mt. Pleasant and home.

They had another day of excitement, however. Probably parties of local "scouts" were riding every neighborhood, each looking like rebels to another. Some two miles up the road, word came to Bostwick that the rebels were in Georgetown again; soon after, they were reported at Smithfield, going to Warrenton. The militia divided, with posted pickets and battle lines on Long Run road, and other companies racing down two roads to the river. By night, when they learned Morgan had been captured in Columbiana County, the militia were "pretty well tired out." They slept in Mt. Pleasant, and the next morning rode home in wagons from Cadiz. "Thus ended the chase…, and we are certain that no troops have done harder marching since Morgan crossed the Ohio than they did. The fortitude with which they bore the hardships of the march would do credit to old troops," Frank Hatton concluded—but after noting that "At almost every house the occupants would furnish them with something to eat" (*CR* 29 Jl).

To the governor, the military committee sent a laudatory report of their "hot" pursuit, by which they saved three towns from "sacking," and drove the rebels "rapidly into the trap set for their capture": "both officers and men manifested the utmost ardor to meet the enemy in combat; and if he could have been induced to fight, our forces would certainly either have destroyed or captured the whole force" (*CR* 12 Ag).

In post-war history of Morgan's raid, the most curious fact is that Stewart Beebe Shotwell received the credit for deterring Morgan. Uniformly, the men who gathered and marched have been termed "Shotwell's militia." He was not recorded as an officer in it, only as secretary of the military committee. Shotwell, however, had gained the attention of the governor; he perhaps signed the dispatch requesting arms, and he may have remained at the telegraph during the event sending out reports, under his name. However he gained the fame, it started early. In 1867, James M. Shackleford, the leader of the pursuing cavalry, wrote to the president of Franklin College that Morgan avoided Cadiz due to the militia led by Shotwell (Beauregard, *Franklin* 84).

The young man who carried his sword into the thick of the action fared far worse in reputation. Thomas Smith came home from his capture to calumny, so that he had to defend himself from charges "that I told Morgan the names and locations of the different banks" and wealthy men in Cadiz, "that I intended piloting Morgan through this place, and God knows *what* all *has* been said by certain gossipers." Smith's misadventure into Morgan's force had taken him beyond Smithfield to Alexandria, cost him his horse, and kept him on the road a week (*CR* 26 Ag).

In Warrenton, Va., 28 July, Capt. McCready began a letter: "We are nearly killed marching and yet we gathered under a shade tree and took a good laugh this morning.... Accidentally I got a paper of Saturday's date. I was soon surrounded by a fine audience and read to them various items of interest to us, among them of Morgan's Raid into Indiana and *across Ohio* and that they were ... even near the Cadiz Junction; within eight miles of Steubenville. 'Good!' one would say. 'Bully for Morgan!' 'I wish he would go to our town!' 'Go it Morgan!'—'He will go it like a shoot!' 'It will make the Copperheads roll their eyes in astonishment as Morgan turns out an old, worn-out horse and mounts the 'bay filly,' tips his hat and sets off at a gallop,' &c., were the comments of the boys. It only increased the merriment (not mine, of course) when some one suggested that they might take 'Jim' (my horse). 'O they have him now.' 'Jim is in the Southern Confederacy,' added others. If they take 'Jim,' henceforth I will be down on the Confederacy, sure.

"Well, in these expressions you have a clue to the sentiments of the soldiers.... The war has not been brought home to your own doors — nay, you really don't know what it is at all. Else your young men would not be lying about the corners, whiffing their cigars.... We think you need a few Morgan blisters and we don't object to their 'drawing,' *in places*, sharply."

The 126th had marched all month, many nights lying in the rain without tents, after leaving the railroad at Frederick, Md. On 8 July they climbed up South Mountain to the scene of the 30th Ohio's battle last September, into a camp of the 3rd corps of Meade's army, which had nearly been demolished in the peach orchard and wheatfield at Gettysburg. "We had fallen in with the Army of the Potomac. Poor fellows! they had marched all the way to Gettysburg, fought, and marched back, and they were about used up. They were covered with mud from head to foot and it might fitly be said of them 'faint yet pursuing.'

"Near a chestnut tree in a clear field on South Mountain stands a stone about two feet high inscribed as follows: — 'Here General Reno fell.' I saw a grave in a shaded spot with the inscription 'W. Tidrick, of the 30th Ohio.' The bones of rebels (as I suppose) are sticking out of several graves. Their graves seem greatly to outnumber the Union graves....

"We began now to get in the neighborhood of the enemy. Indeed the day we reached here there was quite a skirmish going on but a little beyond us. Our marches were short and shifting; first to this or that side as the enemy's line changed." Lee's army was backed up against the Potomac, which the rains had made too high to ford. On 11 July McCready's regiment reached the Antietam battlefield, and that Saturday the "army began to rush forward. We felt sure the battle was opening, and listened every moment for the shock of contending armies. The day passed without it, however. I confess I felt rather disappointed that it did not open, though well aware that the day of battle might be the day of death to me. But where we have anything of great importance before us, we feel impatient that it come, especially if we have expected it. Then I confess that I have always felt a curiosity to witness a battle, which I have been unable to repress, though I regarded it as sinful and cruel — just as I have to see the ocean, the storm, the volcano, or the prairie on fire.

"But I was afraid it would come on Sabbath. It was my prayer, and I heard it mentioned in several prayers…. And sure enough, on Saturday night the order was issued by Gen. Meade stating that he intended moving on the enemy the next morning and ordering all things to be put in readiness."

On Sabbath, Frank Grove chronicled, they "marched in line of Battle to the road leading from Sharpsburg to Williamsport & lay till evening & then fell back & encamped for the night. July 13th Weat weather Lay in Camp all day. July 14th Drawn up in line of Battle in the morning & moved up to the enemies front to make an attac but behold they ware gone. We then moved on towards Williamspoart & camped. Great dissatisfaction amongst the soldiers for letting them escape. July 15th Marched across the Antietam Battle ground & encamped below Sharpsburg verry warm day. several men gave out. 5 dropped down & died."

McCready believed that the Sabbath "day's work was the cause of Lee's escape. Up to that time God seemed to be on our side. He sent the rains of Heaven and shut them in. By disregarding God's day he [Meade] offended God. Lee said that we were ready and would attack, and that day he began to cross. On Monday we lay in camp *when we should* have been led against the enemy. — True the ground was not in good condition for moving artillery, but it could have been done, for Lee moved his to the river. On Wednesday we moved on the enemy's line, but were a day too late, the bird had flown…. We cheated God out of His day and then when we came to reckon, lo! we have lost a day and a day too that will never return to us.

"Poor fellows of the old Potomac Army who had so long followed and so often faced in battle Lee's army. Some swore. Some scolded. Some sat down and almost cried. Some said they would go home — it was no use….

"But Meade was out-generaled by that wily chieftain Lee. With a heavy heart we took up our line of march for — where? … The first day we marched about ten or twelve miles before dinner — hard as we could go, our officers constantly hurrying us. The day was exceedingly warm. We were not after the enemy. The road was very bad and many of our men sick. We knew that we were led by some drunk General or foolish one who was not fit to drive mules. Six men dropped down apparently dying…. We were not surprised to hear afterwards that several bottles of liquor were bet on which Regiment could do the best marching, but whether it is true I can't say….

"Our course was now for Harper's Ferry. We reached there, next day, the 16th inst. On the 17th we crossed on a pontoon bridge and went up through the town, a little band, somewhere, singing the John Brown song. About two o'clock in the morning we encamped in the Loudon Valley, Va." They trekked down the valley under the Blue Ridge, and on 23 July climbed Mannassas Gap in battle lines to Wapping Heights, coming under fire behind a charge which drove the enemy back into the Shenandoah Valley. The pursuit of Lee's army ended here, and they went east to Warrenton, having marched, according to the regimental history, 136 miles (Gilson 12-4).

The entry into the main army as Gilson recorded it brought impressions of "immensity and grandeur — the vast multitude, the martial music, the tramp, tramp, tramp of soldiers; colors flying, horses neighing, cattle lowing, the immense trains of wagons and artillery stretching for miles" (12). McCready gave a far different description, of spoiled land, embittered citizens, and a demoralized army. For the last, he blamed the officers: "There is scarcely an officer — I don't know one — above the rank of Captain and but a few below it who do not drink and sometimes drink to excess. It is not unusual for a General to have a wagon for little else than to haul his liquor. I don't doubt but old alcohol has decided many a battle. I am not certain that it had not something to do with Lee's escape. Our Generals have no fear of God before their eyes — care nothing for God or his day.— There is no Sabbath in this army.— General Meade has had no Sabbath since he took command."

Concluding his long indictment of the army, McCready revealed the one attachment which kept him in its service: "Were it not for my boys I could not consent to continue under the command of those who disregard the Lord's day. But in them I have a trust that I could not lightly lay down. All we can do is to have what religious services we can [to] mourn, as we do not cease to do, our Sabbaths. How precious they now seem. May God restore them to the army and to us. J. S. McCready" (*CR* 12 Ag).

By contrast, the soldiers who had been in the western army for a year had developed high military morale, which they conveyed home in characteristic ways. John Finley Oglevee and "P" of the 98th wrote long letters for publication justifying the occupation of Tennessee and denouncing the peace Democrats. Fin Oglevee, in consummate rhetoric, condemned the July New York riot as one result of poisoning minds against the government and army, and rose to this peroration: "War to the knife, from the knife to the hilt; a bloody, unrelenting war; show no quarters, then the war will soon be over" (*CR* 12 Ag).

Robert Mitchell, though shrunk by illness ("liver complaint") from 150 pounds to 117, was growing up in the army, in the tutelage of Oglevee and Gray, and Nancy's correspondence. Increasingly he could express himself in coherent sentences, and even his spelling improved. He wrote from Shelbyville on 24 July: "Dear Sister ... I would rather be here than any where else. we have a nice time here and I am some beter than I was. The boys is in good spirits. They think war will soon be over.... we can get plenty to eat. new potoes and mutton and lite bread and ripe apples and peaches and freh butter. the most of the sitizen are union.... we are camp on the bank of Duck River where the bridge broke down with the rebles. som of hour boys was in a swimming and found a dead reble....wrte soon. Robert."

They soon moved eight miles east to Wartrace, where Thompson Gray wrote Nancy on 18 August: "Kind Friend, This is the first anniversary of Company C's leaving the old homestead, its kind friends and tender associations....Yes, Friend, one year ago today we first entered camp and were introduced into the mysteries of military science. Then we did not expect to be in the field till this time. Then we hardly knew how much a few disasters would retard and injure us....Our little company of 100 men now numbers but sixty. And nearly one half the missing have passed to their last account. All that was mortal of them lies mouldering in the dust. The cemeteries of New Albany, Louisville, Lebanon, Nashville, and Franklin and the Battlefield of Perryville are all dear to this little company on account of companions who sleep there; while some of them have been interred beneath the soil of their own loved and native State of Ohio. Think not that the soldiers heart has become so inured to death that these things are never thought of. Ah, no, we still miss them. Our little band is broken and each absent one has left a vacancy no other can fill. But one thing more.

"That year has learned many of us to love soldiering, to pride ourselves in doing it well. I for one feel that I have learned to love it. There is something fascinating in it and though I long to see the war ended, yet not as I once did, as when I first quit home for the field. But enough of this....

"The adventures of the Militia after Morgan's band have been the theme of frequent criticism and merry making. Not because they did not do their duty bravely and timely. But because of their exalting their own deeds and also at the many excited accounts we had received of their doing and valor. Of one thing however we are well satisfied and that is his safe quarters at present. Sabbath evening we heard that John L. Mitchell was no more. That his freed spirit had taken its flight to another — and we hope a better — world. Poor fellow, we criti-

cised his conduct too severely during his first illness. May God forgive the wrong and teach us to judge not. May the consolations of Christ's own promises support and sustain the afflicted family...."

John did not die a deserter; in his last days a discharge was obtained for him. But no obituary or memorial tribute was published for Daniel Mitchell's bright son. A slate tablet in Dickerson's graveyard numbered the months and days of his twenty-five years. His sisters soon left their mournful home and depleted neighborhood for the more cheerful clime of Londonderry.

"I learn that there is still much sickness about Cadiz. Amanda says more than has been known there for fifteen years.... [The bane of soldiers' camps, diarrhea, particularly struck the Cadiz children. One week, it wrenched the life from seven of them, including the infant daughter of Josiah and Amanda Estep; and more were expected soon to die (*CDS* 19 Ag)].

"Some of the boys are trying to obtain furloughs....James Dickerson is one. I suppose he wants to be at Sue's wedding. For the first time since Robt's late illness I feel at liberty to encourage you by saying he is fast recovering. He is now able for duty. Eats hearty and is as lively as you ever saw him....Eliza Ritchey has never answered my letter....Uncle Sam Cochran has never found time to write to me either. My Butternut friends don't seem to like me very well....

[The wedding of Susan Dickerson gathered families of numerous Ridge soldiers and their political opponents; Susan was marrying Eliza Ritchey's younger brother Robert.]

"Well friend, I was happy to see that still your trust for peace and deliverance was not placed in an arm of flesh.... I think our nation is beginning to see that large armies will not do unless by our humility we secure the blessings of God upon them.... But thanking you for your kind letter and its encouraging sentiments I will close by requesting you to write as soon as convenient. Your Friend, Thomps. Remember me in your Prayers."

Thus a bitter year taught some to endure and others to love soldiering. The 126th would face Lee's fire this fall at Brandy Station and elsewhere, and the next May fight through the Wilderness and the Bloody Angle of Spotsylvania Court House, losing nearly half its men. The 98th and other local soldiers were on their way to Chickamauga, and many more battles.

The men who enlisted in the 55th Massachusetts and the 3rd regiment of U. S. Colored Infantry went to the South Carolina islands. There on 26 August, the 3rd attacked Fort Wagner, where the 54th Mass. had lost over 200 men on 18 July; the 3rd had eighteen casualties, but the fort was besieged and captured. The 1st, 4th, 5th, and 22nd U.S.C.I., in which local men also served, joined the battles in Virginia. In the trenches and charges on the fortresses at Petersburg in 1864, many lost their lives: of the 4th, 18 enlisted men were killed and 140 wounded or missing; of the 22nd, 17 were killed, and 139 wounded or missing (U.S.A.-G. *Register* 8: 315-16, 169-75, 193).

At the end of the diary Frank Grove filled in his first year's service, he composed some lines that can stand as a valediction for all these soldiers, as he remembered the beautiful landscape he had left:

Farewell native hills. Many a time
have I scaled your heights and sat
beneath the sturdy oaks that deck
your verdant brows. But adieu to your
enchanting scenes till the sun of peace
dispels the dark cloud of rebellion
and smiles upon your looming heights.

Works Cited or Used

Andrews, J. K. "The Sick Soldier's Talk With the Grass Growing in the Hospital." Appendix in *Concise History of the One Hundred and Twenty-sixth Regiment, Ohio Volunteer Infantry*, edited by J. H. Gilson. Salem, Ohio: Walton, Steam Job and Laurel, 1883. 213–18.

Ash, Stephen V. *Middle Tennessee Society Transformed 1860–1870: War and Peace in the Upper South*. Baton Rouge: Louisiana State University Press, 1998.

Baas, William P. "Preliminary Analysis of Post-Battle Deaths at Perryville." *Action Front: The Newsletter of the Perryville Battlefield Preservation Association* 6, no. 4 (1997): 3.

Baskerville, Barnet. *The People's Voice: The Orator in American Society*. Lexington: University Press of Kentucky, 1979.

Beatty, John. *Memoirs of a Volunteer, 1861–63*. Reprint of *The Citizen-Soldier, or, Memoirs of a Volunteer*, 1879. Alexandria, Va.: Time-Life Books, 1983.

Beauregard, Erving E. *Bingham of the Hills: Politician and Diplomat Extraordinary*. American University Studies: Ser. 9, History; vol. 68. New York: Peter Lang, 1989.

_____. *Old Franklin, the eternal touch: a history of Franklin College, New Athens, Harrison County, Ohio*. Lanham, Md.: University Press of America, 1983.

[Beers]. *Commemorative Biographical Record of the Counties of Harrison and Carroll, Ohio....* Chicago: J. H. Beers, 1891.

Belmont Chronicle (St. Clairsville, Ohio). Microfilm, Ohio Historical Society.

Benedict, H. T. N. *Murray's English Grammar, Revised ... to the Inductive and Explanatory Mode of Instruction*. Frankfort, Ky.: A. G. Hodges, 1832.

Blair, Hugh. *Lectures on Rhetoric and Belles Lettres*. 2nd ed. 3 vols. London: 1785. Reprint, New York: Garland Publishing, 1970.

Brandt, Nat. *The Town That Started the Civil War*. New York: Dell-Laurel, 1991.

Brewer, James D. *The Raiders of 1862*. Westport, Ct.: Greenwood Press, Praeger Imprint, 1997.

Burkett, Eva Mae. *American Dictionaries of the English Language Before 1861*. Metuchen, N.J.: Scarecrow Press, 1979.

Butler, Noble. *Butler's Fourth School Reader*. Louisville, Ky.: John P. Morton, 1873.

_____. *Introductory Lessons in English Grammar*. American School Series. Louisville, Ky.: John P. Morton, 1846.

Cadiz Democratic Sentinel (Cadiz, Ohio). 11 Jan. 1860–4 May 1864. Microfilm Roll 20030, Columbus: Ohio Historical Society.

Cadiz Republican (Cadiz, Ohio). 8 Jan. 1862–26 Dec. 1866. Microfilm Roll 19930, Columbus: Ohio Historical Society.

Calder, Angus. "Editor's Notes and Scott's

Notes." In *Old Mortality*, by Sir Walter Scott. London: Penguin, 1975.

Caldwell, J. A. *Caldwell's Atlas of Harrison Co. Ohio 1875.* Condit, Ohio: J. A. Caldwell, 1875.

Cheeseman, May. "Boydville." *The Berkeley Journal* (Martinsburg, W.Va.) 7 (1978): 45–49.

Compiled Military Service Records of Volunteer Soldiers Who Served with the United States Colored Troops: 1st U.S.C.T.... Microfilm Roll M1819, Washington: National Archives.

Compiled Military Service Records of Volunteer Soldiers Who Served with the United States Colored Troops: 2nd Through 7th Colored Infantry.... Microfilm Roll M1820, Washington: National Archives.

Compiled Military Service Records of Volunteer Soldiers Who Served with the United States Colored Troops: 55th Massachusetts Infantry (Colored). Microfilm Roll M1801, Washington: National Archives.

Crèvecoeur, J. Hector St. John De. *Letters from an American Farmer.* In *The Norton Anthology of American Literature*, edited by Nina Baym et al. 3rd ed. Vol 1. New York: Norton, 1989. 556–82.

Crooks, George R. *The Life of Bishop Matthew Simpson, of the Methodist Episcopal Church.* New York: Harper and Brothers, 1890.

[*DAB*]. *Dictionary of American Biography.* Edited by Allen Johnson. 19 vols. New York: Charles Scribner's Sons, 1994.

Denney, Robert E. *Civil War Medicine: Care and Comfort of the Wounded.* New York: Sterling, 1994.

Dyer, Gustavus W., and John Trotwood Moore. *The Tennessee Civil War Veterans Questionnaires.* 5 vols. Easley, S.C.: Southern Historical Press, 1985.

Eckley, H. J., and Wm. T. Perry. *History of Carroll and Harrison Counties, Ohio.* 2 vols. Chicago: Lewis Publishing, 1921.

Federal Writers' Project of the Work Projects Administration for the State of Kentucky. *The WPA Guide to Kentucky.* Edited by F. Kevin Simon. Reprint ed. Lexington: University Press of Kentucky, 1996.

[Fox, Charles Barnard]. *Record of the Service of the Fifty-fifth Regiment of Massachusetts Volunteer Infantry.* Printed for the Regimental Association, Cambridge, Mass.: J. Wilson and Son, 1868. Microfiche, Louisville, Ky.: Lost Cause Press, 1971.

Franklin College Board of Trustees. *Franklin College Register: Biographical and Historical.* Wheeling: West Virginia Printing Company, 1908.

Gilson, J. H. *Concise History of the One Hundred and Twenty-sixth Regiment, Ohio Volunteer Infantry.* Salem, Ohio: Walton, Steam Job and Laurel, 1883.

Glasgow, William Melancthon. *Cyclopedic Manual of the United Presbyterian Church of North America....* Pittsburgh: United Presbyterian Board of Publication, 1903.

Golden, James L., and Edward P. J. Corbett, eds. *The Rhetoric of Blair, Campbell, and Whateley.* New York: Holt, Rinehart and Winston, 1968.

The Goodspeed Histories of Maury, Williamson, Rutherford, Wilson, Bedford, and Marshall Counties of Tennessee. Goodspeed's History of Tennessee. 1886. Reprint, Columbia, Tenn.: Woodward and Stinson, 1971.

[Goodspeed]. *History of Tennessee....* Numerous vols. Nashville: Goodspeed, 1886–87. Reprint, Easley, S.C.: Southern Historical Press, 1979.

Greer, Dorothea. "Underground Railroad in Harrison County." *Our Harrison Heritage* 13, no. 1 (1995): 1–4.

Grimshaw, William. *The Ladies' Lexicon and Parlour Companion....* Philadelphia: John Grigg, 1835.

Hafendorfer, Kenneth A. *Perryville: Battle for Kentucky.* Rev. ed. Louisville, Ky.: K H Press, 1991.

Hall, Susan G. "At Antietam: Custer's First Writing for Publication." *Ohioana Quarterly* 41, nos. 2 and 3 (1998): 83–7 and 175–9.

Hanna, Charles A. *Historical Collections of Harrison County, in the State of Ohio, With Lists of the First Land-Owners, Early Marriages (to 1841), Will Records (to 1861), Burial Records of the Early Settlements, and Numerous Genealogies.* New York: 1900. Reprint, Evansville, In.: Ohio Genealogical Society, 1973.

[Harper]. *The Church Memorial, containing important historical facts and reminiscences connected with the Associate and Associate Reformed Church previous to their union as the United Presbyterian Church of North America.* Edited by R. D. Harper. Columbus, Ohio: Follett, Foster; Fleming and Crawford, 1858.

Harrison, Lowell H. *The Civil War in Kentucky.* Lexington: University Press of Kentucky, 1975.

Heitman, Don. *Heitman's Simplified Hardee's and Skirmish Drill.* Indianapolis: Volunteer Publishing, n.d.

Historic Properties of Martinsburg. Pamphlet, Martinsburg, W.Va.: City of Martinsburg Walking Tour Brochure Committee, 1994.

Howe, Henry. *Historical Collections of Ohio In Three Volumes: An Encyclopedia of the State....* Ohio Centennial Edition. Vol. 2. Columbus: Henry Howe and Son, 1891.

Howells, William Cooper. *Recollections of Life in Ohio from 1813–1840.* 1895. Reprint, Gainsville, Florida: Scholars' Facsimiles and Reprints, 1963.

Index to Questionaires of Civil War Veterans. Nashville: Tennessee State Library and Archives, 1962.

Jarvis, Jacob. *Harrison County, Ohio, 1862 Land Ownership Map.* Cadiz, Ohio: 1862. Compiled by Mary E. Hovorka Beebe, Ashland, Ohio: Mary Beebe, 1985.

Johnston, Charles A. *Lebanon As I Have Known It: Recollections.* Lebanon, Ky.: *Lebanon Enterprise,* 1921. Typescript, Filson Club, Louisville, Ky.

Keller, Allan. *Morgan's Raid.* Indianapolis: Bobbs-Merrill, 1961.

Klement, Frank L. *The Limits of Dissent: Clement L. Vallandigham and the Civil War.* Lexington: University Press of Kentucky, 1970.

Knott, W. T. *History of Marion County, Kentucky.* [Lebanon, Ky.]: *The Standard,* 1888. Typescript, Filson Club, Louisville, Ky.

_____. *History of the Presbyterian Church in … Marion County and … Lebanon, Kentucky.* Typescript, Filson Club, Louisville, Ky.

Ladies' Indispensable Assistant.... New York: E. Hutchinson, 1852. Reprint, n.p.: n.p., n.d.

Lambert, D. Warren. *When the Ripe Pears Fell: The Battle of Richmond, Kentucky.* Richmond, Ky.: Madison County Historical Society, 1995.

Le Grand, Louis. *The Military Hand-Book, and Soldier's Manual of Information....* New York: Beadle and Company, 1861. Reprint, n.p.: n.p., n.d.

Lincoln, Abraham. *Complete Works of Abraham Lincoln.* Edited by John G. Nicolay and John Hay. 12 vols. New York: Century, 1894.

Leyburn, James G. *The Scotch-Irish: A Social History.* Chapel Hill: University of North Carolina Press, 1962.

Lucas, Marion B. *From Slavery to Segregation, 1760–1891.* Vol. 1 of *A History of Blacks in Kentucky.* N.p.: Kentucky Historical Society, 1992.

McAlester, Virgina and Lee. *A Field Guide to American Houses.* New York: Knopf, 1993.

McClellan, George B., translator. *Manual of Bayonet Exercise: Prepared For The Use Of The Army Of The United States.* Translation of M. Gomard. Printed by Order of the War Department, Philadelphia: J. B. Lippincott, 1862.

McDonough, James Lee. *War in Kentucky: From Shiloh to Perryville.* Knoxville: University of Tennessee Press, 1994.

McElroy, J. F. *History of Lebanon.* Lebanon, Ky.: *The Enterprise,* 1910; reprint 1954. Typescript, Filson Club, Louisville, Ky.

McGavran, Samuel B. *A Brief History of Harrison County, Ohio.* Cadiz, Ohio: Harrison Tribune, 1894.

McKinney, William W. "Changes Through Controversy." In *The Presbyterian Valley,* edited by William W. McKinney. Pittsburgh: Davis and Warde, 1958. 233–66.

McPherson, James M. *Abraham Lincoln and the Second American Revolution.* New York: Oxford Univ. Press, 1990.

_____. *Battle Cry of Freedom: The Civil War Era.* The Oxford History of the United States, vol. 6. New York: Oxford Univ. Press, 1988.

_____. *For Cause and Comrades: Why Men Fought in the Civil War.* New York: Oxford Univ. Press, 1997.

_____. *What They Fought For, 1861–65.* Baton Rouge: Louisiana State Univ. Press, 1994.

The Merck Manual of Diagnosis and Therapy. Edited by Robert Berkow and Andrew J. Fletcher. 16th ed. Rathway, N.J.: Merck Research Laboratories, 1992.

Miller, Marion Mills. "The War Is A Failure." In *The Civil War.* Vol. 6 of *Great Debates in American History: From the Debates in the British Parliament on the Colonial Stamp Act (1764–1765) to the Debates in Congress at the Close of the Taft Administration (1912–1913),* edited by Marion Mills Miller. 14 vols. New York: Current Literature Publishing, 1913. 6: 255–79.

Moebs, Thomas Truxtun. *Black Soldiers–Black Sailors–Black Ink: Research Guide on African-Americans in U.S. Military History, 1526–1900.* Chesapeake Bay: Moebs Publishing Company, 1994.

Monaghan, Jay. *Custer: The Life of General George Armstrong Custer.* Boston: Little, Brown, 1959.

The Official Atlas of the Civil War. New York: Thomas Yoseloff, 1958.

Ohio Adjutant General. *Civil War Muster Rolls. U.S. Colored Troops.* Microfilm, Columbus: Ohio Historical Society, GR2057.

_____. *Muster Roll, Fifth Regiment, U. S. Colored Troops, July 1863.* Microfilm, State Archives Series 2141, Columbus: Ohio Historical Society, GR3987.

Ohio Adjutant General's Office. *Roll of Deserters in Ohio Regiments of Infantry.* Manuscript ledger, Archives Series 108, Columbus: Ohio Historical Society.

Ohio Roster Commission. *Official Roster of the Soldiers of the State of Ohio in the War of the Rebellion, 1861–1866.* 12 vols. Akron: Werner Company, 1886–95.

[OR]. *The War of the Rebellion: A Compilation of the Official Records of the Union and Confederate Armies.* 4 series. 70 vols. in 1 to 3 parts. Washington: Government Printing Office, 1881–1901.

O'Neil, Tom. "Hero, To Anti-Hero, To Hero: George Armstrong Custer in Monroe's Newspapers." *Newsletter — Little Big Horn Associates* 28, no. 6 (1994): 4–7.

Parker, Ron. *The Sheep Book: A Handbook for the Modern Shepherd.* New York: Charles Scribner's Sons, 1983.

Porter, Lorle. *A People Set Apart: Scotch-Irish in Eastern Ohio.* Zanesville, Ohio: New Concord Press, 1998.

Prentice, George D., editor. *Louisville Daily Journal.* September 1862. Microfilm, Louisville Free Public Library, Louisville, Ky.

Reed, Connie M. Telephone conversation with author, 23 August 1999.

Riggs, C. Russell. *The Ante-Bellum Career of John A. Bingham: A Case Study in the Coming of the Civil War.* Ann Arbor, Mich.: UMI, 1967.

The Roster of Union Soldiers 1861–1865. Edited by Janet B. Hewett. 33 vols. Wilmington, N.C.: Broadfoot Publishing, 1997.

Ruger, Edward, and Anton Kilp, surveyors. *Map of the Battlefield of Perryville, Ky.* N.p.: U. S. Army Engineers, 1877.

St. Clairsville Gazette (St. Clairsville, Ohio). Microfilm, Ohio Historical Society.

Schmidt, Martin F. *Kentucky Illustrated: The First Hundred Years.* Lexington: Univ. of Kentucky Press, 1992.

Shotwell, Walter Gaston. *Driftwood: Being Papers on Old-Time American Towns and Some Old People.* New York: Longmans, Green, 1927. Reprint, Freeport, N.Y.: Books for Libraries Press, 1966.

Spalding, Hughes, compiler. *The Catholic Spalding Family of Georgia and Its Antecedents in Kentucky and Maryland 1658–1962.* N.p.: n.p., [1962]. Typescript, Filson Club, Louisville, Ky.

Spalding, Thomas W. "The Maryland Catholic Diaspora." *U. S. Catholic Historian* 8, no. 3 (1989): 163–71.

Stevenson, Brenda E. *Life in Black and White: Family and Community in the Slave South*. New York: Oxford University Press, 1996.

Stewart, Nixon B. *Dan. McCook's Regiment, 52nd O.V.I.: A History of the Regiment, Its Campaigns and Battles from 1862 to 1865*. Alliance, Ohio: Nixon B. Stewart, 1900.

Thomas, Benjamin P., and Harold M. Hyman. *Stanton: The Life and Times of Lincoln's Secretary of War*. New York: Knopf, 1962.

Tuscarawas Advocate (New Philadelphia, Ohio). Microfilm, Ohio Historical Society.

U. S. Adjutant-General's Office. *Official Army Register of the Volunteer Force of the United States Army for the years 1861, '62, '63, '64, '65....* 8 vols. Washington: [Government Printing Office], 1865–67.

[U. S. Census Office]. *Agriculture of the United States in 1860; Compiled from the Original Returns of The Eighth Census....* Washington: GPO, 1864.

_____. *Manufactures of the United States in 1860; Compiled from the Original Returns of the Eighth Census....* Washington: GPO, 1865.

_____. *Population of the United States in 1860; Compiled from the Original Returns of the Eighth Census....* Washington: GPO, 1864.

_____. *Statistics of the United States, (Including Mortality, Property, &c.) in 1860....* Washington, GPO, 1866.

[Kentucky indexes]. Johnson, Joseph E., transcriber. *Washington County Kentucky Tax List 1799*. Louisville, Ky.: n.p., 1936.

_____. Lawson, Rowena, transcriber. *Washington County, Kentucky, 1810–1840 Censuses*. Bowie, Md.: Heritage Books, 1986.

_____. McFarland, Judy, transcriber. *Marion County, Kentucky, 1860 Census*. Vacaville, Cal.: n.p., 1984.

[Ohio Indexes]. Harshman, Lida Flint et al. *Index to the 1860 Federal Population Census of Ohio*. 2 vols. Mineral Ridge, Ohio: Lida Flint Harshman, 1979.

_____. Steuart, Raeone Christensen, ed. *Ohio 1870 Census Index*. 6 vols. Bountiful, Utah: Heritage Quest, 1999.

[Virginia Index]. Schreiner-Yantis, Netti, and Florence Speakman Love, compilers. *The 1787 Census of Virginia*. 3 vols. Springfield, Va.: Genealogical Books in Print, 1987.

Vallandigham, Clement L. "The Constitution — Peace — Reunion." Speech in the House of Representatives 14 January 1863. In *Congressional Globe ... of the Third Session of the Thirty-Seventh Congress*. 1863. Part 2: Appendix, 52–60.

Van Ness, W. W. *The National School For The Soldier: An Elementary Work on Military Tactics in Question and Answer*. National Military Series, Part First. New York: Carleton, 1862. Reprint, n.p.: n.p., n.d.

Views of Louisville since 1766. Edited by Samuel W. Thomas. Louisville, Ky.: The Courier-Journal and The Louisville Times, 1971.

Walker, William. *The Southern Harmony and Musical Companion ... 1854*. Edited by Glenn C. Wilcox. Lexington: University of Kentucky Press, 1987.

Wallace, Charles B. *Custer's Ohio Boyhood: A Brief Account of the Early Life of Major General George Armstrong Custer*. 2nd ed. Cadiz, Ohio: Harrison County Historical Society, 1987.

Wallechinsky, David, and Irving Wallace. *The People's Almanac*. Garden City, N.Y.: Doubleday, 1975.

Watson, Geo. F. *United States Rifle and Light Infantry Tactics: An Official Text Book*. Cincinnati: Mumford, 1861. Reprint, n.p.: n.p., n.d.

Wert, Jeffry D. *Custer: The Controversial Life of George Armstrong Custer*. New York: Simon and Schuster, 1996.

Whittaker, Frederick. *A Complete Life of General George A. Custer*. Vol. 1. New York: 1876. Reprint, Lincoln: University of Nebraska Press, 1993.

Wilcox, Glenn C., editor. *The Southern Harmony and Musical Companion ... 1854*, by William Walker. Lexington: University Press of Kentucky, 1987.

Wills, Garry. *Lincoln at Gettysburg: The Words That Remade America*. New York: Simon and Schuster, Touchstone imprint, 1992.

Wishart, William. "Rev. Capt. Jonathan S. McCready: Extract of sketch prepared by Rev. William Wishart, New Athens, Ohio." Appendix in *Concise History of the One Hundred and Twenty-sixth Regiment, Ohio Volunteer Infantry*, edited by J. H. Gilson. Salem, Ohio: Walton, Steam Job and Laurel, 1883. 222–35.

Wood, Don C. "Old County Jail and King's Daughters Hospital." *The Berkeley Journal* (Martinsburg, W.Va.) 7 (1978): 18–21.

Index

Names of Ohio area citizens and soldiers are followed by the initial of their known or probable county in parentheses: Belmont (B), Carroll (C), Guernsey (G), Harrison (H), Jefferson (J), Tuscarawas (T). Variant spellings of the surnames which are used in records also appear in parentheses.